IMPORTANT INFORMATION

Please return this book to:

____

____

____

____

Phone: ________________

Examination Date: ____________________

Time: ____________________

Location: ____________________

____

____

To obtain an application or information about the GMAT, contact:

GMAT
Educational Testing Service
P.O. Box 6103
Princeton, NJ 08541-6103
(609) 771-7330

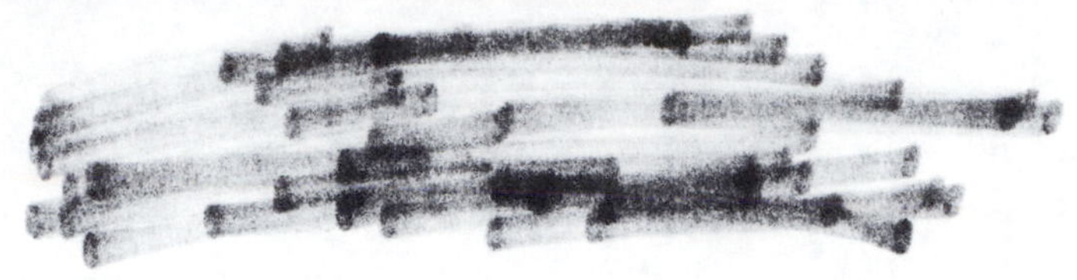

ISBN 1-881018-10-5

All comments and inquiries should be addressed to:
Great Lakes Press
PO Box 483
Okemos, MI 48805
Phone (517) 339-3336.

Library of Congress
Cataloging-in-Publication Data

Printed in the USA by Braun & Brumfield, Inc. of Ann Arbor, Michigan.

10 9 8 7 6 5 4 3 2 1

From The Professors Who Know It Best...

GMAT Time·Saver™

Second Edition

A concise, effective review for the Graduate Management Admission Test

Written by:

Merle C. Potter, Ph.D.
Professor of Engineering, Michigan State University

George I. Mavrodes, Ph.D.
Professor of Philosophy, University of Michigan

James W. Ney, Ed.D.
Professor of English, Arizona State University
with
Kathryn Harris, M.A., Arizona State University

Edited by:

Merle C. Potter, Ph.D.

Great Lakes Press, Inc.
PO Box 483
Okemos, MI 48805
(517) 339-3336

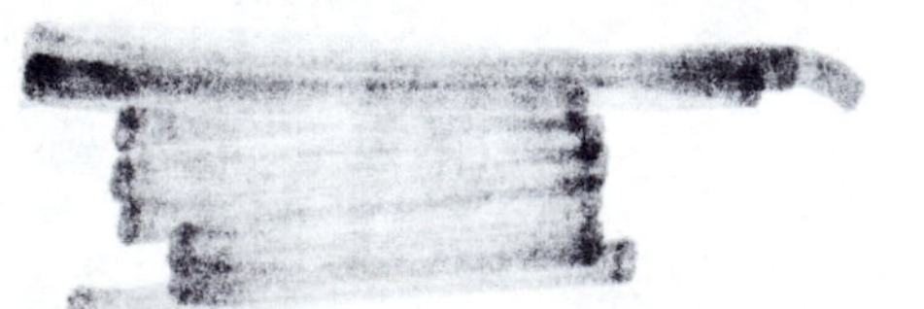

TABLE OF CONTENTS

Acknowledgments

Thanks are hereby accorded the following: Alfred A. Knopf, Inc. for permission to use portions of McConnell Private Power and American Democracy (1966); JAI Press for permission to reprint a section from Rowland and Feiock "Environmental Regulation . . ." and another section from Harris and Milkis "Regulatory Regimes . . ." both from Public Policy and Economic Institutions (1991); Belknap Press for permission to reprint portions of Chandler Scale and Scope (1990); University of Chicago Press for permission to quote from Heyek The Constitution of Liberty (1978); and Cambridge University Press to use material from Hounshell and Smith Science and Corporate Strategy . . . (1988).

Preface

This review manual is intended to aid you in your preparation for the GMAT, the Graduate Management Admission Test. Your ability to score relatively high on this exam increases your likelihood of acceptance to graduate school and may even result in a scholarship award or a teaching assistantship. So, it is important that you prepare as well as time permits.

This manual has been designed to allow you to maximize your score on the GMAT in a minimal amount of time. We have not burdened you with excessive verbiage but have designed a review that recognizes your need for efficiency.

As you begin your review, you are first given an opportunity to evaluate where you are presently—your strengths and your weaknesses. The Diagnostic Test in Chapter 2 allows you to score yourself on a simulated GMAT. An evaluation sheet will show you where you should spend your study time to maximize your score.

With this second edition we have included a chapter on effective writing for the new GMAT writing component. We have added the required analytical writing exercises to each of the three exams. We will also evaluate your two analytical writings and score them according to GMAT guidelines if you send or fax them to us. The fee for this service is $20 per pair of evaluations. Include a Visa or Mastercharge number with expiration date (or a check for $20) and send to: Great Lakes Press, POB 483, Okemos, MI 48805-0483. Fax # (517) 339-4455. We will return an evaluation of your writings within two weeks.

Many thanks to those who aided in compiling, editing and developing this book:

Michelle Gruender . . . Jeff Potter . . . John Gruender. . . . Thanks to all.

If you have any suggestions or comments, we would appreciate hearing from you. Please fill out the enclosed reply card at the front of the book and drop it in the mail.

Merle C. Potter
Ph.D., Engineering

James W. Ney
Ed.D., English

Kathryn Harris
M.A., English

George I. Mavrodes
Ph.D., Philosophy

1 · Introduction

1. INTRODUCTION

Information about the GMAT

The Graduate Management Admission Test (GMAT) consists of a series of multiple-choice exams and two writing assignments designed to provide universities with information used to predict success in graduate business school. It is used by most business schools in the United States.

The GMAT is an exam that measures your aptitude—your ability to think logically—and your ability to employ the verbal and mathematical skills you have developed throughout your years of schooling. The exam does not measure knowledge of any specific undergraduate course. In fact, it resembles the Scholastic Aptitude Test (SAT) you undoubtedly took prior to college admission. Both the SAT and GMAT are produced by the same organization, the Educational Testing Service (ETS). Both exams are designed to test your aptitude.

The GMAT is composed of nine sections with a total exam time of four hours. A possible exam format is outlined below. Every exam contains at least one multiple-choice section covering each of these five categories: Reading Comprehension, Sentence Correction, Critical Reasoning, Problem Solving, and Data Sufficiency. Two additional multiple-choice sections can be any of the previous five, but only six of those seven sections are counted in your test score. The seventh is an experimental section used to calibrate different exams or to try out new questions. You will never know which section of the seven is experimental so you must do your best when taking each section. Two analytical writing sections, described in detail later, make up the nine sections of the examination.

The order in which the sections are positioned on the GMAT is not predictable. The experimental section may be located anywhere in the exam. So if there are two Reading Comprehension sections, either the first or the second or neither may be experimental; you'll never be able to tell when taking the exam. Both analytical writing sections must be completed.

The actual GMAT may be presented in a variety of formats. The description below is just one possibility. The time allowed for each section should be the same as shown below, which is also the same as you will find in each practice test in this book. The number of questions, in each multiple-choice section, however, may vary from that shown in the following table.

It should be noted that as of the fall of 1994, the two analytical writing sections were added to the GMAT. Prior to 1994, applicants wrote an essay in their applications to graduate school. Since there was no control over the writing of the essay, it has been included in the GMAT where it is certain that the applicants write their own essays in the controlled environment.

Possible Format of the GMAT

	Question Type	Number of Questions	Time Allowed
Section 1	Reading Comprehension	18	25 minutes
Section 2	Sentence Correction	22	25 minutes
Section 3	Critical Reasoning	16	25 minutes
Section 4	Problem Solving	16	25 minutes
Section 5	Analytical Writing	—	30 minutes
		—15-minute break—	
Section 6	Data Sufficiency	20	25 minutes
Section 7	Reading Comprehension	25	30 minutes
Section 8	Problem Solving	16	25 minutes
Section 9	Analytical Writing	—	30 minutes
			4 hours

GMAT Registration

The advising/counseling offices of business schools and colleges can provide you with information about the GMAT. This information will give you the exact dates and times in October, January, March, and June that the exam is offered. If your religion discourages Saturday test-taking, arrangements can usually be made for an alternate date.

You may obtain an application for the GMAT from your dean's office or by contacting the Educational Testing Service at:

GMAT
EDUCATIONAL TESTING SERVICE
PO BOX 6103
PRINCETON, NJ 08541-6103

(609) 771-7330

ETS will send you an application and information regarding fees, test dates and times, and sample questions.

The registration fee for the GMAT is $70 in the United States (this can increase without notice), and an additional $15 for late registrants and $25 for standby registrants. If taken at a supplementary test center, an additional $18 may be required. Further review material for the GMAT and information on MBA programs and financial aid may also be requested from ETS at the above address.

Registration forms must be received at least one month prior to the test date. An additional week is allowed for late registration. If you do not register in time for the GMAT you may attempt a day-of-test standby registration; you must have proper identification (with a photograph), a completed registration form (and envelope), and a check or money order made out for the correct amount. Standby registration is allowed only if sufficient space, staff, and test materials are available. Do not attempt to contact the test center prior to the exam time; direct all contacts to ETS in Princeton, New Jersey.

The GMAT is also available in large print, Braille, and cassette if disabilities do not allow you to take the regular-print edition of the test. You must contact ETS and make advance arrangements to accommodate such needs. Special readers are also allowed and/or provided.

Exams are given at numerous test sites throughout the United States; there should be one near you. Your department, college or the ETS can provide you with the location that is best for you.

The exams are written and graded by the ETS at the above address. All inquiries and comments regarding the examinations should be addressed to the ETS.

How the GMAT is Scored

The GMAT is divided into three major areas: Verbal, Quantitative and Analytical Writing. Reading Comprehension, Sentence Correction, and Critical Reasoning make up the Verbal area; Problem Solving and Data Sufficiency make up the Quantitative area; and two writing assignments make up the Analytical Writing area. You will receive a Verbal Score (range: 0–60), a Quantitative Score (range: 0–60), a Total Scaled Score (range: 200–800), and an Analytical Writing Score (range: 0-6), as well as a percentile ranking for each of the first three. An average test taker will receive a Verbal and Quantitative score of about 30, and a Total Scaled Score of about 500. The percentile ranking that you receive will rank you relative to all test takers in the last three years, so if you place in the 80th percentile you can infer that 80 percent of all test takers in the last three years placed below you.

The Analytical Writing is graded as follows:

6—Outstanding. A well-articulated analysis or critique that demonstrates mastery of the elements of effective writing.

5—Strong. A well-developed analysis or critique that demonstrates good control of the elements of effective writing.

4—Adequate. A competent analysis or critique that demonstrates adequate control of the elements of writing.

3—Limited. Some competence in analyzing an issue or critiquing an argument. There are clear flaws in the writing.

2—Seriously flawed.

1—Fundamentally deficient.

0—Totally deficient.

The final score is the average of four independent ratings of your two analytical writing exercises. There may be some subjectivity in this grade, but the average of four grades should result in a fair rating of your writing ability.

The three multiple-choice scores that you will receive about 4 to 6 weeks after the test will be based on your raw score, the total number of correct answers minus one-fourth the number of wrong answers. You are obviously penalized for incorrect answers. If you can eliminate at least two of the five answers to a question, make your best guess; otherwise, leave the answer blank.

If you know you did poorly on the exam (if, for example, you become ill during the exam), you may either notify the test supervisor at the time of the exam, or notify ETS by mail immediately after the exam and cancel your score. Because all cancellations are reported to your future graduate school, it may be better to simply retake the GMAT and use the detailed results of your first try (available from ETS for $8 within 90 days of your test date) to improve your second attempt. An explanation of the first score could then be given to your selected graduate school (be sure and enclose some proof of your reason for not doing well, e.g., a doctor's note, etc.).

How Your GMAT Score is Used

Most graduate business schools require applicants to have their score on the GMAT reported to them by the ETS. Decisions regarding admission, scholarships, fellowships, and assistantships are made using the GMAT score as an important indicator of probable success in the graduate program. Other information, such as your undergraduate grade point average, an interview, references, your under-graduate major, and your social and athletic activity may also be considered. The weighting of the different factors varies between graduate schools, but they invariably regard your GMAT score highly since it measures all applicants relative to the same scale. Make sure you are well prepared for the GMAT. Admission to the program of your choice may depend on how well you do.

Tips to Maximize Your Score

The GMAT is separated into nine sections, as previously outlined. You are allowed exactly 25 or 30 minutes to complete each section. After the first four or five sections you will be allowed a fifteen-minute break, so plan on about four hours and fifteen minutes to complete the exam.

Since there is a penalty for incorrect answers on the multiple-choice sections of the GMAT, you should plan a strategy for smart guessing beginning with common techniques for taking a multiple-choice examination. Here are a few strategy suggestions:

- **Mark your answer sheet after you complete each page**. Write the answer beside each question number clearly (don't make light, difficult-to-read marks). Then transfer the answers to the answer sheet as a block of answers. Do not keep going back and forth for each question; this may interrupt your line of thought or lead to errors in transferring your answers. It is more efficient to mark answers as a block, giving you more time to concentrate on the questions.

- **Make sketches, diagrams or marks in your test booklet** whenever you feel it will be helpful to your thought process. In the math sections, write down all equations clearly. Even though you may be able to work a problem in your head, be careful!

- **Budget your time**. You will not have enough time to do everything you want to do. (Neither will the other people taking the GMAT.) So you need to make the best use of the time you do have. And you don't want to waste time during the test deciding how to use your time. You must decide how to use your time *before you go into the test site.*

  We suggest the following budget. You can see how it works for you on the two practice tests. Modify it if you want, but have a plan. We suggest that you save about one minute at the end for the final "wrap-up." That leaves an average of approximately a minute and a half per question. That may not sound like much, and it isn't, but it is more than you will need for some of the items. We suggest that you spend no more than about a minute on any one question for the first attempt. Some questions will take less time than that, so you will build up a surplus. Be careful not to spend the surplus on the very next question.

  When you've gone through the whole set in this way, then come back to work on some of the items that you left out, starting with those for which you had a good idea of how to proceed but didn't have enough time. On these questions you will probably have to do some "seat of the pants" time budgeting, so as not to spend all of your surplus time on just one or two questions. When there is just a minute or so left, then go into the "wrap-up" operation in which you make final selections of answers to questions in which you have eliminated at least 2 choices—your final guesswork.

  Some people can soon learn to pace themselves pretty accurately by working on practice exams. For other people it might be worthwhile to use a stop watch. If you do that, be sure that you are fully familiar with how to use the watch before you go into the exam. You don't want to waste time trying to remember what sequence of buttons to push. However, for most people the stop-watch is more trouble than it is worth.

- **Put a circle around each question number that you are unsure of** but that you want to return to.

- **Forget about questions you are sure you cannot answer correctly**. There may be a question that you know you cannot answer confidently, no matter how much time you spent on it. Do not waste time trying to select an answer. Do not circle the question number either, since you should not return to such a question. Rather, put an "X" through that question number. Each GMAT question has the same value in the final score, even though some of them are harder than others. A minute spent on an easy question essentially has a higher payoff than a minute spent on a hard question. Don't waste a lot of time on a hard question—one that seems very puzzling to you, one for which you don't know how to get started.

- **Use partial knowledge to guess intelligently**. The regimentation of the GMAT, especially the fact that you are selecting an answer rather than constructing one, makes guessing a valuable strategy. Of course, if you can positively identify one of the alternatives as the correct answer, then mark it on your answer sheet and be done with it. Sometimes, however, you won't be able to do that. But, even so, you will often be able to *eliminate one or more alternatives* as being incorrect. In fact, you can often do that pretty quickly.

It is hard for the people who construct the test to think up five attractive alternatives for each question. So there is often one or two "throw-away" alternatives which you can quickly eliminate. Ruling out alternatives represents use of partial knowledge, and the structure of the GMAT provides a way for you to take advantage of that partial knowledge—by guessing among the remaining alternatives. Of course, you'll guess wrong sometimes, and then you will lose a little in the scoring. But you will also guess right sometimes.

The GMAT scoring is set up in such a way that if you can eliminate even one alternative before you guess, then the odds are in your favor, although we recommend that you *eliminate at least two alternatives before you guess*. You will probably gain more than you lose by guessing. And the more alternatives you can eliminate before you guess, the better your odds become.

As soon as you are satisfied that you can eliminate a particular alternative, *cross out the choice letter* (A, B, C, D, or E) clearly in the question booklet. You will not have to think about that particular alternative again.

You don't have to guess yet. You may have time left at the end to be able to figure out the correct answer. Circle the question number if you would like to return to the problem later to eliminate more choices. If you have to guess in the end, you won't have to think again about what two alternatives to eliminate. (Go ahead and make other quick notes in the question booklet, too, to help jog your memory when you return.)

- **The final wrap-up**, for which you've saved the last minute or so, consists of going back quickly over those questions for which you have circled and still haven't entered an answer. You don't have time enough now to do any more worthwhile reasoning about them. But, at least for those in which you have eliminated at least two alternatives, it's time now to guess. Just pick one of the remaining choices at random and enter it quickly on the answer sheet. If you put in the last answer just as the session ends, then you've done the best you can!

- **Questions are often arranged in order of difficulty**, with the easiest questions first. Make sure of your answers on the easy questions. Do not be surprised if the last questions are quite difficult; answer only those that you are sure of or that have at least two choices that can be eliminated.

How to Use this Review to Score High

The Diagnostic Test in Chapter 2 allows you to score yourself on a simulated GMAT. We suggest that you take note of the following instructions:

- Set aside 4 hours and 15 minutes to take the Diagnostic Test, simulating the actual GMAT as closely as possible. After the first 5 test sections, take a fifteen-minute break and then complete the test.

- Pay strict attention to the time. Use a timer that will buzz when 25 or 30 minutes are up. Stop as soon as the timer buzzes. (You may want a 5-minute warning to allow time for your final review of the problems you may have circled.) Also, have a watch nearby so you know how much time is left as you are working.

- Use these suggestions: circle the numbers of questions you are not sure of, transfer answers in blocks, do not return to problems that are too difficult, and make sketches and write freely in open spaces in the test booklet.

After you complete the Diagnostic Test, analyze your score on the multiple-choice sections with the Analysis Sheet provided at the end of that test. This evaluation sheet will identify your weaknesses and show you where you should spend your study time to maximize your score. Spend additional time on those weak areas, but make sure you review all areas so that you maximize your score.

You may wish to have a friend or colleague grade your writing using the scoring guidelines presented on page 3. Or, should you desire a professional assessment of your writings, you may send the two essays to: Great Lakes Press, POB 483, Okemos, MI 48805-0483. Or fax to (517) 339-4455. You must also provide your Visa/MC # and expiration date (or a check or money order). We will return a well-informed GMAT-type score, an evaluation of your writing and some suggestions for improvement for $20.

A review of each of the five major areas of the GMAT follows the Diagnostic Test. You may have pursued an academic curriculum that prepared you well for some areas of the GMAT, but find yourself weak in others. Based on your performance on the Diagnostic Test, you should spend time in the area(s) identified as weak.

After you review the subject matter, you should then take the two Practice Tests. Remember, a top score on the GMAT may result in admission to the school of your choice.

Types of GMAT Questions

Before you take the Diagnostic Test, we want to give you an idea of the types of questions asked in the five categories, and a description of the analytical writing requirements. A short description follows here, with a detailed analysis of each subject area in the chapters following the Diagnostic Test.

Reading Comprehension

The Reading Comprehension questions typically follow a paragraph or two from selected readings, with 5 to 10 questions following each passage. The questions will be based on information contained in the passage and on implications and inferences suggested by the passage. You may be required to apply the information contained in the passage to a different situation, or deduce the meaning of an unknown word.

If you quickly scan the questions before you read the passage, you will have an idea of what you are seeking. Also, underline the main idea of the passage along with any supporting ideas, specific details, and conclusions to allow for a quick review of the passage as you answer the questions.

Sentence Correction

To answer the questions in the Sentence Correction sections of the GMAT, you must be familiar with English grammar and the usage of English words. Punctuation, spelling, and capitalization will not be tested. Emphasis is on verb tense and verb complements, pronoun case, adverbs and adjectives, comparatives, parallel usage of words, and proper usage of words, to name a few.

Each question will contain a sentence with part of the sentence underlined. The error will always be in the underlined part, and answer (A) will always be an exact duplication of the underlined part. If you think there is no error, then (A) is the correct response. If, as usual, there is an error, then select the best response from (B), (C), (D), and (E). By reviewing the four alternate responses, you may be able to identify the error; then select the response that you think is correct. Note that the correct response never changes the original meaning of the sentence.

Critical Reasoning

The Critical Reasoning questions will test your ability to evaluate an inference, assumption, or argument. Each question includes a short passage of one or more sentences or a set of statements that usually includes a claim or a conclusion. You must then respond to a question about the passage by selecting the best of five responses.

The questions asked about the short passage will require that you identify a flaw in an argument, recognize stated facts, evaluate an inference, or decide if an assumption is acceptable. When formulating your response, you should identify the conclusion and the evidence that supports the conclusion. After carefully considering all the answers, you should select the best response.

Problem Solving

The Problem Solving sections of the GMAT test your mathematical skills learned in arithmetic, algebra, and geometry and possibly require that you interpret tables and graphs. The problems are typically not very difficult and can often be answered with minimal calculation, but if you have not used your mathematical skills very often in your undergraduate courses you may be surprised at how rusty those skills have become.

Do not spend too much time on one problem. If a problem gives you trouble, go on to the next. Write out any equations in the margins of the test—do not work the problems in your head; it is too easy to make simple mistakes. After the Diagnostic Test you will know if you are prepared for the mathematics that you will encounter on the GMAT.

Data Sufficiency

The Data Sufficiency questions on the GMAT test your ability to reason mathematically. As in the Problem Solving sections, the Data Sufficiency questions depend on your arithmetic, algebra, and geometry skills. The important difference, however, is that you do not actually solve problems in the Data Sufficiency sections. You must decide if there is sufficient information given to solve a problem.

Each Data Sufficiency question will begin with a mathematics problem in the form of a question or statement, followed by two statements, (1) and (2), that contain additional information relative to the problem. The correct answer is selected by reasoning that the problem can be solved:

(A) from (1) alone but not from (2) alone.

(B) from (2) alone but not from (1) alone.

(C) using (1) and (2) together. Both are needed.

(D) using (1) alone or using (2) alone. Both provide an answer.

(E) not using (1) and (2); more information is needed.

Undoubtedly, you are not familiar with this type of question in which you do not actually solve a problem to obtain an answer, but merely decide what information is needed to allow you to solve a problem. You should always ask the following three questions:

1. Can the problem be solved with (1) alone?

2. Can the problem be solved with (2) alone?

3. Can the problem only be solved with both (1) and (2) together?

To answer the three questions you must carefully consider both statements (1) and (2).

- If the answer to question 1 is YES and question 2 is NO, then (A) is correct.
- If the answer to question 1 is NO and question 2 is YES, then (B) is correct.
- If the answers to question 1 and 2 are NO but 3 is YES, then (C) is correct.
- If the answer to question 1 is YES and question 2 is YES, then (D) is correct.
- If the answer to all three questions is NO, then (E) is correct.

Because Data Sufficiency questions are so unusual, let's demonstrate with an example to better illustrate the above options.

Example

A company invests $100,000 in a flower-growing venture. How much money did the company earn the first year?

(1) The expenses for the first year were $62,500.
(2) The income from flower sales the first year was $75,600.

Solution. The earnings are the income minus the expenses. Consequently, both (1) and (2) are needed to solve the problem. Hence, answer (C) is selected. It is not required that you solve the problem; you only have to determine what information is needed so that the problem can be solved.

Analytical Writing

There are two Analytical Writing exercises. The first requires that you analyze and explain your views on an issue that is presented. There are no right or wrong answers, just different perspectives as you develop your own position. The second requires that you critique an argument that is presented. You should discuss any questionable assumptions, provide alternate explanations or counter-examples that weaken the conclusion, or evidence that refutes or strengthens the argument. You must write with a #2 pencil in a legible way on the fronts and backs of the three unlined pages which will be provided for each essay.

Getting Started

You should now take the Diagnostic Test. Set aside 4 hours and 15 minutes and simulate an actual exam with exactly 25 or 30 minutes per section and a 15-minute break after Section 5. Time is extremely important on this type of exam so it is very important to time yourself. Keep a watch nearby so you know how much time is left on each section. Do not look ahead at other sections, and do not guess unless you can eliminate at least 2 answers.

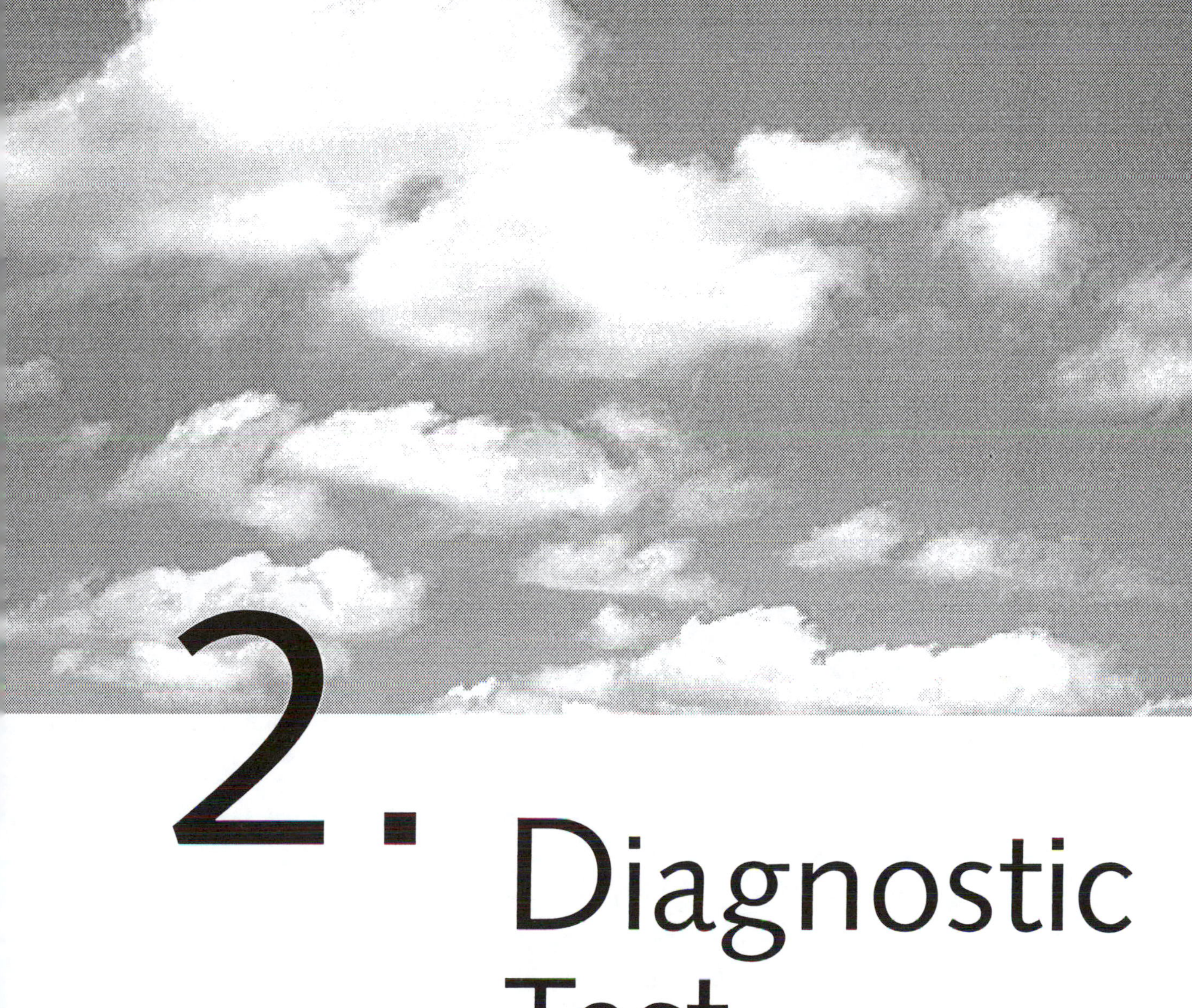

2. Diagnostic Test

Sections:

1. Reading Comprehension
2. Sentence Correction
3. Critical Reasoning
4. Problem Solving
5. Analysis of an Issue
6. Data Sufficiency
7. Reading Comprehension
8. Problem Solving
9. Analysis of an Argument

Followed by:

Score Analysis Charts
Explanations To All Answers

Practice these suggestions while taking this Diagnostic Test:

1. Write your answers next to the questions on each page. Then transfer your answers to the answer sheet a block at a time.

2. On a difficult question, if you cannot eliminate at least two choices, leave the question blank and do not guess.

3. Put a circle around a question number if you are uncertain of the correct answer and think you may return to it if time permits. Before moving on to the next question, guess an answer if you can eliminate at least two choices; you may not have time to return.

4. Construct diagrams, draw sketches, and write equations in the empty space on the exam. Such aids are often helpful in your thought process.

5. Try to simulate actual exam conditions and time yourself very carefully. Do not exceed the allotted 25 or 30 minutes per section. Take a break after the fifth section to simulate the actual exam.

6. Do not worry if you leave some questions unanswered. The GMAT is quite difficult and students often leave questions unanswered. If you cannot eliminate at least two choices on a question, do not guess.

7. Write each of your Analytical Writing exercises on the front sides of three of the six <u>unlined</u> 8.5″x11″ sheets that you should have at hand for this exam. Practice writing legibly, with a #2 pencil. Try to fill all three front sides, but leave an inch or so margins all around and don't write too small or too large. We recommend that you write 4-8 paragraphs of 4-8 sentences each. [To have your essays graded professionally by a team coordinated by our Writing section author, mail them to: GLP, POB 483, Okemos MI 48805, or fax to: 517-339-4455. Your writing will be graded and returned within 2 weeks. The fee is $20.00. Include your Visa/MC number with expiration date or a check or money order.]

How to handle the answer sheet:

- Each section begins with number 1.
- If a section has fewer than 25 questions, ignore the extra answer blanks.
- If you change an answer, erase it completely.
- Do not make any extraneous marks on the answer sheet.

GMAT

SIGNATURE: ____________________

ANSWER SHEET

(simulated GMAT form)

BE SURE EACH MARK IS DARK AND COMPLETELY FILLS THE INTENDED SPACE AS ILLUSTRATED HERE: ●.
YOU MAY FIND MORE RESPONSE SPACES THAN YOU NEED. IF SO, PLEASE LEAVE THEM BLANK.

SECTION 1	SECTION 2	SECTION 3	SECTION 4	SECTION 6	SECTION 7	SECTION 8
1. Ⓐ Ⓑ Ⓒ Ⓓ Ⓔ	1. Ⓐ Ⓑ Ⓒ Ⓓ Ⓔ	1. Ⓐ Ⓑ Ⓒ Ⓓ Ⓔ	1. Ⓐ Ⓑ Ⓒ Ⓓ Ⓔ	1. Ⓐ Ⓑ Ⓒ Ⓓ Ⓔ	1. Ⓐ Ⓑ Ⓒ Ⓓ Ⓔ	1. Ⓐ Ⓑ Ⓒ Ⓓ Ⓔ
2. Ⓐ Ⓑ Ⓒ Ⓓ Ⓔ	2. Ⓐ Ⓑ Ⓒ Ⓓ Ⓔ	2. Ⓐ Ⓑ Ⓒ Ⓓ Ⓔ	2. Ⓐ Ⓑ Ⓒ Ⓓ Ⓔ	2. Ⓐ Ⓑ Ⓒ Ⓓ Ⓔ	2. Ⓐ Ⓑ Ⓒ Ⓓ Ⓔ	2. Ⓐ Ⓑ Ⓒ Ⓓ Ⓔ
3. Ⓐ Ⓑ Ⓒ Ⓓ Ⓔ	3. Ⓐ Ⓑ Ⓒ Ⓓ Ⓔ	3. Ⓐ Ⓑ Ⓒ Ⓓ Ⓔ	3. Ⓐ Ⓑ Ⓒ Ⓓ Ⓔ	3. Ⓐ Ⓑ Ⓒ Ⓓ Ⓔ	3. Ⓐ Ⓑ Ⓒ Ⓓ Ⓔ	3. Ⓐ Ⓑ Ⓒ Ⓓ Ⓔ
4. Ⓐ Ⓑ Ⓒ Ⓓ Ⓔ	4. Ⓐ Ⓑ Ⓒ Ⓓ Ⓔ	4. Ⓐ Ⓑ Ⓒ Ⓓ Ⓔ	4. Ⓐ Ⓑ Ⓒ Ⓓ Ⓔ	4. Ⓐ Ⓑ Ⓒ Ⓓ Ⓔ	4. Ⓐ Ⓑ Ⓒ Ⓓ Ⓔ	4. Ⓐ Ⓑ Ⓒ Ⓓ Ⓔ
5. Ⓐ Ⓑ Ⓒ Ⓓ Ⓔ	5. Ⓐ Ⓑ Ⓒ Ⓓ Ⓔ	5. Ⓐ Ⓑ Ⓒ Ⓓ Ⓔ	5. Ⓐ Ⓑ Ⓒ Ⓓ Ⓔ	5. Ⓐ Ⓑ Ⓒ Ⓓ Ⓔ	5. Ⓐ Ⓑ Ⓒ Ⓓ Ⓔ	5. Ⓐ Ⓑ Ⓒ Ⓓ Ⓔ
6. Ⓐ Ⓑ Ⓒ Ⓓ Ⓔ	6. Ⓐ Ⓑ Ⓒ Ⓓ Ⓔ	6. Ⓐ Ⓑ Ⓒ Ⓓ Ⓔ	6. Ⓐ Ⓑ Ⓒ Ⓓ Ⓔ	6. Ⓐ Ⓑ Ⓒ Ⓓ Ⓔ	6. Ⓐ Ⓑ Ⓒ Ⓓ Ⓔ	6. Ⓐ Ⓑ Ⓒ Ⓓ Ⓔ
7. Ⓐ Ⓑ Ⓒ Ⓓ Ⓔ	7. Ⓐ Ⓑ Ⓒ Ⓓ Ⓔ	7. Ⓐ Ⓑ Ⓒ Ⓓ Ⓔ	7. Ⓐ Ⓑ Ⓒ Ⓓ Ⓔ	7. Ⓐ Ⓑ Ⓒ Ⓓ Ⓔ	7. Ⓐ Ⓑ Ⓒ Ⓓ Ⓔ	7. Ⓐ Ⓑ Ⓒ Ⓓ Ⓔ
8. Ⓐ Ⓑ Ⓒ Ⓓ Ⓔ	8. Ⓐ Ⓑ Ⓒ Ⓓ Ⓔ	8. Ⓐ Ⓑ Ⓒ Ⓓ Ⓔ	8. Ⓐ Ⓑ Ⓒ Ⓓ Ⓔ	8. Ⓐ Ⓑ Ⓒ Ⓓ Ⓔ	8. Ⓐ Ⓑ Ⓒ Ⓓ Ⓔ	8. Ⓐ Ⓑ Ⓒ Ⓓ Ⓔ
9. Ⓐ Ⓑ Ⓒ Ⓓ Ⓔ	9. Ⓐ Ⓑ Ⓒ Ⓓ Ⓔ	9. Ⓐ Ⓑ Ⓒ Ⓓ Ⓔ	9. Ⓐ Ⓑ Ⓒ Ⓓ Ⓔ	9. Ⓐ Ⓑ Ⓒ Ⓓ Ⓔ	9. Ⓐ Ⓑ Ⓒ Ⓓ Ⓔ	9. Ⓐ Ⓑ Ⓒ Ⓓ Ⓔ
10. Ⓐ Ⓑ Ⓒ Ⓓ Ⓔ	10. Ⓐ Ⓑ Ⓒ Ⓓ Ⓔ	10. Ⓐ Ⓑ Ⓒ Ⓓ Ⓔ	10. Ⓐ Ⓑ Ⓒ Ⓓ Ⓔ	10. Ⓐ Ⓑ Ⓒ Ⓓ Ⓔ	10. Ⓐ Ⓑ Ⓒ Ⓓ Ⓔ	10. Ⓐ Ⓑ Ⓒ Ⓓ Ⓔ
11. Ⓐ Ⓑ Ⓒ Ⓓ Ⓔ	11. Ⓐ Ⓑ Ⓒ Ⓓ Ⓔ	11. Ⓐ Ⓑ Ⓒ Ⓓ Ⓔ	11. Ⓐ Ⓑ Ⓒ Ⓓ Ⓔ	11. Ⓐ Ⓑ Ⓒ Ⓓ Ⓔ	11. Ⓐ Ⓑ Ⓒ Ⓓ Ⓔ	11. Ⓐ Ⓑ Ⓒ Ⓓ Ⓔ
12. Ⓐ Ⓑ Ⓒ Ⓓ Ⓔ	12. Ⓐ Ⓑ Ⓒ Ⓓ Ⓔ	12. Ⓐ Ⓑ Ⓒ Ⓓ Ⓔ	12. Ⓐ Ⓑ Ⓒ Ⓓ Ⓔ	12. Ⓐ Ⓑ Ⓒ Ⓓ Ⓔ	12. Ⓐ Ⓑ Ⓒ Ⓓ Ⓔ	12. Ⓐ Ⓑ Ⓒ Ⓓ Ⓔ
13. Ⓐ Ⓑ Ⓒ Ⓓ Ⓔ	13. Ⓐ Ⓑ Ⓒ Ⓓ Ⓔ	13. Ⓐ Ⓑ Ⓒ Ⓓ Ⓔ	13. Ⓐ Ⓑ Ⓒ Ⓓ Ⓔ	13. Ⓐ Ⓑ Ⓒ Ⓓ Ⓔ	13. Ⓐ Ⓑ Ⓒ Ⓓ Ⓔ	13. Ⓐ Ⓑ Ⓒ Ⓓ Ⓔ
14. Ⓐ Ⓑ Ⓒ Ⓓ Ⓔ	14. Ⓐ Ⓑ Ⓒ Ⓓ Ⓔ	14. Ⓐ Ⓑ Ⓒ Ⓓ Ⓔ	14. Ⓐ Ⓑ Ⓒ Ⓓ Ⓔ	14. Ⓐ Ⓑ Ⓒ Ⓓ Ⓔ	14. Ⓐ Ⓑ Ⓒ Ⓓ Ⓔ	14. Ⓐ Ⓑ Ⓒ Ⓓ Ⓔ
15. Ⓐ Ⓑ Ⓒ Ⓓ Ⓔ	15. Ⓐ Ⓑ Ⓒ Ⓓ Ⓔ	15. Ⓐ Ⓑ Ⓒ Ⓓ Ⓔ	15. Ⓐ Ⓑ Ⓒ Ⓓ Ⓔ	15. Ⓐ Ⓑ Ⓒ Ⓓ Ⓔ	15. Ⓐ Ⓑ Ⓒ Ⓓ Ⓔ	15. Ⓐ Ⓑ Ⓒ Ⓓ Ⓔ
16. Ⓐ Ⓑ Ⓒ Ⓓ Ⓔ	16. Ⓐ Ⓑ Ⓒ Ⓓ Ⓔ	16. Ⓐ Ⓑ Ⓒ Ⓓ Ⓔ	16. Ⓐ Ⓑ Ⓒ Ⓓ Ⓔ	16. Ⓐ Ⓑ Ⓒ Ⓓ Ⓔ	16. Ⓐ Ⓑ Ⓒ Ⓓ Ⓔ	16. Ⓐ Ⓑ Ⓒ Ⓓ Ⓔ
17. Ⓐ Ⓑ Ⓒ Ⓓ Ⓔ	17. Ⓐ Ⓑ Ⓒ Ⓓ Ⓔ	17. Ⓐ Ⓑ Ⓒ Ⓓ Ⓔ	17. Ⓐ Ⓑ Ⓒ Ⓓ Ⓔ	17. Ⓐ Ⓑ Ⓒ Ⓓ Ⓔ	17. Ⓐ Ⓑ Ⓒ Ⓓ Ⓔ	17. Ⓐ Ⓑ Ⓒ Ⓓ Ⓔ
18. Ⓐ Ⓑ Ⓒ Ⓓ Ⓔ	18. Ⓐ Ⓑ Ⓒ Ⓓ Ⓔ	18. Ⓐ Ⓑ Ⓒ Ⓓ Ⓔ	18. Ⓐ Ⓑ Ⓒ Ⓓ Ⓔ	18. Ⓐ Ⓑ Ⓒ Ⓓ Ⓔ	18. Ⓐ Ⓑ Ⓒ Ⓓ Ⓔ	18. Ⓐ Ⓑ Ⓒ Ⓓ Ⓔ
19. Ⓐ Ⓑ Ⓒ Ⓓ Ⓔ	19. Ⓐ Ⓑ Ⓒ Ⓓ Ⓔ	19. Ⓐ Ⓑ Ⓒ Ⓓ Ⓔ	19. Ⓐ Ⓑ Ⓒ Ⓓ Ⓔ	19. Ⓐ Ⓑ Ⓒ Ⓓ Ⓔ	19. Ⓐ Ⓑ Ⓒ Ⓓ Ⓔ	19. Ⓐ Ⓑ Ⓒ Ⓓ Ⓔ
20. Ⓐ Ⓑ Ⓒ Ⓓ Ⓔ	20. Ⓐ Ⓑ Ⓒ Ⓓ Ⓔ	20. Ⓐ Ⓑ Ⓒ Ⓓ Ⓔ	20. Ⓐ Ⓑ Ⓒ Ⓓ Ⓔ	20. Ⓐ Ⓑ Ⓒ Ⓓ Ⓔ	20. Ⓐ Ⓑ Ⓒ Ⓓ Ⓔ	20. Ⓐ Ⓑ Ⓒ Ⓓ Ⓔ
21. Ⓐ Ⓑ Ⓒ Ⓓ Ⓔ	21. Ⓐ Ⓑ Ⓒ Ⓓ Ⓔ	21. Ⓐ Ⓑ Ⓒ Ⓓ Ⓔ	21. Ⓐ Ⓑ Ⓒ Ⓓ Ⓔ	21. Ⓐ Ⓑ Ⓒ Ⓓ Ⓔ	21. Ⓐ Ⓑ Ⓒ Ⓓ Ⓔ	21. Ⓐ Ⓑ Ⓒ Ⓓ Ⓔ
22. Ⓐ Ⓑ Ⓒ Ⓓ Ⓔ	22. Ⓐ Ⓑ Ⓒ Ⓓ Ⓔ	22. Ⓐ Ⓑ Ⓒ Ⓓ Ⓔ	22. Ⓐ Ⓑ Ⓒ Ⓓ Ⓔ	22. Ⓐ Ⓑ Ⓒ Ⓓ Ⓔ	22. Ⓐ Ⓑ Ⓒ Ⓓ Ⓔ	22. Ⓐ Ⓑ Ⓒ Ⓓ Ⓔ
23. Ⓐ Ⓑ Ⓒ Ⓓ Ⓔ	23. Ⓐ Ⓑ Ⓒ Ⓓ Ⓔ	23. Ⓐ Ⓑ Ⓒ Ⓓ Ⓔ	23. Ⓐ Ⓑ Ⓒ Ⓓ Ⓔ	23. Ⓐ Ⓑ Ⓒ Ⓓ Ⓔ	23. Ⓐ Ⓑ Ⓒ Ⓓ Ⓔ	23. Ⓐ Ⓑ Ⓒ Ⓓ Ⓔ
24. Ⓐ Ⓑ Ⓒ Ⓓ Ⓔ	24. Ⓐ Ⓑ Ⓒ Ⓓ Ⓔ	24. Ⓐ Ⓑ Ⓒ Ⓓ Ⓔ	24. Ⓐ Ⓑ Ⓒ Ⓓ Ⓔ	24. Ⓐ Ⓑ Ⓒ Ⓓ Ⓔ	24. Ⓐ Ⓑ Ⓒ Ⓓ Ⓔ	24. Ⓐ Ⓑ Ⓒ Ⓓ Ⓔ
25. Ⓐ Ⓑ Ⓒ Ⓓ Ⓔ	25. Ⓐ Ⓑ Ⓒ Ⓓ Ⓔ	25. Ⓐ Ⓑ Ⓒ Ⓓ Ⓔ	25. Ⓐ Ⓑ Ⓒ Ⓓ Ⓔ	25. Ⓐ Ⓑ Ⓒ Ⓓ Ⓔ	25. Ⓐ Ⓑ Ⓒ Ⓓ Ⓔ	25. Ⓐ Ⓑ Ⓒ Ⓓ Ⓔ

SECTIONS 5 & 9 ARE "WRITING ANALYSIS"
—TO BE COMPLETED ON 6 SEPARATE SHEETS
OF PAPER THAT YOU SHOULD HAVE READY.

SECTION 1 Reading Comprehension

18 Questions
Time: 25 minutes

Directions: In this group, each passage is followed by questions based on its content. On the basis of what is stated or implicit in the passage, please select the best answer to each question.

Passage 1:

One of the most persistently troubling parts of national domestic policy is the development and use of water resources. Because the technology of water management involves similar construction skills, whether the task is the building of an ocean jetty for protection of shipping or the construction of a river dam for flood control and irrigation, the issues of water policy have mingled problems of navigation and agriculture. A further inherent complexity of water policy is the frequent conflict between flood control and irrigation, between the requirements for abundance and those for scarcity of water. Both problems exist in America, often in the same river basins; the one is most typically the problem of the lower part of the basin and the other the problem of the upper part. Then there are the problems of cities located along the major American rivers, not infrequently directly on the very flood plains of highly erratic streams. In the arid parts of the land it has recently become clear that climate varies over time, with irregular periods of serious drought followed by wet periods marked by occasional floods. The problems of land and water, then, are inherently difficult. For this reason alone, shortcomings and failures have probably been inevitable. In the scale of the undertakings that have been attempted, moreover, involving on occasion no less than the reversal of stream flow and the altering of the natural features of whole river basins, it is inevitable that some of the shortcomings should also be large.

Nevertheless, the most startling fact about the history of water projects in the United States is the degree to which their shortcomings have been associated with administrative failures. Again and again these shortcomings have proved to be the consequences of inadequate study—of water flow, of soils, of factors other than construction technology . . . and of faulty organization. In 1959, the Senate Select Committee on National Water resources . . . found . . . that twenty different national commissions or committees . . . charged with examining these problems and seeking solutions . . . [had] emphasized with remarkable consistency the need for coordination among the agencies dealing with water.

Perhaps the most common argument has been that a river basin is a natural unit and projects affecting it should treat it as such.

Grant McConnell. Private Power and American Democracy. New York: Alfred A. Knopf, Inc., 1966. pp. 212-213

1. According to the passage, the shortcomings of water projects in the U.S. are primarily the consequences of
   A) conflict between flood control and irrigation
   B) inadequate study and faulty coordination among agencies
   C) problems of land and water
   D) inadequate construction technology
   E) the scale of the projects

2. Of the issues named below, which is more typically the problem of the upper part of a river basin?
   A) navigation
   B) shipping
   C) flood control
   D) drought followed by wet period
   E) scarcity

3. Which of the following is not a problem associated with the development of water resources?
   A) conflict between flood control and irrigation
   B) problems of navigation and agriculture
   C) location of cities on flood plains
   D) inadequate design technology
   E) variations in climate

4. According to the passage, the recommendation that agencies dealing with water coordinate their activities rests upon which basic scientific argument?
   A) requirements for abundance and against scarcity often conflict
   B) abundance and scarcity coexist in the same river basins
   C) a river basin is a natural unit and projects affecting it should treat it as such
   D) shortcomings and failures are inevitable
   E) the technology of water management involves narrow construction skills

5. Which statement below may be inferred from the information given in this passage?
   A) The intersection of problems of climate, geography, purpose, technology, and administration complicates the development of water projects.
   B) Innovative design and construction technology eliminate conflict in demand for flood control and for irrigation.
   C) In the design of a water project, upper and lower parts of a river basin must be regarded as identical entities.
   C) In the design of a water project, predominant problems derive from the presence of erratic streams.
   E) Irregularity of climate is the most critical impediment to the development of water projects.

Passage 2:

. . . There was much immediate experience to justify the view of the state that Gompers and his followers took. Labor's experience with the courts, in particular, seemed to confirm the severest cynicism as to their function, for the machinery of the law had repeatedly been twisted to labor's disadvantage. Whereas the Sherman Act appeared to be proving ineffective in dealing with the trusts, it was quickly and devastatingly turned against unions. The labor injunction as developed by corporation lawyers turned into a perversion of law and justice, and the courts were willing accomplices in the process. In view of the courts' record in using the Sherman Act against labor, Gompers can perhaps be forgiven for terming the Act "that legislative monstrosity." Nevertheless, labor's attitude toward the courts and the law was much more hostile during Gompers' time than any likely to be taken today. The difficulty, as it was seen then, lay not merely in a particular law or a distortion of certain legal processes, but in a fundamental fraud in the entire body of law and the entire court system: "Place it in the power of the courts to take jurisdiction, to assume jurisdiction, or to have jurisdiction accredited to them, and they will leave no stone unturned to exercise it to the detriment of the men and women of labor, who, after all, in all times have been compelled to suffer the tyranny and the oppression of an oligarchy, under whatever name it might be known."

Although the immediate reasons for the AFL (American Federation of Labor) leaders' mistrust of the legal system were wrong, it is worth observing that it went beyond the idea that the courts had abused their trust or that the law had been perverted. In comments made by AFL leaders on the law and the courts was an implicit dislike for the very idea of law, and not merely for the law that touched labor. As one modern observer has said, the AFL made "a principled attack on law and on the state." And beyond this was a simple but firm conviction that the essence of law was compulsion.

. . . An AFL vice president asked in 1902 why there should be any wait for the slow process of the law, "when we can exert sure and certain economic power."

Reliance on economic power—which largely meant collective bargaining (including ultimate recourse to strikes) and the boycott and a rather minimal reliance on friendly benefits—was the converse of hostility to the state and to political action. . . . Economic action was self-help, "the best help"; it represented the nearest approximation of individualism in the context of organization. Above all it was most congenial to solution of the very troubling problem of keeping the labor movement united in any organization whatsoever. . . .

Grant McConnell. Private Power and American Democracy. New York: Alfred A. Knopf, Inc., 1966. pp. 81-83

6. According to the passage, the AFL leaders' mistrust of the legal system rested primarily upon
   A) fundamental fraud in the law and the courts
   B) the labor injunction
   C) the use of the Sherman Act against labor
   D) defects in particular laws and distortion of legal processes
   E) an implicit dislike for the idea of the law

7. In order to advance its interests, the AFL preferred to rely on
   A) economic power instead of legal power
   B) legislative redress instead of litigation
   C) economic and legal power
   D) political pressure and boycott
   E) judicial and legislative relief

8. Gompers termed the Sherman Act "that legislative monstrosity" because
   A) its essence was compulsion
   B) it divided the labor movement
   C) it was turned destructively against the unions
   D) it made the courts accomplices in the perversion of the law
   E) the redress it brought was too slow

9. According to the passage, the view of the state taken by Gompers and his followers was
   A) unprincipled in the extreme
   B) justified by experience
   C) realistic
   D) derived from misunderstanding
   E) skeptical

10. Which of the following is not a feature of reliance on economic power as described in this passage?
    A) collective bargaining
    B) strikes
    C) labor injunction
    D) boycott
    E) minimal reliance on benefits

Passage 3:

The problem of the aged is particularly serious, for in most parts of the Western world today it is the fault of governments that the old have been deprived of the means of support that they may have endeavored to provide for themselves. By failing to keep faith and [to] . . . maintain a stable currency, governments everywhere have created a situation in which the generation going into retirement in the third quarter of our century has been robbed of a great part of what they had attempted to put aside for their retirement and in which many more people than there would otherwise have been are undeservedly facing poverty, despite their earlier efforts to avoid such a predicament. . . .

Yet, even if we approach the problem of provision for old age . . . in full awareness of the special responsibility which governments have incurred, we can but question whether the damage done to one generation . . . can justify the imposition upon a nation of a permanent system under which the normal source of income above a certain age is a politically determined pension paid out of current taxation. . . . In our efforts to remedy one ill, we may well saddle future generations with a burden greater than they will be willing to bear, so tying their hands that, after many efforts to extricate themselves, they will probably in the end do so by an even greater breach of faith than we have committed.

The problem arises in serious form as soon as government undertakes to secure not only a minimum but an "adequate" provision for all the aged, regardless of the individual's need or the contribution made by him. There are two critical steps that are almost invariably taken, once the state assumes the monopoly of providing this protection: first, the protection is granted not only to those who have through their contributions gained a claim to it, but to those who have not yet had time to do so; and second, when the pensions are due, they are not paid out of the yield of an additional capital accumulated for the purpose and therefore out of additional income due to the efforts of the beneficiary, but are a transfer of part of the fruits of the work of those currently producing.

. . . It is vain to believe that any objective standard of justice will set a limit on the extent to which those who have reached the privileged age, even if capable of continued work, can insist on being "adequately" maintained by those still at work. . . .

Assiduous propaganda has completely obscured the fact that this scheme of adequate pensions for all must mean that many who have at least reached the long hoped for time of retirement and who can retire on their savings will nevertheless be the recipients of a gratuity at the expense of those who have not yet reached it . . . and that in a wealthy society not devastated by inflation it is normal that a large proportion of the retired should be more comfortably off than those still at work. How seriously public opinion has been deliberately misguided in this matter is well illustrated by the often quoted assertion . . . that in the United States in 1935, "approximately 3 out of 4 persons 65 and older were probably dependent partly or wholly on others for support"—a statement based on statistics which explicitly assumed that all property held by old couples was owned by the husbands and that consequently all the wives were "dependent"!

Friedrich A. Hayek. The Constitution of Liberty. Chicago: The University of Chicago Press, 1978. pp. 294-296

11. In this passage, the major argument against a government-imposed system of financial support for old age concerns what aspect of this system?
    A) justice
    B) political popularity
    C) monetary feasibility
    D) unpredictability
    E) paternalism

12. How has public opinion of financial support for the aged been shaped?
    A) informed through publication of survey data
    B) misinformed through propaganda
    C) inflamed through fraudulent analysis of statistical data
    D) persuaded by public education programs
    E) kept ignorant of the responsibility government has incurred

13. Which condition worsens the damage done to one generation by a politically determined pension paid from current taxation?
    A) government limits privileged age of recipients
    B) government limits amount of benefits
    C) government determines adequate provision for all, regardless of need
    D) government redistributes wealth among generations
    E) government monopolizes provision of old age support

14. The author suggests that future generations burdened by funding pensions for the aged might
    A) limit privileged age of recipients
    B) rid themselves of the financial burden
    C) support only those whose contributions give them a claim to a pension
    D) pay pensions from interest accumulated for that purpose
    E) limit amount of benefits

<u>Passage 4</u>:

It is true . . . that developments since the last war in Britain . . . have so increased the progressive character of the income tax as to make the burden of taxation progressive throughout and that, through redistributive expenditure on subsidies and services, the income of the very lowest classes has been increased . . . by as much as 22 per cent. But the latter development is little dependent on the present high rates of progression but is financed mainly by the contributions of the middle and upper ranges of the middle class.

. . . [A]ll arguments in support of progression can be used to justify any degree of progression. Its advocates may realize that beyond a certain point the adverse effects on the efficiency of the economic system may become so serious as to make it inexpedient to push it any further. But the argument based on the presumed justice of progression provides for no limitation, as has often been admitted by its supporters, before all incomes above a certain figure are confiscated and those below left untaxed. Unlike proportionality, progression provides no principle which tells us what the relative burden of different persons ought to be. It is no more than a rejection of proportionality in favor of a discrimination against the wealthy without any criterion for limiting the extent of this discrimination. Because "there is no real rate of progression that can be demonstrated by formula," it is only the newness of the principle that has prevented its being carried at once to punitive rates. But there is no reason why "a little more than before" should not always be represented as just and reasonable. . . .

It is the great merit of proportional taxation that it provides a rule which is likely to be agreed upon by those who will pay absolutely more and those who will pay absolutely less and which, once accepted, raises no problem of a separate rule applying only to a minority. Even if progressive taxation does not name the individuals to be taxed at a higher rate, it discriminates by introducing a distinction which aims at shifting the burden from those who determine the rates onto others. In no sense can a progressive scale of taxation be regarded as a general rule applicable equally to all—in no sense can it be said that a tax of 20 per cent on one person's income and a tax of 75 per cent on the larger income of another person are equal. Progression provides no criterion whatever of what is and what is not to be regarded as just. It indi-

cates no halting point for its application, and the "good judgment" of the people on which its defenders are usually driven to rely as the only safeguard is nothing more than the current state of opinion shaped by past policy.

Friedrich A. Hayek. The Constitution of Liberty. Chicago: The University of Chicago Press, 1978. pp. 313-315

15. What is the primary focus of this passage?
    A) subsidies and services
    B) punitive rates of taxation
    C) progressive taxation
    D) proportional taxation
    E) rate of proportionality determined by formula

16. This passage argues against a separate rate of taxation for a minority on the grounds that it is
    A) financially infeasible
    B) monetarily irresponsible
    C) unjustly discriminatory
    D) based on changing public opinion
    E) reactive to major social change

17. Which of the following is an effect of the progressive-income tax?
    A) It has increased the income of the lowest classes by as much as 22 per cent.
    B) It provides a principle by which taxation may be limited.
    C) It limits discrimination against the wealthy.
    D) It applies generally to all.
    E) It cannot be carried to punitive rates.

18. Which of the following is not a characteristic feature of progressive taxation?
    A) It is a general rule applicable equally to all.
    B) It rejects proportionality.
    C) It is discriminatory against the wealthy.
    D) It is harmful to the economic system.
    E) It is confiscatory.

STOP!

If you finish before time is up (25 minutes), you may return to any of the questions in Section 1. Do not turn to any other section of the test.

SECTION 2 Sentence Correction

22 Questions
Time: 25 minutes

Directions: Some part of the following sentences, or the entire sentence, is underlined. The first of the five versions beneath each sentence is identical to the underlined portion. If you think the text is most correct as written in the problem, select (A); otherwise, choose the best sentence correction from the four remaining choices. Follow the requirements of written English when making your selection. Pay attention to grammar, word choice, and general sentence construction. Select the version that expresses most effectively and accurately what is contained in the original sentence.

1. Every year in the spring, the wind and the rain comes through the mountain pass just when the night falls with unbelievable force.
   A) comes through the mountain pass just when the night falls with unbelievable force
   B) come through the mountain pass just when the night falls with unbelievable force
   C) come through the mountain pass with unbelievable force just when the night falls
   D) will be coming through the mountain pass just when the night falls with unbelievable force
   E) comes through the mountain pass with unbelievable force just when the night falls

2. When his motorcade passed the reviewing stand, the president saluted his lady, standing rigidly and tense because of the vibrations from the heavy vehicle.
   A) saluted his lady, standing rigidly and tense because of the vibrations from the heavy vehicle
   B) saluted his lady, standing rigid and tense because of the vibrations from the heavy vehicle
   C) saluted his lady, standing rigid and tense because of the vibrations from his heavy vehicle
   D) , standing rigid and tense because of the vibrations from the heavy vehicle, saluted his lady
   E) , standing rigidly and tense because of the vibrations from the heavy vehicle, saluted his lady

3. Leave the maintenance man to his own resources, using the kind of a mop that he prefers.
   A) Leave the maintenance man to his own resources, using the kind of a mop that he prefers.
   B) Let the maintenance man use the kind of mop that he prefers.
   C) Let the maintenance man use the kind of a mop that he prefers.
   D) Leave the maintenance man use the kind of mop that he prefers.
   E) Leave the maintenance man to his own resources, using the kind of mop that he prefers.

4. The United Auto Workers Union, which represented all the workers at the Milk Run plant, demanded a higher wage for them.
   A) Union, which represented all the workers at the Milk Run plant, demanded
   B) Union which represented all the workers at the Milk Run plant demanded
   C) Union which represented all of the workers at the Milk Run plant demanded
   D) Union, which represented all of the workers at the Milk Run plant, demanded
   E) Union, which will have represented all the workers at the Milk Run plant, demanded

5. Jacques Roessel looks like his father, talks like his father and walks like he owned five cattle ranches.
   A) looks like his father, talks like his father and walks like he owned five cattle ranches
   B) looks and talks like his father and walks as if he owned five cattle ranches
   C) looks like his father, talks like his father and walks as if he owned five cattle ranches
   D) looks and talks like his father and walks like he owned five cattle ranches
   E) looks like his father, talks like his father and walks like he is owning five cattle ranches

6. It's as clear as crystal, Sabrina and Mark are the proud possessors of prodigious progeny.
   A) It's as clear as crystal, Sabrina and Mark are the proud possessors of prodigious progeny.
   B) It is quite evident that Sabrina and Mark are the proud possessors of prodigious progeny.
   C) It's as clear as crystal; Sabrina and Mark have prodigious progeny.
   D) It's quite evident that Sabrina and Mark have wonderful children.
   E) It's as clear as crystal, Sabrina and Mark have wonderful children.

7. The prophet announced quite boldly, "It is him whom all the sages adore."
   A) "It is him whom all the sages adore."
   B) "It is he whom all the sages adore."
   C) "It is him who all the sages adore."
   D) "It is he who all the sages adore."
   E) "It is him whom all the sages had adored."

8. Neither the personnel manager nor the director of sales could determine the cause for the breakdown of morale in the department of product promotion.
   A) Neither the personnel manager nor the director of sales could determine
   B) Either the personnel manager nor the director of sales couldn't determine
   C) Either the personnel manager nor the director of sales could not determine
   D) Neither the personnel manager or the director of sales could determine
   E) Neither the personnel manager or the director of sales could not determine

9. During the meeting, the parliamentarian ruled that the secretary needs first to file the report with the membership.
   A) the secretary needs first to file the report with the membership
   B) the secretary need first to file the report with the membership
   C) the secretary needs to file first the report with the membership
   D) the secretary need to file the report with the membership first
   E) the secretary needs to file the report with the membership first

10. Had the president made a better decision, he would have averted the catastrophe which ensued.
    A) Had the president made a better decision, he would have
    B) If the president made a better decision, he would have
    C) Had the president made a better decision, he had
    D) If the president would have made a better decision, he had
    E) Had the president made a better decision, he would had

11. Struggling to save the company, management poured twice as much money into it's operations this year then they did the year before.
    A) into it's operations this year then they did the year before
    B) into its operations this year than they did the year before
    C) into it's operations this year then they did the year before
    D) into it's operations this year than they had done the year before
    E) into its operations this year than they had done the year before

12. Trying to find the reason for a discrepancy in his computer printout, the accountant discovered a case of fraudulent reporting to the IRS.
    A) Trying to find the reason for a discrepancy in his computer printout, the accountant
    B) Trying to find a discrepancy in his computer printout, the accountant
    C) As he was trying to find a discrepancy in his computer printout, the accountant
    D) Having tried to find the reason for a discrepancy in his computer printout, the accountant had
    E) Since he is trying to find the reason for a discrepancy in his computer printout, the accountant

13. Because labor-management negotiations had ground to a halt, the CEO did his best to find a uninterested arbitrator.
    A) had ground to a halt, the CEO did his best to find a uninterested
    B) had completely stopped, the CEO did his best to find a uninterested
    C) had completely stopped, the CEO did his best to find an uninterested
    D) had completely stopped, the CEO did his best to find a disinterested
    E) had ground to a halt, the CEO did his best to find a disinterested

14. The vice-president discovered a way to augment profits, reduce costs and how to increase efficiency.
    A) augment profits, reduce costs and how to increase efficiency
    B) augment profits, to reduce costs and how to increase efficiency
    C) augment profits, reduce costs and increase efficiency
    D) augment profits, to reduce costs and to increase efficiency
    E) augment profits, how to reduce costs and how to increase efficiency

15. The shop foreman is the kind of person who I know nothing about.
    A) the kind of person who I know nothing about
    B) the person about whom I know nothing
    C) the person about who I know nothing
    D) the kind of person whom I know nothing about
    E) the kind of person about whom I know nothing

16. If the federal government would give us money we would integrate our pools.
    A) If the federal government would give us money we would integrate our pools.
    B) If the federal government would give us money we would desegregate entirely our pools.
    C) If we would integrate our pools, the federal government would give us money.
    D) If we would integrate our pools completely, the federal government would give us money.
    E) On the condition that we integrate our pools, the federal government would give us money.

17. If Sammy had not made the monthly payment, the bank might have repossessed his all-terrain vehicle.
    A) had not made the monthly payment, the bank might have
    B) had not made the monthly payment, the bank had
    C) should not have made the monthly payment, the bank would have
    D) did not make the monthly payment, the bank might have
    E) is not making the monthly payment, the bank will have

18. Since fluorocarbons are destroying the ozone layer, they should stop manufacturing them.
    A) Since fluorocarbons are destroying the ozone layer, they should stop manufacturing them.
    B) Since fluorocarbons had been destroying the ozone layer, the industrialized nations should stop manufacturing them.
    C) Since fluorocarbons have been destroying the ozone layer, the industrialized nations should stop manufacturing them.
    D) Since fluorocarbons have been destroying the ozone layer, they should stop manufacturing them.
    E) Since fluorocarbons will have been destroying the ozone layer, the industrialized nations should stop manufacturing them.

19. Because the vice-president did not review the contract from cover to cover the night before, he seemed nervous during the meeting.
    A) did not review the contract from cover to cover the night before, he seemed
    B) had not reviewed the contract from cover to cover the night before, he seemed
    C) had not reviewed the contract completely the night before, he seemed
    D) had not reviewed the contract completely the night before, he seems
    E) did not review the contract completely the night before, he seemed

20. On Christmas Eve in 1620, the rainy weather and gray skies could not effect the happy group of pilgrims huddled in front of the warm fire.
    A) could not effect
    B) could not have effected
    C) will not have affected
    D) could not affect
    E) could not have affected

21. Jimmy Fisher showed himself a better chess player than any man in the world when he won the world championship.
    A) showed himself a better chess player than any man in the world
    B) showed himself a better chess player than any other man
    C) showed himself a better chess player than any other man in the world
    D) that he was a better chess player than any man in the world
    E) that he was a better chess player than any man

22. The discoverer of the new world who everybody called a foolhardy navigator was relatively unknown in both the old world and in the new world.
    A) who everybody called a foolhardy navigator was relatively unknown in both
    B) whom everybody called a foolhardy navigator was relatively unknown in both
    C) who everybody called him a foolhardy navigator was relatively unknown in both
    D) who everybody called a foolhardy navigator was relatively unknown both in
    E) whom everybody called a foolhardy navigator was relatively unknown both in

STOP!

If you finish before time is up (25 minutes), you may return to any of the questions in Section 2. Do not turn to any other section of the test.

SECTION 3 Critical Reasoning

16 Questions
Time: 25 minutes

<u>Directions</u>: Select the best answer for each of the following questions.

1. You are given twelve cards—four aces, four kings, and four queens—which you can distribute any way you want on two table-tops. When you have distributed the cards to your satisfaction, they are turned face down. Then a small child is brought in and asked to turn over one card on each table. If she turns over two aces, you win a large prize.

   What is the best way for you to distribute the cards on the two tables?

   A) Put two aces, two kings, and two queens on one table, and the other six cards on the other table.
   B) Put one ace by itself on one table, and the other cards on the other table.
   C) Put four aces on one table, and the remainder of the cards on the other table.
   D) Put one ace and four kings on one table, and the other seven cards on the other.
   E) Put two aces on one table, and the other ten cards on the other table.

2. Jerry and Ellen, a retired couple, are hiking the Grand Canyon. They are up early, and start going down the Bright Angel trail from the south rim at 6:00 a.m. They make a leisurely hike of it, arriving at the foot-bridge over the Colorado River at the bottom of the canyon at about 11:30 a.m. They stop several times to rest beside the trail, but they do not leave the trail nor double back on their tracks.

   They camp overnight near the river, and are up early again the next day to begin their climb, crossing the foot-bridge at 6:00 a.m. Naturally, the ascent is slower than the previous day's hike, and they stop more often. Again, they do not leave the trail nor double back on it. They arrive on the south rim at about 3:45 p.m.

   Is there any place on the trail where Jerry and Ellen would have been at the same time of day on both days?

   A) Yes, there must be one such place.
   B) No, there cannot be such a place.
   C) There may be such a place, and there may not. We cannot tell without knowing more about their speed and just when they stop.
   D) There may not be such a place, but if there is then there are two such places.
   E) There must be at least one such place, but we cannot tell how many there may be.

<u>Items 3 and 4 pertain to the following scenario</u>.

A gift shop has been selling a line of greeting cards at $5.00 a box. They buy them wholesale for $2.00 per box, and any wholesale purchase of a reasonable volume is available at that same price. An employee who worked in a similar store in another city has some data which strongly suggests that reducing the selling price to $4.00 will generate a 50% increase in sales of this item. He urges the manager to make this move.

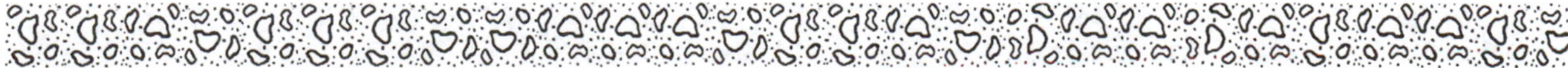

The manager is loath to change. He argues that the increased sales volume will just balance the reduced profit margin, so there will be no net improvement in the profitability of this line of goods.

3. The most promising way for the employee to strengthen his argument would be to
   A) show that the manager is mistaken in computing the overall profits generated by a 50% increase in the sales volume of this item.
   B) point out that fixed costs—such as rent and utilities—could be pro-rated over a larger number of transactions, thus reducing the amount of fixed cost per transaction.
   C) argue that the lower price would draw greeting card customers away from competing stores.
   D) point out that the increased volume would enable the store to hire an additional sales clerk.
   E) argue that the increased volume of card sales would mean more customer traffic in the store, and these additional customers would be likely to make other purchases at the same time.

4. The manager may now be inclined to make the change. Before making that decision final, however, he might consider some further arguments against it. A serious consideration of that sort would be that
   A) additional stocks of cards may not be available to meet the increased demand.
   B) competitors may lower their prices.
   C) there are variable costs—such as the wages of additional employees—which increase with increased sales volume. These may offset any additional profits.
   D) the wholesale cost of cards may increase.
   E) there has been a modest, but steady, increase in card sales over the past few years.

5. A certain college routinely gives the entering freshman class a math proficiency test. In 1992, they re-tested the graduating class with the same test that was used for the entering class in 1988. Surprisingly, the average score for the graduating seniors in 1992 was slightly lower than the average score four years earlier. College officials expressed embarrassed concern over the apparent fact that students were actually losing mathematical competence throughout their college careers.

   Before hastily introducing corrective programs, the officials might well consider whether their conclusion is on shaky grounds, because

   A) most of the courses in this college require little or no use of mathematics.
   B) the increasing use of calculators and computers has made mathematical skills less important for most college graduates.
   C) there is good evidence that the mathematical skills of high school students declined in the period from 1988 to 1992.
   D) those students in the incoming class in 1988 who were the strongest in mathematics may have left the college in disproportionate number prior to 1992.
   E) it is known that mathematical competence declines with age more rapidly than do most other skills.

6. In a certain strongly monogamous culture, over 90% of the adults of reproductive age are married. The average number of children per family is almost five, and over-population is now a serious threat. Programs to encourage the general use of birth-control have been ineffective. It has been suggested that this failure is largely due to the fact that these programs ignored a long tradition which values male children very highly, so that almost every parent wants to have at least one son. It is now proposed that couples be encouraged to use birth-control measures after the birth of their first son.

   If this proposal is widely accepted in the culture, we may expect that

   A) the rate of population increase will be slowed, and future generations will contain a disproportionately high number of females.
   B) the rate of population increase will be slowed, and the gender balance in future generations will remain as it is at present.
   C) the rate of population growth will remain the same, and future generations will contain a disproportionately high number of females.
   D) there will be no significant effect either on population growth or on gender balance.
   E) the population will decline precipitously, because approximately half of all families will have only a single child.

7. After the sinking of their ferry in a freak accident, the 239 passengers and crew members made their way to safety in a total of 20 small boats and rafts. Each boat carried 10 persons, and each raft carried 13.

   Of the 20 craft, how many were rafts?

   A) 7
   B) 15
   C) 5
   D) 13
   E) 11

8. Sharon is Paul's older sister. John is the son of Carl. Helen is older than John. Helen and Paul are twins.

   Which one of the following can be inferred from these statements taken together?

   A) Richard is older than Sharon.
   B) Richard is older than Helen.
   C) Sharon is older than John.
   D) Paul is younger than Richard.
   E) Paul is younger than John.

Items 9 and 10 refer to the following scenario.

An extensive survey, done by an independent and highly respected research institution, shows that over 80% of practicing dentists in the U.S. buy toothpaste fortified with the poly-carbonate additive for their own use and that of their families. There can be little doubt that these figures are accurate. These results are subsequently cited as evidence for the claim that poly-carbonate toothpaste makes a substantial contribution to dental health.

9. Which of the following, if they are facts, tend to weaken that argument?
   i. By the time the survey was taken, all major U.S. manufacturers were already including the poly-carbonate additive in most of their toothpaste brands.
   ii. The poly-carbonate additive improves the luster of teeth.
   iii. The additive is now so inexpensive that toothpaste with it regularly sells for about the same price as toothpaste without.

   A) ii and iii
   B) i and iii
   C) ii only
   D) iii only
   E) i and ii

10. Which of the following, if they are facts, tend to strengthen the standing of the conclusion of the original argument above?
   i. Poly-carbonate is expensive, and toothpaste which includes it sells for a noticeably higher price than others.
   ii. Poly-carbonate sometimes causes a slight discoloration of the teeth.
   iii. Laboratory studies show that dental enamel which has been treated with poly-carbonate is markedly more resistant to the sort of acids produced by oral bacteria.

   A) i and ii
   B) i, ii, and iii
   C) ii and iii
   D) iii only
   E) i only

11. In 1973, a remote Canadian community acquired television for the first time. Shortly before TV broadcasts began there, a study was made of aggressive behavior in first- and second-grade children. A similar study in the same community, after two years of TV, showed that the aggression rate among children of this age had increased by 160%. The tentative conclusion drawn was that TV plays an important role in generating aggressive behavior in children.

    A similar study, covering the same years, was made in two similar communities, but these were communities which had had television for several years prior to 1973. This study showed no change in the aggression rate from 1973 to 1975.

    The result of the second study

    A) suggests that the prevalence of violent themes in TV programming may be explained by the tendencies toward violence which are deeply-rooted in human nature.
    B) tends to show that different social groups may react quite differently to similar stimuli.
    C) tends to show that long-term exposure to TV has no more severe effects than short-term exposure.
    D) tends to confirm the conclusion drawn from the first study.
    E) tends to disaffirm the conclusion drawn from the first study.

12. The Kuwaiti oil-well fires, unlike the nuclear accident at Chernobyl, turned out not to be as serious an ecological disaster as was at first feared.

    From which of the following statements can the statement above be properly inferred?

    A) The Kuwaiti oil-well fires were extinguished much more rapidly than was first expected, and consequently their ecological impact was more limited than had been expected. The Chernobyl accident, on the other hand, was not taken seriously enough at first, either in the Soviet Union or in the West, and its baleful effects continue to outstrip most predictions.
    B) The Kuwaiti oil-well fires, though serious enough in ecological terms, have not had any widespread impact on the global ecology.
    C) The Kuwaiti oil-well fires involved the combustion of hydro-carbons, a process which releases compounds which are already fairly common in the environment. The Chernobyl accident released radio-active debris which has an extremely long half-life.
    D) The effects of the Chernobyl accident will be felt in the world for thousands of years to come, while most of the ecological damage done by the Kuwaiti oil-well fires has already been pretty well dissipated.
    E) The dire predictions of ecological catastrophe which were made about the fires in the Kuwaiti oil-fields have not been borne out in the subsequent course of events.

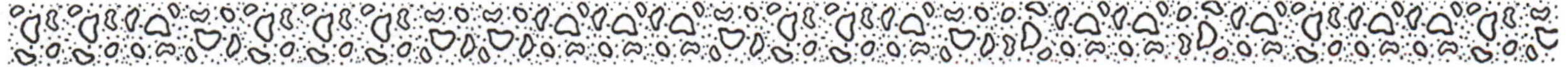

13. If Prince Henry was telling the truth, then John O'Groats was lying.

    If John O'Groats was not lying, then Prince Henry was telling the truth.

    What follows from these two statements taken together?

    A) Prince Henry was telling the truth.
    B) Prince Henry was not telling the truth.
    C) John O'Groats was lying.
    D) John O'Groats was not lying.
    E) The two initial statements are mutually contradictory.

14. A mother promises her children, "If it rains later on in the morning, then we will eat lunch at home and then go to a movie, provided that your father doesn't need the car himself. If it doesn't rain later on in the morning, then we will have lunch in the park and go to a movie afterward." The children promise their father, "If we go to a movie, we will clean up the basement afterward, and if we have lunch in the park, then we will wash the car this evening." The father promises their mother, "If it rains today, then you can use car to take the children, but if it doesn't rain I'll need it myself to get to the golf course."

    If each person keeps his/her promise, then

    A) the children will wash the car.
    B) the children will clean up the basement and wash the car.
    C) if the father goes to the golf course, the children will clean up the basement.
    D) if the father goes to the golf course, the children will eat lunch at home and go to a movie.
    E) if the children wash the car, the father must have gone to the golf course.

15. Mihajlo Markovic, a Serbian official and professor, has defended the Serbian project of "ethnic cleansing" in Bosnia and the tragic fighting there, by comparing it with the U.S. civil war. In a civil war, he says, the destruction of cities such as Sarajevo is to be expected. He is quoted as adding, "General Sherman not only occupied Atlanta, but burned it to the ground, and then did the same up and down the coast." (*The Chronicle of Higher Education*, 7 April 1993.)

    Which of the following claims would, if added to this comparison or analogy, lead plausibly to a strong moral conclusion?

    A) Sherman's burning of Atlanta weakened the Confederacy and contributed in an important way to the final Union victory.
    B) Neither Sherman nor Lincoln authorized the burning of Atlanta; it was the result of lawless acts by renegade Union soldiers.
    C) Sherman believed that the burning of Atlanta was necessary for a Union victory in the war, though he was probably mistaken in that.
    D) The burning of Atlanta, though a tragic event, was morally justified by the noble ends for which the war was fought.
    E) Sherman himself soon thereafter bitterly regretted his part in the burning of Atlanta and in the bloody "march through Georgia."

16. "Why do I know more than other people? Why, in general, am I so clever?" —Friedrich Nietzsche

Questions such as these may be seriously misleading, because

A) Nietzsche was actually insane, at least at some times in his life.
B) these questions refer to inner psychological states, which cannot be directly observed.
C) they are strongly colored by "ego involvement," so that an honest answer to them is likely to arouse strong feelings and unpredictable responses.
D) they involve cross-cultural and trans-temporal comparisons, which are always difficult at best.
E) to answer them just as they stand requires one to accept highly controversial and doubtful claims, which one might really wish to deny.

STOP!

If you finish before time is up (25 minutes), you may return to any of the questions in Section 3. Do not turn to any other section of the test.

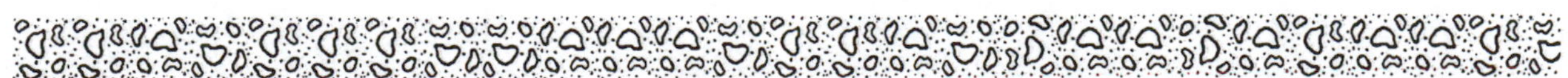

SECTION 4 Problem Solving

16 Questions
Time: 25 minutes

<u>Directions</u>: Solve each problem and mark the best answer on the Answer Marking Sheet provided. You may use the open space on the test paper for scratch work (in the actual exam no scratch paper is permitted). Figures are drawn to scale unless otherwise noted. All numbers are real numbers (no imaginary numbers).

1. The area of a circle is 25π. The area of the square circumscribed by the circle is
   A) $25/\sqrt{2}$ B) 100 C) $50/\sqrt{2}$ D) 50 E) $50\sqrt{2}$

2. A coat was purchased on sale for $140. If it was marked down 30%, what was the original price?
   A) $174 B) $182 C) $196 D) $200 E) $210

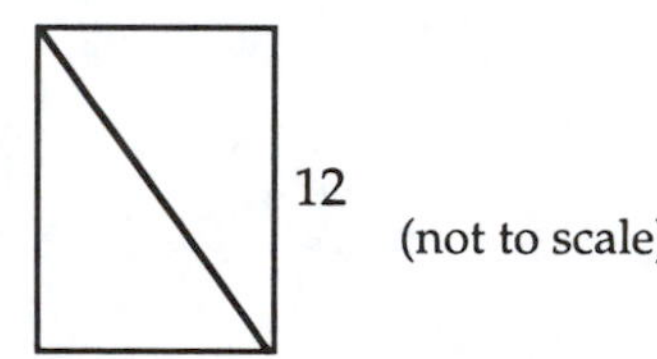

3. If the rectangle above has area 108, what is the length of the diagonal?
   A) 14 B) 15 C) 16 D) 17 E) 18

4. If $x^2 - 4x > 5$ then
   A) $x > -5$ B) $x < 5$ C) $x > -1$ D) $x < 1$ E) $x < -1$

5. A cylindrical, vertical tank is half full of water. When 10 gallons are added, the tank is 7/8 full. How many gallons does the tank hold?
   A) $24\frac{3}{8}$ B) $26\frac{2}{3}$ C) $28\frac{1}{3}$ D) $30\frac{3}{8}$ E) $32\frac{1}{8}$

6. A train travels 100 miles in 2 hours, the next 200 miles in 3 hours, and the last 150 miles in $2\frac{1}{2}$ hours. Calculate the average speed of the train.
   A) 52 mph B) 54 mph C) 56 mph D) 58 mph E) 60 mph

7. If $a - (b/3) = 1/3$ and $a + (b/4) = 3/2$, find $a + b$.
   A) 1 B) 2 C) 3 D) 4 E) 5

8. Jeff earns $12 per hour and John earns $10 per hour. About how much less, as a percentage, does John earn than Jeff?
   A) 25% B) 20% C) 17% D) 15% E) 10%

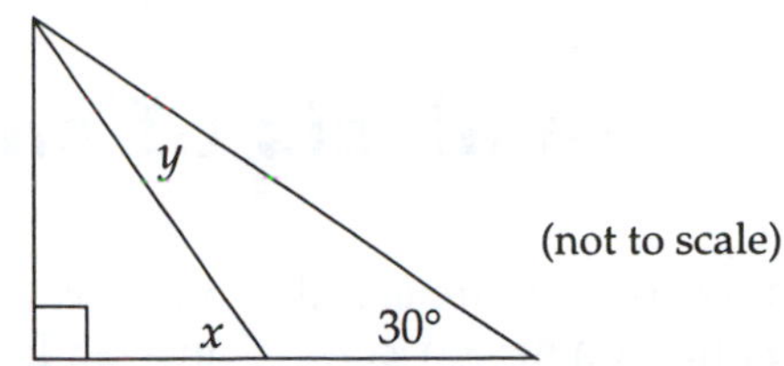

9. If $\angle y$ is 40° in the above triangle, calculate $\angle x$.
A) 75° B) 70° C) 65° D) 60° E) 50°

10. If $x + 2y = 2$ and $2x - y = 4$, then which of the following are true?
i. $x = 2$ ii. $y = 2$ iii. $x - y = 2$
A) i only B) ii only C) iii only D) i and ii E) i and iii

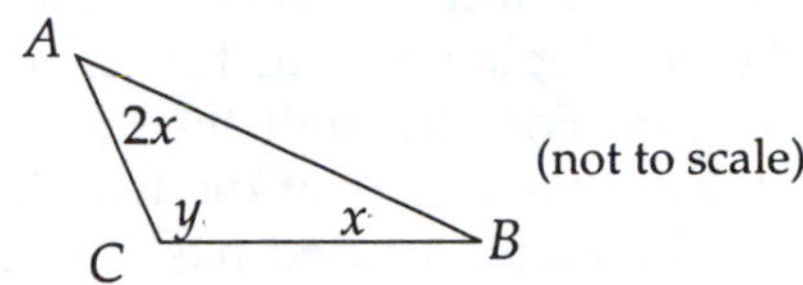

11. If $x + y = 120°$ for the angles in the above triangle, find the angle y.
A) 90° B) 100° C) 110° D) 120° E) none of these

12. Select the largest number from the following:
A) $3/10$ B) $5/20$ C) $\frac{1}{6} + \frac{1}{5}$ D) $\frac{1}{8} \div \frac{7}{5}$ E) 10% of 2

13. Five pickers can pick 10 acres of peaches in 20 hours. How many hours would it take 8 pickers to pick the peaches?
A) $12\frac{1}{2}$ B) 14 C) 15 D) $15\frac{1}{2}$ E) 16

14. If $0 > x > -1$, which of the following is greatest?
A) x^3 B) x C) $1/x$ D) $1/x^2$ E) $1/x^3$

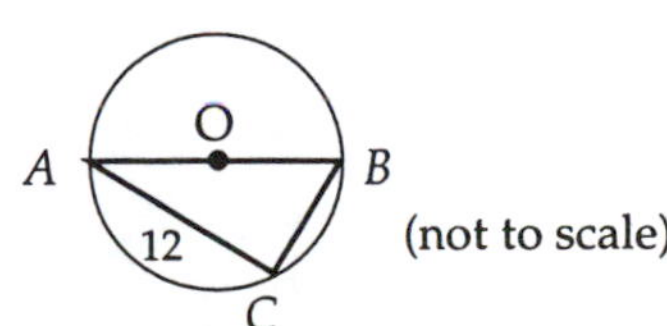

15. Find the area of the above triangle ABC if AB is a diameter.
A) 24 B) 28 C) 30 D) 36 E) 42

16. $7\frac{1}{5}$ inches is what fraction of a yard? (1 yd = 3 ft)
A) $2/15$ B) $1/5$ C) $4/15$ D) $1/6$ E) $7/18$

STOP!

If you finish before time is up (25 minutes), you may return to any of the questions in Section 4. Do not turn to any other section of the test.

SECTION 5 Analysis of an Issue

Directions: In this section you are asked to analyze and explain your views on the issue presented below. The question has no 'correct' answer. Instead, you should consider various perspectives as you develop your own position on the issue.

Read the statement and directions, and then make any notes in your test booklet that will help you plan a response. Begin writing your response on the separate answer document. Make sure that you use the answer document that goes with this writing task.

> At the end of the twentieth century, the civilizations of the industrial nations and the developing nations find themselves living with the specter of mass destruction. For although the collapse of Russian communism has eased tensions in many parts of the world, yet the ease with which nuclear weapons may be manufactured has created even greater, less predictable threats from any terrorist group or rogue nation.

(For your own informal test essay—to be graded by us or your own service—use three of the six unlined 8.5"x11" pages which you have ready, writing on one side only.)

STOP!

If you finish before time is up (30 minutes), do not turn to any other section of the test.

SECTION 6 Data Sufficiency

20 Questions
Time: 25 minutes

Directions: Each data sufficiency problem includes a question followed by two statements, labeled (1) and (2), that contain certain information. Using your knowledge of mathematics and common facts, you must determine if the information in the statements is sufficient to solve the problem. Select:

A if (1) alone is sufficient, but (2) alone is not sufficient;

B if (2) alone is sufficient, but (1) alone is not sufficient;

C if (1) and (2) together are sufficient, but neither alone is sufficient;

D if each statement alone is sufficient;

E if you cannot solve the problem with the information given.

Numbers: Only real numbers are used; no imaginary numbers are used or implied.

Diagrams: Diagrams reflect the information contained in the question, not necessarily the information contained in the two statements.

---

1. Is x^2 greater than x^3?
   (1) $x > 1$
   (2) $x < 1, \quad x \neq 0$

2. Line m is parallel to line n. What is angle y?
   (1) $x = 120°$
   (2) $z = 30°$

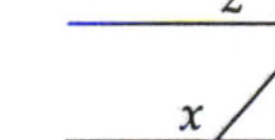

3. What is $x - y$?
   (1) $x = 7y$
   (2) $4x - 5y = 67$

4. What is the sum of the first eight terms of a geometric progression that contains all positive terms?
   (1) The first term of the sequence is 2.
   (2) The third term of the sequence is 6.

5. What is $\overline{BC}$ if $\overline{AB} = 10$ and $x = 30°$?
   (1) $z = 110°$
   (2) $\overline{AC} = 6$

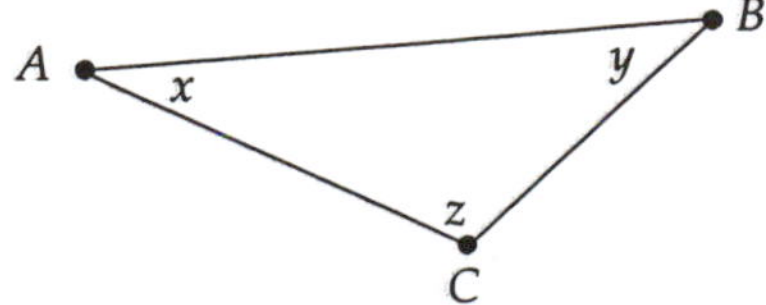

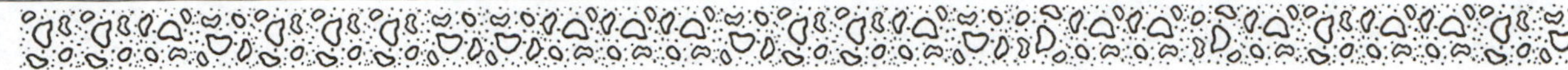

6. An airline company pays \$10,000 less for each additional airplane ordered. What would be the total price for 5 airplanes?
   (1) The first 2 airplanes cost 50% of the total price.
   (2) The last airplane costs half as much as the first.

7. Is the area of a circle equal to the area of a square?
   (1) The square has sides of length 10.
   (2) The circle's diameter is 20% greater than the length of the square's side.

8. Is $a^2 - a - 12 > 0$?
   (1) $a < 4$
   (2) $a < -3$

9. What is the ratio of John's salary in 1992 to John's dad's salary in 1952?
   (1) John worked 1000 hours to buy a car in 1992.
   (2) John's dad worked 2000 hours to buy a car in 1952.

10. What is h?
    (1) The angle opposite h is 90°.
    (2) The triangle is a right triangle.

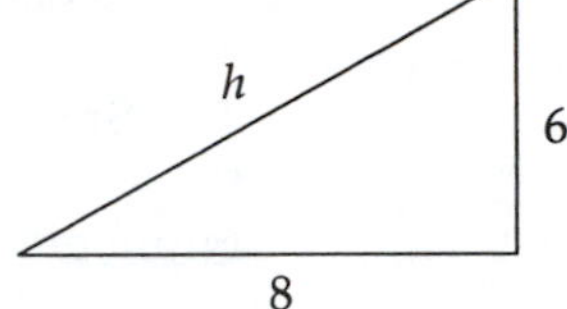

11. What is the average of five numbers?
    (1) The median of the five numbers is 8.
    (2) The sum of the five numbers is 27.

12. Is $1/x$ less than y?
    (1) $y > 1$
    (2) $x^2 < 1$

13. Is the volume of a rectangular tank less than 1000 liters?
    (1) The tank measures 2 m × 0.8 m × 0.5 m.
    (2) The tank holds 250 gallons of water.

14. Calculate the length b if $h = \sqrt{3}$.
    (1) Angle A is 60°
    (2) Angle B is 60°

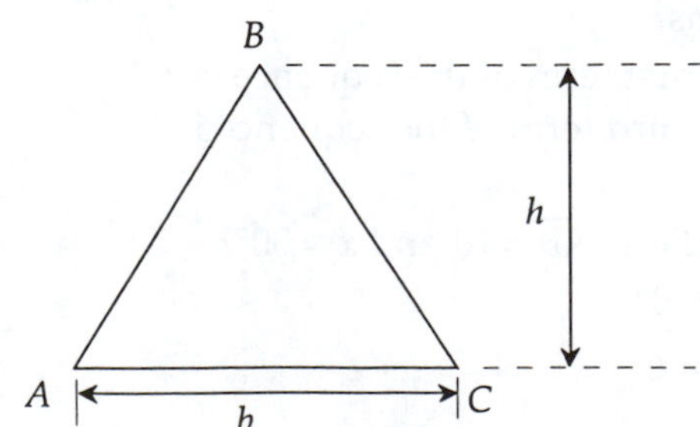

15. Does a perpendicular from B to $\overline{AC}$ bisect $\overline{AC}$ in the above triangle?
    (1) Triangle ABC is an isosceles triangle.
    (2) Angle A equals angle B.

16. What is a two-digit number with first digit x and second digit y?
    (1) The product of the digits is 12.
    (2) The sum of the digits is 8.

17. Is x^9 greater than y^{10}?
    (1) $x < 0$ and $y > 0$
    (2) $x = y + 1$

18. The radius of the circle is 5. What is $\overline{BC}$?
    (1) $\overline{AC} = 8$
    (2) Angle CAB is 30°

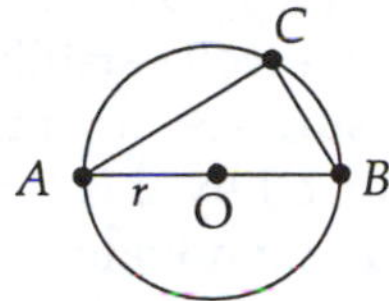

19. m and n are integers less than –2. Is $m < n$?
    (1) m and n are factors of 12
    (2) n is odd

20. What is the length of a line that connects the origin with point (x, y)?
    (1) $x = 4y$
    (2) $x + y = 5$

STOP!

If you finish before time is up (25 minutes), you may return to any of the questions in Section 6. Do not turn to any other section of the test.

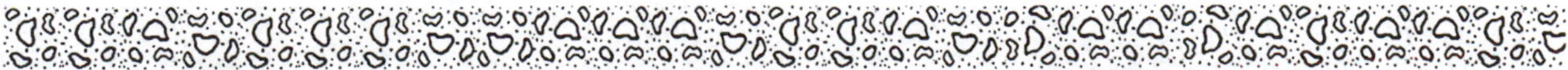

SECTION 7 Reading Comprehension

25 Questions
Time: 30 minutes

Directions: In this section, each passage is followed by questions based on its content. On the basis of what is stated or implicit in the passage, please select the best answer to each question.

Passage 1:

The record of the American Federation of Labor (AFL) in the long struggle for social legislation in the United States was truly remarkable. Conceptions of social insurance were developed in Europe during the nineteenth century and were well established in a number of countries before the twentieth. Old age insurance, unemployment insurance, and even health insurance were recognized by this time in many places as quite free of radical taint; indeed, the great innovator in this field was Bismarck. The contest for social insurance came after the turn of the century, but was largely won before the beginning of World War I. In America, however, the story was very different. Although Americans watched the English controversy on social legislation closely, there was no comparable political movement for its enactment in the United States. In the labor movement, the response to suggestions for a system of social legislation was generally hostile.

One of the early controversies within the AFL on social legislation related to laws regulating hours of work. The limitation of hours had long been a major objective of trade unionism, and in the years just before World War II, the eight-hour day was the goal of the most able and aggressive unions. In 1913, however, Gompers had denounced the idea of achieving this objective through legislation. . . . Presumably such legislation would have been compulsion.

. . . On the greater issue of social insurance, the AFL was bleakly antagonistic. The array of arguments brought forward in opposition to state insurance, whether for old age, health, or unemployment, was at once long and abstract. All these forms of insurance were "paternal." They would increase taxation. They would create a special bureaucracy for their administration. They would require the registration of workingmen as a class. They would divide people into two groups: those eligible for benefits and those ineligible. They would be undemocratic; they would destroy freedom.

Old age pensions under a governmental system were discussed with some heat in AFL conventions. . . . Resolutions favoring such pensions were defeated . . . until 1909, when a very mild and dilute form of approval was reluctantly given. . . . The debate on health insurance did not even produce transitory approval.

Unemployment insurance was the really big issue, and also the most revealing of AFL attitudes. . . . Resolutions in favor of an American system of unemployment insurance proffered in AFL conventions were soundly defeated in the years before American entry into the war. Thereafter, the issue lapsed, although there was some desultory discussion in the 1920s. With the onset of the Great Depression it once more came alive. After 1929, unem-

ployment increased rapidly and the membership of the AFL dwindled. Nevertheless, a resolution favoring unemployment insurance was defeated in . . . 1930. . . . [F]inally, in 1932, a resolution in favor of unemployment insurance was approved, although substantial opposition remained. In 1933 there was a unanimous favorable vote. History offers few comparable examples of doctrinaire rigidity in the face of adverse circumstances and in the name of pragmatism.

Grant McConnell. Private Power and American Democracy. New York: Alfred A. Knopf, Inc., 1966. pp. 84-85

1. According to the passage, the issue to which the AFL directed its most durable opposition was
   A) health insurance.
   B) unemployment insurance.
   C) laws regulating conditions of work.
   D) laws limiting hours of work.
   E) old age pensions.

2. After 1929, when unemployment increased rapidly, the AFL again considered the issue of unemployment insurance and
   A) allowed the issue to lapse.
   B) proposed new forms of unemployment insurance.
   C) made no decision regarding its adoption.
   D) continued to oppose it.
   E) reluctantly approved its adoption.

3. Regarding the origin of the concept of social insurance, the passage indicates that it
   A) originated in the U.S. before the American entry into World War I.
   B) originated in Europe after 1929.
   C) originated in the U.S. with the onset of the Great Depression.
   D) originated in the U.S. in 1933.
   E) originated in Europe during the nineteenth century.

4. The information given in this passage indicates that
   A) the AFL closely patterned its plans for social insurance on the postwar British model.
   B) the AFL sought to achieve social insurance through political pressure and legislation.
   C) the AFL, fearing radicalism, opposed social insurance.
   D) the AFL approved of health insurance only.
   E) the AFL was receptive of innovative social programs within the labor movement.

5. The major arguments of the AFL against social insurance were primarily
   A) monetary.
   B) economic.
   C) political.
   D) rhetorical.
   E) legal.

6. According to the passage, unanimous AFL approval was directed solely to
   A) health insurance.
   B) laws limiting hours of work.
   C) laws regulating conditions of work.
   D) unemployment insurance.
   E) old age pensions.

7. Which of the following is the major conclusion reached by the author?
   A) The AFL was long opposed in its struggle to obtain enactment of legislation on sc cial insurance in the U.S..
   B) The great innovator in legislation of social insurance for workers was Bismarck.
   C) Legislation of social insurance followed closely major social upheaval and war.
   D) The American labor movement lagged well behind the European movement i: political promotion of social benefits for workers.
   E) The AFL provides a distinctive example of fidelity to political principle even in th face of great disadvantage to its own interests.

<u>Passage 2</u>:

[It is paradoxical that] the old countries involve themselves in the most absurd complexities to prevent a shrinkage of their agricultural population [and] the new countries seem even more anxious to speed up the growth of the industrial population by artificial means. Much of this endeavor on the latter's part seems to be based on a rather naive fallacy of the *post hoc ergo propter hoc* variety: because historically the growth of wealth has regularly been accompanied by rapid industrialization, it is assumed that industrialization will bring about a more rapid growth of wealth. This involves a clear confusion of an intermediate effect with a cause. It is true that, as productivity per head increases as a result of investment in knowledge and skill, more and more of the additional output will be wanted in the form of industrial products. It is also true that a substantial increase in the production of food in those countries will require an increased supply of tools. But neither of these considerations alters the fact that if large-scale industrialization is to be the most rapid way of increasing average income, there must be an agricultural surplus available so that an industrial population can be fed. If unlimited amounts of capital were available and if the mere availability of sufficient capital could speedily change the knowledge and attitudes of an agricultural population, it might be sensible for such countries to impose a planned reconstruction of their economies on the model of the most advanced capitalist countries. This, however, is clearly not within the range of actual possibilities. It would seem, indeed, that if such countries as India and China are to effect a rapid rise in the standard of living, only a small portion of such capital as becomes available should be devoted to the creation of elaborate industrial equipment and perhaps none of it to the kind of highly automatized, "capital-intensive" plants that are characteristic of countries where the value of labor is very high, and that these countries should aim at spreading such capital as widely and thinly as possible among those uses that will directly increase the production of food.

The essentially unpredictable developments that may be produced by the application of advanced technological knowledge to economies extremely poor in capital are more likely to be speeded up if opportunity for free de-

velopment is provided than if a pattern is imposed which is borrowed from societies in which the proportion between capital and labor is altogether different from what it will be in the newer economies in the foreseeable future. However strong a case there may exist in such countries for the government's taking the initiative in providing examples and spending freely on spreading knowledge and education, it seems to me that the case against over-all planning and direction of all economic activity is even stronger there than in more advanced countries.

Friedrich A. Hayek. The Constitution of Liberty. The University of Chicago Press.

8. According to this passage, which term below describes the argument that industrialization will accelerate the growth of wealth?
   A) illogical
   B) probabilistic
   C) possible
   D) economic
   E) deterministic

9. What does the author of this passage recommend in order to produce a rapid rise in standard of living in India and China?
   A) direction of capital to the creation of industrial equipment
   B) direction of capital to automatized, capital-intensive plants
   C) direction of capital to increased production of food
   D) modeling of their economies on those of advanced capitalist countries
   E) increased investment in knowledge and skill

10. Capital-intensive plants are characteristic of countries where
    A) all economic activity is planned and directed.
    B) economies are poor in capital.
    C) the value of labor is very high.
    D) the value of labor is low.
    E) capital is spread thinly and widely.

11. The application of advanced technical knowledge to economies extremely poor in capital may produce
    A) rapid increase in wealth.
    B) substantial increase in the production of food.
    C) unpredictable developments.
    D) growth of industrial population.
    E) increased need for tools.

12. The major objective of this passage is
    A) to argue that developing countries should increase productivity per head.
    B) to compare industrial/agricultural policies of developing countries to those of the most advanced countries.
    C) to argue against overall planning and direction of all economic activity in developing countries.
    D) to advocate management of proportion between capital and labor in developing countries.
    E) to link increased standard of living with increased industrialization.

Passage 3:

The belief that friendly sociopolitical climates and low costs of government may be important [to competition among states to attract, keep, and enlarge high tech and manufacturing resources] has been reinforced by anecdotal evidence from business publications and business lobbyists who threaten to shift resources among states in response to costs or inconveniences imposed by state governments.

. . . Imbedded within the larger question of whether state policy initiatives affect the interstate movement of developmental resources is the more specific question of whether state-imposed environmental costs affect the interstate allocation of these resources. Do the actual or anticipated costs of complying with expensive environmental regulations in some states encourage producers to shift resources to other states? . . . [E]xtant evidence is mixed.

One set of scholars argues that interstate competition for economic development initiates a process analogous to Gresham's Law in which low regulatory costs in one state "drive out" higher costs in competing states because states that impose higher marginal costs of government will lose in the competition for economic resources. Empirical tests of the Gresham's Law analogy have produced inconsistent results; however, recent research suggests that, while they have by no means supplanted traditional locational factors, these environmental costs-of-government are increasingly important determinants of plant location, especially of intraregional location choices among states with comparable extra-governmental characteristics.

Others argue that the environmental costs of government, like other costs of government, remain a trivial factor in industries' resource allocation decisions. Christopher Duerkson's extensive study for the Conservation Foundation (1981) found little effect of state regulation on plant siting decisions, corroborating Healy's finding two years earlier that environmental regulation had an insignificant impact on the location of industry. Moreover, industry publications have consistently ranked environmental regulation as one of the least important elements of "business climate" influences on location decisions.

What is one to make of this contradictory evidence? To some degree it reflects inherent research design difficulties. Multicollinearity, for example, makes it extremely difficult to distinguish the attractiveness of environmental regulation from other aspects of "business climate." Likewise, the concentration of energy and other natural resources in states with relatively low costs of government make it difficult to distinguish the effects of these two potential influences. But the inherent design difficulties should not obscure the possibility that both sets of evidence are partially correct.

C. K. Rowland and Richard Feiock. "Environmental Regulation and Economic Development," Public Policy and Economic Institutions. Melvin J. Dubnick and Alan R. Gitelson, eds. Greenwich, Connecticut: JAI Press, 1991. pp. 206-207

13. This passage discusses which two major influences on business competition among states?
    A) locational factors and business climate
    B) state policy initiatives and state-imposed environmental costs
    C) interstate flight of capital and declining business capital
    D) actual and anticipated costs of compliance with environmental regulation
    E) sociopolitical climate and business climate

14. Which statement below most comprehensively states the central idea of this passage?
    A) Anecdotal evidence from business publications and lobbyists is suspect.
    B) The relative weight of critical factors in plant siting decisions is difficult to determine.
    C) Environmental regulation is a major deterrent in plant siting decisions.
    D) Anticipated and actual costs of environmental regulation differ.
    E) Evidence concerning factors in plant siting decisions is consistent.

15. Which statement below best describes difficulties of research design in this study?
    A) Potential influences are collinear, and their effects are not easily separable.
    B) Potential influences intersect, and their effects are readily separable.
    C) Potential influences are parallel, and their effects are measurable.
    D) Potential influences are interdependent, and their effects are fixed.
    E) Potential influences shift, and their effects are inseparable.

16. In the search for the critical factor in plant siting decisions, the weight of the evidence indicates that
    A) higher costs of government outweigh traditional locational factors.
    B) environmental costs are critical determinants.
    C) environmental costs are a trivial factor.
    D) state policy decisions are critical determinants.
    E) concentration of energy is a critical factor.

Passage 4:

The answers to our research questions can easily be summarized. States do vary substantially in the pollution abatement expenses (PAE) they impose on the chemical industry and in their ability to attract that industry's capital. This variance is not accounted for by frostbelt-sunbelt differences; variance within each region rendered differences between regions insignificant. Variance in ability to attract new capital shares is, however, related to private PAE; interstate variance in pollution abatement expense explains more than half the 1977-1981 change in states' ability to attract a share of the chemical industry's new capital.

In addition to the straightforward statistical findings, these data suggest that, for the chemical industry, the relationship between resource allocation and environmental costs may not be linear. . . . [W]hile states which impose high pollution abatement costs tend to compete unsuccessfully for new capital, those who impose the lowest marginal costs are not necessarily the most successful in increasing their share of new capital. Rather, there appears to be a PAE threshold; when a state exceeds it, the state loses capital to states that remain below it. In all likelihood states with limited capacity to socialize the costs of environmental regulation must exceed that marginal-cost threshold to meet federally imposed environmental standards while states with greater fiscal capacity can meet such standards without exceeding the threshold and compete for developmental resources on the basis of other incentives.

. . . [F]irmer conclusions are limited by some implicit caveats and design limitations. First, . . . our findings tell us little about the relationship between

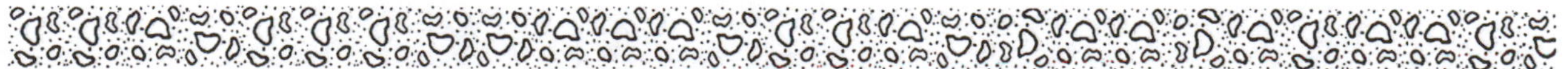

overall quality of environmental protection and the allocation of CAP (chemical and allied producers') resources. We do not, therefore, know whether the adequacy of regulation is affected by economic development. Second, our conclusions are limited to our sample and time frame. Third, we could not, in this exploratory study, control the possibility that our statistical relationships are the spurious artifact of other, unexamined, effects. . . . Finally, we have not controlled for the possibility that a large relative pollution abatement expenses in 1977 may be accounted for partially by an exodus of resources before 1977 that left relatively fixed expenses to be balanced against a shrinking pool of shipments.

C. K. Rowland and Richard Feiock. "Environmental Regulation and Economic Development," Public Policy and Economic Institutions. Melvin J. Dubnick and Alan R. Gitelson, eds. Greenwich, Connecticut: JAI Press, 1991. pp. 215-216

17. Which inference below may be derived from the information given in this passage?
    A) The relationship between resource allocation and environmental costs is linear.
    B) States that impose lowest pollution abatement expenses compete most successfully for new chemical industry capital.
    C) States that impose highest pollution abatement expenses compete least successfully for new chemical industry capital.
    D) Pollution abatement expenses are a negligible factor in competition for new chemical industry capital.
    E) Variance in ability to attract new chemical industry capital appears to relate to a threshold figure for pollution abatement expenses.

18. According to the passage, what impedes the ability of states to keep within the marginal-cost threshold of pollution abatement expenses?
    A) other, unexamined effects
    B) frostbelt-sunbelt differences
    C) lower fiscal capacity to meet federal standards
    D) unequal allocation of chemical producers' capital
    E) loss of other incentives

19. Which of the following is not a statistical finding summarized in this passage?
    A) The ability of states to attract chemical industry capital varies greatly.
    B) Variance in ability to attract chemical industry capital is not explained by frostbelt-sunbelt differences.
    C) Pollution abatement expenses imposed by states on the chemical industry vary greatly.
    D) Quality of environmental protection and attraction of new capital correlate strongly.
    E) Variance within regions renders differences between regions insignificant.

20. Implicit caveats that limit firmer conclusions to this study are
    A) flaws
    B) warnings
    C) gaps in statistical data
    D) unexplained artifacts of research
    E) spurious effects of research

21. States with greater fiscal capacity
    A) can meet federal environmental standards and compete for resources on the basis of other incentives.
    B) must exceed marginal-cost threshold.
    C) can control quality of environmental protection.
    D) can adjust pollution abatement costs to increase share of new capital.
    E) can balance quality and cost of environmental protection.

Passage 5:

Whatever the initial motivation for its investment in new operating units, the modern industrial enterprise has rarely continued to grow or maintain its competitive position *over an extended period of time* unless the addition of new units (and to a lesser extent the elimination of old ones) has actually permitted its managerial hierarchy to reduce costs, to improve functional efficiency in marketing and purchasing as well as production, to improve existing products and processes and to develop new ones, and to allocate resources to meet the challenges and opportunities of ever-changing technologies and markets.

. . . Reductions in costs and efficient resource utilization have resulted, the explanation continues, from the exploitation of economies of scale in production and distribution, from exploiting economies of joint production or joint distribution, or from reduction in the costs of transactions involved.

Economies of scale may be defined initially as those that result when the increased size of a single operating unit producing or distributing a single product reduces the unit cost of production or distribution.

Economies of joint production or distribution are those resulting from the use of processes within a single operating unit to produce or distribute more than one product. (I use the increasingly popular term "economies of scope" to refer to these economies of joint production or distribution.)

Transaction costs are those involved in the transfer of goods and services from one operating unit to another. When these transactions are carried out between firms or between individuals, they usually involve the transfer of property rights and are defined in contractual terms. When they are carried out within the enterprise, they are defined by accounting procedures. The costs of such transactions are reduced by a more efficient exchange of goods and services *between* units, whereas the economies of scale and scope are closely tied to the more efficient use of facilities and skills *within* such units.

. . . It was the development of new technologies and the opening of new markets, which resulted in economies of scale and of scope and in reduced transaction costs, that made the large multi-unit industrial enterprise come when it did, where it did, and in the way it did. These technological and market changes explain why the institution appeared and continued to cluster in certain industries and not in others, why it came into being by integrating units of volume production with those of volume distribution, and finally, why this multifunctional enterprise continued to grow . . . by becoming multinational and multiproduct.

Alfred D. Chandler, Jr. Scale and Scope: The Dynamics of Industrial Capitalism. Cambridge, Massachusetts: The Belknap Press of Harvard University Press, 1990. pp. 17-18

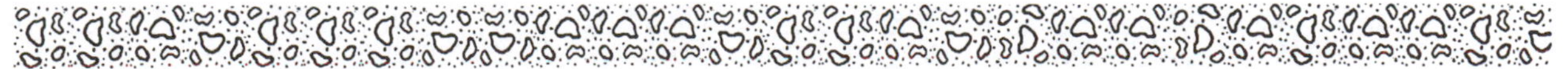

22. Which of the items below encouraged the formation of the multi-unit industry?
    A) control of transaction costs and opening of new markets
    B) technological change and market imperfections
    C) volume production and volume distribution
    D) economies of scale, economies of scope, and reduced transaction costs
    E) addition of new units and reduction of costs

23. According to this passage, which of the following is not included in the efforts of management to promote growth or maintain its competitive position?
    A) concentration of facilities of production
    B) development of new products
    C) improvement in existing products
    D) improved efficiency of marketing, purchasing, and production
    E) allocation of resources to meet changing technologies and markets

24. When transaction costs are carried out within an enterprise, they are defined by
    A) contractual terms.
    B) accounting procedures.
    C) transfer of property rights.
    D) concentrated source of supply.
    E) efficient use of resources.

25. Economies of scope are those in which
    A) the same processes within a single unit produce or distribute more than one product.
    B) increased size of a production unit reduces unit cost of production or distribution.
    C) multi-unit industrial enterprises cluster in certain industries.
    D) multi-unit enterprise integrate volume production and distribution.
    E) transaction costs are carried out within an enterprise.

STOP!

If you finish before time is up (30 minutes), you may return to any of the questions in Section 7. Do not turn to any other section of the test.

SECTION 8 Problem Solving

16 Questions
Time: 25 minutes

Directions: Solve each problem and mark the best answer on the Answer Marking Sheet provided. You may use the open space on the test paper for scratch work (in the actual exam no scratch paper is permitted). Figures are drawn to scale unless otherwise noted. All numbers are real numbers (no imaginary numbers).

1. The plans of a building are drawn so that $\frac{1}{8}$ inch equals 1 foot. A measurement of $5\frac{7}{8}$ inches equals how many feet?
   A) 41 B) 47/64 C) 45 D) 47 E) 25/32

2. If $x - \frac{y}{2} = \frac{3}{4}$ and $y = \frac{7}{4}x$ find x.
   A) 6 B) 2 C) $\frac{1}{4}$ D) $-\frac{1}{4}$ E) -4

3. Select the fraction that has the largest value.
   A) $\frac{1}{3}$ B) $\frac{2}{5}$ C) $\frac{3}{7}$ D) $\frac{4}{9}$ E) $\frac{5}{13}$

4. Three corners of a rectangle are at (3, 1), (3, – 3), and (– 4, 1). What are the coordinates of the fourth corner?
   A) (4, 1) B) (3, – 1) C) (– 4, – 1) D) (– 4, – 3) E) (– 3, – 1)

5. Dale walks 3 miles north, 2 miles east, and 5 miles north. He then walks east again. If he is discovered exactly 10 miles from his starting point, how many miles east did he walk?
   A) 2 B) 3 C) 4 D) 5 E) 6

6. Find the angle x, in degrees, in the diagram.
   A) 75° D) 95°
   B) 80° E) 105°
   C) 85°

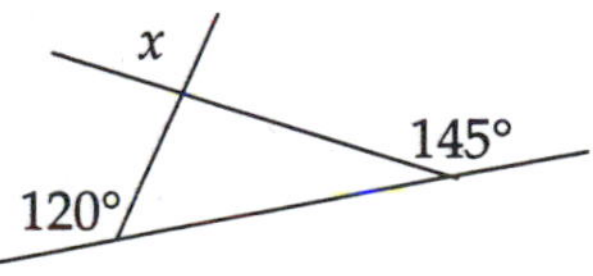

7. A farmer harvested x bushels of corn, y bushels of soy beans, and z bushels of wheat. What portion of his harvest was corn?
   A) $x / (x + y + z)$ B) $(x + y + z) / x$ C) $x + y + z / x$
   D) $(y + z) / (x + y + z)$ E) $x / x + y + z$

8. If the sum of $x - 5$ and a second number is 4, what must the second number be?
   A) $5 + x$ B) 9 C) $x + 9$ D) $x + 4$ E) $9 - x$

9. If $x = t + t^2$ and $y = t - t^2$, find a possible value for y at $x = 2$.
   A) -6 B) -4 C) -2 D) 2 E) 4

10. A biker rides 100 miles at 30 miles per hour and returns the next day against the wind at 20 miles per hour. What was his average speed?

    A) 24 mph B) $24\frac{1}{2}$ mph C) 25 mph D) $25\frac{1}{2}$ mph E) 26 mph

11. Write $\frac{4.11}{300}$ as a decimal.

    A) 0.137 B) 0.0137 C) 0.00137 D) 0.000137 E) 0.0000137

12. A pie graph depicts the budget of an organization. A pie piece represents $40,000 of a $300,000 total budget. What angle is represented by the pie piece?

    A) 30° B) 42° C) 48° D) 56° E) 60°

13. Calculate the angle z.

    A) 15° D) 30°
    B) 20° E) 35°
    C) 25°

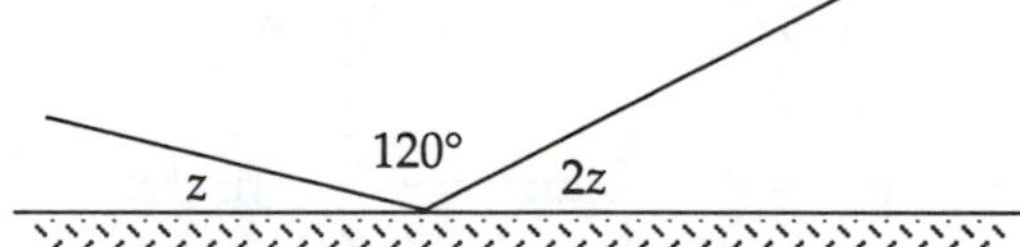

14. The longest side of an isosceles right triangle is 8. How long is one of the other sides?

    A) $2\sqrt{5}$ B) $3\sqrt{2}$ C) $5\sqrt{3}$ D) $4\sqrt{2}$ E) $3\sqrt{3}$

15. If x and y are two acute angles of a right triangle, and $y > 30°$, then

    A) $x < 60°$ B) $x > 60°$ C) $x < 90°$ D) $x > 90°$ E) $x < 180°$

16. Each edge of a cube is 6 ft. If it takes one quart of paint to cover 100 ft^2, how many pints of paint should be purchased to cover the entire exterior surface of the cube?

    A) 5 B) 6 C) 7 D) 8 E) 9

STOP!

If you finish before time is up (25 minutes), you may return to any of the questions in Section 8. Do not turn to any other section of the test.

SECTION 9 Analysis of an Argument

Directions: In this section you will write a critique of the argument presented below. You may, for example, consider what questionable assumptions underlie the thinking, what alternative explanations or counter examples might weaken the conclusion, or what sort of evidence could help strengthen or refute the argument. Read the argument and directions, and then make any notes in your test booklet that will help you plan a response. Begin writing your response on the separate answer document. Make sure that you use the answer document that goes with this writing task.

> Although biologists think that food production cannot keep pace with population growth, economists say that science comes up with new technologies when free markets offer inducements for change. They, therefore, believe that food production can outpace population growth, thus providing sufficient food for all of the peoples on the earth.

(For your own informal test essay—to be graded by us or your own service—use three of the six unlined 8.5"x11" sheets of paper you have ready, writing on front and back sides.)

STOP!

If you finish before time is up (30 minutes), do not turn to any other section of the test.
This is the last section of the Diagnostic Test.

Answer Key to the Diagnostic Test

Section 1 *Reading*	Section 2 *Sentences*	Section 3 *Reasoning*	Section 4 *Problems*	Section 6 *Data*	Section 7 *Reading*	Section 8 *Problems*
1. **B**	1. **C**	1. **B**	1. **D**	1. **D**	1. **B**	1. **D**
2. **E**	2. **D**	2. **A**	2. **D**	2. **D**	2. **D**	2. **A**
3. **D**	3. **B**	3. **E**	3. **B**	3. **C**	3. **E**	3. **D**
4. **C**	4. **A**	4. **C**	4. **E**	4. **C**	4. **C**	4. **D**
5. **A**	5. **B**	5. **D**	5. **B**	5. **D**	5. **C**	5. **C**
6. **E**	6. **D**	6. **B**	6. **E**	6. **D**	6. **D**	6. **C**
7. **A**	7. **B**	7. **D**	7. **C**	7. **B**	7. **E**	7. **A**
8. **C**	8. **A**	8. **C**	8. **C**	8. **B**	8. **A**	8. **E**
9. **B**	9. **D**	9. **E**	9. **B**	9. **E**	9. **C**	9. **A**
10. **C**	10. **A**	10. **B**	10. **E**	10. **D**	10. **C**	10. **A**
11. **A**	11. **E**	11. **D**	11. **A**	11. **B**	11. **C**	11. **B**
12. **B**	12. **A**	12. **A**	12. **C**	12. **C**	12. **C**	12. **C**
13. **C**	13. **D**	13. **C**	13. **A**	13. **D**	13. **B**	13. **B**
14. **B**	14. **C**	14. **C**	14. **D**	14. **C**	14. **B**	14. **D**
15. **C**	15. **B**	15. **D**	15. **C**	15. **E**	15. **A**	15. **A**
16. **C**	16. **A**	16. **E**	16. **B**	16. **E**	16. **C**	16. **A**
17. **A**	17. **A**			17. **A**	17. **E**	
18. **A**	18. **C**			18. **D**	18. **C**	
	19. **C**			19. **C**	19. **D**	
	20. **E**			20. **C**	20. **B**	
	21. **B**				21. **A**	
	22. **E**				22. **D**	
					23. **A**	
					24. **B**	
					25. **A**	

Note: Sections 5 & 9 are "Writing Analysis," to be answered on 6 separate sheets.

Self-Grading & Score Conversion

Upon completing the Diagnostic Test, it is extremely beneficial for you to grade yourself. This will enable you to identify your weak areas so that you can organize a review that will give you the greatest improvement.

Using the Answer Sheet, determine your Raw Score using the following formula for each of the seven sections of the test and fill in the following table:

$$\text{Raw Score} = \text{\# Correct} - \tfrac{1}{4}\,(\text{\# Incorrect})$$

Your rating (poor to excellent) in each section is determined using the second table.

Self-Grading Table

Section	Correct	Incorrect	Blank	Raw Score	Rating
1					
2					
3					
4					
6					
7					
8					

<u>Note</u>: Sections 5 & 9 (Analytical Writing) are to be graded by a peer or by our FAX service.

Rating Determination (use Raw Scores)

Section	Poor	Fair	Good	Excellent
1	0-6	7-10	11-15	16-18
2	0-8	9-13	14-18	19-22
3	0-6	7-9	10-13	14-16
4	0-6	7-9	10-13	14-16
6	0-8	9-12	13-17	18-20
7	0-10	11-16	17-21	22-25
8	0-6	7-9	10-13	14-16

Your Verbal and Quantitative scores and your total score can be converted to approximate percentile rankings using the following formulas:

Verbal Raw Score = Sum of Raw Scores from Sections 1, 2, and 3
Quantitative Raw Score = Sum of Raw Scores from Sections 4, 6, and 8
Total Score = Sum of Verbal and Quantitative Raw Scores

Top Quarter Percentile	Middle Half Percentile	Bottom Quarter Percentile
Verbal > 37	37 > Verbal > 17	Verbal < 17
Quantitative > 34	34 > Quantitative > 16	Quantitative < 16
Total > 69	69 > Total > 35	Total < 35

Explanations to the Answers

SECTION 1 Reading Comprehension

1. B The passage makes it quite clear that no conflict of purpose or use, no complexity of land or water, no complexity of technology or scale is a primary cause of the shortcomings of water projects in the U.S. (A), (C), (D), and (E) are, as a result, incorrect.

2. E The passage makes it clear that in the lower part of the basin, flooding is the problem; in the upper part, scarcity is the problem. Scarcity is the **only** problem identified with the upper part of a basin. (A), (B), (C), and (D) are irrelevant to this question and, as a result, are incorrect.

3. D The passage makes it plain that (A), conflict of purpose; (B), practical problems of use; (C), vulnerability of cities on flood plains; and (E), climatic variations, impede the development of water resources. Design technology is not one of the impediments identified by this passage.

4. C The key here is in the last part of the sentence: "projects affecting it should treat it as such." (A) and (B) are factual statements, but neither answers the question relative to coordination of activities. (D) and (E) are incorrect, for they are generalizations unsupported by evidence from the passage.

5. A It is a limited inference. The passage makes it clear that problems of climate, geography, purpose, and technology complicate the development of water projects, but the most serious impediment is the impediment of inadequate study and faulty coordination. The inference in (B) is wholly unsupported by the passage. (C) directly contradicts the major scientific argument of the passage. The inferences in (D) and (E) are not supported by information in the passage.

6. E The passage makes it clear that (A), (B), (C), and (D) were events that contributed to the AFL leaders' mistrust of the legal system, but it makes the point that their dislike went beyond these injustices to a profound political conviction, "an implicit dislike for the idea of the law."

7. A (B) is incorrect, for the passage indicates that Gompers had called the Sherman Act "that legislative monstrosity" and that labor's attitude toward the law was hostile. (C) is incorrect, for the point of the passage is that the AFL mistrusted legal power. (D) is incorrect, since the AFL approved of economic action precisely because it was "the converse of political action." (E) is incorrect, for the passage makes it quite clear that the AFL leaders mistrusted the judiciary.

8. C (A) is incorrect, since it was the "essence of law" that was seen as compulsion, not one particular act. (B) is incorrect, for nowhere does the passage mention division of the labor movement, only a means of keeping it united. (D) is incorrect because it was the labor injunction, not the Sherman Act, that made the courts accomplices in the perversion of the law. (E) is incorrect, since nothing in the passage mentions redress.

9. B The passage declares, "There was much immediate experience to justify the view of the state that Gompers and his followers took." (A), (C), and (E) are incorrect, for the passage makes no judgment on Gompers' and his followers' view of the state. (D) may be an accurate statement, but it is an incorrect answer, since it is not supported by evidence from the passage.

10. C The labor injunction was not a feature of labor's reliance on economic power. It was used destructively against labor. The passage enumerates (A), (B), (D), and (E) as **parts** of reliance on economic power.

11. A Key words are "undeservedly," "justify," and "objective standard of justice." (B), (C), (D), and (E) are not supported by information given in the passage.

12. B Key phrases are "assiduous propaganda" and "public opinion has been deliberately misguided in this matter." (A) is incorrect, since the passage says nothing of survey data. (C) is incorrect, for although the passage does mention fraudulent analysis of statistical data, it does not indicate that the public has been inflamed by it. (D) is incorrect, for public information programs are mentioned nowhere in the passage. (E) may be implicit in this passage, but it does not answer the question concerning the "shaping" of public opinion. In this passage, propaganda shapes public opinion.

13. C "The problem arises in serious form as soon as the government undertakes to determine adequate provision for all, regardless of need." (A) and (B) are incorrect, for they name limits, not standardization of benefits. The accuracy of (D) may be implicit in this argument, but it does not answer the question, "Which condition worsens the damage. . .?" (E) contributes to the author's argument against government control of old age support, but it does not answer the question, "Which condition worsens the damage. . .?" It is the standardization of provision for all, regardless of need, that worsens the damage.

14. B (A), (C), and (D) are incorrect, for nowhere does the passage indicate selective reform of the funding system. (E) is incorrect, since it is not mentioned in association with the burden on future generations.

15. C (A) is incorrect because it is an effect of progressive taxation, not the primary focus of the passage. (B) is incorrect because it is a feature of progressive taxation, not the primary focus of the passage. (D) is incorrect, for it is the alternative to progressive taxation, the primary focus of this essay. (E) is incorrect, since it is a feature of the proportional tax, and the proportional tax is a secondary focus of the passage.

16. C This passage argues against progressive taxation on the basis of its injustice. (A), (B), (D), and (E) are incorrect, for nowhere are they mentioned in the passage.

17. A It is the only measurable effect of the progressive income tax mentioned in the passage. (B) is incorrect, for it is inaccurate according to the information given in the passage. (C) is incorrect, since the passage argues the opposite effect of the progressive tax. (D) is incorrect, for it is an advantageous feature of the proportional tax. (E) is inaccurate because the passage argues the opposite effect of the progressive tax.

18. A It is precisely because it does not provide a general rule applicable equally to all that the author argues against the progressive tax. (B), (C), (D), and (E) accurately describe features of progressive taxation.

SECTION 2 Sentence Correction

1. C The problem with (A) is that the phrase *with unbelievable force* is not next to the phrase which it modifies: *the wind and the rain comes through the mountain pass*. Neither is the verb *come* in agreement with the plural subject. These are both remedied by (C).

2. D *Rigidly* and *tense* are not parallel, (A) and (E). The modifier starting with *standing* is not close to the noun it modifies, *the President*.

3. B *Leave . . . to his own resources* is a cliché, (A), (D) and (E). In *kind of a*, the *a* is completely unnecessary, (A) and (C). *Leave* as a synonym for *let* is colloquial. Only (B) could be correct.

4. A Proper nouns cannot have restrictive clauses, (B) and (C). The *of* in *all of* is unnecessary, (C) and (D). The future does not fit the situation, (E). There is nothing wrong with (A).

5. B The repeated words in *looks like his father, talks like his father* are unnecessary, (A), (C) and (E). *Like* cannot be used as a conjunction, as in (A), (D) and (E). Only (B) is correct.

6. D Like many clichés, *it's as clear as crystal* adds nothing to the meaning and is unnecessary; this rules out (A), (C) and (E). The same could be said for *prodigious progeny* and *proud possessors*. Only (D) is left.

7. B The subjective case of the pronoun must be used after *it is*; thus, only (B) and (C) could be right. *Whom* is the object of *adore* and must be in the objective case (B).

8. A *Neither* and *nor* travel together in negative sentences. Only (A) could be right.

9. D *First* is a misplaced modifier. It cannot come between a verb and its complement. In sentences having to do with parliamentary procedure, the subjunctive should be used, (D).

10. A The clause starting with *had . . . made* is equivalent to a clause with *if the President had made*. Thus there is nothing wrong with the original.

11. E There are several problems in this sentence: *it's* (it is) instead of *its*, the possessive pronoun; *then* for *than*; and the use of the past tense rather than the past perfect tense.

12. A The accountant had already found the discrepancy; what he needed was a reason for it. (C) and (E) are more wordy than the correct form (A).

13. D *Ground to a halt* is a cliché and should not be used. No one would want to use uninterested arbitrators in a dispute. Disinterested arbitrators would be better.

14. C The basic problem is a matter of parallelism; two infinitives, *to augment profits* and *to reduce costs*, are paired with a *how*-infinitive clause, *how to do it*. This is corrected in (C).

15. B Actually, there is nothing wrong with ending a sentence with a preposition in speech. But it should be avoided in writing, (A) and (D). *Kind of* adds nothing in this sentence and is, therefore, redundant. *Who* is object and needs the *-m*.

16. A The main idea must be in the main clause as in (A). The comma is not necessary. In (B) *entirely* is unnecessary.

17. A The past perfect in the *if*-clause and the present perfect in the main clause with a conditional is correct since the time in the *if*-clause is anterior to the time in the main clause.

18. C Since the indefinite *they* does not refer to anybody specific, and since it thus does not have an antecedent, it should not be used. Since the time in the first clause is antecedent to the present tense in the main clause, the present perfect tense is required (C).

19. C A time anterior to a time in the past must be expressed by the past perfect, (B) and (C). It also must be followed by a past tense, excluding (D). *From cover to cover* is a trite cliché for *completely*.

20. E *Effect* is usually a noun. Only the contrary to fact conditional phrase *could not have affected* fits the context.

21. B Jimmy Fisher could not be a better chess player than any man in the world for that would make him better than himself. *In the world* is unnecessary since chess-playing men only exist in this world.

22. E *In both* destroys the parallelism in the two prepositional phrases since the second phrase does not have *both* following *in*. *Who* is the object of *call* and must be in the objective case.

SECTION 3 Critical Reasoning

1. B If you don't catch that (B) is the best answer right away, you should at least quickly identify (C) as the worst. That arrangement guarantees that an ace is drawn from one table, and makes it impossible to get an ace at the other, since the other table has no aces. But that fact contains a clue to the best answer—if you want to guarantee at least one ace, the most economical way of doing so is to put one ace by itself. That leaves the largest possible number of aces for the other table, thus giving you the best chance of getting an ace there. So (E) cannot be as good as (B). With (A), at each table the chance of getting an ace is 1/3, so the chance of getting two aces is 1/9. With (D), the chance of getting an ace at the first table is 1/5, and at the other table it is 3/7. The chance of getting two aces is thus 3/35, or less than one in ten. With (B) however, the child is sure to draw an ace at the first table, since that is the only card there. So the probability of getting two aces is just the probability of getting an ace at the second table, which is 3/11, better than one in four.

2. A The easiest way to see this is to imagine that two different couples exactly duplicate the two parts of Jerry and Ellen's hike, but on a single day. Since the entire time for the descent is included within the time for the ascent, the upward-bound couple is on the trail during the whole time the other couple is on the trail. Since neither couple leaves the trail, they must meet somewhere. That is the place where the two couples are at the same time. And since they do not double back, they cannot meet again. So there can be only one such place. And that place is where Jerry and Ellen, duplicating the movements of these two parties but on two different days, arrive at the same time on those two days.

3. E Probably it is best seen that (E) is the best answer by eliminating the others. (A) is unsuitable because the manager is not mistaken on this point. Two boxes of cards now sell for a total of $10.00 and cost the store $4.00, for a gross profit of $6.00. A 50% increase in sales, at the new price would result in selling three boxes for $12.00. The cost of the three boxes would be $6.00, again leaving a gross profit of $6.00, just as the manager says.

(B) is correct, but not relevant. No matter how they are pro-rated, the fixed costs have to be paid out of the gross profit. If there is no increase in gross profit, then the fixed costs will take the same bite regardless of the sales volume. (C) suffers much the same fate. Additional customers may be drawn, but if their purchases do not generate additional profit there is no advantage in it. And (D) is, if anything, a point against the employee's plan. An additional clerk is an additional expense.

(E), however, does contain the promise of additional profit overall, from additional sales of other items in the store. It is, therefore, the most attractive argument to strengthen the employee's suggestion.

4. C (C) directly addresses the question of overall profits, which must be a major concern in the business, and it suggests a plausible way in which the promised increase in profits may be eaten up. And (C) is compatible with all of the assumptions in the problem. (A) is unlikely to be correct, since it contradicts an assumption of the problem. (B) may be true, but the data from the other store suggests that either competitors do not lower their prices or else that the increased volume is achieved despite that lowering. (D) also seems to contradict an assumption, and in any case, if these prices do increase, the same principle of lowered profit margins could still be applied. (E) is good news for card sellers, but it doesn't seem to have any clear relevance to the decision at hand.

5. D Notice that the question is about the conclusion which the officials have drawn, a conclusion they have possibly drawn prior to considering corrective measures. What is that conclusion? It is that students have been losing math skills while in college. (D) is the only answer which suggests that this conclusion may be poorly founded, for (D) suggests a way in which average scores may decline, even if no students who took the 1992 test did worse on it than they did in 1988. If (D) is true, then average scores may decline even if no student loses mathematical skills while in college.

(A) might explain the apparent fact which the officials concluded, but does not suggest that their conclusion is shaky. The same goes for (E). (B) suggests that remedial action may not be very urgent, but it does not call the officials' conclusion into question. (C) is an additional claim—perhaps true, but not relevant to the officials' conclusion about what happens to college students during their college careers.

6. B Since almost all the young adults are monogamous and married, this society (like most human groups) has approximately equal numbers of males and females at the younger ages. Presumably this extends to a rough parity at birth. On the average, then, there is one girl born for every boy that is born. If, in this society, each family were to have exactly one boy, then somewhere in the society (though not in each individual family) there would have been an equal number of female births. Thus the average number of children per family would be two. Since that is considerably lower than the present average of almost five, population growth would be slowed. So neither (C) nor (D) can be correct.

The use of birth-control cannot affect the gender balance of the births that do occur. In any given cycle of births—in a given year, say, or a given month—there may be fewer births than if no one had practiced birth-control. But whatever births there are will be about evenly divided between males and females. Thus, this proposal cannot affect the gender balance of future generations. (It is true that there will be families with two, three, four, or more daughters, and only one son. But this is balanced by the fact that about half of all families will have one son and no other children.) So (A) and (C) are ruled out.

Although half of all families will have only one child (a son), this will be balanced by the fact that there will be other families with several children (mostly daughters). Since the average number of children per couple will be two, there will not be a precipitous decline in the population. So (E) is incorrect.

7. D This is the kind of problem which is probably best to leave to the end, unless you see your way through it right away. If you remember your algebra, this problem can be readily solved by using a fairly simple equation. It can also be solved by trial and error, which is especially useful here since you have only five alternatives to consider.

There is also a third way. Think of the captain assigning people to these vessels. He knows that each vessel will carry at least 10 people, so he puts 10 in each one. That takes care of 200 people, leaving 39. These must go into the rafts. The rafts already have 10 people in each one, and we know that they wind up with 13. So each raft gets 3 additional passengers. To account for the 39 remaining people there must be 13 rafts.

Problems of this sort, especially if they appear in this part of the GMAT, often have "common-sense" solutions such as this one. If you find yourself getting into complicated computations you are probably overlooking a much simpler approach.

8. C This problem is also best left to the end, unless you see how to solve it right away. The first thing to catch onto is that this is really about ages. That becomes evident when you read the items among which you have to choose, for they are all about age relationships. So the stuff about sons and twins in the initial information can just be translated into ages. After that, the main problem is keeping all the information in mind and in the right order. That's easy to do with a diagram. If you didn't make one, try it now, before you read the solution.

The first statement in the initial description is represented by writing an "S" (for Sharon) above a "P." We don't know how much older she is, or whether someone else comes in between, so leave some space. The second statement introduces two new people, with no relation so far to the first pair. Leave them out for the moment, and leave out also the third pair for the same reason. The fourth statement links up with the first, because Helen and Paul are the same age. Write "H" off to the side of "P," and link them with a horizontal line. Then you can go to the third statement and write "J" under "H." To represent the second statement we need to write "R" above "J." But we don't know how far above. So draw a line which curves out and up from "J," and write "R" at the top end of it. That shows that Richard is above John, but is non-committal as to where he is in relation to the others.

Now you can easily check the alternative answers by referring to the diagram. (A) is unsupported by the diagram, since Richard is off to the side, with his relation to Sharon unspecified. (A) is also unsupported for the same reason, as is (D). (E) is

false, because Paul is above John in the diagram. But (C) is true, because Sharon is above John in the diagram.

9. E In this sort of item, a "multiple-multiple" set of responses, you can concentrate on the first set of alternatives. Mark those which you take to be clearly correct and those which are clearly wrong. Even if you can do this only in part, it will probably enable you to eliminate at least some of the combinations in the final set of alternatives. And, of course, if you find a combination that matches your judgment exactly, that's the one you go for.

The original argument starts with a fact, the actions of the dentists in buying toothpaste for their own use. It suggests a plausible explanation of that fact—the dentists believe that this sort of toothpaste improves dental health. On the assumption that dentists are especially knowledgeable about that sort of thing, the conclusion is drawn that the toothpaste probably does contribute to dental health.

(i), however, provides a plausible alternative explanation for the buying practices of the dentists. Maybe they buy the poly-carbonate toothpaste because it is readily available and it is hard to find any other kind, and not because they believe it to be especially beneficial. So i weakens the original argument.

(ii) works the same way. Maybe dentists buy this sort of toothpaste, not because it is more healthful than other kinds, but because it has a desired cosmetic effect. So ii also weakens the original argument.

(iii), on the other hand, does not provide an alternative explanation as to why the dentists buy what they do. It may well be true, but it has no effect on the original argument.

10. B All three of these suggestions strengthen the original argument, but only in conjunction with the information about dentists' buying habits. If i is true, then dentists buy poly-carbonate toothpaste <u>despite</u> its higher cost. It is plausible to think that this is because they believe this toothpaste is more beneficial than others. ii also suggests that dentists use this toothpaste despite an undesirable side-effect—the discoloration. Presumably, then, they expect some benefit other than cosmetics, and health benefit seems like a plausible candidate. i and ii, however, without the information that dentists regularly use poly-carbonate toothpaste themselves, do not tend to support the conclusion.

(iii) also strengthens support for the conclusion, but in a different way. It operates independently of the information about the buying habits of dentists. It provides some free-standing evidence that poly-carbonate makes teeth resistant to decay.

11. D It is important to keep in mind just what the reported results are. Perhaps most important, nothing is said about the absolute values of the aggression rates, but only about <u>changes</u> in the rates. And nothing is said about how the rates in the other two communities compared with those of the first.

The first study correlated two changes—the change from no TV to TV in 1973 and the change in aggression rates from 1973 to 1975. And the tentative conclusion is that the first of these changes was the cause of the second change. The second study focused on communities in which there was no change of the first sort—they were already well accustomed to TV in 1973. (Thus the second study focuses on a sort of natural

"control group.") That study found that there was no change of the second sort—aggression rates in those communities remained constant from 1973 to 1975. The second study thus tends to reduce the plausibility of the suggestion that some change other than the introduction of TV caused the rise in aggressiveness in the first community. If there was some other cause, at least it doesn't seem to have been acting in the communities of the second study. And that reduces the range of possible candidates. Thus the second study tends to make more probable the conclusion drawn from the first.

If the second study had found that the aggression rates in the other two communities were no higher than in the first, then (C) would also be a plausible answer. But nothing is reported about the rates in one community compared with those in another.

(B) cannot be correct. The stimulus studied in the first case is the <u>change</u> from no TV to TV. But in the second case there was no such change. So there is nothing here about how different social groups react to similar stimuli. Similarly, there is nothing bearing on the conjecture included in (A).

12. A This is a fairly easy question about inference, but you need to be careful about the direction of the inference. The question asks about inferring the initial statement from one of the alternatives, not *vice versa.* To be a proper inference, the conclusion must be inferred from something which contains, in some way or other, all of the information which the conclusion contains. (A) does contain all of that information, and in a fairly open way. So the inference from (A) to the initial statement is proper. (A) also contains some additional information, so the inference in the other direction would not be proper. None of the other alternatives contain all of the information in the initial statement. (Note that the initial statement asserts that some ecological effects were, or were not, <u>as bad as initially expected</u>.) If the question had asked for an inference in the opposite direction, then (E) would have been correct. (B), (C), and (D) are not correct, since all of them contain information which cannot be found in the initial statement.

13. C If you think through the second statement carefully you will see that it is equivalent to "If Prince Henry was not telling the truth, then John O'Groats was lying." So the two statements taken together imply that, whatever Prince Henry was doing, John O'Groats was lying. Nothing, however, follows about what Prince Henry was doing.

This combination strikes some people initially as contradictory, but it is not. It simply reflects a rather common sort of situation, that of a state of affairs (John O'Groats' lying) which is <u>not</u> conditional on how a certain other state of affairs (Prince Henry's telling the truth) turns out.

14. C This is a fairly easy problem, and the key to it is that, according to the mother's promise, the children will go to a movie regardless of whether it rains, provided that they can use the car if it rains. The father's promise covers that eventuality, so the children are guaranteed a movie. They in turn have guaranteed that if they go to a movie they will clean up the basement. So they are bound to clean up the basement, regardless of whether their father goes to the golf course. So, if he does go to the golf course they will clean the basement, just as (C) says.

Their promise binds them to washing the car if they have lunch in the park, and that will happen only if it doesn't rain. But they might wash the car anyway (after all, they didn't promise <u>not</u> to wash it). So their washing it doesn't guarantee that their

father went to the golf course. (E), therefore, is not correct. (A), (B), and (D) may or may not turn out to be true, but (C) is bound to be true, so it is the stronger response.

15. D (D) seems to be the best response. The question asks for an additional premise or claim which will generate a "strong moral conclusion" from Markovic's analogy. Any one of the alternatives might be used to squeeze some moral juice out of the analogy; any one of them might be thought to have some moral significance. But (D) is the one which most openly and plainly has a moral content. If (D) is true, and if the destruction of Sarajevo is morally similar to the burning of Atlanta, then the destruction of Sarajevo is morally justified. So (D) seems to be a stronger candidate than the others.

Notice that in answering this question (and in general for taking the GMAT) you need not agree with Markovic's analogy, nor with the moral judgment expressed in (D). You are asked to decide whether this premise would, if true, lead to a strong moral claim. You need not believe it to be true in fact.

16. E Nietzsche's questions are classic examples of what some logicians call a "complex question." They ask for an explanation of a certain fact—i.e., that Nietzsche is unusually clever. If we undertake to answer that question on its own terms, then no matter what answer we give, we appear to accept the claim that Nietzsche is, in fact, unusually clever. The form of the question tends to trick one into accepting the concealed claim.

Responses (B), (C), and (D) tend to show, at best, that the question is difficult. But the crucial thing in this item is the misleading character of such questions. (A) is an interesting conjecture, and perhaps true, but irrelevant to an elucidation of the misleading character of his questions.

SECTION 4 Problem Solving

1. D $\pi r^2 = 25\pi$. $\therefore r^2 = 25$. $r = 5$.

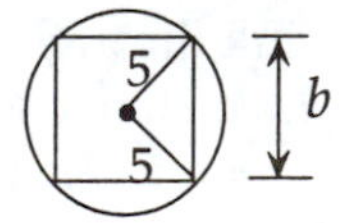

The side of the square is $b = \sqrt{5^2 + 5^2} = \sqrt{50}$.

Area of square $= b^2 = \sqrt{50}\sqrt{50} = 50$.

2. D Let x = original price. $x - 0.30x = 140$. $0.7x = 140$.

$\therefore x = \dfrac{140}{0.7} = 200$.

3. B $A = bh = b \times 12 = 108$. $\therefore b = \dfrac{108}{12} = 9$.

The diagonal is the hypotenuse of a 3-4-5 triangle of multiple 3.

$\therefore$ diagonal $= 3 \times 5 = 15$.

4. E $x^2 - 4x - 5 > 0$. $\therefore (x-5)(x+1) > 0$. If we set it equal to zero we find $x = 5, -1$. Hence, we try $x < -1$. Then $(x-5)$ is negative and $(x+1)$ is also negative. The product is positive. $\therefore$ this is acceptable. If we select $x > -5$ (say 0), then $(-5)(1) = -5$, which

is not acceptable. If we select $x > -1$ (say 0), ditto! If $x > 5$ this is also acceptable, but this answer is not present.

5. B Let x represent the gallons the tank holds. Then $\frac{x}{2} + 10 = \frac{7}{8}x$. This is rewritten as $10 = \frac{7x}{8} - \frac{4x}{8} = \frac{3x}{8}$. $\therefore x = \frac{8 \times 10}{3} = \frac{80}{3} = 26\frac{2}{3}$ gallons.

6. E The average speed is the total distance divided by the total time. It is

$$\frac{100+200+150}{2+3+2\frac{1}{2}} = \frac{450}{7\frac{1}{2}} = \frac{450}{15/2} = 450 \times \frac{2}{15} = 30 \times 2 = 60.$$

7. C Eliminate the fractions. Multiply the first equation by 3: $3a - b = 1$. Multiply the second equation by 4: $4a + b = 6$. If we add the equations, the variable b subtracts out: $7a = 7$. $\therefore a = 1$. Then $b = 2$. Hence, $a + b = 1 + 2 = 3$.

8. C $\frac{12-10}{12} \times 100 = \frac{2}{12} \times 100 = \frac{200}{12} = \frac{100}{6} = 16.67\%$, or about 17%.

9. B Let z be the angle next to x so that $x + z = 180°$, i.e., a straight line. From the triangle, $z + y + 30 = 180°$ since the sum of the 3 angles in a triangle is always 180°. Thus, $z + 40 + 30 = 180$, or $z = 110$. Finally, $x + 110 = 180$ or $x = 70°$.

10. E $\begin{aligned} x+2y&=2 \\ 2x-y&=4 \end{aligned}$ or $\begin{aligned} x+2y&=2 \\ 4x-2y&=8 \\ \hline 5x\quad&=10 \end{aligned}$ $\therefore x = 2$ and $y = 0$.

Both I and III are correct.

11. A $x + 2x + y = 180$ or $\begin{aligned} 3x+y&=180 \\ x+y&=120 \\ \hline \end{aligned}$

(subtract) $2x = 60$. $\therefore x = 30$ and $y = 90$.

12. C $3/10 = 0.3$. $5/20 = 0.25$. $\frac{1}{6} + \frac{1}{5} = \frac{5+6}{30} = \frac{11}{30} = 0.367$. $\frac{1}{8} \div \frac{7}{5} = \frac{1}{8} \times \frac{5}{7} = \frac{5}{56} < 0.1$. $0.1 \times 2 = 0.2$. 0.367 is the largest.

13. A One picker would take $20 \times 5 = 100$ hr. Eight pickers would take $100/8 = 12.5$ hr.

14. D Since x is negative, all answers are negative except $1/x^2$ which is positive. Positive > Negative.

15. C If AB is a diameter, $\angle C$ is a right angle so that $AB = 13$ is a hypotenuse. This is a 5-12-13 triangle, with $BC = 5$. Using the base as 12 and the height as 5, Area $= \frac{1}{2}(12 \times 5) = 30$.

16. B $7\frac{1}{5} = x(36)$. $7\frac{1}{5} = \frac{36}{5}$. $\frac{36}{5} = 36x$. $\therefore x = \frac{36}{5(36)} = \frac{1}{5}$.

SECTION 5 Analysis of an Issue

You may wish to have a friend or colleague grade your writing using the scoring guidelines presented on page 136 in 'Analytical Writing.' Or, should you desire a pro-fessional assessment of your writings, you may send the two essays to: Great Lakes Press, POB 483, Okemos, MI 48805-0483. Or fax to (517) 339-4455. You must also provide your Visa/MC # and expiration date (or a check or money order). Within 2 weeks, we will return a well-informed GMAT-type score, an evaluation of your writing and some suggestions for improvement for $20. Essays will be graded through an expertly-staffed program managed by Dr. James Ney, the author of this chapter.

SECTION 6 Data Sufficiency

1. D If $x > 1$, then x^2 is less than x^3 (e.g., $2^2 < 2^3$), so for (1) the answer is "No." For negative numbers, a positive x^2 is always greater than a negative x^3. If $x > 0$ and $x < 1$, then x^2 is also greater than x^3 (e.g., $\left(\frac{1}{2}\right)^2 > \left(\frac{1}{2}\right)^3$), so for (2) the answer is "Yes." Both answers are sufficient.

2. D The small box implies a right angle (90°). Corresponding angles are equal so $120 + a = 180$. $\therefore a = 60°$. Also, $a + b = 90°$. $\therefore$ $b = 90 - 60 = 30°$. Finally, $b + y = 180$. $\therefore y = 150°$ and (1) is sufficient. (2) states that $z = 30°$ and hence $30 + 90 + a = 180$ and $a = 30°$. And again we can calculate y so that (2) is also sufficient.

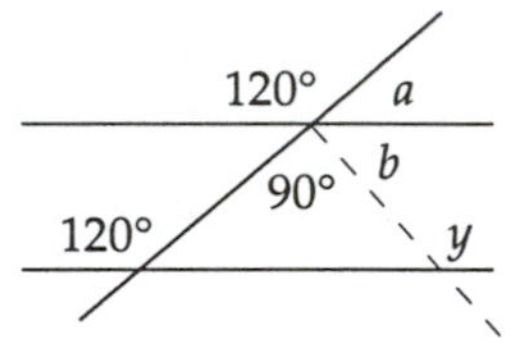

3. C (1) and (2) are two equations from which x and y can be determined. Then $x - y$ can be found. (Substitute (1) into (2): $4(7y) - 5y = 67$. $\therefore 23y = 67$ and $y = 67/23$, etc.)

4. C If the first term is 2 and the third term is 6, let the second term be x. In a geometric progression each term is the common factor multiplied by the preceding term: $x = 2y$ and $6 = xy$. These two equations can be solved for the two unknowns so the terms in the progression can be determined. ($6 = 2y^2$. $\therefore y = \sqrt{3}$. The terms are 2, $2\sqrt{3}$, 6, $6\sqrt{3}$, etc.)

5. D It is not necessary to actually solve for $\overline{BC}$; sketch a line 10 units long and sketch another line through A with $x = 30°$. It is obvious that if we pass another line through B such that $z = 110°$, $\overline{BC}$ is fixed and could be measured using the same scale used to measure the 10 units. Hence, we could calculate $\overline{BC}$. Thus, (1) is sufficient. Likewise, if we measure 6 units along the line at 30°, we also fix point C and hence $\overline{BC}$ is known.

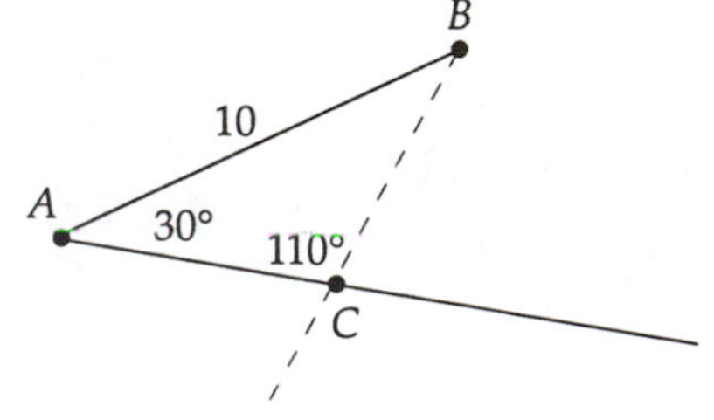

6. D Let x be the purchase price of the first airplane. Let y be the total price which is $x + x - 10{,}000 + x - 20{,}000 + x - 30{,}000 + x - 40{,}000$. We know that x can be calculated and then the total price because (1) states that $x + (x - 10{,}000) = 0.5y$. (1) is sufficient. But (2) states that $x - 40{,}000 = \frac{x}{2}$ so we can calculate x with (2) alone and subsequently the total price. (2) is also sufficient.

7. B (1) is not sufficient. (2) states that $d = 1.2h$; then the question becomes, is $\frac{\pi(1.2h)^2}{4} > h^2$? Obviously, the question can be answered with a calculation, so (2) is sufficient and (1) is of no interest.

8. B First, factor the quadratic: $(a-4)(a+3) > 0$? If $a < 4$, then the first factor is negative, but the second is positive if $a > -3$ and negative if $a < -3$; the answer cannot be determined. If $a < -3$, then both factors are negative and the answer is "Yes"; (2) is sufficient.

9. E The cost of the car in 1992 is not known, and neither is the cost of a car in 1952. So the question cannot be answered using (1) and (2).

10. D If the angle opposite h is 90°, then the right triangle permits $6^2 + 8^2 = h^2$ so that (1) is sufficient. (2) states that the triangle is a right triangle, providing the same result. Hence, (2) is also sufficient.

11. B The median is not related, in general, to the average. The average is the total divided by the number of entries: Average = $\frac{27}{5}$; (2) is sufficient.

12. C If $y > 1$, then $\frac{1}{x} < 1$ or $x > 1$. If $x^2 < 1$, then $x < 1$ and $x > -1$. Consequently, the answer is "No." Since we can answer the question, (1) and (2) are sufficient.

13. D The volume of the tank is $2 \times 0.8 \times 0.5 = 0.8\ \text{m}^3$. Thus, there are 800 liters in the tank since each cubic meter holds 1000 liters, and (1) is sufficient. (2) is also sufficient since there is a known conversion between a gallon and a liter, even if we do not remember the conversion!

14. C (1) is not sufficient since only one angle is known. With (1) and (2) we know that all angles are 60° and that all sides are equal to b. A perpendicular from point B bisects the base so b can be determined. $\left(b^2 = \left(\frac{b}{2}\right)^2 + \left(\sqrt{3}\right)^2. \quad \therefore \frac{3}{4}b^2 = 3 \text{ or } b = 2.\right)$

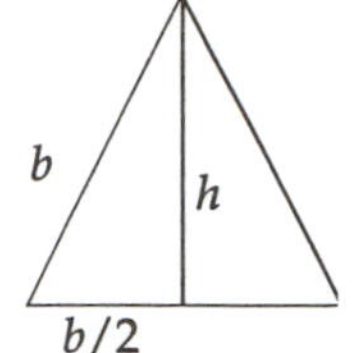

15. E A perpendicular from B bisects $\overline{AC}$ if angle A = angle C. An isosceles triangle has two angles equal but the angles could be angles *A and B*. So (1) is not sufficient. Neither is (2).

16. E (1) states that $xy = 12$ and (2) states that $x + y = 8$. These two equations can be solved for x and y. Substituting for x in the second equation gives $\frac{12}{y} + y = 8$ so that $12 + y^2 = 8y$ or $y^2 - 8y + 12 = 0$. This can be factored into $(y-6)(y-2) = 0$ so that $y = 6$ or 2. Then x is 2 or 6. The two-digit number is then 26 or 62. To select one of these more information is needed.

17. A If x is negative and y is positive, then the question can be answered since a negative is always less than a positive. The answer would be "No" and (1) is sufficient. (2) is not sufficient since if $x = 2$ then $y = 1$ and $2^9 > 1^{10}$. But, if $x = -2$ then $y = -3$ and $\left(-2^9\right) < (-3)^{10}$.

18. D We know that a triangle inscribed in a circle with one side a diameter is a right triangle. Since $\overline{AB} = 10$ and $\overline{AC} = 8$ we can calculate $\overline{BC}$, so (1) is sufficient. $\left(10^2 = 8^2 + \overline{BC}^2. \quad \therefore \overline{BC}^2 = 36 \text{ and } \overline{BC} = 6.\right)$ Also, (2) is sufficient since the right triangle is a 30–60–90 triangle which has the side opposite the 30° angle equal to one half the hypotenuse. $\left(\overline{BC} = \frac{1}{2}\overline{AB} = 5.\right)$

19. C (1) states that m and n are any of the integers 1, 2, 3, 4, 6, 12, or their negative values, –1, –2, –3, –4, –6, –12. If n is odd and less than –2 it must be –3. Since m is less than –2 also, it must be –4, –6, or –12 and the answer is "Yes" using both (1) and (2).

20. C The length of a line is given by $\sqrt{(x_1 - x_2)^2 + (y_1 - y_2)^2}$. Since one point is the origin ($x_2 = 0$ and $y_2 = 0$) the length is given by $\sqrt{x^2 + y^2}$. Both (1) and (2) are needed to determine x and y. (Substitute $x = 4y$ into the second equation: $4y + y = 5$ or $5y = 5$ so that $y = 1$ and $x = 4$. The length is then $\sqrt{1^2 + 4^2} = \sqrt{17}$.)

SECTION 7 Reading Comprehension

1. B The passage explicitly states that "unemployment was the really big issue." (A), (C), (D), and (E) are indeed forms of social insurance, but they are not the issue to which the AFL directed its most durable opposition.

2. D (A) is incorrect, because the AFL action was more aggressively hostile than the phrase "allowed to lapse" indicates. (B) is incorrect, for nothing in the passage indicates that the AFL proposed any form of unemployment insurance at all. (C) and (E) are incorrect, because the passage clearly declares the contrary.

3. E According to the passage, "Conceptions of social insurance were developed in Europe during the nineteenth century." (A), (B), (C), and (D) are all inaccurate.

4. C (A) is incorrect, since the passage does not indicate that the AFL copied the British model. (B) is incorrect, for the passage explicitly indicates that the AFL avoided political and legislative solutions in favor of economic solutions. (D) is incorrect, since the passage indicates the contrary. (E) is incorrect, because every example in the passage argues the contrary.

5. C The AFL argued that all forms of social insurance "would be undemocratic; they would destroy freedom." These are political, not monetary, economic, rhetorical, or legal arguments.

6. D According to the passage, the AFL gave unanimous approval to unemployment insurance. (A), (B), (C), and (E) are incorrect, because the passage declares the contrary.

7. E Clearly, the author ties the consistent attitudes of the AFL toward all forms of social insurance to an historic example of doctrinaire rigidity in the face of adverse circumstances and in the name of pragmatism. (A) is incorrect, for nothing in the passage mentions outside opposition to the AFL. (B) is an accurate statement but not the major conclusion. (C) and (D) may be accurate inferences, but neither is the major conclusion of this passage.

8. A The author declares that the argument is based on a naive fallacy (a flaw resulting from ignorance of logic) of the **post hoc ergo proper hoc** variety. (B) is incorrect, for what is probable is not at issue here. (C) is incorrect, since what is possible is not at issue here. (D) is incorrect, for although the passage concerns economic conditions, the central argument is not an economic argument but a logical argument. (E) is incorrect; nowhere does the passage mention deterministic impetus for economic conditions.

9. C (A), (B), and (C) are incorrect, for the passage flatly declares the contrary. (E) may be partially correct, but the best answer is (C), direction of capital to increased production of food. Everything in the passage points to this answer.

10. C (A) is incorrect, for nowhere does the passage associate planning and direction of all economic activity with the creation of capital-intensive plants. (B) is incorrect, because the passage does not associate economies poor in capital with capital-intensive plants. (D) is incorrect, since the passage flatly declares the contrary. (E) is incorrect; nowhere does the passage describe a country where capital is spread thinly and widely.

11. C (A), (B), (D), and (E) may be partially correct, but the passage explicitly indicates that "essentially unpredictable developments may be produced by the application of advanced technical knowledge to economies extremely poor in capital."

12. C (A) is incorrect, for the passage connects productivity per head to increased need for industrial products, yet the passage argues most strongly for increased production of

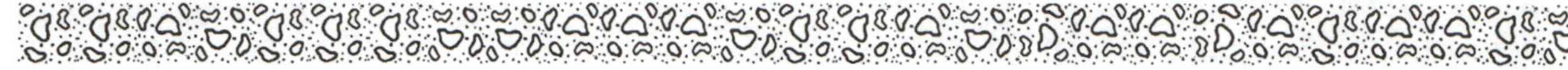

food. (B) is incorrect, since the task of the passage is not detailed comparison but argument. (D) is incorrect, because the passage advocates nothing about the management of proportion between capital and labor. (E) is incorrect, for although it may be objectively true, it is not a position argued by this passage.

13. B (A) is incorrect, since it names factors too broadly and too abstractly. Plainly, the passage focuses on state policy initiatives and environmental costs. (C) is incorrect, because interstate flight is a consequence, not an influence. (D) is incorrect, for it names only costs of environmental regulation, not state policy initiatives. (E) is incorrect, because it is too abstract.

14. B (A) is incorrect, because it cites a flaw in the data gathering concerning critical factors in plant siting decisions. (C) is incorrect. According to the passage, evidence from research declares the contrary. (D) is incorrect, since the passage says nothing about the difference between actual and anticipated costs of environmental regulation. (E) is incorrect, because the passage flatly indicates that evidence concerning factors in plant siting decisions is inconsistent.

15. A According to the passage, it is multicollinearity (the arrangement of many corresponding parts in the same linear order) that makes it difficult to distinguish effects of certain factors. (B) is incorrect, since multicollinearity is not intersection. (C) is incorrect, because multicollinearity is not parallelism. (D) is incorrect, for the passage says nothing about interdependence. (E) is incorrect, because the passage says nothing about the shift of potential influences.

16. C Duerkson's finding corroborates Healy's earlier finding that environmental costs are a trivial factor. Industry publications confirm this finding. (A) may be an accurate statement, but it does not answer the question. (B), (D), and (E) are incorrect, for the passage flatly declares the contrary.

17. E (A) is incorrect, since the passage clearly declares that the relationship "may not be linear." (B) and (C) are incorrect, since neither accurately identifies the cause of variance in ability to attract new chemical industry capital. (D) is incorrect, for the passage does not give enough evidence to warrant the conclusion that pollution abatement expenses are a negligible factor. The only acceptable inference is (E), that variance appears to relate to a threshold figure.

18. C Relying upon information given, that states with greater fiscal capacity can meet environmental standards without exceeding a threshold figure, we can reason that states with lower fiscal capacity to meet federal standards cannot meet environmental standards without exceeding a threshold figure. (A), (B), (D), and (E) are analytic criteria proposed by the authors but discarded because they do not explain variance.

19. D It is not a statistical finding summarized in this passage, and it is unwarranted by the evidence given in the passage. (A), (B), (C), and (E) are all statistical findings mentioned in this passage.

20. B A **caveat** is a warning. (A), (C), (D), and (E) may each be present in the analysis of research findings, but they are not caveats.

21. A The passage asserts this judgment straightforwardly. (B) is incorrect, for the advantage of states with greater fiscal capacity is that they need not exceed marginal-cost

threshold. (C), (D), and (E) are incorrect, since none of them is warranted by evidence in the passage.

22. D The passage makes it plain that these three advantages "made the large multi-unit industrial enterprise come when it did." (A) is incorrect in its second part. (B) is incorrect, for nothing in the passage supports it. (C) is incorrect, since volume production and distribution are **parts** of economies of scope. (E) is incorrect, because addition of new units is a **part** of economies of scale.

23. A The passage makes it plain that (B), (C), (D), and (E) are all results of the addition of new units. Concentration of facilities of production is not mentioned in the passage.

24. B (A) and (C) are incorrect, because they are the result of transactions carried out between firms or between individuals. (D) and (E) are incorrect, for they are not related to transaction costs in this passage.

25. A (B) is incorrect, since it defines economy of **scale,** not of scope. (C) and (D) are incorrect, for they are merely broadly descriptive of multi-unit industrial enterprises. (E) is incorrect, because it does not define economies of scope.

SECTION 8 Problem Solving

1. D $5\frac{7}{8} = \frac{47}{8}$. $\frac{47}{8} \div \frac{1}{8} = \frac{47}{8} \times \frac{8}{1} = 47$ feet.

2. A Substitute $y = \frac{7}{4}x$ into the first equation: $x - \frac{1}{2}(\frac{7}{4}x) = \frac{3}{4}$.

   $\therefore\ x - \frac{7}{8}x = \frac{3}{4}$ or $\frac{x}{8} = \frac{3}{4}$. $\therefore\ x\ \frac{3}{\not{4}} \times \overset{2}{\not{8}} = 6$.

3. D 1/3 = 0.33. 2/5 = 0.4. 3/7 = 0.43. 4/9 = 0.44. 5/13 = 0.38. ∴ 4/9 is the largest.

4. D Make a sketch. The corner is at (– 4, – 3).

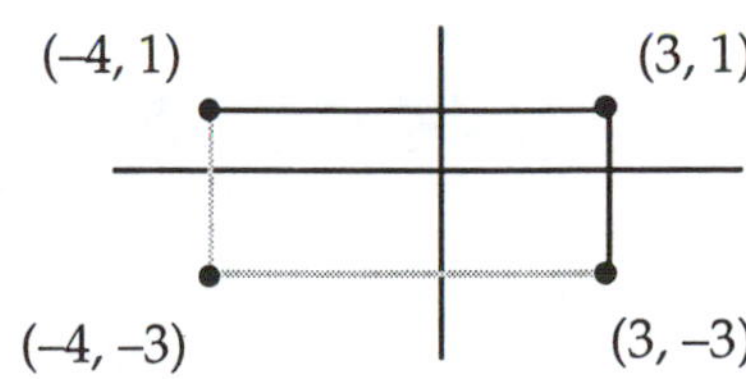

5. C Make a sketch.

   This is twice the base size of a 3-4-5 triangle. ∴ $x = 6$ and $d + 2 = 6$ so that $d = 4$.

6. C There are 180° in a straight line. Next to the 120° angle there is a 60° angle. Next to the 145° angle there is a 35° angle. The three angles in a triangle add to 180°. Hence, $60 + 35 + x = 180$. ∴ $x = 85°$.

Note: Vertical angles are equal, so that the angle just below x is also equal to x.

7. A The total bushels = $x + y + z$. Corn represents $\frac{x}{x+y+z}$ of the crop.

8. E $x - 5 + y = 4$. $\therefore y = 4 - x + 5 = 9 - x$.

9. A $x = 2$. $\therefore 2 = t + t^2$ or $t^2 + t - 2 = 0$. Factor this: $(t + 2)(t - 1) = 0$. Thus, $t = -2$ or 1. If $t = -2$, $y = -2 - (-2)^2 = -6$. If $t = 1$, $y = 1 - 1 = 0$.

10. A The total distance is 100 + 100 = 200 miles.

    The total time is $100/30 + 100/20 = 3\frac{1}{3} + 5 = 8\frac{1}{3} = \frac{25}{3}$.

    The average speed is $200 \div \frac{25}{3} = 200 \times \frac{3}{25} = 24$.

11. B $\frac{4.11}{300} = \frac{.0411}{3}$ (move the decimal two places in both numerator and denominator.)

    $\frac{.0411}{3} = .0137$.

12. C There are 360° in a circle graph. $\frac{40{,}000}{300{,}000} \times 360 = \frac{4}{30} \times 360 = 48°$.

13. B $z + 120 + 2z = 180$. $\therefore 3z = 180 - 120 = 60$. $\therefore z = 20$.

14. D The longest side is the hypotenuse. Let x be the length of each of the legs (they are equal because the triangle is isosceles). Then $x^2 + x^2 = 8^2$. $\therefore 2x^2 = 64$ and $x^2 = 32$. $\therefore x = \sqrt{32} = \sqrt{16 \times 2} = 4\sqrt{2}$.

15. A $x + y = 180$. $\therefore x = 180 - y = 180 - 30 = 60$. This is the maximum x.

16. A There are six sides to a cube. $\therefore$ Area $= 6(6 \times 6) = 216$. $216/100 = 2.16$ quarts or 4.32 pints. $\therefore$ Buy 5 pints.

SECTION 9 Analysis of an Argument

You may wish to have a friend or colleague grade your writing using the scoring guidelines presented on page 12 of chapter 6 ('Writing Analysis'). Or, should you desire a professional assessment of your writings, you may send the two essays to: Great Lakes Press, POB 483, Okemos, MI 48805-0483. Or fax to (517) 339-4455. You must also provide your Visa/MC # and expiration date (or a check or money order). Within 2 weeks, we will return a well-informed GMAT-type score, an evaluation of your writing and some suggestions for improvement for $20. Essays will be graded through a expertly-staffed program managed by Dr. James Ney, the author of this chapter.

3 Reading Comprehension

How To Identify:

- Passage Subjects
- Central Ideas
- Organization of Passages
- Limiting Conditions

3. Reading Comprehension

The reading comprehension portion of the Graduate Management Achievement Test (GMAT) is designed to test how well you read as measured by how accurately you perceive major and minor subjects, abstract main ideas and discriminate between contributing ideas, devise reasonable applications, and construct inferences from given passages. In your preparation for the GMAT, a direct and profitable approach is to study reading passages and examination questions typical of those that appear on the test itself.

You may be surprised that the passages for reading and study are not drawn from professional business or trade publications. Instead, in accordance with the precedent set by the GMAT in which passages are drawn from scholarly, research-based writing in the humanities, social sciences, and physical sciences, this guide presents passages from a wide range of such writing in economics, law, scientific reporting, government policy writing, and philosophy. These passages concern such issues as civil liberty and the private market, the economics of developing countries, the political interests of the labor movement—issues that arise in disciplines outside business operations but that have clear implications for business policy.

The level of complexity of these passages for reading and practice approximates the level of complexity of the passages in the reading comprehension tests of the GMAT. It is, of course, impossible to predict from the range of possible questions the exact kinds of questions you will be asked. Close study of the GMAT shows that it places a high value on the **retrieval of information:** that is, the GMAT is more likely to ask what a sentence **says** or what a passage **declares or generalizes or claims** than what a sentence or passage means or what an author intends. It is more likely to ask what the **subject** is, what the **central idea** is than to ask about the **tone** or the **relative emphasis** of a passage. Understanding these facts will help guide your reading and will give you insight into the kinds of questions most frequently asked on the GMAT.

3.1 Identifying the Subject of a Passage

The most frequently occurring question concerns the **subject** or **topic** of a passage—the **what** of a passage. The **subject** is to be distinguished from the **central idea** of a passage, which is the central assertion, declaration, or claim **about** the subject. If you are unsure what the subject of a passage is, you should study the grammatical **subjects** and **objects** of sentences in order to find repetitions of terms. Generally, when a term appears repeatedly in the grammatical position of either the subject or the object of a sentence, that term constitutes the **subject** of the passage.

Consider the following example in which the terms **railroads, management,** and **managerial enterprises** are repeated in varying form or in synonym, and thus determine a **subject**:

> During the 1850s American railroads became the pioneers in modern management. Because of the complexities of their operations, they [the railroads] formed almost overnight the nation's first managerial enterprises. In the larger railroads, managers with almost no equity in the enterprise made the operating decisions. And as the [rail]roads grew, these managers came to play a critical role in determining the strategy of their growth and competition.

A question might ask the following:

Q1: The purpose of this passage is to
- A) analyze the formation of early railroad and telegraph companies.
- B) identify the origin of modern management systems in the organization of the early railroad companies.
- C) describe operations of the railroads.
- D) analyze coordination of routes and schedules.
- E) analyze working out of essential inter-company relationships.

In order to answer it, you have to know the **purpose** or **task** as well as the **subject**. Clearly, the **subject** of the passage is the origin of modern management systems in the organization of the early railroads, (B). The verb "identify" accurately states the **purpose** or **task** of the passage.

Consider the sentence subjects and objects in the following passage:

> Until recently, the generation and tabulation of toxicological and environmental data in the United States has been carried out in an unsystematic fashion by several federal and state government agencies, industry, and the medical profession. . . . Generally, chemicals were considered to be harmless unless proven otherwise. It was not until the 1960s that Americans began to believe that systematic investigation and regulation of toxicological and environmental impact of chemicals was necessary. By this time, however, DuPont had been doing research on the

> toxic effects of chemicals for thirty years at its Haskell Laboratory for Toxicology and Industrial Medicine.

What is the **subject** of this passage? Plainly, it is DuPont's research into the toxic effects and environmental impact of chemicals.

3.2 Identifying the Central Idea of a Passage

Often, but not always, the **central idea** will be stated in the first paragraph of a passage. A **central idea** is not a **subject** of a passage. Rather, a **central idea** is expressed in a declarative statement, an assertion, a thesis, a claim **concerning the subject.** It is the most comprehensive, overarching statement in a passage, drawing into a central abstraction or generalization the threads of supporting data.

For example, in the passage on the origin of modern management systems in the organization of the early railroad companies, the following sentence expresses the **central idea:**

> Thus, during the 1850s American railroads became the pioneers in modern management.

The **subjects** are **railroads** and **managers** or **managerial systems**. The **central idea** is the thesis that modern management originated from the need of the early American railroads to organize their operations.

Often, you can identify the comprehensive **central idea** by the presence of what is called the **designating term.** The designating term begins sentences whose full explanation will be in parts. For example, if a sentence states that **four legislative powers** affect economic planning in the U.S., or **five issues** preoccupied the founders of the labor movement, or the relative **weight of critical factors** in plant siting decisions is difficult to determine, then that sentence states the **central idea** of the passage.

In the next example, the **designating term** operates differently. The purpose of the following passage is to identify a major finding about the failures of water projects in the United States. In this passage, a **designating term** sums up the details in preceding sentences and draws them together into a comprehensively stated **central idea**:

> **One** of the most persistently **troubling parts** of national domestic policy is the development and use of water resources.
> **Issues** of water policy have mingled **problems** . . .
> Inherent **complexity** . . . is the frequent **conflict** . . .
> Both **problems** exist in America . . .
> There are the **problems** . . .
> **Problems** of land and water . . . are inherently **difficult.**
> **Shortcomings** and **failures** have . . . been inevitable.

The next sentence expresses the **central idea**:

> The most startling fact about the history of water projects in the United States is the degree to which their shortcomings have been associated with administrative failures.

Note that the **designating term** of this passage, "the most startling fact," summarizes and restates the contributing terms (troubling parts, problems, conflict, shortcomings, failure) and shapes them into a **central idea:** Of all the factual problems detailed above, the most startling fact is . . .

3.3 Identifying the Organization of a Passage

Identifying the **central idea** of a passage is critical to clear understanding of that passage, partially because the **organization** or **pattern** of the passage will be derived from it. Often, you may take your clue as to the **pattern** of the passage from the order in which the central idea is expressed.

Of the two conventional ways to organize writing—sequentially and categorically—the simplest is sequentially. A text that is arranged sequentially is developed according to a **chronological** or **hierarchical** pattern. The major advantage of patterns is the regularity with which they order information. Identifying the principle of order in a chronological or hierarchical pattern will promote understanding of the general framework of the passage. An understanding of these patterns of development is valuable to your preparation for the GMAT, for the organization of passages frequently prompts questions on the reading comprehension examination .

Chronological Organization

A text that is organized **chronologically** takes as its central idea the chronology of events it describes. Consider the example below:

> Resolutions in favor of an American system of unemployment insurance proffered in AFL conventions were soundly defeated in the years before American entry into the war. Thereafter, the issue lapsed, although there was some desultory discussion in the 1920s. With the onset of the Great Depression, it once more came alive. After 1929, unemployment increased rapidly and the membership of the AFL dwindled. Nevertheless, a resolution favoring unemployment insurance was defeated in . . . 1930. [F]inally, in 1932, a resolution in favor of unemployment insurance was approved . . .

The following kinds of questions may be prompted by the chronological pattern:

1. **When** did X-event take place?
2. What was the **duration** of X-process?

3. Was the **sequence** of X-process interrupted/continuous?
4. What are the **stages** of X-process or **steps** in X-procedure?
5. What **precedes/follows** X-event/process?

You may encounter these kinds of questions phrased in varying ways. Consider the question below:

Q2: Resolutions in favor of an American system of unemployment insurance proposed in AFL conventions before World War I were

A) allowed to lapse.
B) reluctantly discussed.
C) heatedly opposed.
D) soundly defeated.
E) tentatively approved.

The correct answer is (D). Plainly, the significant fact is that at **each stage** in the history of these proposals, different reactions ensued. And questions on the GMAT that concern chronology test whether you understand the specific **times** at which particular events took place.

Hierarchical Organization

A passage organized by **hierarchy** (a ranked series) creates an order to information where none inherently exists. For example, if no chronological significance exists in the subject to be described, then the author may group information according to a system that promotes meaning of another kind. In order to understand organization by hierarchy, you must identify the principle of order that informs the passage. Once you have identified the principle by which the information is ordered (for example, trivial to critical, or easy to difficult, or simple to complex), you may anticipate and assimilate later information into this framework of understanding as the information is presented.

A text organized by hierarchy will present causes and effects, advantages and disadvantages, or features of various kinds in **ascending** or **descending order of quality** of some kind.

Consider the following passage:

> The legislative branch holds the broadest authority of any agency . . . to define standards and rules of official and private conduct. Its powers to tax, borrow, and spend provide it a role in allocating economic resources. . . . Legislatures hold plenary power to create new forms of organization for public or private action. Legislatures have authority to investigate matters of fact . . ., [and] in some respects, the power of investigation is potentially the broadest, most significant legislative power.

The hierarchical pattern may prompt the following kinds of questions:

1. In **increasing order of importance,** what are the features, traits, advantages, causes implicit in X-object or process?
2. Which is the **most/least** urgent, critical, beneficial, expensive, controversial feature of X-object or process?

Or, as you might encounter the question on the reading comprehension test,

Q3: Which power of the legislative branch is potentially its broadest, most authoritative power?

A) power to tax, borrow, and spend
B) power to define standards of official and private conduct
C) investigative power
D) plenary power to create new forms of organization
E) power to allocate economic resources

The correct answer is (C).

Categorical Organization

Organization by **categorical pattern** is more complicated, and the relationships it describes may be more difficult, although certainly not impossible, for you to perceive. In a categorical pattern, the author establishes **categories of information** that fit the purpose of the writing. These categories name arbitrary bases of judgment. For example, the author may write of **immediate causes** or **long-range causes, liberal** or **conservative publication policies** of the National Institutes of Health, **managerial procedures that reduce manufacturing costs**, etc.

In organization by category, the point is not to establish a hierarchy or progression but merely to identify categories. So, **managerial procedures that reduce manufacturing costs** may be presented in a list, with none necessarily more valuable or more beneficial than another, as in the following example:

> Reductions in costs . . . have resulted . . . from the exploitation of economies of scale . . ., from economies of scope, or from reduction in the costs of transactions involved.

These procedures are listed in no particular ascending or descending order of importance. They are merely grouped according to category.

Or, as you might encounter a question concerning **category** on the reading comprehension test of the GMAT:

According to the passage, which of the procedures below helped reduce costs and encourage the formation of multi-unit industries?

A) control of transaction costs and opening of new markets
B) technological change and market imperfections
C) volume production and distribution
D) economies of scale, economies of scope, reduced transaction costs
E) addition of new units and exploitation of technological innovation

The correct answer is (D).

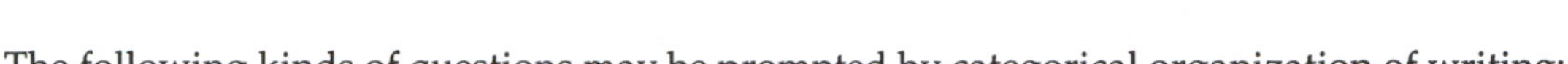

The following kinds of questions may be prompted by categorical organization of writing:

1. What is the motivation, inducement, view, cause of X-event/process?
2. What approaches explain X-event/process?
3. What models simulate X-event/process?

General-to-Specific

A variation of the categorical pattern may be seen in the **general-to-specific pattern.** This pattern is most frequently encountered in argumentation. Argumentative writing makes a general claim, develops it by a grouping of specific examples that support the claim, and concludes by restating the general claim. You may understand claim to mean also premise, conclusion, or controlling generalization. You will recognize argumentative writing by such characteristic phrases as "A strong case may be made for . . ." or "The progressive income tax is arguably. . . ." Characteristically, the argumentative claim expresses a judgment concerning such matters as **quality** or **responsibility.** These are matters typical of argument.

Consider the passage below:

> The problem of the aged is **particularly serious,** for in most parts of the Western world today it is the **fault** of governments that the old have been deprived of the means of support that they may have endeavored to provide for themselves. By failing to keep faith and [to] maintain a stable currency, governments everywhere have created a situation in which the generation going into retirement in the third quarter of our century has been **robbed** of a great part of what they had attempted to put aside for their retirement and in which many more people than there would otherwise have been are **undeservedly** facing poverty, despite their earlier efforts to avoid such a predicament.

In this passage, the general claim (stated in the first sentence) is followed by a cause-and-effect statement in support of the claim. This pattern might prompt the following question:

Q4: This passage argues that the action of government with respect to the ability of the aged to provide for themselves has been

A) paternalistic
B) discriminatory
C) unjust
D) intolerant
E) monopolistic

The correct answer, according to the passage, is (C): The aged have been **robbed,** and they **undeservedly** (unjustly) face poverty.

3.4 Identifying Conditions that Limit the Extent of Assertions

A final aspect of text that governs the full meaning of a passage is the attribute function of language. If an author stipulates a point of view (**from the modern standpoint, for contemporary scholars, from the perspective of the professional politician**), then that stipulation governs the breadth of a claim, and you will have to give it due weight when you infer from that claim. If an author uses a **condition** that limits the extent of assertions (**particularly serious, critically injured, intolerably burdened**), then you will likewise have to give it due weight when you infer from the thesis or claim. Attention to **conditions** is critical to close, accurate reading.

In the passage below, the general claim is expressed in the following:

> All arguments in support of progression can be used to support any degree of progression.

What can you and can you **not** logically derive from this general claim? Remember, the general claim covers all arguments in support of progression. This **condition** is critical to accurate understanding of the claim. You can derive an inference concerning the statement: **all arguments** (no other modes of discourse) in support of **progression** (no other subject) can be used to justify any degree of progression. You may not derive the inference that **only some arguments** can be used or that **no arguments** can be used. You must attend to the condition when you make your inference.

Consider another general claim modified by a close, specific condition:

> Progression provides no criterion whatsoever of what is and what is not to be regarded as just.

The claim is that progression provides **no** criterion **whatsoever** of what is/is not to be regarded as just. You may not derive the inference that it provides a criterion or a few criteria; nor may you derive the inference that progression is just/unjust. The argumentative claim is bounded unequivocally by its **conditions** expressed in "no criterion whatsoever."

When you read the passages on the reading comprehension test of the GMAT, pay very close attention to the **conditions** that limit the extent of assertions. You will have to infer or reason from these assertions, and understanding the conditions that limit the extent of these assertions will be critical to your success.

4. Sentence Correction

General Grammar Principles
Grammatical Terms
Grammatical Problems

With Examples, Problems and Full Solutions

4. Sentence Correction

The Sentence Correction portion of the GMAT is intended to test your ability to improve incorrect or ineffective grammatical expressions based on your familiarity with grammatical rules and stylistic conventions of standard written English. It will test the skill with which you can express yourself grammatically and with clarity.

Questions in this section will ask you to determine if the underlined portion of a given sentence expressing some idea or relationship is correct as presented, or if one of four other options is preferable. These questions will challenge your knowledge of proper grammar, your diction, and your ability to recognize concise, effective expression. In this review section we will present over twenty grammatical points you will need to understand and retain to master the Sentence Correction questions on the GMAT.

4.1 General Principles

Each question on the Sentence Correction section of the GMAT generally involves three "points of grammar" to be considered. By this we mean that there will be a decision to be made regarding the proper handling of three different rules of grammar throughout the five potentially correct answers (choices). Often, the decision regarding two of these points of grammar will be more challenging, while the third will be more obvious. Generally, four of the answer choices for each question will challenge you on the two more difficult points, and the fifth choice will challenge you on the third (easiest) point.

For example, assume the three points of grammar being evaluated are the use of commas, word order, and verb tense, and that they are represented by the letters J, K and L, respectively. For this example, we will assume that L happens to be the most obvious of the grammatical challenges—the easiest. (Often, this more obvious grammatical challenge deals with perfect tenses of verbs, which will be discussed in the pages that follow.) This point of grammar is usually only presented in one of the five choices and is not even involved in the other four. One possible presentation of the challenges regarding points of grammar could be as follows (in no predictable order):

A) point of grammar J correct; point K incorrect; L absent
B) point of grammar K correct; point J incorrect; L absent
C) points of grammar J and K correct; L absent
D) points of grammar J and K incorrect; L absent
E) points J and K either correct or incorrect; point L incorrect

In this case, option C would obviously be the correct choice, for only that option provides a situation in which there is no incorrect handling of any point of grammar. Note that only in choice E is point of grammar L, the most obvious infraction, present and incorrect. This would generally be the first choice to dismiss as you go about determining the correct answer. Only rarely will the choice containing the more obvious challenge regarding a point of grammar be the correct choice. Consider the following example.

Q1: Every year in the winter, Jacques with Gizelle migrates to Florida just when the snows begin up north in their old station wagon.

A) migrates to Florida just when the snows begin up north in their old station wagon
B) migrate to Florida in their old station wagon just when the snows begin up north
C) had migrated to Florida in their old station wagon just when the snows begin up north
D) migrates to Florida in their old station wagon just when the snows begin up north
E) migrate to Florida just when the snows begin up north in their old station wagon

Here, there are two strong problems: (i) Subject-verb agreement: Jacques migrate/migrates, and, (ii) placement of the modifier "in their old station wagon." The weak problem is in (C) and it is simply wrong; the past perfect tense does not 'fit' with "Every year." (See the section on sequence of tenses below.) In (A), the agreement is right, but the placement of the adverb is wrong. In (B), the agreement is wrong, but the placement of the adverb is right. In (E), the agreement is wrong and the placement of the adverb is wrong. In (C), the agreement is irrelevant but the placement of the adverb is right; the perfect tense is wrong, however. In (D) the agreement is right and the placement of the adverb is right. Thus, the answer is (D). This kind of question construction is very common on the Sentence Correction portion of the GMAT.

The less common type of question on the GMAT may be constructed as in the following example where there is a single problem, the modifier of the dangling participle.

Q2: Trying to find a parking space, a vagrant accosted them with a request for some money.

A) Trying to find a parking space, a vagrant accosted them
B) Trying to find a parking space, they were accosted by a vagrant
C) Before they had tried to find a parking space, they were accosted by a vagrant
D) After trying to find a parking space, a vagrant accosted them
E) Trying to find a parking space, a vagrant had accosted them

In this case, there is only a single problem, the dangling participial modifier or phrase. Five options for correcting the problem are offered, only one of which is correct (B). As per the discussion in the section below, the subjects of the participial phrase and the main clause must be the same. This is accomplished in (B) in which the subject "they" is the subject of try and accost. The (C) and (D) answers change the meaning of the original. (A) and (E) do not correct the problem with the dangling participial phrase. It is interesting to note that the correct answer includes a passive. (Passive is defined below.) Usually, the passive is to be avoided, but in instances like this it is acceptable.

4.2 Grammatical Terms

Subject is usually the doer-of-the-action; *object* is usually the receiver-of-the-action. Thus, in the sentence, Charlotte kicked the mule, "Charlotte" is the subject because she's doing the action, kicking, and the "mule" is the object because it is receiving the action; that is, it is the mule that is getting kicked. The verb expresses the actions such as "kicking" in the sentence above. Sometimes the subject is not the doer-of-the action. For instance, in passive sentences the subject is the receiver of the action as in (2) on the following page.

(1) ACTIVE SENTENCE: Charlotte kicked the mule.
(2) PASSIVE SENTENCE: The mule was kicked by Charlotte.

Obviously, in this case the sentence has been turned around so that the subject is now the receiver-of-the-action. The doer-of-the action follows the verb, and it is preceded by the preposition *by*.

Many English verbs are *inflected* (the grammatical term for a change in form that comes with a change in tense) so that they have the three forms as follows:

Present	Past	Past Participle
eat	ate	eaten
drink	drank	drunk
sing	sang	sung

Many more English verbs, including 'regular' verbs, are inflected so that they have only two forms, as in the following:

Present	Past	Past Participle
bring	brought	brought
call	called	called
catch	caught	caught

A few English verbs are inflected so that they have only one form as in the following:

Present	Past	Past Participle
hit	hit	hit
cost	cost	cost

Passives are formed by the use of the past participle and a form of *be*:

(3) A ball hit Carl on the hand. (active)

(4) Carl was hit on the hand by a ball. (passive)

The present participle of any English verb can be formed by adding *-ing* to the present: eat—eating; bring—bringing; hit—hitting.

4.3 Problems with Verbs

It is a standard principle of GMAT grammar that the active voice is to be preferred over the passive.

In English, the passive voice is formed with some form of the verb *be* and the past participle, a verb form which usually then ends with *-ed* or *-en*. Thus, the sentences in the A-column are active and the sentences in the B-column are passive:

	(A)	(B)
(5)	The mule kicked John.	John was kicked by the mule.
(6)	Jack ate the pie.	The pie was eaten by John.
(7)	A foul ball hit the fan.	The fan was hit by a foul ball.

Besides the formation of passives with some form of *be*, some inceptive passives formed with *get* emphasize the beginning of the action. Compare "He was shot by an assassin," and "He got shot by an assassin." It should be apparent from the above that changing an active sentence into a passive sentence requires more than a change in the voice of the verb. It requires in addition a reversing of the nouns in the sentence. The subject as actor is shifted into the position usually occupied by the object and the object as receiver of the action is put into the position of the subject. In any case, the active voice is usually preferred over the passive voice, which is generally condemned as being "weak." Only when the writer is intent on maintaining focus is the passive voice preferred, as in the following:

(8) A bear ambled through the woods on a fall day. Just then, a shot rang out and the bear fell dead on the leaves. It was killed by a single bullet.

In the last sentence, the passive voice is used to keep the focus on the bear, "it," as subject. Thus, the active is almost always preferred over the passive in GMAT Sentence Correction questions; the passive is used reluctantly only to maintain focus and permit the correction of a nongrammatical sentence (as in sentences such as Example 2(B) from Section 4.1 earlier).

4.4 Problems with the Objective Case of Pronouns

One problem that frequently forms the basis for questions on the GMAT Sentence Correction section is the selection of the correct form of pronouns. In English, the pronouns are more highly inflected than all other words except the verb *be*; the form of the pronoun differs as the case differs. In English, the four recognized grammatical cases are the subjective, objective, possessive and predicate nominative.

	Singular First Person	Singular Third Person	Plural First Person	Plural Third Person	"WH-" Pronoun
Subjective	I	he she	we	they	who
Objective	me	him her	us	them	whom
Possessive	my	his her	our	their	whose
Predicative	mine	his hers	ours	theirs	whose

There is a second person pronoun in English, *you*, but it is not inflected for the objective case. Besides this, there is some inflection in the third singular neuter pronoun *it*, but since it does not have an objective case marker, *it*, like *you*, does not figure into GMAT questions in this dimension. However, the contrast between the possessive *its*, the pronoun *it*, and the contracted form of *be* (*it's*) figures rather prominently in GMAT questions. Never confuse *it's*, which comes from *it is*, with *its*, the possessive case of the pronoun *it*!

Although these pronoun forms are few, they are used in a number of problems on the GMAT. Very often, in spoken English, such ungrammatical sentences as the following will occur:

(9) It's me.

(10) Those are the people who I don't like at all.

(11) She is the lady about who I know nothing.

(12) They gave gifts to whomever held a pass.

The correct version of all these sentences is as follows:

(13) It's I. (Grammatical on the GMAT.)

(14) Those are the people whom I don't like at all.

(15) She is the lady about whom I know nothing.

(16) They gave gifts to whoever held a pass.

The use of whoever/whomever in (16) is determined by the function in the clause. Since *to* is outside the clause, it does not influence the selection of the relative pronoun *whoever*. *Whoever* is always the subject of the clause in which it functions and must be selected on this basis.

Actually, there are two rules that govern the use of the objective case of the pronouns:

<u>Rule One</u>. The objective forms of the pronouns are used after prepositions: words such as *to, at, in, of, between, among, over, in back of,* and so on. The following sentences should illustrate this point.

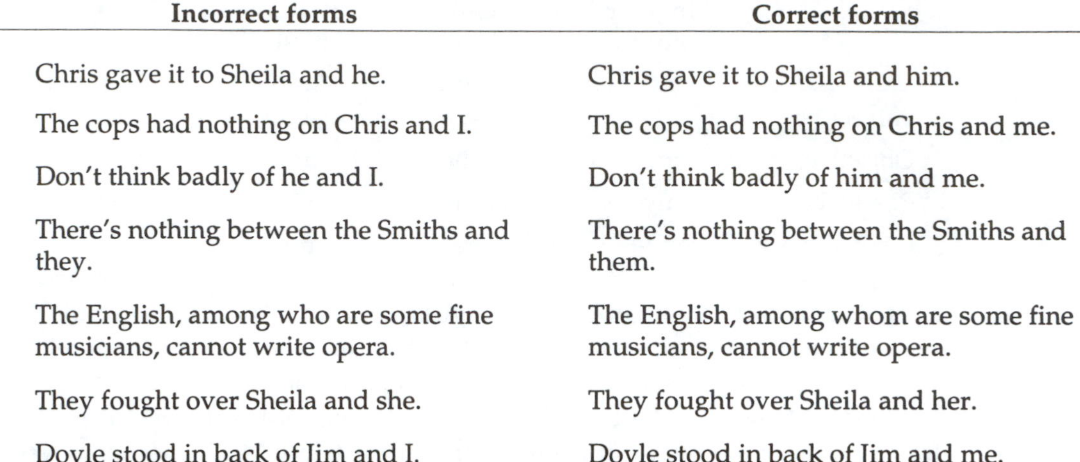

Incorrect forms	Correct forms
Chris gave it to Sheila and he.	Chris gave it to Sheila and him.
The cops had nothing on Chris and I.	The cops had nothing on Chris and me.
Don't think badly of he and I.	Don't think badly of him and me.
There's nothing between the Smiths and they.	There's nothing between the Smiths and them.
The English, among who are some fine musicians, cannot write opera.	The English, among whom are some fine musicians, cannot write opera.
They fought over Sheila and she.	They fought over Sheila and her.
Doyle stood in back of Jim and I.	Doyle stood in back of Jim and me.

Rule Two. The objective forms of the pronouns also fit after verbs; that is, they are used after action words such as *kick, like, kill, grow, believe, breathe, bathe*, and so on. In such a position they are objects; that is, things are done to them. Thus, all of the sentences on the left are wrong, and those on the right are correct.

Incorrect forms	Correct forms
Chris kicked he and I twice.	Chris kicked him and me twice.
The cops liked Chris and I.	The cops liked Chris and me.
Don't kill both she and I.	Don't kill both her and me.
The Smiths believe both they and their story.	The Smiths believe both them and their story.
The English, who the Russians usually beat at chess, can really play cricket.	The English, whom the Russians usually beat at chess, can really play cricket.
Mother spanked Sheila and I.	Mother spanked Sheila and me.

Essentially, the sentence should still make sense if you were to remove the conjunction *and* (and words such as *both*) and **either** pronoun.

The one true exception to the objective forms fitting after verbs occurs with the verb *be*. Many people use the objective form after *be* in their spoken English; they say, "It's me." This is considered incorrect in the grammatical systems that underlie the GMAT. On the GMAT, "It's I" is correct. The subject form of the pronoun must be used after any form of the verb *be*. In other words, in the predicate position after any of the forms of the verb *be* including the contracted form of *is*, *'s*, the correct form is the subjective form as in the sentences: "It is I," **not** "It is me"; "This is he," **not** "This is him"; "That's she," **not** "That's her." The only exception to this rule is the possessive form: That's mine, hers, his, ours, theirs or whose. If it is after the bare form of *be*, the use of the objective case may look deceptively close to being the right answer; nevertheless, it is wrong as in: "They need the quarterback to be (him/he) who has a cool head and a strong throwing arm." In this case, the use of *him* is wrong, *he* is right.

All of the pronoun forms following other verbs as objects, or following prepositions, must be in the objective case as in the sentences 9-12 and 13-16. The problem here is that in some clauses the object actually precedes the subject as in sentences 11 and 15. These create the tricky cases which actually show up on the GMAT Sentence Correction section. There are also correct sentences such as the following: "He is the gentleman who grew fruit for whoever would come to pick it." Here, although *whoever* follows a preposition, it is a subject of the verb *would come*.

Principle: The object form of pronouns must always be used after verbs in positions where the pronoun is the object and after prepositions, even if a conjunction such as *and* appears between the verb or preposition and its object, as in the case of "Mother spanked Sheila and me."

4.5 Dangling Participles—How To Handle Them

The favorite question on the GMAT usage section involves what is known as a dangling participial phrase. This is a reference-less phrase which starts a sentence or clause, as is demonstrated in the following:

(17) Going downtown, a strange occurrence was witnessed by Jack.

The way to figure out the correct form for such sentences is to ask who is doing what for each part of the sentence and to make sure the same person or thing is doing the action in both parts of the sentence. For instance, in (17) above, you should ask the question: Who is going downtown? The answer is Jack. In the same sentence, the next question should be: Who witnessed the strange occurrence? The answer is Jack. Therefore the sentence should read:

(18) Going downtown, Jack witnessed a strange occurrence.

Not all dangling participial phrases are so easy to spot. Some of them may be as follows:

(19) Looking at the main intellectual trends growing into the human consciousness, it can be determined that idiocy is not yet dead.

Again, who is doing the looking? It certainly cannot be "it." Therefore the sentence is wrong. Obviously the doer of the action, *looking*, must be a person of some kind or another. Consequently, if the test offers you the following choices, only one of them is correct:

A) Looking at the main intellectual trends growing into the human consciousness, it can be determined
B) Having looked at the main intellectual trends growing into the human consciousness, it can be determined
C) It can be determined, looking at the main intellectual trends growing into the human consciousness
D) Looking at the main intellectual trends growing into the human consciousness, it could easily be determined
E) Looking at the main intellectual trends growing into the human consciousness, any thinking person can determine

Only (E) has a human referent that can do the looking in answer to the question: Who is doing the looking? To be correct, the "who" should appear first in the part of the sentence following the comma. Therefore, (E) is the correct answer. Another way to look at this is to understand that the focus of both parts of the sentence must be the same.

Principle: The answer to the question who (or what) is doing the action, for both parts of sentences starting with an *ing*-word, must be the same, and reference to the person or thing doing the action (the subject) usually must be at the beginning of the second part of the sentence.

A similar problem can occur with prepositional phrases as modifiers. For instance, sentence (20) is considered wrong, and (21) correct.

(20) As an adult, the forces of evil seemed always to overwhelm him.

(21) As an adult, he seemed always to be overwhelmed by the forces of evil.

The problem here, again, is a matter of focus. The second part of the sentence must focus on the same individual or thing that has the focus in the first part of the sentence. Again, note how correct grammar can occasionally force the sentence into using the usually undesirable passive voice.

4.6 Problems with Double Negatives

Sentences with double negatives are ungrammatical—and should be closely watched out for on the GMAT. These are sentences where the negative words serve to cancel the intent when looked at logically. For example, a sentence such as "He don't know nothing," although heard occasionally in spoken English, is ungrammatical on the GMAT. The correct form of this sentence is "He doesn't know anything." The rule about double negatives doesn't apply to sentences such as "No, I won't go," which are quite all right.

The problem with double negatives is most difficult to spot when it involves three adverb-like words which are negative: *hardly*, *never*, and *seldom*. These cannot be used with the negative *not*. If they are used together, they produce a double negative. For example, consider the following sets of sentences:

(22) a. They hardly ever go by way of the coast road.
b. They don't hardly ever go by way of the coast road.

(23) a. They seldom go by way of the coast road.
b. They don't seldom go by way of the coast road.

(24) a. They never go by way of the coast road.
b. They don't never go by way of the coast road.

The second sentence in each set is obviously ungrammatical.

Principle: Look for double negatives and make sure no sentence contains them.

4.7 Problems in Agreement

In English, the third singular form of the verb is marked with an *-s*. Hence, the grammatically correct sentence is (26).

(25) He see streams in the desert everyday.

(26) He sees streams in the desert everyday.

In some forms of spoken English, sentences like sentence (25) may occur, but in written English, they are never acceptable. However, when the words around the subject and verb disguise the situation, some sentences like (25) appear to be correct. Don't be deceived! One of these sentences is:

(27) His uncle, together with his two cousins, recommend that he go to the doctor for a checkup.

The confusing thing about the two verbs in (27), *recommend* and *go*, is that one is quite correct as it is but the other is not. The first verb *recommend* may appear to have a plural subject, "uncle and two cousins." But it really has a singular subject, "uncle." The noun phrase, "two cousins," is embedded in a prepositional phrase and does not count as the subject in determining the marking on the verb. On the other hand, the verb *go* has a singular subject *he*, and normally would be marked with an *-s*. But here *go* is in a *that*-clause following a verb that requires a subjunctive (a proposed action). As a result, the correct form of the sentence is:

(28) His uncle, together with his two cousins, recommends that he go to the doctor for a checkup.

Fortunately, there are not too many verbs that take a *that*-clause with the subjunctive. And just as fortunately, often these verbs occur in documents coming out of parliamentary procedure; the verbs include *insist, suggest, move*, and *recommend*, as in the following examples:

(29) a. I move that the lady from Virginia be seated.
b. I recommend that the speaker require silence.
c. I insist that one member of parliament be removed.
d. I suggest that he end his filibuster.

Theoretically, with sentences that start with *there* followed by some form of *be*, the subject follows the verb and from that position determines the number in the verb. Thus, although sentence (30a) is quite all right in speech, it is wrong on the GMAT and in prescriptive grammar. The form of the sentence should be as it is in (30b) for the GMAT.

(30) a. There is Molly and Phil.
b. There are Molly and Phil. (two nouns, plural subject)

There is another apparent exception to the rule about singular subjects requiring a special form of the verb with *-s*. If the noun entails a group, such as family, team, and government, it is described as a collective noun and can be in agreement with either a plural or singular verb as both variants of the following sentence:

(31) a. The family need a lot of loving warmth.
b. The family needs a lot of loving warmth.

Besides this, there are some constructions which are confusing. For example, if two singular nouns are joined by *and*, the construction counts as a plural subject. But if the same nouns are joined by *or* or *nor*, the construction counts as a singular subject, since on the level of an idea the construction is singular, as in the following:

(32) a. In the story, John and Betty travel in Japan.
b. In the story, neither John nor Betty travels in Japan.
c. In the story, either John or Betty travels in Japan.
d. In the story, John or Betty travels in Japan.

4.8 Problems with Nouns and Pronouns

Problems with agreement in number occur not only with subjects and verbs but also with nouns and other words in front of them. Thus, the number of the fronting word is determined by some other word in the sentence that is some distance from the noun, as in sentence (33):

(33) a. Every person feels that their needs are the most crucial.
b. Every person feels that his needs are the most crucial.

Since person is a singular noun, the pronoun that refers to it must be singular, too. Hence, (33a) is incorrect. The correct version is (33b). These problems become particularly irksome in sentences with the indefinite pronouns: one, none, anybody, everybody and nobody. For most of the speakers of the language, sentence (34) is quite all right, but on the GMAT it is wrong.

(34) Everybody shaved their heads.

The argument is that since "everybody" is singular, the personal pronoun should be singular, and since there are no two-headed people in the frame of reference, "head" must also be singular.

(35) Everybody shaved his head.

The use of "his" is correct. Sentence (35) depicts a 'genderless' use of the gender-oriented pronoun *his*.

In the sentence below, it appears that the noun "boys" is the subject and it is plural.

(36) Every day, one of the touring choir boys lose their wallets.

The sentence is correct only in the form given in (37).

(37) Every day, one of the touring choir boys loses his wallet.

In any case, agreement between subject and verb or between a noun or pronoun and its antecedent is extremely important.

4.9 Problems with the Marked Infinitives

In English, the infinitive is usually marked by *to*, the sign of the infinitive, as in:

(38) They were admonished to love their country greatly and to obey its laws completely.

In the use of infinitives, however, there is a law: Never split an infinitive as in sentence (39):

(39) They were admonished to greatly love their country and to completely obey its laws.

On the GMAT, the rule has no exceptions. The *to* of the marked infinitive must always be right up close to the verb form. It must not be separated from the verb—that is, split. One other problem occurs with infinitives. GMAT examiners love to ask questions that force a choice between "try and" and "try to." Thus they ask the test-taker to choose between sentence (40a) and (40b).

(40) a. The government will try and put him away on charges of sedition.

b. The government will try to put him away on charges of sedition.

The "try and" construction is never correct, because the "and" implies a second action. Always choose the "try to" construction.

4.10 Problems of Parallelism in Form

The principle of parallelism insists that phrases or clauses of similar status or importance must be of similar form. Thus, phrases or clauses must be parallel in form when they are in a series or when they are joined by a conjunction such as *and*: that is, if there is one verb with *-ing* in a series, then all of the verbs must have *-ing*, or if there is one *who*-clause in a series, then all of the members of the series must be in the form of a *who*-clause. A simple example can be used to make the point. Sentences should not have the form of (41a) below; they should rather be cast in the form of (41b).

(41) a. Charles likes swimming, hiking and to ski.

b. Charles likes swimming, hiking and skiing.

Not all cases of faulty parallelism in the GMAT usage section are so easy to spot; some are more complex. For instance, sentence (42) violates the principle of parallelism, but (43) does not.

(42) The police came to arrest Paul Jones, a devout church-goer who also belongs to the fraternal order of the Eagles.

(43) The police came to arrest Paul Jones, a devout church-goer and member of the fraternal order of the Eagles.

In sentence (42), an appositive, "a devout church-goer," is matched with a *who*-clause, producing a sentence that has faulty parallelism. This can be cured only by matching the first appositive with a second appositive, as in sentence (43).

The most common question involving faulty parallelism on the GMAT usually strings together many *ing*-forms of the verb having the marked infinitive with *to*. Thus, the kind of sentence like (44) is frequently found on the GMAT; it is corrected by sentence (45).

(44) Many businessmen like singing German songs, dancing with German ladies and to guzzle German beer when they are in Bonn.

(45) Many businessmen like singing German songs, dancing with German ladies and guzzling German beer when they are in Bonn.

The parallelism might be in the verb form, as in the following where an imperative without a subject is paired with a full verb form with a subject.

(46) First, exit the fuselage and then you should inflate the life jacket.

(47) First, exit the fuselage and then inflate the life jacket.

Parallelism must also be preserved in sentences with *be*. The noun forms on either side of *be* must be similar. Thus, a sentence such as (48) is wrong, but sentence (49) is quite all right.

(48) For a sculptor, completing a perfect figurine is as satisfying as to finish a life-sized statute.

(49) For a sculptor, completing a perfect figurine is as satisfying as finishing a life-sized statute.

Principle: The principle of parallelism requires that phrases or clauses of similar status or importance be of similar form. Sentences which are not constructed in conformity to this principle are incorrect.

4.11 Problems with Comparison

In English, there are three degrees for the comparison of adjectives and two types of adjectives, the *regular* and the *irregular*. These are illustrated below:

	Positive	Comparative	Superlative
Regular	slow	slower	slowest
	fast	faster	fastest
	beautiful	more beautiful	most beautiful
	quickly	more quickly	most quickly
	lovely	more lovely	most lovely
Irregular	good	better	best
	bad	worse	worst

Adjectives and adverbs with three or more syllables require comparison with *more* and *most*. For adjectives and adverbs with two syllables, the form can require either *-er/-est* or *more/most*.

	Positive	Comparative	Superlative
Regular	easy	easier	easiest
		more easy (WRONG)	most easy (WRONG)
	ready	more ready	most ready
		readier (WRONG)	readiest (WRONG)

Both the form and nature of comparison appear on the GMAT. Questions on the form of comparatives require a decision between the correctness of (50) and (51).

(50) Could you please drive more slowly? I'm getting car sick.

(51) Could you please drive slower? I'm getting car sick.

When in doubt pick the *more/most* form, sentence (50).

Generally, if there are only two things being compared, then only the comparative degree can be used; the superlative is used only with three or more entities.

(52) Of the two runners, he is the best. (*ungrammatical*)

(53) Of the two runners, he is the better.

(54) Of all the runners on the OSU track team, he is the best.

In a comparison of the part versus the whole, be sure not to include the part in the whole. For instance, sentence (55) is wrong, but sentence (56) is right.

(55) Charles Atlas was stronger than any man in the world. (*ungrammatical*)

(56) Charles Atlas was stronger than any other man in the world.

The logic behind the difficulty with sentence (55) is this: In the second part of the comparison, all the men in the world are included; thus, the sentence says that Charles Atlas is stronger than Charles Atlas, an obvious absurdity.

Although many forms of spoken language use *than* in phrasal comparison, that is, comparison between nouns and noun phrases, the preferred form in the written language is *from*, as in grammatical sentence (58).

(57) He was quite different than all his brothers. (*ungrammatical*)

(58) He was quite different from all his brothers.

GMAT questions always require *different from* for phrasal comparison of adjectives in the positive degree. Comparison using adjectives marked for comparison, however, can use *than* as in (59) and (60):

(59) Eating corn chips is better for you than eating french fries.

(60) The life of a king seems more restricted than the life of a peasant.

The difference, then, is between adjectives in the positive degree which require *from* in comparisons, and compared adjectives which require *than*.

4.12 Problems with Relative Clauses and the Restrictive/Non-Restrictive Distinction

Most of the grammarians who write about this distinction will say that a non-restrictive clause (with commas) simply adds additional information to the sentence, information not essential to the meaning of the sentence. They will also tell you that a restrictive relative clause (without commas) is essential to the meaning of the sentence. If such a clause is taken out of a sentence, the sentence will no longer mean the same. It will mean something quite different. As examples they give sentences such as the following:

(61) The man, who ate nine green apples before breakfast, was quite ill by noon. (non-restrictive)

(62) Anyone who eats nine green apples before breakfast will be quite ill by noon. (restrictive)

Obviously, sentence (61) is still a good sentence when the relative clause is taken out: "The man was quite ill by noon." This is not true of sentence (62). In (62), if the relative clause is omitted the sentence no longer makes sense: "Anyone will be quite ill by noon." But what happens if the two sentences are more similar in form such as sentences (63) and (64)?

(63) The sailor, who ate five cans of sardines before breakfast, was quite ill by noon. (non-restrictive)

(64) The sailor who ate five cans of sardines before breakfast was quite ill by noon. (restrictive)

The first sentence refers to a single sailor. The second sentence refers to a group of sailors, one of whom receives special reference. In these two sentences, (63) and (64), there is no real difference in the concept essential to the meaning of the sentence. Therein lies the difficulty: Sentences on the GMAT do not provide much context, yet test-takers must figure out just what (or who) is the referent of the noun in the sentence before any determination of the status of a following clause can be made.

Restrictive clauses are attached to nouns that refer to one of a group of things or a number of such things which are distinct from other groups of things. Non-restrictive clauses do not thus identify things or individuals: they simply add more information to the sentence. For example, compare sentences (65) and (66):

(65) The sailors who ate sardines from the officers' mess became quite ill. (restrictive)

(66) The sailors, who ate sardines from the officers' mess, became quite ill. (non-restrictive)

In (65), there are obviously two groups of sailors: those who ate sardines from the officers mess and those who did not. Only those who ate the sardines from the officers' mess became ill. In (66), there is obviously only one group of sailors who happened to eat sardines from the officers mess and they all became ill. Thus, spotting the difference between restrictive and non-restrictive relative clauses is relatively difficult. There are, moreover, two easy-to-apply rules concerning restrictive and non-restrictive clauses: (i) Proper nouns are never followed by restrictive clauses and (ii) *that* never starts non-restrictive clauses, as in the examples below:

(67) Jimmy, who ate sardines from the officers' mess, became quite ill. (non-restrictive)

(68) Jimmy who ate sardines from the officers' mess became quite ill. (non-restrictive, ungrammatical)

(69) The sailors that ate sardines from the officers' mess became quite ill. (restrictive)

(70) The sailors, that ate sardines from the officers' mess, became quite ill. (non-restrictive, ungrammatical)

Thus, in questions that have restrictive and non-restrictive clauses, that is, clauses beginning with who (whom, whose), there are four strategies to be followed: (i) Check to see if the noun antecedent is a proper noun, that is, check to see if the noun starts with capital letters. If it does, the clause following it is non-restrictive—it needs the commas. (ii) Check the context to see if one individual or one group of individuals is singled out and separated from another group of individuals. If it is, the clause is a restrictive clause, and no commas should be used. (iii) If one individual or one group is referenced alone in the sentence under consideration, then the clause is non-restrictive. Commas should be used. (iv) If the noun antecedent is an indefinite pronoun: one, none, anyone, no one, etc., then the clause is restrictive. No commas should be used.

4.13 Problems with Indefinite Pronouns and the Pronoun Shift

Generally, writers of the questions on the GMAT usage section view the use of the indefinite pronoun *one* as something akin to a disease. They do not like it at all, and they will invariably expect the test taker to view sentences (71)–(73) as exhibiting various degrees of 'incorrectness.'

(71) One can never be happy doing only what one likes, can you?

(72) You can never be happy doing only what you like, can you?

(73) The roads are terrible. They ought to do something about it.

There is nothing wrong with the use of pronouns. It is the indefinite use of these pronouns that is to be avoided. Thus, in sentence (73), *they* is used indefinitely. There is no possible referent for *they*. There is no answer to the question: "Who is *they*?" Nor is there an answer to the question: "What is *it*?" *They* and *it* function as indefinite pronouns in (73). Sentence (73) can be repaired by making the referents definite as in (74).

(74) The roads are terrible. The Highway Department should do something about them.

The *them* in sentence (74) is definite since *it* refers to the noun "roads" in the first part of the example. The aspect of sentence (71) that is wrong in the minds of the authors of questions on the GMAT is the shift of the pronoun from *you* to *one*. On the GMAT any shift of this nature is wrong. Thus sentence (76) is to be preferred over sentence (75).

(75) If U.S. citizens study their history, we will come to understand that we are quite warlike.

(76) If U.S. citizens study their history, they will come to understand that they are quite warlike.

From this it should be apparent that within the GMAT system of grammar, shifts in both definite and indefinite pronouns should be avoided, and the use of indefinite pronouns should be shunned.

4.14 Problems with Correlative Conjunctions

Even though correlative conjunctions are few they occupy a disproportionately important place on the GMAT. There are basically only three sets of correlative conjunctions in English: *either/or, neither/nor, not only/but also*. The secret to their use lies in keeping a balance on either side of them. Thus sentence (77) is ungrammatical, but sentence (78) is correct.

(77) The car salesman bid either on a nod or call basis.

(78) The car salesman bid either on a nod or on a call basis.

(79) The car salesman bid on either a nod or a call basis.

For sentence (78), since the two words *on* and *a* follow *either* they must also follow *or* to maintain a proper balance. Sentence (77) can also be corrected by the sentence at (79) where again the same kind of word follows both *or* and *either*.

This is also true for the correlative conjunction *not only/but also*. Thus sentence (80) is not grammatical in the framework of the GMAT but (81) is.

(80) A big raise has not only been given to the janitors but also to the maintenance workers.

(81) A big raise has been given not only to the janitors but also to the maintenance workers.

So, then, correlative conjunctions travel together, and (i) they must never be separated, and

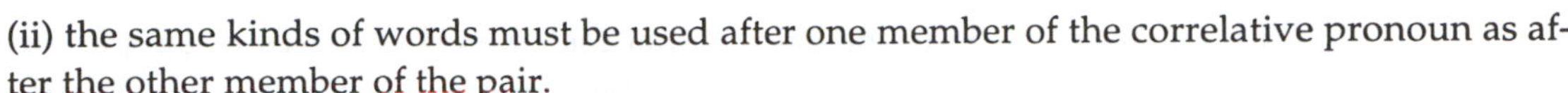

(ii) the same kinds of words must be used after one member of the correlative pronoun as after the other member of the pair.

4.15 Problems with Deletion

Different kinds of deletion can occur in a variety of places. If two parts of a sentence are identical, one can be deleted. Thus, in the following examples, parts of the sentences on the left can be deleted, yielding the sentences on the right.

(82)	Jack has fallen down and Jack has broken his crown.	Jack has fallen down and broken his crown.
(83)	John has frequently tried and John will ultimately be able to fix his crown.	John has frequently tried and will ultimately be able to fix his crown.
(84)	Mike has frequently tried to fix his bike and will finally succeed in fixing his bike.	Mike has frequently tried to and will finally succeed in fixing his bike.

What sometimes goes wrong is that on occasion non-identical parts of the sentence are deleted. Thus sentence (84) might have a deletion so that a sentence such as (85) is produced:

(85) Mike has frequently tried and will finally succeed in fixing his bike. (*ungrammatical*)

What has gone wrong in (85) is that *to* was not in both clauses of sentence (84); that is, the part of the sentence before the *and* has *to*, but the part of the sentence after the *and* does not. Therefore, both parts of the sentence are not identical, and *to* cannot be deleted as it has been in sentence (85).

Principle: For sentences like (85) on the GMAT, make sure that only the parts of sentences that are the same get deleted.

4.16 The Details Behind Sequences of Tenses

There are clearly defined rules for using tenses in the right order in sentences which have more than one clause. On the GMAT, the most popular tense to ask about is the perfect tense. This tense in English shows certain peculiarities. Its meaning, and consequently its use, can be contrasted with the 'simple' tenses—past, present and future—as per the following diagram:

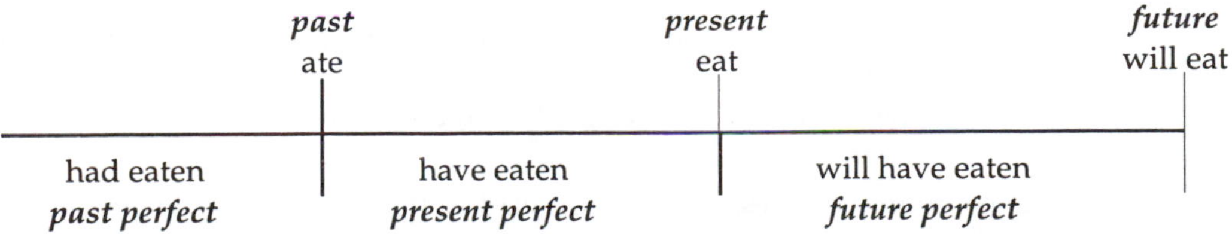

From the diagram, it should be evident that the past tense expresses simple time in the past, the present tense expresses simple time in the present, and the future tense expresses simple time in the future. It should also be evident that the past perfect tense expresses time leading up to a time in the past, the present perfect tense expresses time leading up to a time in the present, and the future perfect tense expresses time leading up to a time in the future. Thus, sentences (86)–(88) in the A-column are all correct; those in the B-column are incorrect:

	A- column	B- column
(86)	Although I had asked him last year to pay back the money, as of yesterday, Joe had not paid it back.	Although I asked him last year to pay back the money, as of yesterday Joe did not pay it back.
(87)	Although I have asked him repeatedly to pay back the money, Joe is not listening to me.	Although I asked him repeatedly to pay back the money, Joe is not listening to me.
(88)	Although I will have asked him to pay back the money for a year by the end of next week, Joe probably still won't have paid it back.	Although I asked him to pay back the money for a year by the end of next week, Joe will probably still not have paid it back.

As in sentences (86)–(88), the perfect tenses describe time anterior (prior) to a time in the present, past or future. Besides these, sequence of tense problems occur in dialogues with reported speech.

	Original	Reported Speech
(89)	"I will go."	I said that I would go.
(90)	"You can leave now."	She said that you could leave.
(91)	"Jack is sleeping."	She said that Jack was sleeping.

In "reported" sentences (89)–(91), the tense in the first clause must be the same as the tense in the second clause. Interestingly, the present perfect tense with *would, should, might, could* and *may* produces contrary-to-fact conditionals. Thus the action in the following sentences (92)–(96) did not occur; it was never performed.

(92) Philip would have paid the monthly installment on the house.

(93) Philip should have paid the monthly installment on the house.

(94) Philip might have paid the monthly installment on the house.

(95) Philip could have paid the monthly installment on the house.

(96) Philip may have paid the monthly installment on the house.

In sentences with *if*-clauses, normally the clauses that are contrary to fact require *would, should, might, could* or *may*, and the present perfect. With the *if*-clause, the past perfect is preferred:

(97) If Philip had paid the monthly installments on the house, the bank would not have foreclosed.
Compare: If Philip paid the monthly installments on the house, the bank would not have foreclosed. (*ungrammatical*)

Very often *would have, should have, might have, could have* and *may have* are pronounced as if they were "would of," "should of," etc. They must never be written this way, however.

Principle: The selection of the 'correct' sequence of tenses requires that the tense in one clause of a sentence be the same as the tense in another clause of the sentence. If the time-frame in one clause of a sentence is anterior to the time in another part of the sentence, then the perfect tense should be used.

4.17 Problems with the Choice of Tense

If an extended period of time is addressed in a sentence, then the durative (or progressive) tenses are needed. These tenses are marked by some form of *be* and the verb ending *-ing*.

(98) She has been living in Destin for fifteen years and she is living there now.

Some verbs, called *stative verbs*, do not take these tenses. These are verbs such as *know, believe, resemble* and *have* (in some usages):

(99) I am knowing that he is finished. (*ungrammatical*)
Compare: I know that he is finished.

(100) I am believing that you are a genius. (*ungrammatical*)
Compare: I believe that you are a genius.

(101) I am having some money. (*ungrammatical*)
Compare: I have some money.

4.18 Special Problems with Adverbs in English

In English, there are two sets of adverbs of manner. The first set is composed of words ending in *-ly* like *slowly, quickly, carefully* and others in the sentences below:

(102) a. Please drive slowly.
b. Please run quickly.
c. Please drive carefully.

The second set is composed of words like *slow, fast, hard, low* and others in the sentences below:

(103) a. Drive slow.
b. Hit hard.
c. Swing low.
d. Drive fast.

These are known as *flat adverbs* because they do not end in *-ly*. Furthermore, if there is a choice between the use of the flat adverb form and the *inflected adverb* form on the GMAT, the inflected form is the correct form. "Drive slow" is ungrammatical; "Drive slowly" is the correct form. b., c. and d. are correct as is. Besides this, the *-ly* adverbs are problematic when they are compared. Supposedly, words of two syllables take the comparative *-er* suffix, but sometimes these are problematic. As a result, the comparison with *more* is preferred.

(104) a. Henry drives slower than Grada. (*ungrammatical*)
b. Henry drives more slowly than Grada.

4.19 Problems with Ambiguous Antecedents

Make sure that the pronouns which you use refer to only one antecedent. If a pronoun can refer to either of two antecedents it is ambiguous.

(105) Since Janet treated Marilynn rather rudely, there seems to be no joy in her life.

Here, the pronoun, "her," can refer either to Marilynn or Janet. It is therefore ambiguous. The sentence should be revised so that the pronoun reference is clear.

(106) Since she treated Marilynn rather rudely, Janet seems to have no joy in her life.

Principle: Avoid any sentence with an ambiguous reference of pronoun.

4.20 Problems with Wordiness

The *principle of parsimony* states that extra words should be deleted from a statement. Generally, the shorter statement should be preferred over the longer statement. Another similar principle requires that redundancy be reduced to a minimum or be eliminated. If a concept is expressed in two different words, one of them should be eliminated. Thus, a sentence such as (107) should be reduced to sentence (108).

(107) They entered into a darkened room with a table. (*ungrammatical*)

(108) They entered a darkened room with a table.

The most common of the redundant phrases appearing on the GMAT is *The reason . . . is . . . because*. Thus sentence (109) is correct but sentence (110) is not.

(109) The reason that I like Doyle is that he is so consistent.

(110) The reason that I like Doyle is because he is so consistent. (*ungrammatical*)

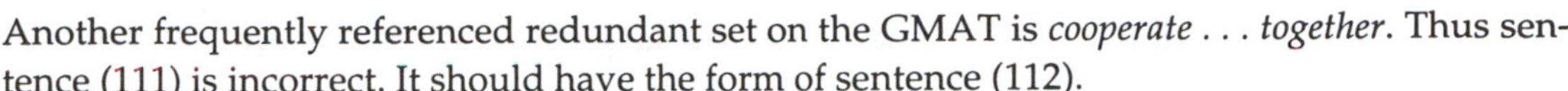

Another frequently referenced redundant set on the GMAT is *cooperate . . . together*. Thus sentence (111) is incorrect. It should have the form of sentence (112).

(111) They decided to cooperate together on the project.

(112) They decided to cooperate on the project.

The notion behind "together" is entailed by the notion of "cooperate." It makes no sense to have the notion repeated.

4.21 The Dominant Sentence Type

The *dominant sentence type* is a type of cumulative sentence in which the subject and the verb are followed by all of the attributes which develop the meaning in the first part of the sentence. Such a sentence follows:

(113) **Cumulative sentence**: Jennifer is undoubtedly one of the best artists in the country, although few people like her wild colors or undisciplined brush strokes.

It appears that at least some of the question-writers for the GMAT prefer *periodic* sentences for effect. Periodic sentences hold the main meaning-based elements to the end of the sentence, as in the following (114):

(114) **Periodic sentence**: Although few people like her wild colors or undisciplined brush strokes, Jennifer is undoubtedly one of the best artists in the country.

It is difficult to know when the test writer will expect the answer to be the periodic sentence, but if all other criteria fall short, select the periodic sentence.

4.22 Lexical Infelicities...

...And awkward phrasings. There are some proscribed forms which frequently occur and re-occur on the GMAT. It is difficult, if not impossible, to offer a general principle which covers the correct use of all these forms. Generally, however, it can be said that if the form occurs in the speech of the test-taker, and if the test-taker learned it from peers at an early age, then its usage is probably wrong. Some examples follow on the next two pages.

Uninterested vs. *disinterested*: An uninterested person is one who has no interest in a person or project. A disinterested person is one who has no favored interest in one side or another.

Imminent vs. *eminent*: Something that is imminent is close by or near at hand. Someone who is eminent is someone who is famous.

Differ with vs. *differ from*: It is impossible to differ with an individual since *with* implies agreement.

Despite vs. *in spite of*: Despite is a colloquial form which is sometimes used for the more formal in spite of.

Irregardless of vs. *regardless of*: Irregardless is a low colloquial (and incorrect) form which is sometimes used for the more formal, correct regardless.

Aggravated vs. *irritated*: A wound can be aggravated. Irritated can be applied to human beings.

Had ought vs. *should*: Had ought is a colloquial form which is used in speech for the correct form should.

Try and vs. *try to*: Try and is colloquial for the more formal (and correct) try to:

Due to the fact that vs. *because*: Due to the fact that is a wordy version of because.

Allude vs. *elude*: Allude is a literary term meaning 'to make an indirect reference to something.' It is related to the term allusion. Elude is a term meaning 'to escape from' or 'to stay out of someone's way.'

Accept vs. *except*: To accept, a verb, implies a willingness to receive something; except is usually a preposition which has the effect of excluding someone or something.

Everywheres, anywheres, nowheres vs. *everywhere, anywhere, nowhere*: Everywheres, anywheres, nowheres are low prestige, dialectal variants of everywhere anywhere, nowhere. They should not be used in writing.

Beside vs. *besides*: Beside is a preposition that means 'by the side of.' Besides is a connecting word that means 'in addition to.'

Agree to vs. *agree with*: In standard written English, people agree to a proposal but they agree with a person.

Personal vs. *personnel*: If something is personal, it belongs to or is peculiarly the possession of a person. Personnel refers to an aggregation or collection of individuals usually in a company or some other organization such as the personnel department or the personnel manager.

Ingenious vs. *ingenuous*: Ingenious is usually applied to things, such as in the term ingenious device, which signifies a cleverly constructed device. Ingenuous is usually applied to people and it refers to people who have frank and open personalities.

Insure / ensure / assure. Ensure is the same as insure but it has a variant spelling. Assure means to give confidence to or build confidence in. It is related to reassure, which means to assure again as in "I assure you Joel does not need to be reassured."

Notoriety vs. *fame*: Notoriety connotes that type of fame which is gained on the basis of a bad or notorious reputation. Fame is generally positive.

Revue vs. *review*: A revue is something on the order of a Broadway musical show. A review can be anything from a book review to a reviewing of troops on a parade ground. They should not be confused.

Effect vs. *affect*: Affect means 'to influence or to have some influence on.' It usually occurs as a verb although there is a psychological term, affect, a noun, which is related to the term affection. On the other hand, effect is usually a noun which means 'result.'

Avoid selecting answers with trite expressions such as the following. They are always wordy and, because of their frequent use, they do not have much impact.

a good time was had by all
all too soon
after all is said and done
at death's door
at loose ends
a sigh of relief
beat a hasty retreat
beyond the shadow of a doubt
specimen of humanity
replete with interest
the proud possessor
clear as crystal
never in the history
grind to a halt
kind of a / sort of a
leave / let
all / all of
like / as
needless to say

(This page is intentionally blank.)

5. Critical Reasoning

Strategies for the Test
The Process of Reasoning
Suggestions

5. CRITICAL REASONING

Reasoning is what we do when we try to "figure something out" by thinking about it. Reasoning is a kind of skill, a "know how." It is something we can do well or poorly, something we can get right or wrong. Furthermore, this is a very generalized skill, one that we can apply to just about any kind of subject matter. If you're taking the GMAT, then you have already had many years of experience in reasoning.

It's useful to think of two kinds of reasoning. Sometimes we want to start with something we already know (or at least something we think we know), and then go further by thinking about that knowledge and building something more on it. This is reasoning "from scratch." When you do it, you have to invent the course of reasoning yourself. You have to decide what premises to use, what evidence to appeal to, what facts are relevant, how they connect with each other, and so on. And you have to think of how to go from those premises and evidence to a conclusion. That is what we might call *original reasoning* or *constructive reasoning*.

Sometimes, however, we already have some course of reasoning in hand, and we are trying to evaluate it. We want to know whether it really succeeds in providing a firm basis for an advance in knowledge—whether it is a good piece of reasoning or a bad one, that is. Strictly speaking, that's the project of *critical reasoning*. You may perform critical reasoning on an argument of your own, taking a second look at it after you've invented it. Often, however, you perform critical reasoning on arguments and reasoning that someone else gives you. You find this reasoning in books, papers, lectures, casual talk, and so on. And you try to evaluate it, so as to know whether to adopt it yourself, or, on the other hand, reject it. In critical reasoning you're thinking about a prior piece of thinking, either your own or someone else's.

This section of the GMAT is mostly about critical reasoning, though some items may have a part which requires some constructive reasoning. Each question will start by giving you a text which may itself involve a piece of reasoning. And you will then be asked to do a piece of reasoning about that text.

5.1 STRATEGIES

There is no strategy at all which will compensate for a complete lack of skill in critical reasoning. But if you're taking the GMAT, then of course you already have developed a great deal of skill in this area. You could hardly have arrived at your present position without it. And you can improve your skill even more before taking the test. First, however, let's think about some strategies which will help you make the most of your ability in this test.

The Test Situation

The bottom line. On the GMAT, *the bottom line is your score*. Your answer sheet will be run through a machine which will compute a numerical score based on how many questions you answered correctly and how many you got wrong. That score is what will be reported to the people who use the results of this test—the admissions officers in graduate school. So far as this test is concerned, that is what they will have to go on. Your task, then, is to get the best score you can. That may seem obvious, but you have to really stress to yourself the fact that the other things you do in taking this test are useful only if they serve to improve your score. You might make a brilliant analysis of the arguments in the critical reasoning section, but if that analysis doesn't raise your score—the bottom line—then it doesn't count for anything on this test.

A very tight structure. Compared to almost any other situation you are likely to encounter—a job interview, for example—the GMAT is very highly structured and regimented. Within this test you can't really fight that. You have to adapt to it, and even make it work for you.

One example of this regimentation is the time limitation for the test. The critical reasoning section allows just 30 minutes for a total of 20 questions; that's it. What you think of after that time has passed doesn't affect the bottom line. And almost surely, *you won't have time enough to do everything you would like to do in this test*. But don't panic. The people you're competing with will have the same problem with time. But it is essential that you give some thought to how you are going to use that limited amount of time, and that you then follow your plan.

The other important part of the tight regimentation is that in the GMAT *all the answers are provided for you*. In most other contexts, if someone asks you a question, you have to come up with your own answer. Then you have to express your answer as clearly and convincingly as possible. Maybe the questioner will follow up by asking you to explain your answer a little more, or to give your reasons for it, and so on.

None of that happens in the GMAT. There are questions, but you do not have the open-ended task of thinking up the answers, expressing them, defending them, etc. Your task, instead, is that of *selecting an answer* from a small set (five) of alternatives. Selecting an answer from a set that someone else gives you is much different than making up your own answer in your own way. Some people are very uncomfortable with this kind of regimentation, and that's understandable. But there are ways of taking advantage of this restriction and making it work for you. And that brings us to the following strategies.

Critical Reasoning Strategies

These strategies are specialized for the type of items in the Critical Reasoning section of the GMAT. Each item in the Critical Reasoning section of the GMAT begins with a brief passage—a paragraph or two. You are then asked a question about that text, and are provided with five alternative answers to the question.

Read the question first. Usually you will save time if you read the question before you read the text to which it refers. Remember, during this test you are not reading these items for enjoyment, nor to expand your general knowledge of interesting subjects. Nor are you to distract yourself with whether or not you agree with statements or conclusions drawn in the passages. These are fine things to do, and often we do read for these purposes, but this is not the time for that.

Here your task is to get the best possible score. In order to get a good score you don't need to know everything about the given topics. You just need to know enough to select the right answer to the question (or, at least, to eliminate some of the wrong answers). And you don't need to prepare yourself to answer a "surprise" question. No, the question is right out in the open from the very beginning. You might as well take advantage of that fact. *If you read the question first, then you'll have a good idea of what to look for in the text.* That will save time and effort.

If you find the question puzzling at first, don't worry about it. It may well become clear when you read the text. And sometimes glancing quickly through the answers will help to clarify the question, as you see what kind of things are suggested as plausible answers.

After you've read the text, read the question again. Read the question a second time, to assure yourself that you really do know what the question is. One of the most common ways people go wrong on this test is by answering a different question from the one asked. That answer may represent a real piece of knowledge, a genuine and insightful analysis of the text, but the GMAT has no way of recognizing that knowledge or insight. It simply gets counted as a wrong answer. It counts for nothing—actually, for less than nothing—on the bottom line, since wrong answers count against your score.

Almost always, the question will be clear enough, at least on a careful second reading. If it isn't, then probably you are better off going on to another item and coming back to this one later, if there is time.

When you understand the question, read the answers. Remember that you do not have to construct an answer to the question. You have to *select an answer*. Get a good idea of what your choices are. Now and then, you may see right off what the best answer must be. If so, good! If not, then go back to the text and start to do your critical reasoning in a systematic way, seeking to choose among those five alternatives by analyzing the text.

Don't worry about special knowledge. The Critical Reasoning passages will involve many different subject areas—the natural sciences, social sciences, history, literature, etc. Don't worry if the text is about a subject in which you have very little expertise, or none at all. You should be able to do just as well on these as on any other item. The questions are constructed in such a way that you don't need any special knowledge to handle them. You don't need to know whether any of the alleged special facts asserted in the text are in fact true.

What you are asked to do is to assess the way in which these alleged facts "hang together," the extent to which some of them support others. So you don't need any special knowledge of chemistry, for example, or Russian history, to do well on this section. And the vocabulary will be such that any well-educated person will be able to understand it.

The other side of the coin is that special knowledge probably won't be of much advantage in dealing with a particular item. In fact, it may well be a detriment. You may happen to know a lot about astronomy, for example, and you may find an item about astronomy. That's OK. But if you find yourself thinking about the special things you know about astronomy, and using that knowledge to evaluate the material in the text, look out! You're probably focusing on the wrong thing. Remember, that whole item was meant to be accessible to people who are not astronomers. Look at the question again, and see to it that you are answering that question and not some other.

5.2 THE PROCESS OF CRITICAL REASONING

Applying Critical Reasoning to a passage involves making a set of decisions about it. These decisions are related to one another. We'll discuss them here one after another, but you will see that they tie back into one another.

Is the text an argument? An "argument" here doesn't mean a dispute or controversy. Roughly, it means an attempt to provide a reason for believing something by citing something else. Or, to put it in a somewhat different way, it is an attempt to show that something is true, or probably true, by appealing to something else, some reason or evidence, which indicates that it is true.

The following text includes an argument:

> "New evidence shows that the AIDS virus may not be as lethal as it has been thought to be, and that some people may be able to develop a defense against it. Or maybe they have some sort of natural immunity. The evidence involves an appreciable number of people who have been HIV positive for many years—some of them for twelve years or more. Lab tests show that the virus is present in their blood. But they have not developed any symptoms of AIDS. They continue to be in good health, and show no signs of developing the disease. Some researchers estimate that as many as 5% of those infected by the virus may be in this category, and that they will never develop the disease."

In this text a claim is made about how lethal the AIDS virus is. It may not be 100% lethal. Some people may be able to resist it, perhaps because of a natural immunity. And some evidence is cited to show that this claim is true. That evidence is the (alleged) fact that some people have had the AIDS virus in their system for many years, and show no signs at all of developing the disease. It is plausible to think that the person who wrote that text intended to cite that fact as a reason for believing the claim about the lethality of the AIDS virus.

Not every passage contains an argument. It is important to remember that there are other kinds of passages. In every kind of subject matter we often make claims, and assert alleged facts, without even pretending to give any argument or reason in support of those claims. For example, someone who says, "I have a terrible cold," has made a claim. But she has not put forward any argument or reason to show that it is true.

In ordinary contexts she can probably count on her friends believing her just because she says it. Or they may be able to gather their own evidence by noticing her puffy eyes and hoarse voice. If she adds, "I hardly slept a bit all night," she still hasn't produced an argument. She makes a second statement, all right, but it probably is not intended as a support for the first one. (For one thing, hearers are not likely to be in a better position to judge or accept the second statement than they are with respect to the first.)

The most plausible way to think of her second statement is that it is an elaboration of the first one, a further and more detailed description of the state of her health. Expanding on a topic, adding interesting or important details, conveying more information—these are very common aspects of ordinary speech and writing. But they need not, and often do not, involve any argument at all.

A little further on we will discuss the most important kind of passage which might be confused with an argument, and we will say something about telling them apart. But first let's look a little more at arguments.

Premises and Conclusions

In an argument some claims are put forward in support of others. The claim which is being supported is the *conclusion*. The claims which are alleged to support the conclusion are the *premises*. There may be more that one conclusion in an argument, and there are often more than one premise. In the argument above about AIDS, there is a closely related set of conclusions.

> "AIDS may not be as lethal as it was thought to be. Some people may have a natural immunity to it, or they may develop an effective defense."

And in support of these conclusions the author cites the (alleged) fact that some people have been infected with the virus for a long time without showing any signs of the disease itself. This latter assertion is the premise in this argument.

Notice that in this argument no reason at all is given in support of the claim that there really are people of the sort described who have had the virus for many years without developing the disease. We are left to take that simply on the authority of the writer, or on some basis not stated here, if we accept it at all.

Every argument begins with something. It begins with an attempt to provide some support for its conclusion. It does not provide support for its premises (though there may be some other argument which supports them).

No claim or statement is a conclusion or a premise inherently, or by itself. To be a conclusion, or to be a premise, is to perform a certain role in a particular argument. One and the same claim may be a conclusion in one argument, a premise in another argument, and an independent statement, neither premise nor conclusion, in still another text.

How do you identify premises and conclusions? There is a tendency to put the premises first in the paragraph, and the conclusion at the end. But that is not very reliable, since the conclusion is often put first, or in the middle. In the argument about AIDS, for example, the conclusions introduce the paragraph, then comes the premise, and the paragraph ends with a further elaboration which doesn't seem clearly to be either a premise or a conclusion.

More reliable clues are provided by certain key words which are often used to identify premises and conclusions. The following words and phrases are quite often used to introduce conclusions:

So . . .
This shows that . . .
Therefore . . .
We can infer that . . .
Hence . . .
Consequently . . .
It follows that . . .
This indicates that . . .
For that reason, we can say . . .

This is, of course, only a partial list. But it should give you a pretty good feel for conclusion-marking expressions. There are also certain expressions which often mark the premises of an argument. These include the following:

The reason is that . . .
Because . . .
Since . . .
Evidence . . .
On the basis of . . .
It follows from . . .
In view of . . .
We can infer from . . .

Again, this list is only partial, and there are many other expressions which do more or less the same job as the ones listed here. They too are premise indicators.

While these words and phrases are *indicators* of premises and conclusions, they are not used exclusively as indicators. Sometimes they have other uses, or at least most of them do, so we will often look for additional clues.

So, how do we tell whether a passage presents an argument, and, if so, what are its premises and conclusion? In the case of the AIDS passage above, we have one of the most reliable indicator words, "evidence." If a passage is said to be evidence for something else, this certainly suggests that it either puts forward, or else reports, an argument. Either it is hoped that readers will accept a certain claim because they accept certain other claims, or else the author is claiming that researchers accept some of those claims on the basis of the others.

This suggestion gains further plausibility when we observe that some alleged facts—e.g., that a certain disease is lethal to some degree, or that some people are immune to that disease—are comparatively hidden. They don't look like the sort of facts which we would ordinarily expect to discover directly. Compared to them, however, other alleged facts—e.g., that a certain person has not died, that he is not severely incapacitated, and even that his lab tests for the HIV virus came back "positive"—seem more open, more easily ascertained (if they are true at all). And so it seems plausible that we, or the researchers, might come to accept facts of the first sort by first collecting some facts of the second sort and then reasoning to facts of the first sort on the basis of those facts of the second sort.

It looks like the AIDS paragraph cited above either invites or reports just this sort of inferential reasoning. So it is plausible to think that it involves an argument. And the same considerations which indicate that it is an argument also make pretty clear its premises and its conclusion.

Let's look now at the other kind of texts which are most easily confused with arguments.

Is the text an explanation? Some texts purport to explain some fact or state of affairs by citing some other facts which are related to the first one in relevant ways. The following short statement is an example of an explanatory text. In fact, this single sentence involves a sequence of two explanations.

> "The victim, though apparently in good health, died because of a massive heart attack, brought on by over-exertion during the recent storm."

In this passage, a certain fact—the victim's death—is explained by another fact—the heart attack. And the heart attack, in turn, is explained by still a third fact—the over-exertion. Notice that the text asserts still another fact, that the victim was apparently in good health. But nothing is said in the text to explain that fact, nor is it used to explain anything else. It serves only to provide a fuller picture of the whole situation, adding a (perhaps surprising) detail.

We said above that the explanatory facts (sometimes called the *explanans*) are related to the fact to be explained (sometimes called the *explanandum*) in some relevant way. One of the most common explaining relations is that of cause and effect. Something is explained by showing that it was caused in a certain way. The example we have just been considering is of that sort. The over-exertion caused the heart attack, and the heart attack caused the death.

The other common sort of explanation is in terms of purposes, intentions, desires, and similar attitudes on the part of some agent. The following is an example:

> "In the Spring of 1944, the German High Command proposed transferring the 42nd Division, probably the finest infantry division in the German army, from the Russian front to a position in northern France. Germany's top generals were anticipating the Allied invasion from Britain, and they wanted to have this crack unit in position for a quick counter-strike. Hitler, however, over-ruled this proposal, because he assigned a higher priority to preventing the advance of the Russian forces."

Note, before we leave this topic, that there exists another type of passage which may at first appear to be an argument, but in fact is not. A passage in which the conclusion merely restates, in so many words, a premise, is not truly an argument, but is commonly referred to as a *circular argument*.

Arguments and Explanations

Arguments and explanations are sometimes confused with each other. One frequent source of this confusion is the fact that the word "because" is often used to identify the premise of an argument, and it is also used to identify the explaining fact (the *explanans*) in an explanation. There isn't any mechanical way of clearly distinguishing an argument from an explanation. You have to make a judgment about which classification makes more plausible sense of the text. If it is plausible to think that the author is citing evidence to show that some claim is true, then there probably is an argument there. Such an author is trying to give us a basis on which to believe something, or, to put it another way, telling us why we can safely take his conclusion to be true.

If, on the other hand, the author is trying to tell us why a certain event happened (not why we should believe that it happened) or why a certain state of affairs is the way it is, then the text probably involves an explanation. In the AIDS example above, it seems plausible to think that the author is stating the evidence which shows that his claim (about the possibility of resisting AIDS) is true. In the Hitler example, the author appears to be telling us why the 42nd division was not moved to France. In the first text there is an argument, and in the second an explanation.

Often the situation is more complex. The claim that X is the explanation of Y is itself a claim for which we might want to have some evidence, some argument. So, *there can be an argument in support of an explanation*. The historian, for example, might be able to show entries in Hitler's diaries which indicated Hitler's thinking about the threat of a Russian advance in 1944. That argument would tend to support his claim about why the 42nd was not shifted. In such cases it is important to be clear about what the alleged explanation is, so that we will be clear about what the argument is supposed to establish.

Arguments about explanations—that is, arguments intended to show that one thing is the cause of another, or that a certain purpose lies behind a certain action—constitute an important subset of arguments. The GMAT often includes examples of such arguments.

Deductive and Inductive Arguments

In some arguments there is a really tight connection between the premises and the conclusion. There is no possible way in which the conclusion could fail to be true if the premises are true. (That's not to say, of course, that the premises are true.) These are the *deductive* arguments. Arguments in mathematics and in pure logic are often of this sort: "If no one watered my plants during my vacation, they are all dead now. No one watered my plants during my vacation. Therefore, they are all dead now." The premises of that argument might possibly be false. But if they are both true, then there is no way the conclusion can be false. Arguments with that tight link are deductive arguments.

There are other arguments with a looser connection. If the premises are true, then the conclusion is *likely* to be true also; it would be *surprising* if the conclusion were false; we have *good reason* to think that the conclusion is true, and so on. These are the *inductive* arguments. The AIDS argument above is inductive. It is possible that, even if all of the cited evidence is true, these patients will still develop the disease. But the long time which has elapsed since their infection, and the rather steady state of their health over that time, make it seem unlikely. It seems probable that in some way the disease has been successfully stalled.

In both sorts of arguments, the premises really do support the conclusion *if those premises are true.* But if they are false they provide no such support. Discovering that a premise is false, then, undercuts the force of both deductive and inductive arguments. It is important to remember, however, that discovering a false premise in an argument does not, in general, give us a positive reason for thinking that the conclusion is also false. That discovery takes away one reason we might have for thinking the conclusion true. Except in rather special cases, it does not give us a positive reason for thinking the conclusion to be false.

Because inductive arguments are only probabilistic, and not conclusive, they can be weakened (maybe rejected entirely) even if we continue to recognize that their premises are perfectly true. If, for example, researchers were to identify a virus very similar to the AIDS virus, and if they discovered that the incubation period for this virus in chimpanzees often exceeded 15 years, that discovery would seriously weaken the argument in the example. But it would not tend to show that any of the premises of the original argument were false. It would not tend to show that some people have not survived, and in good health, for 12 years after having been infected. It weakens the argument by introducing another live possibility, that the AIDS virus may have a longer incubation period than previously thought plausible.

Inductive arguments can also be strengthened by the introduction of new data. If it were discovered that there is a similar virus which infects chimpanzees, and for which many chimpanzees develop a resistance which enables them to live out a normal life-span in good health, that would further bolster the conclusion that perhaps some humans can make a similar defense against AIDS.

Questions about what would strengthen or weaken an inductive argument often appear on the GMAT. The sample tests in this book include several such items, along with a discussion of the answers.

Types of Inductive Arguments

We can usefully distinguish three main types of inductive arguments. The first of these makes use of the idea of explanation, but the argument itself is not an explanation. We might call arguments of this sort "explano-inductive." Both the premises (P) and the conclusion (C) of arguments of this type express alleged facts, events, states of affairs, etc. The argument proceeds by claiming that the occurrence or reality of P is some evidence that C is also a fact, because C would be a plausible explanation for P. This latter claim, that C would be a plausible explanation for P, is often left unexpressed in the argument. It may be taken to be obvious, or to be suggested by the context. But it is an essential element in arguments of this sort. So the butler's footprint, found near the scene of the crime, is one piece of evidence tending to show that the butler committed the crime, because his having committed the crime would explain why his footprint is in that location.

Two points must be kept in mind here. First, the evidential relation runs in the opposite direction from that of the explanatory connection. P (the existence of the footprint) is the evidence for C (the crime), but C is the explanation for P. Second, these are not arguments for the conclusion that C does, or would, explain P. These arguments require that we already know, or believe, that C would (if it were real) provide a plausible explanation for P. What these arguments conclude is that, because P is real, C is (probably) real. In general, the idea is that facts like P have an explanation, and if C would be a plausible explanation, then the fact that P has occurred is some evidence that C is also a reality.

The second main type of inductive argument is basically statistical. If it is known that a certain characteristic appears in the members of a certain group with a certain frequency, then we may infer that some otherwise non-selected member of that group has the corresponding probability of having that characteristic. It seems to be the case, for example, that people who live a largely sedentary sort of life suffer from heart attacks at a higher than average rate. Given this data, we can infer that Professor Plushbottom, whom we can find sitting in his office any day of the week, is "at risk" for a heart attack, more likely to have one than the average run of the population. Statistical arguments form the core of actuarial practice, the setting of insurance rates for different groups of people, some gambling strategies, and so on.

The third main type of inductive argument, sometimes called "argument from analogy," proceeds by noting that something, X, is similar to something else, Y, in certain respects. It is then inferred that X is also similar to Y in some further respect. Drugs, for example, are often tested in vertebrate animals, and the results—toxicity or carcinogenic potential—are then tentatively extrapolated to human beings. Behind this procedure lies the knowledge that the test animals are similar to humans in several ways—in important anatomical features, in physiology, and so on. But of course they are not completely similar, and the differences might turn out to be crucial. So, in many cases at least, the final tests must be done on human volunteers.

It is useful to keep in mind, in a schematic way, the essentials of analogical arguments. One essential is that there be two or more things, the analogues, which are similar to each other. We are not arguing about those similarities; they are the starting points of our analogy. Then we have some property or characteristic which one or more of these analogues is known to possess. Again, we are not arguing about that. We also take that as a given fact, a starting point for our argument. But there is one of the analogues in the argument which is not yet known to have that property. The argument consists of saying that because this thing is similar to the other analogues in certain ways, it is probably also similar in having this last property too.

Strengthening or Weakening Inductive Arguments

Because inductive arguments are not conclusive, they can be strengthened or weakened by further considerations. In general, there are two ways of doing this. We might bring in considerations which strengthen, or weaken, the connections between the premises of the original argument and its conclusion. Or we might bring in additional considerations which serve as the premises of additional arguments for, or against, the original conclusion.

Explano-inductive arguments, such as the one in the butler example, are regularly weakened by thinking of, or discovering, alternative explanations for P. So if we discover that the butler regularly walked past that spot in the usual course of his work, then the significance of the footprint is greatly diminished, because the presence of the footprint might be readily explained by the butler's ordinary activities, rather than by his complicity in the crime. The plausible alternative explanation weakens the connection between the original premise and the conclusion.

Merely thinking of possible explanations, as contrasted with discovering that explanatory events actually happened, often does comparatively little to weaken arguments of this sort. Is it possible that the real criminal stole one of the butler's shoes, used it to make the footprint, and then returned it to the butler's closet? Yes, that's possible, but it probably strikes us as rather less likely than that the butler made the footprint himself, wearing his own shoe. Of course, if we were to discover that the shoe actually was missing around the time of the crime, then the theft of the shoe becomes a much stronger candidate for the explanation of the footprint, and it correspondingly weakens the case against the butler. Other more bizarre possible explanations, such as the workings of foreign agents, may seem so implausible and unlikely that we ignore them altogether.

An inductive case like this can also be weakened in another way, without providing an alternative explanation for the original evidence. If an individual of good reputation testifies that the butler was with him in another place at the time of the crime, the case against him is weakened, even without suggesting any other explanation for the presence of his footprint. This really amounts to producing another inductive argument, with different premises and the opposite conclusion from that of the first. This second argument gathers its force from the fact that a plausible explanation for the willingness of the witness to give this testimony would be the fact that the butler really was with him. And in that case, presumably, he could not have committed the crime.

An inductive case of this sort may be strengthened in either of two ways, parallel to the two ways of weakening it. The first way involves discovering facts which serve to rule out, or to make less plausible, alternative explanations of the original evidential facts. Thus, we would strengthen connection between the original premises and the conclusion. If we could show, for example, that on the day in question the butler had no duties which took him near the spot in question, then this discovery would add something to the significance of his footprint there.

The other way of strengthening the case for the original conclusion consists of finding another evidential fact, another P, which is also plausibly explained by the original C. If the butler's fingerprints are found on the murder weapon, or if his coat has blood stains, then the case against him becomes stronger. Each of these items is an independent piece of evidence for the same conclusion, and each one adds a bit of strength to the case.

In medical tests of the effectiveness of a new drug, it is common to give the drug to one group of patients, and to have another group (the "control group") who are treated, so far as possible, in the same way but without the drug. The function of this control group is to make it less likely that some factor other than the drug is responsible for the differential responses observed in the two groups.

Statistical arguments can be strengthened, or weakened, by bringing in additional statistics. Almost every individual is a member of many different groups. Professor Plushbottom, whom we met earlier, is a member of the group of sedentary workers. But it may also be the case that Plushbottom's family tree, for the past several generations, includes no one who died of a heart attack. Among people with that heredity, heart attacks are comparatively rare. If we throw that statistic into the pot, then we should revise downward our estimate of Plushbottom's risk. But he may also be a member of a third group, that of overweight men, for whom the statistics are high. That pushes our estimate upward again. You will probably not meet a problem on the GMAT which requires you to make a fine-grained statistical analysis of conflicting data of this sort. But you should remember that it is possible for an individual to be involved in several groups whose statistics may pull in different directions.

The analogical case for the conclusion that X has a certain characteristic is strengthened by finding additional cases of the analogy—other things which are similar to X and which also have the characteristic in question. And it is weakened by finding "non-analogies"—things which are similar to X but do not have the characteristic in question. These discoveries amount to finding the premises for additional arguments, more or less like the original, tending to support or refute the original conclusion.

A more powerful sort of confirmation is generated by the discovery of a wide variety of positive analogies. If it is found that A, B, and C are all similar to X in certain ways, and A, B, and C all have the characteristic in question, and A, B, and C are otherwise widely different from each other, then the confirmation is much stronger than if A, B, and C were pretty much the same sort of thing. So if an experimental drug is found to have no harmful side effects in rats, pigs, and monkeys, then the inference that it will be harmless to humans is greatly strengthened over what we could reasonably infer from tests on one species alone.

The reason for that is that, in this case, the differences among the experimental animals have not generated a relevant difference in the reaction to the drug. It is therefore less likely that the difference between humans and these animals will generate a different reaction. Simply finding additional cases of the analogy under consideration strengthens the case, but finding a variety of such cases strengthens it much more. This can be taken to be another example of strengthening an inductive argument by strengthening the connection between its premises and its conclusion.

Another way in which analogical arguments can be strengthened or weakened—again by way of strengthening or weakening the connection between premises and conclusion—involves judgments about the *relevance* of various similarities. Imagine that archaeologists, excavating a Bronze Age site in North India, find pottery of a very distinctive and unusual shape. Indeed, no other ancient source is known for this type of pottery. There is, however, a 20th century West African tribal group who made very similar pottery, using an ingenious, eccentric potter's wheel.

Now, reflecting on these facts, we might begin with the assumption that the Bronze Age inhabitants of the archaeological site were similar to modern West Africans in some rather general ways—human anatomy and physiology, etc. We have now turned up another, and rather special similarity—they both make the same very distinctive type of pottery. Could we reasonably infer any further similarities between them on the basis of this similarity in pottery making?

Well, one conjecture we might make, with some analogical basis, is that the ancient potters, like the modern West Africans, knew how to make and use eccentric potter's wheels. The case for this conjecture would be weakened if we could show that it was easy to make those pottery shapes without any potter's wheel at all. On the other hand, it would be strengthened if we could not imagine any practical way of making those pots without such a potter's wheel.

But of course we may know many other things about the West Africans in addition to their use of these potter's wheels. We may know, for example, that their characteristic diet is unusually low in salt. Would we be on any sort of solid ground at all in inferring that the Bronze Age potters were probably similar to them in this respect also? That conjecture seems a lot more shaky than the one about the potter's wheel. In fact, it looks like it gets almost no support at all from the similarity of the pots. Behind that judgment there lies a judgment of relevance. We know (or at least think we know) that the sort of tools potters use is relevant to the sort of pots they make. But we also believe that their diet is not nearly so relevant. And the case for inferring a relevant similarity is much stronger than the case for inferring just any old similarity.

5.3 SUGGESTIONS

When you take the practice tests, you should look carefully at the discussion and analysis of each question. You can learn something from both the items you answered right and those you answered wrong or did not manage to answer at all.

If both your answer and your analysis of the problem match the solution, great! But you may have the same answer having used a different way of analyzing the problem. Try to understand what the differences are. Your analysis may not be wrong just because it is different. It is quite possible that, for some problems, you will come up with a somewhat different way of approaching them which yields the same result in the end, and is just as good. If you understand both approaches and rationales, then you are in a stronger position to take the test than if you adopt only one way.

And what about the items you got wrong? Of course, work through the analyses we present. If you can see where you went wrong, you've learned a lot—you're less likely to make that sort of mistake again. And what if in the end you disagree about what the correct answer is? That's not a tragedy. We are not bound to agree (and you are not bound to agree with the scoring of the actual test either, by the way). Neither we nor the makers of the GMAT are infallible. We might make mistakes too. If you can't agree with our answer and our rationale for it, then try to explain for yourself just how you think we went wrong, and try to formulate your own rationale as clearly and persuasively as you can. That itself is a tremendous learning exercise, and will strengthen your mental "muscles" for the real GMAT.

If you want some more useful learning materials, we have some suggestions. Books of logical puzzles provide an enjoyable way of developing your ability in reasoning. Most such puzzles don't require any specialized knowledge, or sophisticated mathematics. Go to a public library, or a college library, and look for books by Raymond Smullyan and Martin Gardner. (The same shelves will probably have several other books of the same sort.)

If you want some additional practice in identifying arguments and picking out the premises and conclusions, you can find examples and problems in the early chapters of introductory textbooks on logic. Irving Copi's *Introduction to Logic* would be a good choice. Many college libraries will have one or another edition of it.

(This page is intentionally blank.)

6. Analytical Writing

Advice for the Analytical Essay
Hints on Writing the Argument Essay
How GMAT Writing is Scored
Sample Essays

Time·Saver experts can score <u>your</u> practice essays!

6. Analytical Writing

6.1 Advice for the Analytical Essay

Expectations for the Analysis of Issue Essay

The people who write and grade the analysis of issue for the GMAT expect the following: i) a well-developed essay that is logical and coherent; ii) an essay that demonstrates critical thinking skills; iii) an essay which uses varied sentence structure and vocabulary; iv) an essay that uses the language of standard written English; v) an essay that is free of mechanical errors in spelling, punctuation, capitalization; and vi) an essay that follows the conventions of standard written English.

These conventions can be summarized in a single statement: Written English requires that each paragraph be developed directly away from a topic (or thesis) sentence or directly towards a topic (or thesis) sentence. The former is known as deductive development; the latter is known as inductive development. Since this is the case for all English written prose it should be obvious that writers in English have less freedom to wander from the main point of their discourse than writers in other languages. English expository prose style must be direct and to the point even though it is necessary to support each main idea with examples, explanations, and illustrations. The thesis (or topic sentence) must contain the germ of the idea that permeates the entire paragraph. Each example or illustration must be connected to that idea with transitional markers such as for example, or thus or moreover.

Writing the Analysis of Issue Essay

You can produce effective writing in the GMAT analytical writing section on the analysis of an issue by following a few simple rules:

1. Outline the essay briefly before you start to write.
   a. You may outline the essay in your head and hold it in memory.
   b. If you find it difficult to hold an outline in memory, scribble a few words down on paper to help you follow the outline.

2. Make sure that your outline.
   a. states the central idea of the essay clearly and forcefully;
   b. provides a word or phrase for every paragraph in the essay;
   c. relates each paragraph to the central idea of the essay in (2a) above.
   d. includes an opening and closing paragraph which tie the essay together.

3. Build your paragraphs in the essay carefully.
   a. Each paragraph should state a central idea which relates to the central idea of the entire essay.
   b. Every statement in each paragraph should relate to the central idea of the paragraph in (3a) above. In each paragraph, use examples to support the central idea or explain it completely.
   c. Consciously choose paragraph length, for if your paragraphs are all too short (one or two sentences), you will be penalized, and if they are too long you will also be penalized. Two or three paragraphs per written page should be about right.

4. Make sure that you write a lot (about five paragraphs). Work quickly, but keep your handwriting legible so that the examiners can read it easily.

Remember the acronym, OCPA (pronounced 'Oh-See-Pa'), which can be used as a mnemonic device to represent the following:

O = Outline—start with an outline.
C = Central—keep everything relevant to a central idea.
Pa = Paragraph—keep the paragraphs just right -- not too long and not too short.

An Example of an 'Analysis of Issue' Essay Test Question

For example, the GMAT test may present a statement such as the following:

> The Clinton administration has stated that since many Americans do not have health insurance, there is a crisis in health care. Critics have said that if the government intervenes in the health-care industry, costly, inefficient, government bureaucracies will create problems far greater than those they are designed to remedy.

The first step in writing, an issue-for-analysis essay on 'Health Care Reform' is to devise an outline which starts with a central idea.

> Central idea: Government interference in the health care system will create intractable problems.

I. With government intervention, health care will become problematic.
II. The government creates problems in the welfare system.
III. The government creates problems in the defense department.
IV. The government creates problems in the 'war on drugs.'
V. The government creates problems in protecting children.
VI. The government will create problems in the health care system.

Sample Essay

The following would be considered a well-written essay for the GMAT. Note how it follows the advice of "OCPA."

In nearly every avenue of life where the government intervenes, it produces more problems than it solves. This general finding will apply to government intervention in the health care system.

Point I on the Outline

For example, government intervention in the welfare system provides one instance of this general principle. Originally designed to help people who were 'down on their luck' and without enough income for food and shelter, the welfare system has produced a permanent underclass, on the one hand, and a group of middle class bureaucrats and slumlords who prey on the dispossessed, on the other hand, government handouts to the poor and unemployed do not as a rule help these people to obtain productive jobs principally because an army of middle class bureaucrats depends on a class of poverty-stricken individuals for their employment. If there were no unemployed individuals, there would be no need for the people who run the welfare system. Furthermore, if there were no unemployed individuals, there would be no slumlords to prey on them. Thus, it can be said that the welfare system may be one of the causes for the existence of a poverty-stricken underclass an example of a costly problem produced by the government.

Relates to Point I on the Outline

Point II on the Outline

Relates to Point I

The same principle describes the inefficiency in the Defense Department. For example, it is widely known that the defense department is party to huge cost over-runs in the procurement of major weapon systems. For example, the B2 bomber was supposed to cost $800 million. Before it was completed, the total cost was closer to $2 billion or more than twice the original estimate. Besides this, everyone has heard that the army purchases $20.00 hammers that can be procured for less than half that in the local hardware store or $200.00 toilet seats that sell for less than $12.00 outside of the Army procurement system. The point is that government bureaucracies are remarkably inefficient and that the creation of a bureaucracy for the management of health care would produce only one more inefficient organization.

Relates to Point I

Point III on the Outline

Relates to Point I

Similarly, in the war on drugs, the government ,seizes huge shipments of cocaine and other similar contraband. Sometimes, government agents manage to arrest and ultimately incarcerate drug lords and their henchmen. But does the war on drugs man

The word 'similarly' relates to Point I

age to significantly alter the trafficking in banned substances? Hardly. Sometimes the trafficking is slowed somewhat, but it is never stopped. Besides, new drug lords take over where the old had failed and continue the trade. The government effort simply addresses the wrong part of the problem and fails. The same thing would happen in a government run health care system.

Point IV on ***the Outline***

Relates to ***Point I***

In many states, a division of the government called 'Child Protective Services,' or some similar name is in charge of looking after the welfare of children. Undoubtedly, such an organization does some good things. But more obvious are the stories that seem to be in the newspaper on an almost daily basis: 'Tot in Foster Home Dies after Beating' or 'Couple Struggles to Regain Family.' On the one hand, the government bureaucracies fail to investigate fully before placing a tot into foster care; on the other hand, the people acting in the name of government become too zealous and break up a family on insufficient evidence. So the government errs in two directions: it is not zealous enough in some instances and it is overzealous in others. The same would happen with a government run health care system.

Point V on ***the Outline***

Relates to ***Point I***

These examples strongly support the argument that government actions often result in unwanted effects, as in the case of the welfare system. In other instances, they result in the wasting of money as in the case of the defense department spending. Sometimes, government actions simply fail to achieve their intended goals as in the case of the war on drugs and, in others, they simply produce unwanted results as in the case of child protective services. Is it not to be expected, then, that as government enters the field of health care it will produce all of these effects.

Point VI on ***the Outline***

Relates to ***Point I***

For your benefit I have to repeat: Use the acronym OCPA (pronounced 'Oh-See-Pa') to your advantage. The above essay followed it. If you follow it, you won't go wrong. It is a mnemonic device that represents the following:

O = Outline—start with an outline.
C = Central—keep everything relevant to a central idea.
PA = Paragraph—keep the paragraphs just right—not too long, not too short.

6.2 Hints on Writing an Analysis of an Argument

The Nature of Argument

A strong argument attempts to persuade people to accept a point of view. As such, it consists of a proposition, a declarative statement which is capable of being argued, and a proof, a reason or ground which is supported by evidence. The evidence, in turn, is composed of relevant facts, opinions based on facts and careful reasoning. If you are analyzing an argument, you should look for both of these: A proposition and the evidence supporting the proposition.

In the same way that an analysis of issue essay must start with a thesis, so also an essay that analyzes an argument must start with a topic sentence which provides for the analysis of a proposition. In a debate, the proposition starts with "Resolved that ..." In other forms of argument, the proposition can start with a question ("Should logging operations be halted by environmental considerations?") or with a flat statement ("The Federal Government should stop the immigration of Cubans to the USA."). Whether the proposition is framed in a formal statement or whether it takes the form of a question, every argument should have a proposition, and the identification of this proposition is crucial to the writing of an analysis of an argument.

For instance, the following could appear in the analytical writing section of the GMAT:

> Since the world population will double to 11 billion people by the middle of the 21st century and since food production will not show a corresponding increase, efforts should be made to limit population growth. Governments must institute population control policies to insure an adequate food supply for future generations.

The two clauses beginning with since provide evidence in support of the proposition. In turn, the proposition itself is framed by the second sentence.

Expectations for the Analysis of an Argument Essay

One aspect of argumentation that needs special attention is the use of terms. In an argument, all of the terms should be clear and well-defined. If the terms are unclear, proof is likely to be impossible, creating a weak argument. One type of weak term is the emotionally loaded term. Terms such as 'socialized medicine' evoke emotional responses and, thus, obscure the argument. Thus, anyone who writes an analysis of an argument should examine the terms used and be sure that the writer avoids emotive, subjective terms. To the extent of your ability, make sure that the writer defines terms clearly and objectively.

In addition, the people who write and grade the analysis of an argument section for the GMAT expect the following: i) They want an essay that analyzes the several aspects of the argument with critical insight. ii) They want a cogently developed essay that is logical.

iii) They want a coherent essay with well-chosen transitional devices. iv) They also expect an essay which uses varied sentence structure and vocabulary. v) Besides this, they require an essay that is free of mechanical errors in spelling, punctuation, capitalization, grammar and errors in the use of standard written English.

Writing the Analysis of an Argument Essay

Just as the conventions surrounding an analysis of an issue essay can be summarized by a single statement so it is with the conventions surrounding an analysis of an argument. For example, the writing for the analysis of argument requires that each paragraph be developed directly away from a thesis or topic sentence or directly towards a thesis or topic sentence. The former is known as deductive development; the latter is known as inductive development. Inductive argument is the process of thinking from the particular to the general, from individual facts to a generalization which is the proposition. Deductive argument proceeds from a generalization, the proposition, to the particular cases that support the proposition. As in the case of the analysis of the issue, the topic sentence must contain the germ of the idea that permeates the entire paragraph. Each example or illustration must be connected to that idea with transitional markers such as *for example, furthermore, therefore, thus* or *moreover*.

Knowing this, you can produce effective writing in the GMAT analytical writing section on the analysis of an argument by following a few simple rules:

1. Analyze the argument presented in the test section of the GMAT.
   a. Identify the proposition.
   b. Investigate different ways of probing the argument.

2. From your analysis of the argument, develop a brief outline of the essay that you are to record before you start to write.

3. Sketch in the outline in the space provided in the test booklet.
   a. State a clear thesis for the essay.
   b. Make each heading correspond to a paragraph.
   c. Make sure that there are at least five paragraphs.
   d. Make sure that each heading corresponds to a topic sentence.
   e. Be sure that there are a beginning and ending paragraph which tie the essay together.

3. Write your paragraphs in the essay with great care.
   a. Each paragraph should have a topic sentence which relates to the central idea of the entire essay.
   b. Everything in each paragraph should support the idea in the topic sentence of the paragraph in (3a) above. For each paragraph, state an idea then give examples to support the idea or explain the idea completely.
   c. Make your paragraphs just long enough so that your essay is about five paragraphs long.

4. Work rapidly, but keep your handwriting legible so that the examiners can read it easily. If you have time rewrite the entire essay.

Remember the acronym, TOPA (pronounced 'Toe-Pa'), which can be used as a mnemonic device to represent the following:

T = Topic sentence—Keep everything relevant to a topic sentence.
O = Outline—Make sure you follow an outline.
PA = Paragraph—Keep the paragraph length steady so that you have about five paragraphs.

Sample 'Analysis of Argument' Essay Test Question

For example, the GMAT test may present a statement such as the following for the analysis of an issue:

> In many countries, including the USA, the postal service is a quasi-governmental organization whose primary mission is to deliver mail to individuals within the borders of the country. Since, it is argued, mail delivery to rural addresses where the population is sparse cannot be done economically under any acceptable circumstance, the postal service is given a monopoly on mail delivery. Actually, however, mail delivery could be done economically by private corporations as long as each corporation were given a monopoly to service any given area where sparsely populated areas were balanced against densely populated areas.

In the above, argument for analysis, the proposition is contained in the last sentence and so the analysis of the argument must focus on this sentence.

I. The proposition regarding the privatization of the post office is based on two questionable assumptions and is most likely not true:
   A. Population in the USA is distributed in such a way that postal market areas can be divided and costly market areas can be balanced against lucrative market areas.
   B. Private corporations are more cost effective than quasi-governmental organizations.

II. Postal markets cannot be distributed so that service to any given market is economical.
   A. The reason for the distribution of population.
   B. The effect of that distribution on geographically contiguous areas.
   C. The effect of that distribution on geographically non-contiguous areas.

III. Private corporations are not necessarily more cost efficient than quasi-governmental corporations.
   A. The case of defense contractors.
   B. The case of private corporations.

IV. The case for the privatization of the post office department is based on questionable assumptions.

Sample Essay

The following would be considered a well-written essay for the GMAT argument section. Note that the writing follows the acronym 'TOPA.'

The idea that the post office department can be privatized is based on two questionable assumptions: In the first place, it can be shown that population in the USA is not distributed so that postal market areas can be divided with the result that costly market areas are balanced against lucrative market areas. In the second place, it can be shown that private corporations are not necessarily more cost effective than quasi-governmental organizations. It is, therefore most likely that privatization of the post office department cannot be accomplished.

Statement of the Topic: Outline I

In the first place, due to mechanization, one worker on the farm can support at least three hundred people living in the city. Large combines with relatively small crews can roll across the prairies harvesting 500 ton of wheat in a day, enough to feed hundreds of people for a year. As a result, there has been less and less employment in rural areas and, as a further result, people have left the rural areas for life in the city, creating the contemporary dilemma for postal planners. It is easy to distribute tons of mail to big city dwellers in high rise buildings at a reasonable cost. But who is going to find a cost effective way to deliver a single first class letter twenty miles down a country road in a snowstorm in January? Therefore, postal markets cannot be distributed so that service to any given market is economical using contiguous geographical markets.

Statement of Evidence: Outline II.A

Inductive Development

Statement of Evidence II.B

Statement of Topic Sentence II

Perhaps the answer lies in distributing the cost of mail delivery by balancing a cost intensive market area such as rural upstate New York with a lucrative market area such as New York City. On examination, however, this turns out to be an impossibility because population simply is not distributed in neatly balanced areas for reasons noted in the preceding paragraph. Albany, New York, probably has a greater population than the entire state of Wyoming. Is a single company going to be given Wyoming and Albany as a single market area? If so, that company will not be able to service the area economically because the costs of doing business over such a long distance are extremely high. The current post office department, in effect, already does this and it has found it to be not economical. Clearly, it is also true that postal markets cannot be distributed using noncontiguous geographical markets, so that service to any given market is economical.

Statement of Evidence II.C

Inductive Development

Topic Sentence II

Furthermore, not all private corporations are economical. The federal government has always subsidized defense contractors rewarding them for their inefficiencies with huge cost over-runs. Besides this, any number of large private corporations have gone bankrupt including Continental Airlines and Pan American Airways. Would any social planners want postal delivery discontinued to any area because a large, privatized postal company declared bankruptcy?

Topic Sentence *Outline III*

Outline III.A

Outline III.B

The argument that the post office department can be privatized is based on two questionable assumptions. It is therefore most likely that this argument is invalid (1) because populations are not distributed in such a way that large, regional post offices could be run economically, and (2) because private corporations are not necessarily cost efficient and economical.

Restatement of *Topic Outline IV*

Again, the example above demonstrates the effectiveness of the procedure referred to with the acronym, TOPA, which represents the following:

T = Topic sentence—Keep everything relevant to a topic sentence.
O = Outline—Make sure you follow an outline.
PA = Paragraph—Keep the paragraph length steady so that you have about five paragraphs.

6.3 Analysis of Your Writing...

The following are practice essays for you to attempt. There is one analytical type and one argument analysis type. The instructions are as they will be on the exam. You may wish to have a friend or colleague grade your writing using the scoring guidelines presented on page 136. Or, should you desire a professional assessment of your writings, you may send the two essays to: Great Lakes Press, POB 483, Okemos, MI 48805-0483. Or fax to (517) 339-4455. You must also provide your Visa/MC # and expiration date (or a check or money order). Within 2 weeks, we will return a well-informed GMAT-type score, an evaluation of your writing and some suggestions for improvement for $20. Essays will be graded through an expertly-staffed program managed by Dr. James Ney, the author of this chapter.

'Analysis of an Issue' Practice Essay

Directions: In this section, you are asked to analyze and explain your views on the issue presented below. The question has no 'correct' answer. Instead, you should consider various perspectives as you develop your own position on the issue.

Read the statement and directions, and then make any notes in your test booklet that will help you plan a response. Begin writing your response on the separate answer document. Make sure that you use the answer document that accompanies this writing task.

> Loggers and forest industry executives see the need for a continuous supply of wood products. Conservationists and government officials see a rapidly dwindling natural resource which, in some instances, cannot be replaced. In this apparent impasse, the critical issue is the balancing of the need for lumber and other wood products against the need to preserve virgin and primal forests and the habitat of living plants and animals, some of which are endangered.

'Analysis of an Argument' Practice Essay

Directions: In this section you are asked to evaluate the strength of the argument presented below. You may, for example, consider the validity or plausibility or truth of the assumptions that support the argument, or you may uncover objections that might weaken the argument, or you might cite evidence that will either confirm or refute the argument.

Read the argument and directions, and then make notes and an outline in your test booklet for your essay. Begin writing your response on the separate answer document. Make sure that you use the answer document that goes with this writing task.

> The mounting US national debt will change the status of the USA from that of a debtor nation to that of a wholly bankrupt nation. It is quite likely that a prelude to bankruptcy will occur when the US Department of the Treasury will start printing debt free money as the Weimar Republic did before Hitler took over the German state.

6.4 The Scoring of GMAT Writing

Scores for the analytical writing section are given on a 6-to-0 scale, with 6 being the highest possible score for an essay. Details of each score, for both analytical and argument essays, are as follows....

6 = Outstanding

An essay with the score of 6 gives the reader a compact, well-reasoned analysis of the intricacies of the issues, or a convincing evaluation of the argument, and illustrates excellent control of all aspects of effective written composition. An essay assigned the score of 6 is an essay superior in thought and linguistic skills.

Following are the characteristics of an essay assigned the score of 6:

1. It establishes a perspective on the issue supported by perceptive reasons and pertinent examples. Or: It discusses crucial elements of the argument and identifies the merits and demerits of these elements.
2. Its organization derives clearly and logically from the perspective of the issue or the flow of the argument, with clear transitions.
3. It demonstrates proficiency in the use of the English language, as reflected in a judicious choice of words and a varied use of grammatical structures.
4. It shows mastery of the mechanics of spelling, grammar and usage of Standard written English, although minor errors may be present.

5 = Strong

An essay assigned the score of 5 advances a skillful, thoughtfully developed analysis of several aspects of the issue or central points of an argument while maintaining competence in the conventions of good writing.

Following are the characteristics of an essay assigned the score of 5:

1. It constructs a position on the issue with appropriately selected examples. Or: It discerns important aspects of the argument and discusses their strengths and weaknesses in a knowledgeable manner.
2. It is strongly and logically organized.
3. It shows good control of the English language, including a mature choice of words and correct use of different grammatical structures.
4. It shows good control of the mechanics of spelling, grammar and usage of standard written English with some minor flaws.

4 = Adequate

An essay with the score of 4 shows the reader a competent analysis of the issue or argument and an adequate control of the many components of writing.

Following are the characteristics of an essay assigned the score of 4:

1. It presents a consistent point of view on the issue, developed by supporting arguments and examples.
2. It has an adequate organization. Transitional devices not used effectively. Provides some support for ideas in the analysis of an issue or evaluation of an argument.
3. It shows sufficient control of the English language, including a adequate choice of words, but may show some weakness in or unfamiliarity with the use of different grammatical structures.
4. It shows some control of the mechanics of spelling, grammar and the use of standard written English, but it may have errors in mechanics.

3 = Limited

An essay assigned the score of 3 shows that the writer has some ability to analyze an issue or evaluate an argument and to maintain some control of the many components of writing, but both are obviously flawed.

An essay assigned the score of 3 has one or more of the following characteristics:

1. It presents an obscure point of view on the issue and/or fails to examine many of the relevant facets of that issue. Or: It fails to discern and examine many of the important aspects of the argument and/or does not examine many of the facets of that same argument although some analysis is performed.
2. It shows a lack of purposeful, intelligible organization.
3. It fails to present sufficient supporting arguments or examples.
4. It lacks adequate control of the English language and fails to use a variety of grammatical structures.

5. Its shows failure to control the mechanics of spelling, grammar, and the use of standard written English. This essay contains some major errors and many minor errors.

2 = Seriously Flawed

An essay assigned the score of 2 shows that the writer has obvious inadequacies in the manifested ability to write an analysis-of-issue essay or critique an argument.

An essay assigned the score of 2 has one or more of the following characteristics:

1. It fails to make an explicit statement in the presentation of a point of view on the issue or presents a too narrow scope of the issue, or that the writer is unable to identify or analyze the principal aspects of an argument.
2. It shows little skill in the organization of ideas.
3. It presents few supporting arguments or examples.
4. It contains major errors in the use of the English language and in the use of grammatical structures.
5. It contains frequent errors in spelling, grammar and punctuation, errors so frequent and major as to interfere with the reader's understanding of the text.

1 = Fundamentally Deficient

An essay assigned the score of 1 contains elementary mistakes in writing an analysis-of-issue essay or evaluation of an argument.

An essay assigned the score of 1 has one or more of the following characteristics:

1. It presents practically no evidence of an organized response to an issue or ability to dissect an argument.
2. It contains major errors in the use of the English language and in the use of grammatical structures errors, which persist throughout the essay.
3. Its contains errors in spelling, grammar and punctuation which impede understanding of the text.

0 = Unacceptable

An essay that is written in handwriting so poor that it cannot be read or that departs from the assigned topic receives a score of 0.

7 · Mathematics

Arithmetic
Algebra
Geometry
Data Interpretation
Data Sufficiency

With Examples, Problems and Full Solutions

7. Mathematics

The GMAT Mathematics sections test students on their knowledge of the basic elements in the introductory subjects of mathematics: arithmetic, algebra, and geometry. In fact, only some of the elementary notions of algebra and geometry introduced in high school are tested. The more advanced notions introduced in college algebra, trigonometry and analytic geometry need not be reviewed. The GMAT attempts to answer the following questions: How well do you understand the basic elements of mathematics? Can you apply these basic elements in the solution of conventional problems? Can you use your knowledge to solve some non-conventional problems?

The subjects of arithmetic, algebra, and geometry are tested with two very different types of questions: Problem Solving and Data Sufficiency. The Problem Solving questions are the common math questions that you are most familiar with. Simple manipulations in arithmetic and algebra, some word problems that require arithmetic or algebra, and straight-forward geometry questions are included. You may not be able to respond correctly to each question, but you should understand what is being asked. Some questions are quite difficult so you must make sure you do not spend too much time on any one question.

The Data Sufficiency questions do not require you to actually solve the problem; you must decide if there is sufficient information given so that a solution is possible. Each Data Sufficiency problem contains a question followed by additional statements (1) and (2). The correct answer is selected by determining which of the additional statements is needed, or if both are needed, to solve the problem. It is also possible that the problem cannot be solved with the additional information. Since this type of problem is quite unfamiliar, you may find it quite helpful to practice this problem type in Article 7.5.

There may be questions that require you to properly interpret data presented in the forms of bar graphs, circle graphs, line graphs, and tables. Some helpful suggestions and examples will be given in Article 7.4 to help you correctly respond to these questions.

If you have studied subjects for the last several years that do not require significant mathematical calculations, you may be quite surprised at your inability to quickly respond to simple questions. This is quite natural. A quick review, however, will bring back much of the ability needed to correctly respond to a major part of the mathematical portion of this exam. Much can be gained by spending even a minimal amount of time in this review, particularly in the mathematical section of the exam.

7.1 Arithmetic

Arithmetic involves problems in which the numbers are all known. The objective is to add or subtract the numbers, and multiply or divide the numbers. If the problem involves an unknown, it is an algebra problem, although we have included raising a number to a power or finding the square root of a number in our algebra review; this is often done even though an unknown is not involved. This article covers the basics of arithmetic. Depending on your major in college, you may or may not have used a significant amount of arithmetic. If you have used arithmetic extensively, you should be able to skip this article. If not, you may find this quick review helpful.

Integers

A positive number is a number greater then zero, such as +5 (usually written as 5). If it is a *whole number* (a number that does not include a decimal part or a fractional part), it is also called an *integer*. A negative number is a number less than zero, such as – 5. It is also a whole number, or an integer, if it does not contain a decimal or fractional part. The *absolute value* of a number, written as $|-5|$, is the magnitude of the number; the absolute value of + 5 is equal to the absolute value of – 5, written as

$$|+5| = |-5| = 5.$$

The following is true of positive and negative numbers (use example numbers in your mind to illustrate):

Positive × Positive = Positive
Positive × Negative = Negative
Negative × Negative = Positive

Positive ÷ Positive = Positive
Positive ÷ Negative = Negative
Negative ÷ Negative = Positive

An integer that is divisible by 2 is an *even number*. If an integer is not divisible by 2, it is an *odd number*. Any number that is divisible by only itself and 1 is a *prime number*. A set of numbers is *consecutive* if each member of the set is the successor of its predecessor. A consecutive set could be the even numbers 4, 6, 8, 10, or the odd numbers 3, 5, 7, 9, or the prime numbers 3, 5, 7, 11, 13. The following is true of even and odd whole numbers (use example numbers in your mind to illustrate):

Even + Even = Even
Odd + Even = Odd
Odd + Odd = Even

Even – Even = Even
Even – Odd = Odd
Odd – Odd = Even

Even × Even = Even
Even × Odd = Even
Odd × Odd = Odd

Even ÷ Even = Cannot say
Odd ÷ Even = Is not possible
Odd ÷ Odd = Odd

A *factor* is an integer that divides another number resulting in a whole number. Consequently, a number can be expressed as a *multiple* of each of its factors. The number 24 has factors 1, 2, 3, 4, 6, 8, 12, 24. Note that 24 is a multiple of any one of its factors, i.e., 24 is a multiple of 8.

Any integer can be written as a product of factors that are prime numbers. To express an integer as a product of prime numbers we:

- Divide the integer by 2 as many times as is possible.
- Divide the resulting integer by 3 as many times as is possible.
- Divide the resulting integer by 5 as many times as is possible.
- Continue this process, using successive prime numbers, until all factors are obtained.

The *least common multiple* (LCM) of several numbers is the smallest integer which is a common multiple of the several numbers. The LCM of the several numbers is found as follows on the next page.

- Write each of the several numbers as a product of factors that are prime numbers.
- Any factor that occurs more than once retain in only one number.
- Multiply the retained factors.

The following examples illustrate some of the above.

Example 1

Multiply the following sets of numbers:

a) $2, -3$ b) $|-4|, 3$ c) $3, -2, -4$

Solution. a) $2(-3) = -6$ b) $|-4|(3) = 12$ c) $3(-2)(-4) = 24$

Example 2

Compute each of the following:

a) $2 - 3$ b) $4 + 6 - 10$ c) $(-5 + 2)(-3)$

Solution.

a) $2 - 3 = -1$

b) $4 + 6 - 10 = 10 - 10 = 0$

c) $(-5 + 2)(-3) = (-3)(-3) = 9$

Example 3

State why 7, 13, 17, 19, 23 is not consecutive.

Solution. The numbers are prime numbers and would be consecutive if 11 were between 7 and 13.

Example 4

If k is an odd integer, state whether each of the following is odd or even:

a) $k + k + k$ b) $k \times k \times k$ c) $k + 2k$ d) $2k \times k$

Solution.

a) $(k + k)$ is even. Thus $(k + k) + k$ is an even plus an odd, which is odd.
b) $k \times k$ is odd. Thus $(k \times k) \times k$ is an odd times an odd, which is odd.
c) $k + 2k$ is an odd plus an even, which is odd.
d) $2k$ is even. An even times an odd is even.

Note: If you do not remember the rules, merely select an odd number (e.g., 3) and perform the required operation.

Example 5

State all the factors of 63.

Solution. The number 63 can be divided by 1, 3, 7, 9, 21, and 63. Hence, these are its factors.

Example 6

Write 63 as a product of prime numbers.

Solution. The number 63 is obviously not divisible by 2, but is divisible by 3. Hence,

$$\begin{aligned} 63 &= 3 \times 21 \\ &= 3 \times 3 \times 7 \end{aligned}$$

Both 3 and 7 are prime numbers. We do not include 1 as a prime number.

Example 7

Write the LCM of 6 and 12.

Solution. We write each number as a product of prime numbers:

$$\begin{aligned} 6 &= 2 \times 3 \\ 12 &= 2 \times 2 \times 3 \end{aligned}$$

The factor 2×3 is used only once because it occurs in both numbers. Hence, the LCM is

$$\text{LCM} = 2 \times 3 \times 2 = 12$$

Example 8

Find the LCM of the three numbers 20, 30 and 50.

Solution. Write each number as a product of prime numbers:

$$\begin{aligned} 20 &= 2 \times 2 \times 5 \\ 30 &= 2 \times 3 \times 5 \\ 50 &= 2 \times 5 \times 5 \end{aligned}$$

The factor 2×5 occurs in all three numbers, thus it is used only once. The LCM is

$$\begin{aligned} \text{LCM} &= (2 \times 5) \times 2 \times 3 \times 5 \\ &= 300 \end{aligned}$$

Fractions

Definitions

A *fraction* is one number divided by another number. It is a division, such as 3/5. The top number is the *numerator* and the bottom number is the *denominator*. The denominator represents the number of equal parts into which an entity has been divided; the numerator represents the number of parts that are selected. For example, if a garden is divided into 5 equal plots, 3/5 of the garden is represented by 3 of the plots.

A fraction that has 0 as its denominator (e.g., 5/0) is not defined; it is infinitely large and undefined. A fraction with numerator equal to the denominator (e.g., 5/5) is equal to 1.

A *mixed number* is a number that is an integer plus a fraction. The number $4\frac{2}{3}$ is the integer 4 plus the fraction 2/3. Any mixed number can be written as a fraction, and any fraction greater than 1 can be written as a mixed number. To express $4\frac{2}{3}$ as a fraction we multiply 4×3, add the numerator to this product, $12 + 2 = 14$, and divide by the denominator:

$4\frac{2}{3} = \frac{14}{3}$. To convert the fraction 17/5 into a mixed number, divide by the denominator (17 divided by 5 is 3 with 2 remaining) and add the remainder over the denominator: $\frac{17}{5} = 3\frac{2}{5}$.

Example 1

Convert $4\frac{5}{7}$ into a fraction.

Solution. We multiply 4 × 7 and obtain 28. Add 5 to this and obtain 33. Put this over 7 and we find

$$4\frac{5}{7} = \frac{33}{7}$$

Example 2

Convert 79/9 into a mixed number.

Solution. Divide 79 by 9 and obtain 8 with 7 remaining. Now add to the 8 the fraction 7/9:

$$\frac{79}{9} = 8\frac{7}{9}$$

Equivalent Fractions

A fraction that has a common factor in both numerator and denominator is equal to the fraction with the common factor canceled. The fraction 6/10 is equivalent to the fraction 3/5 since the common factor 2 occurs in both numerator and denominator of 6/10. In fact, the following fractions are all equivalent: 3/5 = 6/10 = 9/15 = 12/20. A fraction that has no common factors in the numerator and denominator is said to be expressed in *lowest terms*.

A fraction with a negative numerator or denominator is equivalent to a negative fraction, that is, $\frac{-3}{5} = \frac{3}{-5} = -\frac{3}{5}$. If both numerator and denominator are negative, the fraction is positive, that is, $\frac{-3}{-5} = \frac{3}{5}$.

Example 3

Express 26/16 as a mixed number in lowest terms.

Solution. The mixed number is found by dividing by 16 giving 1 with 10 remaining. Hence

$$\frac{26}{16} = 1\frac{10}{16}$$

The fraction 10/16 has a common factor of 2 in numerator and denominator. It is canceled to give

$$\frac{26}{16} = 1\frac{5}{8}$$

Multiplying and Dividing Fractions

To multiply fractions, cancel out any common factors that appear in both numerators and denominators. Then multiply all numerators to form one numerator, and all denominators to form one denominator. This final fraction may then be written as a mixed number, if desired.

To divide fractions, say $x/y \div a/b$, invert the divisor (the fraction a/b) and multiply the two fractions, i.e., $x/y \div a/b = (x/y)(b/a)$.

Example 4

Multiply the three fractions $6/8 \times 12/5 \times 15/24$.

Solution. First we look for common factors and cancel. Write the product as

$$\frac{6}{8} \times \frac{12}{5} \times \frac{15}{24} = \frac{3\times\cancel{2}}{\cancel{2}\times 4} \times \frac{\cancel{4}\times\cancel{3}}{\cancel{5}} \times \frac{3\times\cancel{5}}{\underset{2}{\cancel{6}}\times\cancel{4}} = \frac{3}{4} \times \frac{1}{1} \times \frac{3}{2} = \frac{9}{8}$$

If we wish to express the answer as a mixed number, we have

$$\frac{9}{8} = 1\frac{1}{8}$$

Example 5

Perform the division $4/7 \div 8/21$.

Solution. Invert the divisor, form the multiplication and simplify:

$$\frac{4}{7} \div \frac{8}{21} = \frac{4}{7} \times \frac{21}{8} = \frac{2\times 2}{7} \times \frac{3\times 7}{2\times 4} = \frac{3}{2}$$

As a mixed number the answer is

$$\frac{3}{2} = 1\frac{1}{2}$$

Example 6

Solution. Perform the division $\dfrac{3/5}{9/30}$.

Write the division in the form $\dfrac{3}{5} \div \dfrac{9}{30}$. Then invert and solve:

$$\frac{3}{5} \times \frac{30}{9} = \frac{\cancel{3}}{\cancel{5}} \times \frac{6\times\cancel{5}}{\cancel{3}\times 3} = \frac{6}{3} = 2$$

Adding and Subtracting Fractions

To subtract one fraction from another, we simply add a negative fraction to a second fraction. Consequently, the rules for adding and subtracting are the same. The first step is to write the fractions such that each fraction has the same denominator. Then add or subtract the numerators. Then simplify.

To write all fractions with the same denominator, a quick choice is to multiply all denominators together. This may, however, give a rather large denominator. To avoid a possible large denominator we could find the *least common denominator* (LCD); it is the least common multiple (LCM) of all the denominators.

Example 7

Add the two fractions $\frac{1}{6} + \frac{1}{4}$.

Solution. The first step is to write the two fractions with the same denominator. A quick choice is $6 \times 4 = 24$. We have

$$\frac{1}{6} + \frac{1}{4} = \frac{4}{24} + \frac{6}{24} = \frac{4+6}{24} = \frac{10}{24} = \frac{5}{12}$$

Alternatively, we could use the LCD, which is $3 \times 2 \times 2 = 12$; there results

$$\frac{1}{6} + \frac{1}{4} = \frac{2}{12} + \frac{3}{12} = \frac{5}{12}$$

Example 8

Find the results of $\frac{3}{5} + \frac{2}{3} - \frac{1}{6}$.

Solution. First, write all fractions with the same denominator. Obviously, if we multiply all denominators $(5 \times 3 \times 6 = 90)$ that would work. We have

$$\frac{3}{5} + \frac{2}{3} - \frac{1}{6} = \frac{54}{90} + \frac{60}{90} - \frac{15}{90} = \frac{54+60-15}{90} = \frac{99}{90} = \frac{11}{10}$$

Or, using the LCD, which is $5 \times 3 \times 2 = 30$:

$$\frac{3}{5} + \frac{2}{3} - \frac{1}{6} = \frac{18}{30} + \frac{20}{30} - \frac{5}{30} = \frac{18+20-5}{30} = \frac{33}{30} = \frac{11}{10}$$

In terms of a mixed number, the answer is

$$\frac{11}{10} = 1\frac{1}{10}$$

Example 9

Express $\frac{x}{2} - \frac{x}{3} + \frac{x}{4}$ as a single fraction.

Solution. Multiply the denominators to get $2 \times 3 \times 4 = 24$. Then

$$\frac{x}{2} - \frac{x}{3} + \frac{x}{4} = \frac{12x}{24} - \frac{8x}{24} + \frac{6x}{24} = \frac{12x - 8x + 6x}{24} = \frac{10x}{24} = \frac{5x}{12}$$

We could have used the LCD, which is $2 \times 3 \times 2 = 12$. The result would be the same.

Decimals

Definitions

A *decimal fraction* is a fraction whose denominator is a power of 10 but not a factor of the numerator. For example, the fraction 3/100 is written in decimal form as 0.03; the fraction 223/10,000 is 0.0223. Note that the number to the right of the decimal point is the numerator of the decimal fraction, and the denominator is 10 raised to the power n where n is the number of places you move the decimal point. To write 0.0031 as a decimal fraction, 31 is the numerator and because we moved the decimal point 4 places, the denominator is $10^4 = 10{,}000$; consequently, the decimal fraction is 31/10,000.

A *mixed decimal* is the sum of an integer and a decimal fraction, quite analogous to the mixed fraction. The integer 5 added to the decimal fraction 35/100 is 5 + 35/100 = 5 + 0.35 = 5.35. The mixed decimal, or a decimal fraction, is usually simply called a *decimal*. (Note: the leading 0 in 0.35 is simply convention; it does not have mathematical significance: 0.35 = .35.)

Example 1

Write the fraction 649/100 as a decimal.

Solution. The numerator 649 can be written as the decimal 649.0 . When we divide by 100, we move the decimal point 2 places to the left so that

$$\frac{649}{100} = 6.49$$

It is not necessary to write any zeros after the 9, that is, 6.490 is equivalent to 6.49.

Example 2

Write $\frac{31.2}{100{,}000}$ as a decimal.

Solution. When we divide by 100,000, which is 10^5, we move the decimal point 5 places to the left. Then

$$\frac{31.2}{100{,}000} = 0.000312$$

Example 3

Express 0.075 as a fraction in lowest terms.

Solution. The decimal is expressed as a fraction

$$0.075 = \frac{75}{1000}$$

The denominator and numerator are factored resulting in

$$\frac{75}{1000} = \frac{25 \times 3}{25 \times 40} = \frac{3}{40}$$

Example 4

Write $3 + \frac{3}{10} + \frac{4}{1000}$ as a mixed decimal.

Solution. The two fractions are added as follows:

$$\frac{3}{10} + \frac{4}{1000} = \frac{300}{1000} + \frac{4}{1000} = \frac{304}{1000}$$

This decimal fraction is equivalent to

$$\frac{304}{1000} = 0.304$$

The mixed decimal is then

$$3 + 0.304 = 3.304$$

Adding and Subtracting Decimals

To add or subtract decimals, we write the decimals in a column with the decimal points aligned vertically. First, add the decimals with a plus sign. Next, add the decimals with a minus sign. Then subtract the sum of the negative decimals from the sum of the positive decimals. In performing these tasks, we add zeros to the right of the decimal point so that each number has an entry in each column. For example, if we subtract 3.021 from 5, we write 5 as 5.000 so that there is an entry in each of the 3 places to the right of the decimal in both numbers.

Example 5

Add 5 + 2.783 + 3.04.

Solution. Write the decimals in a column, with zeros added if none exist:

$$\begin{array}{r} 5.000 \\ 2.783 \\ +\ \underline{3.040} \\ 10.823 \end{array}$$

Example 6

Compute 6.98 + 3.217 - 1.68 + 3 - 1.957.

Solution. Add the positive decimals and the negative decimals:

$$\begin{array}{r} 6.980 \\ 3.217 \\ +\ \underline{3.000} \\ 13.197 \end{array} \qquad \begin{array}{r} \\ 1.680 \\ +\ \underline{1.957} \\ 3.637 \end{array}$$

Subtract the sum of the negative decimals from the sum of the positive decimals:

$$\begin{array}{r} 13.197 \\ -\ \underline{3.637} \\ 9.560 \end{array}$$

Multiplying and Dividing Decimals

Multiply two decimals just like you would multiply two integers. The number of decimal places in the product is then equal to the total of the decimal places in the two decimals.

To divide two decimals, move the decimal point in the divisor (the number doing the dividing) to the right so that the divisor is an integer. Move the decimal point in the dividend to the right the same number of places. Now perform the division, placing the decimal point in the answer directly above the decimal point in the dividend.

Example 7

Compute 0.05 × 12.

Solution. Set up the multiplication as though the decimals are integers:

$$\begin{array}{r} 12 \\ \underline{5} \\ 60 \end{array}$$

The answer must have a total of 2 decimal places: 0.60.

Example 8

Evaluate $2.4 \div 0.006$.

Solution. Set up the division as follows:

$$.006\overline{)2.4} \Rightarrow 6\overline{)2400.}\quad (\text{quotient } 400.)$$

The correct answer is 400.

Example 9

Express 3/75 as a decimal.

Solution. If we simplify the fraction first, the problem is usually easier. Since $75 = 3 \times 25$ the fraction is written as

$$\frac{3}{75} = \frac{1}{25}$$

Now divide:

$$\begin{array}{r} .04 \\ 25\overline{)1.00} \\ \underline{1.00} \end{array}$$

The decimal is 0.04.

Averages and Medians

The *average*, or *arithmetic mean*, is the sum of a set of numbers divided by the total number of elements in the set.

If all the numbers in a set are arranged in ascending or descending order, the middle number is the *median*. Half of the people in a country earn more than the median income and half earn less. The average income does not split the people into a top half and bottom half. For example, if 5 people have weekly incomes of \$200, \$300, \$500, \$1000 and \$6000, the median is \$500 but the average is \$4000. If a large number of people earn very little and a few earn a huge amount, the average would be quite impressive but the median would be surprisingly low.

Example 1

Ten students on an exam scored 20, 30, 30, 25, 30, 35, 80, 60, 40, and 90. Calculate the average and the median.

Solution. The average is the sum of all the numbers divided by 10:

$$\text{average} = \frac{20 + 25 + 3 \times 30 + 35 + 40 + 60 + 80 + 90}{10} = 44$$

The median is, for the case of an even number of entries, the average of the two middle numbers when arranged in order:

$$\text{median} = \frac{30 + 35}{2} = \frac{65}{2} = 32.5$$

Example 2

Mary had 10 students in a recitation section with an average of 62 points. John had 20 students in his recitation section with an average of 70 points. What was the overall average?

Solution. Mary's students had a total number of points of

$$10 \times 62 = 620$$

John's students had a total number of points of

$$20 \times 70 = 1400$$

The overall average number of points is

$$\frac{620 + 1400}{30} = 67.33$$

Practice Problems

—Arithmetic—

Integers

1. $7 - 3 + (-4) - (-3) =$
   A) -3 B) 3 C) 4 D) -4 E) 7

2. $-7 - (-5) - 6 - (-9) =$
   A) -4 B) -3 C) -2 D) 1 E) -1

3. Find the product (3) (– 4) (– 2).
   A) -24 B) 24 C) 12 D) – 12) E) 36

4. Find the product $(-2)\ |-3|\ |-2|$.
   A) 6 B) -6 C) 12 D) -12 E) 24

5. Fill in the missing number of this consecutive set: 4, 9, __ , 25.
   A) 12 B) 14 C) 16 D) 18 E) 20

6. What is the missing element of this consecutive set? 4, 7, __ , 13.
   A) 8 B) 9 C) 10 D) 11 E) 12

7. If k is odd, then
   I. $2k$ is even II. $k + k$ is even III. k^2 is even
   A) I & II B) II & III C) III only
   D) I, II & III E) II only

8. If k is even and n is odd, then

I. $k \times n$ is even II. $k \times (-n)$ is even III. $k \times n \times n$ is even

A) I only B) II only C) III only
D) I & II E) I, II & III

9. All of the factors of 12 are

A) 2, 4, 6, 8, 12 B) 1, 2, 3, 6, 12 C) 1, 2, 4, 8, 12
D) 2, 3, 4, 6, 12 E) 1, 2, 3, 4, 6, 12

10. Express 24 as a product of prime numbers.

A) $2 \times 2 \times 2 \times 3$ B) $2 \times 3 \times 4$ C) $2 \times 2 \times 6$
D) 3×8 E) 2×12

11. Write the LCM of 4, 6, and 16.

A) 24 B) 36 C) 48 D) 64 E) 96

12. Write the LCM of 2, 5, 10, and 30.

A) 30 B) 45 C) 50 D) 60 E) 90

Fractions

13. Express the mixed number $2\frac{1}{3}$ as a fraction.

A) $\frac{7}{2}$ B) $\frac{5}{2}$ C) $\frac{9}{3}$ D) $\frac{7}{3}$ E) $\frac{5}{3}$

14. Express 60/7 as a mixed number.

A) $7\frac{4}{7}$ B) $7\frac{4}{5}$ C) $8\frac{3}{7}$ D) $9\frac{1}{7}$ E) $8\frac{4}{7}$

15. Write 24/42 in lowest terms.

A) $\frac{3}{6}$ B) $\frac{4}{7}$ C) $\frac{8}{14}$ D) $\frac{12}{21}$ E) $\frac{7}{6}$

16. Which of the following fractions are equivalent?

I. 12/15 II. 4/5 III. 60/75

A) I & II B) I & III C) II & III
D) I, II & III E) none of these

17. Evaluate $\frac{-6}{14} \times \frac{35}{-4} \times \frac{8}{15}$.

A) 2 B) $\frac{2}{5}$ C) -2 D) $-\frac{2}{5}$ E) 3

18. Compute $\frac{14}{35} \div \frac{7}{10}$.

A) $\frac{5}{7}$ B) $\frac{4}{7}$ C) $\frac{1}{7}$ D) $\frac{2}{7}$ E) $\frac{10}{7}$

19. Divide 4/7 by 12/35.

A) $2\frac{1}{3}$ B) $\frac{7}{3}$ C) $\frac{4}{3}$ D) $1\frac{1}{3}$ E) $1\frac{2}{3}$

20. Compute $2 - \frac{1}{3} + \frac{1}{5} - \frac{1}{6}$.

A) 101/60 B) 5/3 C) $1\frac{7}{10}$ D) 53/30 E) 19/10

21. Calculate $2\frac{1}{3} + 1\frac{5}{6} - 3\frac{1}{2}$.

A) 2/3 B) 1/2 C) 5/6 D) $1\frac{1}{6}$ E) $1\frac{1}{3}$

22. What fractional part of a yard is $7\frac{1}{5}$ inches?

A) 1/2 B) 1/3 C) 1/4 D) 1/5 E) 1/6

23. A professor had 48 students. A graduate student, Mark, was responsible for 5/8 of the students, but that proved to be too much, so Mallory assumed responsibility for 2/3 of Mark's students. How many students was Mallory responsible for?

A) 16 B) 20 C) 24 D) 28 E) 30

24. Express $\frac{x}{5} - \frac{2x}{6} + \frac{7x}{3}$ as a simple fraction.

A) $\frac{5x}{6}$ B) $\frac{5x}{3}$ C) $\frac{37x}{30}$ D) $\frac{7x}{6}$ E) $\frac{11x}{5}$

25. A job is 2/3 done. A worker finishes another 1/6 of the job. What fractional part of the job is now completed?

A) 1/9 B) 1/2 C) 5/6 D) 7/6 E) 3/4

Decimals

26. Write $\frac{21.3}{500}$ as a decimal.

A) 4.26 B) 0.426 C) 0.0426 D) 0.00426 E) 0.000426

27. Compute $4 + 6.802 + 0.0015 - 7.1625$.

A) 3.739 B) 3.641 C) 3.649 D) 3.749 E) 3.629

28. Compute 3.215×100.

A) 3215 B) 321.5 C) 0.03215 D) 0.3215 E) 32.15

29. Express 0.275 as a fraction in lowest terms.
   A) 275/100 B) 275/1000 C) 11/40 D) 11/4 E) 55/200

30. Express the fraction 9/25 as a decimal.
   A) 0.287 B) 0.278 C) 0.63 D) 0.925 E) 0.36

31. Select the smallest number.
   A) 0.6066 B) 0.6061 C) 0.6006 D) 0.6010 E) 0.6106

32. Compute 7 + 1.216 – 3.007 + 5.1162 – 4.1.
   A) 6.2252 B) 6.2152 C) 6.2358 D) 6.2258 E) 6.2352

33. Write $4+\frac{3}{5}-\frac{1}{2}+2\frac{1}{4}$ as a mixed decimal.
   A) 7.35 B) $7\frac{7}{20}$ C) 6.15 D) 6.35 E) $6\frac{7}{20}$

34. Express $\frac{1}{5}\times\frac{2}{7}\times\frac{15}{8}\times\frac{14}{6}\times\frac{4}{5}$ as a decimal.
   A) 0.15 B) 0.2 C) 0.25 D) 0.3 E) 0.4

35. To multiply by 0.05 is to divide by which number?
   A) 50 B) 1/20 C) 1/50 D) 0.02 E) 20

36. Compute 0.02 ÷ 0.002.
   A) 0.01 B) 0.1 C) 1 D) 10 E) 100

37. Multiply 5.02 × 0.04.
   A) 12.55 B) 0.2008 C) 0.0208 D) 2.08 E) 1.255

38. A pie is cut into 7 equal pieces. What decimal fraction is each piece to the nearest thousandth?
   A) 0.14 B) 0.142 C) 0.143 D) 0.1428 E) 0.1429

39. John inherited 0.8 of his father's 600 acres. John gave 6/10 of his land to Michelle, and she gave 2/5 of her land to Alex. How much land did Alex receive, to the nearest acre?
   A) 210 B) 180 C) 130 D) 115 E) 110

Averages and Medians

40. Compute the average of six stocks valued at 2, 62, 120, 8, 40, 52.
   A) 47 B) 47.3 C) $47\frac{1}{2}$ D) $47\frac{1}{3}$ E) $47\frac{2}{3}$

41. Write the median value of six stocks valued at 2, 62, 120, 8, 40, 52.
   A) 52 B) 8 C) 64 D) 46 E) 40

42. A class receives the following grades: 2 at 70, 4 at 75, 6 at 80, 5 at 85, and 3 at 95. Calculate the average grade.

A) 78 B) 81.5 C) 83 D) 80.5 E) 82

43. Lane receives grades of 80, 86, and 78 on three English essays. He desires an average of 85 on the four required essays. What grade does Lane need on his last essay?

A) 86 B) 88 C) 90 D) 92 E) 96

44. Forty workers have an average weekly salary of \$360. Twenty other workers average \$420. What is the average of all the workers?

A) \$360 B) \$370 C) \$380 D) \$390 E) \$400

45. Calculate the average speed of seven bikers who are timed at speeds of 20, 32, 24, 22, 31, 25, and 30 mph.

A) 25.4 B) $25\frac{6}{7}$ C) 26.1 D) $26\frac{2}{7}$ E) 26.2

46. Find the median speed of the bikers in Problem 45.

A) 25 B) 22 C) 24 D) $24\frac{1}{2}$ E) 31

Answers to Practice Problems

—Arithmetic Section—

Integers		Fractions		Decimals		Averages and Medians	
1.	B	**13.**	D	**26.**	C	**40.**	D
2.	D	**14.**	E	**27.**	B	**41.**	D
3.	B	**15.**	B	**28.**	B	**42.**	B
4.	D	**16.**	D	**29.**	C	**43.**	E
5.	C	**17.**	A	**30.**	E	**44.**	C
6.	C	**18.**	B	**31.**	C	**45.**	D
7.	A	**19.**	E	**32.**	A	**46.**	A
8.	E	**20.**	C	**33.**	D		
9.	E	**21.**	A	**34.**	B		
10.	A	**22.**	D	**35.**	E		
11.	C	**23.**	B	**36.**	D		
12.	A	**24.**	E	**37.**	B		
		25.	C	**38.**	C		
				39.	D		

Explanations to the Answers

Integers

1. B $7 - 3 + (-4) - (-3) = 7 - 3 - 4 + 3 = 3$.

2. D $-7 - (-5) - 6 - (-9) = -7 + 5 - 6 + 9 = 1$.

3. B $(3)(-4)(-2) = 3 \times 4 \times 2 = 24$.

4. D $(-2)|-3||-2| = -2 \times 3 \times 2 = -12$.

5. C 4, 9, __, 25. This set is $2^2, 3^2, \_\_, 5^2$. The missing element is $4^2 = 16$.

6. C 4, 7, __, 13. If we add 3 to each element, we obtain the next element. Hence, $7 + 3 = 10$.

7. A Select an odd number, say k = 3. Then 2(3) = 6, 3 + 3 = 6, 32 = 9. Thus, (1) and (2) are true.

8. E Select k = 2, n = 3. Then $2 \times 3 = 6$, $2(-3) = -6$, $2 \times 3 \times 3 = 18$. Thus, all three are true.

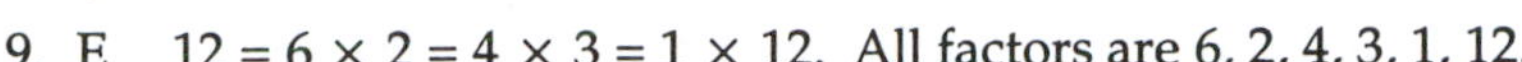

9. E $12 = 6 \times 2 = 4 \times 3 = 1 \times 12$. All factors are 6, 2, 4, 3, 1, 12.

10. A $24 = 12 \times 2 = 6 \times 2 \times 2 = 3 \times 2 \times 2 \times 2$.

11. C

$$\begin{aligned} 4 &= 2 \times 2 \\ 6 &= 3 \times 2 \\ 16 &= 2 \times 2 \times 2 \times 2 \end{aligned}$$

2×2 is common to 4 and 16. Also 2 is common to 6 and 16. The LCM is then found by suppressing 2×2 and 2:

$3 \times 2 \times 2 \times 2 \times 2 = 48$.

12. A

$$\begin{aligned} 2 &= 2 \\ 5 &= 5 \\ 10 &= 2 \times 5 \\ 30 &= 2 \times 3 \times 5 \end{aligned}$$

2 is common to three numbers. 5 is common to three numbers. Retain 2 once and 5 once: $2 \times 5 \times 3 = 30$.

Fractions

13. D $3 \times 2 + 1 = 7$. Thus, $2\frac{1}{3} = \frac{7}{3}$.

14. E $7\overline{)60}$ quotient 8; 56; remainder 4.   Thus, $\frac{60}{7} = 8\frac{4}{7}$

15. B $\frac{24}{42} = \frac{6 \times 4}{6 \times 7} = \frac{4}{7}$.

16. D $\frac{12}{15} = \frac{3 \times 4}{3 \times 5} = \frac{4}{5}$. $\frac{60}{75} = \frac{5 \times 3 \times 4}{3 \times 5 \times 5} = \frac{4}{5}$. Thus, all are equal.

17. A $\frac{-6}{14} \times \frac{35}{-4} \times \frac{8}{15} = \frac{-\cancel{3} \times \cancel{2}}{\cancel{2} \times \cancel{7}} \times \frac{\cancel{7} \times \cancel{5}}{-\cancel{4}} \times \frac{\cancel{4} \times 2}{\cancel{3} \times \cancel{5}} = 2$.

18. B $\frac{14}{35} \div \frac{7}{10} = \frac{14}{35} \times \frac{10}{7} = \frac{7 \times 2}{7 \times 5} \times \frac{5 \times 2}{7} = \frac{4}{7}$.

19. E $\frac{4}{7} \div \frac{12}{35} = \frac{4}{7} \times \frac{35}{12} = \frac{4}{7} \times \frac{5 \times 7}{3 \times 4} = \frac{5}{3}$. $3\overline{)5}$ quotient 1; 3; remainder 2.   Thus, $\frac{5}{3} = 1\frac{2}{3}$.

20. C $2-\frac{1}{3}+\frac{1}{5}-\frac{1}{6}=\frac{60}{30}-\frac{10}{30}+\frac{6}{30}-\frac{5}{30}=\frac{60-10+6-5}{30}=\frac{51}{30}=\frac{3\times 17}{3\times 10}=\frac{17}{10}.$

$$\begin{array}{r} 1 \\ 10\overline{)17} \\ \underline{10} \\ 7 \end{array}$$

Thus, $\frac{17}{10}=1\frac{7}{10}.$

21. A $2\frac{1}{3}+1\frac{5}{6}-3\frac{1}{2}=\frac{7}{3}+\frac{11}{6}-\frac{7}{2}=\frac{28+22-42}{12}=\frac{8}{12}=\frac{2\times 4}{3\times 4}=\frac{2}{3}.$

22. D $7\frac{1}{5}=\frac{36}{5}$. There are 36 inches in a yard. Thus, $\frac{36/5}{36}=\frac{36}{36\times 5}=\frac{1}{5}.$

23. B $\frac{2}{3}\times\frac{5}{8}\times 48=\frac{2}{3}\times\frac{5}{2\times 4}\times\frac{4\times 3\times 4}{1}=20.$

24. E $\frac{x}{5}-\frac{2x}{6}+\frac{7x}{3}=\frac{6x-10x+70x}{30}=\frac{66x}{30}=\frac{6\times 11x}{6\times 5}=\frac{11x}{5}.$

25. C $\frac{2}{3}+\frac{1}{6}=\frac{4}{6}+\frac{1}{6}=\frac{5}{6}.$

Decimals

26. C $\frac{21.3}{500}=\frac{2\times 21.3}{2\times 500}=\frac{42.6}{1000}=0.0426.$ (Move the decimal point 3 places to the left.)

Or:
$$\begin{array}{r} .0426 \\ 500\overline{)21.3000} \\ \underline{2000} \\ 1300 \\ \underline{1000} \\ 3000 \\ \underline{3000} \\ 0 \end{array}$$

27. B $4+6.802+0.0015-7.1625 \Rightarrow$

First add:
$$\begin{array}{r} 4.0000 \\ 6.8020 \\ \underline{+\ 0.0015} \\ 10.8035 \end{array}$$

Then subtract:
$$\begin{array}{r} 10.8035 \\ \underline{-\ 7.1625} \\ 3.6410 \end{array}$$

28. B $3.215\times 100=321.5$. (Move the decimal point 2 places to the right.)

29. C $0.275=\frac{275}{1000}=\frac{25\times 11}{25\times 40}=\frac{11}{40}$. (We divided by 1000 because we moved the decimal point 3 places to the right.)

30. E $\frac{9}{25}=\frac{9\times 4}{25\times 4}=\frac{36}{100}=0.36.$

31. C 0.6006 < 0.6010 < 0.6061 < 0.6066 < 0.6106. Eliminate the decimal point by moving it 4 places to the right on all numbers. Then make your decision.

32. A 7 + 1.216 – 3.007 + 5.1162 – 4.1 ⇒ First add positive numbers to get 13.3322; then add negative numbers to get 7.107; finally, subtract 7.1070 (negative numbers) from 13.3322 (positive numbers) to get the answer, 6.2252.

33. D $4+\frac{3}{5}-\frac{1}{2}+2\frac{1}{4}=4+0.6-0.5+2.25=6.85-0.5=6.35.$

34. B $\frac{1}{5}\times\frac{\cancel{2}}{\cancel{7}}\times\frac{\overset{3}{\cancel{15}}}{\underset{2}{\cancel{8}}}\times\frac{\overset{2}{\cancel{14}}}{\cancel{6}}\times\frac{\cancel{4}}{\cancel{5}}=\frac{1}{5}=0.2$.

35. E $a\times 0.05=a\frac{5}{100}=\frac{a}{20}.$

36. D $0.02\div 0.002=\frac{0.02}{0.002}=\frac{0.02\times 1000}{0.002\times 1000}=\frac{20}{2}=10.$

37. B $5.02\times 0.04 \Rightarrow$ 5.02 Both numbers combine for 4 decimal places.

$$\begin{array}{r} 5.02 \\ \underline{.04} \\ .2008 \end{array}$$

38. C $\frac{1}{7} \Rightarrow$ .1428 rounds off to .143.

$$\begin{array}{r} .1426 \\ 7\overline{)1.0000} \\ \underline{7} \\ 30 \\ \underline{28} \\ 20 \\ \underline{14} \\ 60 \\ 56 \end{array}$$

39. D $\overset{\overset{12}{\cancel{60}}}{\cancel{600}}\times 0.8\times\frac{6}{\cancel{10}}\times\frac{2}{\cancel{5}}=12\times 0.8\times 12=144\times 0.8=115.2$.

Averages and Medians

40. D $(2 + 62 + 120 + 8 + 40 + 52)/6 = \frac{284}{6} = 47\frac{2}{6} = 47\frac{1}{3}.$

41. D Arrange in ascending order: 2, 8, 40, 52, 62, 120. There is no middle number. The average of the two middle numbers is (40 + 52)/2 = 92/2 = 46.

42. B 2 × 70 = 140, 4 × 75 = 300, 6 × 80 = 480, 5 × 85 = 425, 3 × 95 = 285. There are 2 + 4 + 6 + 5 + 3 = 20 grades in all. The average is

$$\frac{140+300+480+425+285}{20}=\frac{1630}{20}=81.5.$$

43. E $85 = \frac{80+86+78+L}{4}$. $4 \times 85 = 80+86+78+L$. $\therefore L = 96$.

44. C $40 \times 360 + 20 \times 420 = 14,400 + 8,400 = 22,800$. There are $40 + 20 = 60$ workers total. The average is $\frac{22,800}{60} = 380$.

45. D $(20+32+24+22+31+25+30)/7 = \frac{184}{7} = 26\frac{2}{7}$.

46. A Arrange in order: 20, 22, 24, 25, 30, 31, 32. The middle number is 25.

7.2 Algebra

Algebra involves problems in which at least one quantity is an *unknown*, also called a *variable.* The unknown quantity is often denoted by the letter x, although any letter can be used. For example, a group of bikers travel x miles in y hours if their speed is v miles per hour. For a particular situation, we may assign values to some of the variables and attempt to determine the remaining unknowns. If the bikers travel at 20 miles/hour for 2 hours, how far do they travel? Obviously, they travel 40 miles. We have just solved an algebra problem. First, we decided that $x = yv$. Then with $y = 2$ and $v = 20$ we found that

$$x = yv = 2 \times 20 = 40.$$

Some algebra problems are quite simple but others can be more complicated and, in fact, quite difficult. We will attempt to help you solve even the more difficult problems. If you majored in one of the physical science fields (engineering, chemistry, geology, etc.) as an undergraduate, you undoubtedly were required to take the mathematics courses of calculus and beyond; if that is your situation, you may be able to skip this material. But make sure you understand it well; most mathematical problems on the GMAT are solved using algebra.

Before we review some of the more common algebra problems, we need to define some terms. An *algebraic term* is any variable, constant, or combination of variables and constants that stands alone. For example , 5, $5y$, $4x/y$, and $3x^2y$ can each be referred to as a term. In the term $3x^2y$, the constant 3 is the *numerical coefficient* of the variables. A single term by itself is often called a *monomial* (e.g., $5y - 3x^2y$ or $2 - 3x + 5y^2$). Two terms are *like terms* (or *similar terms*) if they differ only in their numerical coefficients (e.g., $2xy^2$ and $-3xy^2$).

Algebraic Expressions

Exponents

When attempting to solve algebra problems it is important that the laws concerning exponents be strictly followed.

Law I: Add the exponents when multiplying two powers of the same base. In general

$$a^m a^n = a^{m+n}$$

Law II: Multiply the exponents when obtaining the power of a power. That is

$$(a^m)^n = a^{mn}$$

Law III: Subtract the exponents when dividing a power of a specified base by another power of the same base. This is expressed by

$$\frac{a^m}{a^n} = a^{m-n}$$

If $n > m$ we can avoid a negative exponent by writing

$$\frac{a^m}{a^n} = \frac{1}{a^{n-m}}$$

Law IV: The power of a product of factors is written by raising each factor to the specified power. In general

$$(abc)^n = a^n b^n c^n$$

Law V: The power of a fraction is written by raising the numerator and the denominator to the specified power. This is expressed by

$$\left(\frac{a}{b}\right)^n = \frac{a^n}{b^n}$$

Example 1 (simple)

1. $a^2 a^3 = a^5$
2. $2^2 2^4 = 2^6 = 64$
3. $(r^2)^3 = r^6$
4. $(2^2)^4 = 2^8 = 256$
5. $\dfrac{x^5}{x^3} = x^2$
6. $\dfrac{5^2}{5^3} = \dfrac{1}{5}$
7. $(ax)^3 = a^3 x^3$
8. $(2 \cdot 3)^3 = 2^3 \cdot 3^3 = 8 \cdot 27 = 216$
9. $\left(\dfrac{x}{y}\right)^3 = \dfrac{x^3}{y^3}$
10. $\left(\dfrac{4}{3}\right)^3 = \dfrac{4^3}{3^3} = \dfrac{64}{27}$

Example 2 (more difficult)

1. $\dfrac{2^3}{5^2}\left(\dfrac{3}{4}\right)^2 = \dfrac{8}{25}\,\dfrac{9}{16} = \dfrac{9}{50}$
2. $\left(x^2 x^3\right)^2 = \left(x^5\right)^2 = x^{10}$
3. $\left(\dfrac{2h}{3k^2}\right)^3 = \dfrac{2^3 h^3}{3^3 k^6} = \dfrac{8h^3}{27k^6}$
4. $-2a^3\left(-ab^2\right)^3 = -2a^3\left(-a^3 b^6\right) = 2a^6 b^6$
5. $\dfrac{50r^2 s^5}{-15s^3 r^5} = -\dfrac{5 \cdot 10s^2}{5 \cdot 3r^3} = -\dfrac{10s^2}{3r^3}$

Roots

If $a^2 = b$, we call a the *square root* of b. Each positive number b has two square roots, one positive and one negative, denoted by $\sqrt{b}$ and $-\sqrt{b}$. In the GMAT, *use the positive square root.* We also write the square root as a power: $a = b^{1/2}$. The square root of a fraction is found by finding the square root of the numerator and of the denominator and then dividing the two.

The nth root of b is written as $\sqrt[n]{b}$ or $b^{\frac{1}{n}}$. Since $2^5 = 32$, we say that the 5th root of 32 is 2. Also, since $(-2)^3 = -8$, the cube root of (-8) is -2. The square root of a negative number is not a real number because whenever a negative number is squared it is positive, i.e., $(-2)^2 = 4$. We do not consider non-real numbers in this review.

Example 3

1. $\sqrt{x^4y^8} = x^2y^4$

2. $\sqrt[3]{8x^3/y^6} = \sqrt[3]{2^3x^3/\left(y^2\right)^3} = 2x/y^2$

3. $\sqrt{\dfrac{36}{9x^4}} = \dfrac{\sqrt{36}}{\sqrt{9}\sqrt{x^4}} = \dfrac{6}{3x^2} = \dfrac{2}{x^2}$

4. $\left(-32x^5\right)^{1/5} = \left[(-2)^5x^5\right]^{1/5} = -2x$

Simplifying Expressions

Many complicated algebraic expressions can be simplified by following some basic rules. A review of the rules follows.

Rule I: Perform multiplications and divisions before you perform additions and subtractions. The expression $x + 2y/3$, or equivalently $x + 2y \div 3$, is not the same as $\dfrac{x+2y}{3}$.

Rule II: Combine all like terms in an expression. The expression $2x + x - y^2 + 4y^2$ is simplified by combining the like terms resulting in $3x + 3y^2$.

Rule III: Perform operations inside parentheses first. The expression $(x + 2y)/3$ is not the same as $x + 2y/3$. With the parentheses present, we add first then divide; with no parentheses, we use Rule I and divide first then add.

Rule IV: Eliminate inner parentheses first and the outermost parentheses last. In the expression $x(x + 2(3x + 4) - 3)$, we remove the inner parentheses first obtaining $x(x + 6x + 8 - 3)$; then combine like terms giving $x(7x + 5)$; we may then remove the last parentheses providing $7x^2 + 5x$. Often brackets and braces are used if two or three sets of parentheses are needed.

Example 4

1. $5 + 3x^2/x + (2x-3)/2 - \dfrac{5}{2} = 5 + 3x + x - \dfrac{3}{2} - \dfrac{5}{2} = 4x + 1$

2. $$\begin{aligned} 2(3x - 2(2-x) + x - 1) + 4x &= 2(3x - 4 + 2x + x - 1) + 4x \\ &= 2(6x-5) + 4x \\ &= 12x - 10 + 4x \\ &= 16x - 10 \end{aligned}$$

3. $$2x[(3-5x)y+2xy-3x(1-2y)] = 2x[3y-5xy+2xy-3x+6xy]$$
$$= 2x[3y-3x+3xy]$$
$$= 6xy-6x^2+6x^2y$$

The Products of Monomials and/or Polynomials

To multiply a monomial by a monomial, multiply the numerical coefficients and then follow the laws of exponents with the same base. An example would be

$$(2rs^3)(-3r^3s^2) = 2(-3)(r\cdot r^3)(s^3\cdot s^2) = -6r^4s^5$$

To multiply a polynomial by a monomial, multiply each term of the polynomial by the monomial. This is illustrated by

$$4x(3x^2-2xy+y^2) = 12x^3-8x^2y+4xy^2$$

To multiply two polynomials, multiply one of them by each term of the other, and then combine like terms. The following illustrates the process:

$$(2x-y)(2+x-3y) = 2x(2+x-3y)-y(2+x-3y)$$
$$= 4x+2x^2-6xy-2y-xy+3y^2$$
$$= 4x-2y+2x^2-7xy+3y^2$$

Example 5

1. $$2x^2y\sqrt{9x^6y^2} = 2x^2y(3x^3y) = 2(3)(x^2\cdot x^3)(y\cdot y) = 6x^5y^2$$

2. $$(a+2)(a+3)(a+4) = [a(a+3)+2(a+3)](a+4)$$
$$= [a^2+3a+2a+6](a+4)$$
$$= (a+4)[a^2+5a+6]$$
$$= a[a^2+5a+6]+4[a^2+5a+6]$$
$$= a^3+5a^2+6a+4a^2+20a+24$$
$$= a^3+9a^2+26a+24$$

Factoring

Before we proceed with the rules of division we introduce the notion of factoring. If an algebraic expression can be written as the product of two other algebraic expressions, the two other expressions are called *factors*. Sometimes there may be more than two factors. Factoring an expression will often allow us to simplify a problem, so it is quite important when solving many algebra problems.

There are several algebraic expressions that occur frequently, and you should be able to recognize their factors immediately. Five common types are:

1. $ax + ay = a(x+y)$
2. $x^2 - y^2 = (x+y)(x-y)$
3. $x^2 + 2xy + y^2 = (x+y)^2$
4. $x^2 - 2xy + y^2 = (x-y)^2$
5. $x^2 + (a+b)x + ab = (x+a)(x+b)$

Example 6

Factor $3a^2b^2 - 15a^4b$.

Solution. Note that $3a^2b$ is common to both terms. Factor it out and obtain

$$3a^2b^2 - 15a^4b = 3a^2b\left(b - 5a^2\right)$$

The two factors are $3a^2b$ and $\left(b - 5a^2\right)$.

Example 7

Factor $4x^2 - 9$.

Solution. This is the difference of two perfect squares: $(2x)^2$ and 3^2. Using type No. 2 above we see that

$$4x^2 - 9 = (2x-3)(2x+3)$$

NOTE: This may be the most common expression that you will need to factor so be sure to recognize it quickly.

Example 8

Factor $y^2 + 6y + 9$.

Solution. The number 9 is 3^2 so we try type No. 3 and observe that

$$y^2 + 6y + 9 = (y+3)^2$$

Note that this can be factored using type No. 5: What two numbers add together to give 6 and multiply together to give 9? The answer is 3 and 3 so that

$$y^2 + 6y + 9 = (y+3)(y+3)$$

Example 9

Factor $r^2 - 8r + 16$.

Solution. The number 16 is 4^2 so we try type No. 4 and observe that

$$r^2 - 8r + 16 = (r-4)^2$$

This also can be factored using type No. 5: What two numbers add together to give – 8 and multiply together to give 16? The answer is – 4 and – 4 so that

$$r^2 - 8r + 16 = (r-4)(r-4)$$

Example 10

Factor $3x^4 + 21x^3 + 36x^2$.

Solution. First, we simplify by factoring out the common factor $3x^2$ and write the expression as

$$3x^4 + 21x^3 + 36x^2 = 3x^2\left(x^2 + 7x + 12\right)$$

Now we have a type No. 5 expression $\left(x^2 + 7x + 12\right)$. What two numbers add together to give 7 and multiply together to give 12? They are 3 and 4 resulting in

$$\begin{aligned} 3x^4 + 21x^3 + 36x^2 &= 3x^2\left(x^2 + 7x + 12\right) \\ &= 3x^2(x+3)(x+4) \end{aligned}$$

Division of Algebraic Expressions

There are two common divisions that you may be asked to perform. The first involves dividing an algebraic expression by a monomial, such as

$$\frac{3x + 6ax^2 + 15xa^2}{3x}$$

We first recognize the numerator as a type No. 1 expression and factor out $3x$. The factor $3x$ then cancels out with the denominator and we have

$$\frac{3x + 6ax^2 + 15xa^2}{3x} = \frac{3x\left(1 + 2ax + 5a^2\right)}{3x} = 1 + 2ax + 5a^2$$

The second type of division involves divisions such as

$$\frac{5x^2 - 15x + 10}{5x - 10}$$

We write the denominator as $5(x-2)$ and the numerator as $5(x^2 - 3x + 2)$. The numerator is a type No. 5 expression: What two numbers added together give – 3 and multiplied together give 2? They are – 2 and – 1. Hence, we can write

$$\frac{5\left(x^2 - 3x + 2\right)}{5(x-2)} = \frac{(x-2)(x-1)}{x-2} = x - 1$$

Example 11

Simplify $\dfrac{y^2 - 4y - 12}{y+2}$.

Solution. The numerator is a type No. 5 expression: What two numbers added together give – 4 and multiplied together give – 12? They are – 6 and 2. Consequently, we have

$$\frac{y^2 - 4y - 12}{y+2} = \frac{(y-6)(y+2)}{y+2} = y - 6$$

Example 12

Simplify $\dfrac{x^2+2x-8}{x^2+5x+4}$.

Solution. The numerator and denominator are both type No. 5 expressions so that each can be factored as follows:

$$\frac{x^2+2x-8}{x^2+5x+4}=\frac{(x-2)(x+4)}{(x+1)(x+4)}=\frac{x-2}{x+1}$$

Multiplying and Dividing Algebraic Fractions

When multiplying algebraic fractions, we search for common factors: factors that are common to both numerators and denominators. These factors are canceled and the resulting fraction simplified, if possible. An example illustrates.

When dividing algebraic fractions, we invert the divisor (the fraction we're dividing by) and then multiply, searching for common factors.

Example 13

Multiply the fractions $\dfrac{2x+3}{x-1}$ and $\dfrac{x^2+3x-4}{4x^2-9}$.

Solution. First, we factor the quadratic expressions as follows:

$$x^2+3x-4=(x+4)(x-1)$$
$$4x^2-9=(2x-3)(2x+3)$$

We then have

$$\frac{2x+3}{x-1}\;\frac{x^2+3x-4}{4x^2-9}=\frac{\cancel{2x+3}}{\cancel{x-1}}\;\frac{(x+4)\cancel{(x-1)}}{(2x-3)\cancel{(2x+3)}}$$
$$=\frac{x+4}{2x-3}$$

This is in simplest form.

Example 14

Perform the division $\dfrac{3a-4}{2-3a}\div\dfrac{3ab-4b}{4-9a^2}$.

Solution. First, invert the divisor and express the division as the multiplication

$$\frac{3a-4}{2-3a}\div\frac{3ab-4b}{4-9a^2}=\frac{3a-4}{2-3a}\;\frac{4-9a^2}{3ab-4b}$$

Next, factor any factorable expressions:

$$4-9a^2=(2-3a)(2+3a)$$
$$3ab-4b=b(3a-4)$$

The given division is now written and the common factors canceled:

$$\frac{\cancel{(3a-4)}}{\cancel{(2-3a)}}\;\frac{\cancel{(2-3a)}(2+3a)}{b\cancel{(3a-4)}}=\frac{2+3a}{b}$$

$$\frac{(3a-4)}{(2-3a)}\frac{(2-3a)(2+3a)}{b(3a-4)} = \frac{2+3a}{b}$$

Addition of Algebraic Fractions

When adding (or subtracting) algebraic fractions we proceed as in arithmetic:

- Find the lowest common denominator (LCD) of the fractions.
- Write each fraction using the LCD of the fractions.
- Add (or subtract) the numerators. The denominator will be the LCD.
- Simplify the resulting fraction.

Two examples will illustrate this procedure.

Example 15

Express as a single fraction: $\frac{2x+1}{2a} - \frac{x-3}{3a}$.

Solution. The lowest common denominator is $6a$. Each fraction is written with its denominator as $6a$. This gives:

$$\frac{2x+1}{2a} - \frac{x-3}{3a} = \frac{3(2x+1)}{6a} - \frac{2(x-3)}{6a}$$

$$= \frac{6x+3}{6a} - \frac{2x-6}{6a} = \frac{6x+3-2x+6}{6a} = \frac{4x+9}{6a}$$

Example 16

Express as a single fraction: $\frac{2a}{b} - 3a + \frac{5}{2a}$.

Solution. The lowest common denominator is identified as $2ab$. Each fraction is written with its denominator as $2ab$:

$$\frac{2a}{b} - 3a + \frac{5}{2a} = \frac{2a \cdot 2a}{2ab} - \frac{3a \cdot 2ab}{2ab} + \frac{5b}{2ab}$$

$$= \frac{4a^2 - 6a^2b + 5b}{2ab}$$

This fraction cannot be simplified.

Equations

Definitions

An *equation* is a mathematical statement that two algebraic expressions are equal. The letters in the equation are the *unknowns*. An equation may be thought of as asking the question: what numerical value of the unknown satisfies the equation? (*Satisfies* means to make both sides equal.) The value of the unknown is called the *solution* of the equation, or the *root* of the equation. We *solve* an equation by finding the numerical value of all of its roots.

There are equations that do not have real roots. For example , the equation $x^2 = -4$ does not have a real root; the square of any real number, whether positive or negative (e.g., + 2 or – 2) is positive. Hence, there is no real root to $x^2 = -4$. We will not be interested in solving equations that do not have real roots. (The equation $x^2 = -4$ has non-real roots called imaginary roots; such equations are not of interest in this review.)

Equivalent Equations

Two equations that have the same roots are said to be *equivalent*. To solve an equation we often put the equation in a form that is more easily solved with one or both of the following operations:

- Add or subtract the same term to or from each side of an equation.
- Multiply or divide each side of an equation by the same number or algebraic expression.

Using the above operations, you will be able to solve equations of the *first degree*, also called *linear equations*. Such equations involve the unknown to the first power. An example, $2x + 5 = x/3$. A linear equation could not have a term like $2x^2$ or $3\sqrt{x}$. The operations are also used when solving a *quadratic equation*, an equation that includes the unknown squared, such as $x^2 + 5x + 4 = 0$.

Linear Equations

To solve a linear equation that contains fractions, first remove all fractions by multiplying both sides by the lowest common denominator of all the fractions. Then move all terms containing the unknown to one side and all terms that do not contain an unknown to the other side. Factor out the unknown from all terms that contain the unknown; finally, divide each side by the coefficient of the unknown.

Example 1

Solve $\frac{x}{2a} = \frac{3}{5}$ for x.

Solution. This is solved by multiplying each side of the equation by $2a$ and 5 (cross multiplying). There results

$$(2a)(5)\frac{x}{2a} = \frac{3}{5}(2a)(5)$$
$$(5)x = 3(2a)$$
$$5x = 6a$$
$$x = \frac{6a}{5}$$

Example 2

Solve $2x + 6 = 3x - 4$.

Solution. Move the unknowns to the right side and the constants to the left side, adding 4 to each side:

$$2x + 6 + 4 = 3x - 4 + 4$$
$$2x + 10 = 3x$$

Now subtract $2x$ from each side:

$$2x + 10 - 2x = 3x - 2x$$
$$10 = x$$

The solution is $x = 10$. It could have been obtained by simply moving $2x$ to the right side while simultaneously moving -4 to the left side, remembering to change the sign on any term that is moved from one side to the other.

Example 3

Solve $\frac{3a-4}{2} = \frac{2+a}{3} - 4$.

Solution. First remove the fractions. The lowest common denominator is 6. Multiply each side by 6 as follows:

$$6\left(\frac{3a-4}{2}\right) = \left(\frac{2+a}{3} - 4\right)6$$
$$3(3a-4) = 2(2+a) - 4 \cdot 6$$
$$9a - 12 = 4 + 2a - 24$$

Move $2a$ to the left side and -12 to the right side:

$$9a - 2a = 4 - 24 + 12$$
$$7a = -8$$

The unknown a is found to be

$$a = -\frac{8}{7}$$

Example 4

Solve $a(a+t) = b^2 - bt$ for t.

Solution. Note that this is a quadratic equation if the unknown is either a or b, but it is a linear equation if the unknown is t. To solve for t, first remove the parentheses:

$$a^2 + at = b^2 - bt$$

Move $-bt$ to the left side and a^2 to the right side:

$$bt + at = b^2 - a^2$$

We can factor t out of the two terms on the left side; we can also factor the right side to obtain

$$t(b+a) = (b+a)(b-a)$$

Divide both sides by $(b+a)$ and find the solution to be

$$t = b - a$$

Simultaneous Equations

Two unknowns in two equations are solved by either of two methods.

The substitution method:

1. Solve the first equation for one unknown in terms of the other unknown and substitute the result into the second equation.

2. Solve the resulting equation for the unknown.

3. Substitute the value of this known unknown into either original equation and solve for the second unknown.

The addition or subtraction method:

1. Multiply one equation by a properly chosen number so that one of the unknowns has the same coefficient in both equations.

2. Add or subtract the equations so that one of the unknowns is eliminated.

3. Solve the resulting equation for the remaining unknown.

4. Substitute the value of this known unknown into either original equation and solve for the second unknown.

Let us solve a few problems using both methods.

Example 5

Solve $\begin{matrix} x-y=2 \\ 2x+y=-5 \end{matrix}$ using the substitution method.

Solution. Using the substitution method, the first equation gives

$$x=2+y$$

Substitute this into the second equation and solve for y:

$$\begin{aligned} 2(2+y)+y&=-5 \\ 4+2y+y&=-5 \\ 3y&=-9 \\ y&=-3 \end{aligned}$$

Substitute this value back into the first equation and solve for x:

$$\begin{aligned} x-(-3)&=2 \\ x+3&=2 \\ x&=-1 \end{aligned}$$

The solution is $x=-1,\ y=-3$.

Example 6

Solve $\begin{matrix} x-y=2 \\ 2x+y=-5 \end{matrix}$ using the addition or subtraction method.

Solution. We simply add the two equations since this will eliminate y:

$$\begin{aligned} 2x+x&=2-5 \\ 3x&=-3 \\ x&=-1 \end{aligned}$$

Substitute this value back into the first equation and solve for y:

$$\begin{aligned} -1-y&=2 \\ -y&=3 \\ y&=-3 \end{aligned}$$

The solution is $x=-1,\ y=-3$.

Example 7

Solve the simultaneous equations $3x - y = 7$ and $2x + 3y = 12$ by using the substitution method.

Solution. The first equation provides

$$3x - 7 = y$$

This is substituted into the second equation to give

$$\begin{aligned} 2x + 3(3x - 7) &= 12 \\ 2x + 9x - 21 &= 12 \\ 11x &= 33 \\ x &= 3 \end{aligned}$$

Substitute this value of x back into the second equation and solve for y:

$$\begin{aligned} 2(3) + 3y &= 12 \\ 6 + 3y &= 12 \\ 3y &= 6 \\ y &= 2 \end{aligned}$$

The solution is $x = 3,\ y = 2$.

Example 8

Solve the simultaneous equations $3x - y = 7$ and $2x + 3y = 12$ by using the addition or subtraction method.

Solution. First, write the two equations one above the other so it is more obvious what to do:

$$\begin{aligned} 3x - y &= 7 \\ 2x + 3y &= 12 \end{aligned}$$

Multiply the first equation by 3:

$$\begin{aligned} 9x - 3y &= 21 \\ 2x + 3y &= 12 \end{aligned}$$

Add the two equations and solve for x:

$$\begin{aligned} 11x &= 33 \\ x &= 3 \end{aligned}$$

Substitute this value of x back into the first equation and solve for y:

$$\begin{aligned} 3(3) - y &= 7 \\ 9 - y &= 7 \\ 2 &= y \end{aligned}$$

The solution is $x = 3,\ y = 2$.

Quadratic Equations

A *quadratic equation*, or an equation of the *second degree*, can be written in the standard form

$$ax^2 + bx + c = 0$$

where a, b, and c are constants. If either b or c is zero, the equation is relatively easy to solve. If neither b nor c is zero, we will consider only those equations in which the quadratic expression on the left side can be factored.

Example 9

Solve $x^2 = 16$.

Solution. In this equation both b and c are zero. The solution is

$$x = \pm\sqrt{16}$$
$$= 4,\ -4$$

There are two roots and the solution is $x = 4,\ x = -4$, or equivalently, $x = 4, -4$.

Example 10

Solve $x^2 + 4x = 0$.

Solution. The left side of this equation can be factored so that we can write it as

$$x(x + 4) = 0$$

This equation is satisfied if either factor is zero. Hence we write

$$x = 0$$
$$x + 4 = 0 \qquad \therefore x = -4$$

The solution is $x = 0,\ x = -4$.

Example 11

Solve $x^2 - 5x + 4 = 0$.

Solution. This quadratic equation has all terms present, hence we expect that the left side can be factored. Indeed it can and we write

$$(x-4)(x-1) = 0$$

We set each factor equal to zero and solve for x:

$$x - 4 = 0 \qquad \therefore x = 4$$
$$x - 1 = 0 \qquad \therefore x = 1$$

The solution is $x = 4, 1$.

Example 12

Solve $2x - 3 = (4/x) + x$.

Solution. First, put the equation in standard form by multiplying both sides by x:

$$2x^2 - 3x = 4 + x^2$$
$$x^2 - 3x - 4 = 0$$

This equation is factorable so we write

$$(x-4)(x+1) = 0$$

Set each factor equal to zero and solve for x:

$$x - 4 = 0 \qquad \therefore x = 4$$
$$x + 1 = 0 \qquad \therefore x = -1$$

The solution is $x = 4, -1$.

Word Problems

Problems in real life come to us in verbal form, not in the form of mathematical equations as we have been considering thus far in this review of Algebra. To solve a word problem, we must express the verbal form as a mathematical equation letting x, or some other letter, represent the quantity that we wish to determine.

Let us consider several of the more common categories of word problems that may be encountered on the GMAT.

Percentages

The word *percent* is abbreviated by the symbol % and is a fraction whose denominator is 100. That is, 26% is equivalent to the fraction 26/100. To change a number, usually a decimal, to percent we simply multiply by 100; the number 0.321 is equivalent to 32.1%. If a percentage is given, move the decimal two places to the left to express its equivalent decimal form.

Example 1

Convert 4% into a decimal and a fraction in lowest terms.

Solution. To convert 4% into a decimal, we move the decimal point two places to the left,

$$4\% = 0.04$$

To express 4% as a fraction, we divide by 100:

$$4\% = \frac{4}{100} = \frac{1}{25}$$

Hence

$$4\% = 0.04 = \frac{1}{25}$$

Example 2

If the price of a stock falls from \$50 to \$40, what is the percentage decrease?

Solution. First subtract the numbers resulting in a decrease of 50 – 40 = \$10. Then divide by the original amount:

$$\frac{50-40}{50} = \frac{10}{50} = 0.2$$

Convert to a percentage by moving the decimal point two places to the right:

$$\%\text{ decrease} = 20\%$$

Example 3

An employee is to mark up a piece of jewelry 120%. If it cost the owner \$100, what should be its selling price?

Solution. The amount of the markup is

$$1.2 \times 100 = \$120$$

The selling price is then

$$\$100 + \$120 = \$220$$

Example 4

A college bookstore purchases tradebooks on a 40% margin, i.e., it purchases a tradebook for 40% less than its retail price. What is the percentage markup (based on its wholesale price)?

Solution. Since the retail price is not given, the percentage markup that we seek must be the same for all tradebooks. Therefore, let the retail price of a tradebook be \$100 (rather than the symbol x). Then the bookstore's purchase price is

$$100 - 100 \times 0.4 = 100 - 40 = \$60$$

If a book sells for \$100 and costs \$60, its percentage markup is

$$\%\text{ markup} = \frac{100-60}{60} \times 100 = \frac{40}{60} \times 100 = 66\tfrac{2}{3}\%$$

Example 5

Kathy buys a bike for \$240, which was marked down 40%. What was the original price?

Solution. Let P be the original price. Then

$$P - P \times 0.4 = 240$$
$$0.6P = 240 \qquad \therefore P = \$400$$

Example 6

Find the number of residents of a city if 20% of them, or 6,200 people, ride bicycles.

Solution. Let R be the number of residents. The equation that represents the verbal statement is

$$0.2R = 6,200$$
$$\therefore \quad R = \frac{6200}{0.2} = \frac{62000}{2} = 31,000 \text{ people}$$

Example 7

Kent pays 20% taxes on income between \$10,000 and \$20,000 and 30% on income over \$20,000. The first \$10,000 is tax free. If he pays \$14,000 in taxes, what was his income?

Solution. Let Kent's income be I. Then the total tax is

$$0.2(20,000 - 10,000) + 0.3(I - 20,000) = 14,000$$
$$2,000 + 0.3I - 6,000 = 14,000$$
$$0.3I = 14,000 + 4,000 = 18,000$$
$$\therefore \quad I = \frac{18,000}{0.3} = \$60,000$$

Example 8

How many gallons of pure water must be added to 100 gallons of a 4% saline solution to provide a 1% saline solution?

Solution. Let x be the gallons of pure water to be added. There are $100 \times 0.04 = 4$ gallons of salt and 96 gallons of pure water in a 4% saline solution. The total number of gallons will be $x + 100$. The amount of salt will remain constant. Hence,

$$0.01(x+100)=4$$
$$0.01x+1=4$$
$$0.01x=3$$
$$x=\frac{3}{0.01}=300 \text{ gallons}$$

Interest, Discount, and Markup

The interest I earned on the amount P of money invested depends on the interest rate i and the time T the money is invested. This is represented by the equation

$$I = PiT$$

The interest would be the dollars earned (or paid), the interest rate is always the annual interest rate (unless otherwise stated), and the time is measured in years. *Simple interest* means that the interest I is determined using the total time period, e.g., 10 years, rather than compounding the interest, that is, adding the interest I to the amount P after each year.

Discount is the percent reduced on the price of an item. *Markup* is the amount of increase when the cost of an item is increased a certain percent. Examples will illustrate.

Example 9

A student invests \$1000 at 10% for the summer (3 months). How much interest does the student earn?

Solution. The interest is calculated to be

$$\begin{aligned} I &= PiT \\ &= 1000(0.10)\left(\tfrac{3}{12}\right) \\ &= \$25 \end{aligned}$$

We have expressed the 10% interest rate as 0.10, and the 3 months as 3/12 of a year since the interest rate is assumed to be an annual rate.

Example 10

A professor retires with a retirement fund of \$400,000. If she is paid monthly interest of \$3600, what is the interest rate?

Solution. The interest rate is assumed to be an annual rate. The annual interest income is \$3600 (12) so that

$$I = PiT$$
$$3600(12) = 400,000i(1)$$
$$i=\frac{3600(12)}{400,000}=\frac{3.6(3)(4)}{4(100)}=0.108 \qquad \text{or } 10.8\%$$

Example 11

A pair of aerobic shoes is marked \$120 and is discounted to \$90. What is the percent discount?

Solution. The percent discount is based on the initial cost. It is

$$\% \text{ discount} = \frac{120-90}{120} \times 100$$
$$= \frac{30}{120} \times 100 \quad = \quad 25\%$$

Example 12

A pair of running shoes is purchased for $90 and is sold to a friend for $120. What is the percent markup?

Solution. The percent markup is based on the original cost. It is

$$\% \text{ markup} = \frac{120-90}{90} \times 100$$
$$= \frac{30}{90} \times 100 \quad = \quad 33\frac{1}{3}\%$$

Progressions

A *sequence* is a set of numbers arranged in a definite order. The numbers in the sequence are *terms*. An example of a sequence is $9, 6, 3, 0, -3, \cdots$, where 9 is the first term, 0 is the 4th term, and the three dots mean that the sequence continues indefinitely.

An *arithmetic progression* is a sequence in which each term is derived from the preceding term by adding or subtracting a fixed number called the *common difference*. The example 9, 6, 3, 0, – 3, ··· is an arithmetic progression in which (– 3) is the common difference. The progression – 3, 0, 3, 6, 9, ··· is an arithmetic progression in which 3 is the common difference. If the first term and the common difference are given, the arithmetic progression can be written.

A *geometric progression* is a sequence in which each term is derived by multiplying or dividing the preceding term by a fixed number called the *common ratio*. The sequence 4, – 2, 1, – 1/2, ··· is a geometric progression for which (– 1/2) is the common ratio.

Example 13

Write the seventh term of the sequence $1, \frac{1}{4}, \frac{1}{9}, \cdots$. Is it a progression?

Solution. The sequence appears to be a set of numbers squared. Let us write it as

$$1^2, \left(\frac{1}{2}\right)^2, \left(\frac{1}{3}\right)^2, \cdots$$

The additional terms are obviously

$$1^2, \left(\frac{1}{2}\right)^2, \left(\frac{1}{3}\right)^2, \left(\frac{1}{4}\right)^2, \left(\frac{1}{5}\right)^2, \left(\frac{1}{6}\right)^2, \left(\frac{1}{7}\right)^2, \cdots$$

The seventh term is 1/49.

The difference between terms is not a constant number, neither is the ratio of two successive terms a constant number. Hence, the sequence is neither an arithmetic progression nor a geometric progression.

Example 14

The first term of an arithmetic progression is 5 and the common difference is 4. What is the sum of the first six terms?

Solution. The sequence is

$$5, 9, 13, 17, 21, 25, \cdots$$

The sum is

$$5 + 9 + 13 + 17 + 21 + 25 = 90$$

Example 15

An investment of $1000 is placed into a particular account at the beginning of each year at a simple interest of 8%. How much money is in the account after 5 years?

Solution. The first $1000 will earn interest for 5 years for a total of $80 × 5 = $400. Its value will be $1400. The second $1000 will earn interest for 4 years for a total of $320. Its value will be $1320. The third $1000 will be worth $1240. The progression is

$$\$1400, \$1320, \$1240, \$1160, \$1080$$

The money in account is the total of the above five numbers:

$$\$1400 + \$1320 + \$1240 + \$1160 + \$1080 = \$6200$$

Example 16

Find the 4th term of a geometric progression if the 6th term is 20 and the common ratio is 2.

Solution. The geometric progression is

$$\cdots, 4^{th} \text{ term}, \ 5^{th} \text{ term}, \ 6t^{th} \text{ term}, \cdots$$
$$\cdots, 5, 10, 20, \cdots$$

The 4th term is 5.

Uniform Motion

When an object is moving at constant speed (or velocity), the object is traveling with *uniform motion*. The distance D that the object will travel in time T depends on the velocity V; it is expressed mathematically as

$$D = VT$$

If we desire the distance in miles, we usually express the velocity in miles per hour (mph) and time in hours. If the distance is in kilometers, then the velocity would be in kilometers per hour (kph).

Example 17

A biker travels 60 miles in $2\frac{1}{2}$ hours. Determine the biker's average speed.

Solution. The equation relating distance, velocity and time provides

$$60 = V\frac{5}{2}$$
$$\therefore \quad V = \frac{2 \times 60}{5} = 24 \text{ miles / hour}$$

Example 18

A police officer, traveling at 100 miles per hour, pursues Philip who has a 30 minute start. The police officer overtakes Philip in two hours. Find Philip's speed.

Solution. Let x miles per hour be Philip's speed. The distance traveled by the officer equals the distance traveled by Philip:

$$2 \times 100 = (2 + \frac{30}{60})x$$
$$200 = (2 + 0.5)x$$
$$200 = 2.5x \qquad \therefore x = 80 \text{ mph}$$

Example 19

A car travels between two cities 400 miles apart in 7 hours. The return trip takes 9 hours. Find the average speed of the car.

Solution. The total distance is 2(400) = 800 miles. The total time is 7 + 9 = 16 hours. The average speed is found from $D = VT$:

$$800 = V(16)$$
$$V = \frac{800}{16} = 50 \text{ miles/hour}$$

Example 20

Car A traveling 60 miles per hour starts out from town A, heading for town B, at the same time that car B traveling at 40 miles per hour starts out from town B, heading for town A. If the towns are 400 miles apart, how long will they travel before they meet?

Solution. The time that car A travels equals the time that car B travels. Let x be the distance car A travels. Then $(400 - x)$ will be the distance car B travels. Since the times are equal we write

$$T = \frac{D_A}{V_A} = \frac{D_B}{V_B}$$
$$\frac{x}{60} = \frac{400 - x}{40}$$

Cross multiply and find

$$40x = 60(400 - x) = 24,000 - 60x$$
$$100x = 24,000 \qquad \therefore x = 240 \text{ miles}$$

The time is now found since we know how far car A traveled. We have

$$T = \frac{D_A}{V_A} = \frac{240}{60} = 4 \text{ hours}$$

Work

The amount of work W accomplished in time T depends on the rate R at which the work is being accomplished. This is quite similar to the problems of uniform motion. The equation we use is

$$W = RT$$

The rate R is most often expressed as the job to do divided by the time, where $W = 1$ job. For example, a tractor plows 1/10 of a field each hour; the job is one field so the rate is 1/10 of a field per hour. If it takes x tractors to do one job in 1 hour, then each tractor works at a rate of $1/x$ of the job per hour. If it takes x tractors 4 hours to do one job, then each tractor works at one quarter of the previous rate, or at the rate of $\frac{1}{4x}$ of the job per hour. In general, if it takes x tractors y hours to do one job, the rate that each tractor works is $\frac{1}{xy}$ of the job per hour.

Example 21

It takes 3 men 8 hours to paint a house. How long will it take 5 men to paint the same house?

Solution. The rate at which each man works is

$$R = \frac{1}{3 \times 8} = \frac{1}{24} \quad \text{houses per hour}$$

Hence the rate for 5 men is $(5R)$. The work is 1 house. Our equation gives

$$1 = \frac{5}{24}T$$

$$\therefore T = \frac{24}{5} = 4.8 \text{ hours} \qquad \text{or 4 hours and 48 minutes}$$

NOTE: 0.8 hours is $0.8 \times 60 = 48$ minutes.

Example 22

Michelle can input a day's invoices into the computer system in 40 minutes and John can input the same invoices in 60 minutes. How long will it take both of them , working simultaneously, to input the invoices?

Solution. Michelle's rate for doing the job is 1/40 of the job per minute. John's rate is 1/60 of the job per minute. Let the time they work be T. Then the sum of the work that Michelle does and the work that John does must equal one job:

$$1 = \left(\frac{1}{40}\right)T + \left(\frac{1}{60}\right)T$$

This is most easily solved by multiplying by 40(60):

$$40(60) = \frac{40(60)}{40}T + \frac{40(60)}{60}T$$

$$2400 = 60T + 40T$$

$$\therefore T = 24 \text{ minutes}$$

Example 23

Kelly and Shelley type a manuscript in 8 hours. Kelly can type the manuscript alone in 20 hours. How long does it take Shelley to type the manuscript?

Solution. The rate that Kelly works is 1/20 of the job per hour. Let the rate that Shelley works be R. To do one job in 8 hours we have

$$1 = \frac{1}{20}(8) + R(8)$$

To solve for R, multiply by 20:

$$20 = 8 + 8(20)R$$

$$12 = 8(20)R$$

$$\therefore R = \frac{12}{8(20)} = \frac{3}{40} \quad \text{of the job per hour}$$

To type the entire manuscript alone, Shelley takes

$$T = \frac{W}{R}$$

$$= \frac{1}{3/40} = \frac{40}{3} = 13\frac{1}{3} \text{ hours} \qquad \text{or 13 hours and 20 minutes}$$

Ratio and Proportion

A *ratio* is a fraction that compares two numbers. The ratio of x to y is written as $x : y$ or x/y or $x \div y$. An example would be the ratio of the length of a Toyota to the length of a Cadillac. Ratios are usually used to compare quantities of the same type. We would not form the ratio of the length of a Toyota to the cost of a Cadillac.

A *proportion* states that two ratios are equal. Two ratios involve four numbers: two numerators and two denominators. Most often one of these four numbers is not known; it is found by equating the two ratios, such as

$$\frac{2}{15} = \frac{6}{x}$$

The unknown x is then found by cross multiplying:

$$2x = 15(6) \qquad \therefore x = 45$$

Two quantities are *directly proportional* if one is a constant times the other, i.e., $x = cy$. They are *inversely proportional* (or *indirectly proportional*) if one is a constant divided by the other, i.e., $x = c/y$, or equivalently, $xy = c$. If a quantity is stated to be proportional to another, the word *directly* is implied; so, if x is stated to be proportional to y it means $x = cy$.

To decide if two quantities are directly or inversely proportional, we ask the question, "Do the quantities both increase (or decrease) or does one increase while the other decreases?" If they both increase (or decrease), they are directly proportional; if one increases while the other decreases, they are inversely proportional.

To solve an equation that represents a direct proportion, such as $x = cy$, we set up the equation as

$$\frac{x_1}{x_2} = \frac{y_1}{y_2}$$

where the subscript 1 refers to the first situation and the subscript 2 to the second situation. If the equation results from an inverse proportion, such as $xy = c$, we have

$$\frac{x_1}{x_2} = \frac{y_2}{y_1}$$

To solve problems involving proportions, 3 of the 4 numbers will usually be known and the problem will be to calculate the fourth. Examples will illustrate.

Example 24

Calculate x if $4 : 15 = 16 : x$.

Solution. The equation is written in a more obvious form as

$$\frac{4}{15} = \frac{16}{x}$$

Cross multiplication gives

$$4x = 16(15) \qquad \therefore x = 60$$

Example 25

The ratio of two numbers is 4 and their sum is 40. Find the two numbers.

Solution. This is expressed mathematically as

$$\frac{x}{y} = 4$$
$$x + y = 40$$

The first equation can be written in the form

$$x = 4y$$

This is substituted into the second equation to yield

$$4y + y = 40$$
$$5y = 40 \qquad \therefore y = 8$$

Since $x = 4y$ we find that $x = 4(8) = 32$. The two numbers are 8 and 32.

Example 26

If an airplane travels 1200 miles in 2.5 hours, how far will it travel in 10 hours?

Solution. This represents a direct proportion: both the distance traveled and time increase. Consequently, if we let x = distance the airplane will travel, we have

$$\frac{1200}{x} = \frac{2.5}{10}$$

$$12{,}000 = 2.5x \qquad \therefore x = 4{,}800 \text{ miles}$$

Example 27

Renee paints 500 ft^2 in 45 minutes. How many ft^2 can Renee paint in 9 hours?

Solution. This is a direct proportion: both time and area increase. Let x represent the area painted. Then

$$\frac{500}{x} = \frac{45}{9(60)}$$

where 60 converts hours to minutes. The result is

$$500(9)(60) = 45x$$
$$500(3)(\cancel{3})(\cancel{15})(4) = \cancel{3}(\cancel{15})x \qquad \therefore x = 6000 \text{ ft}^2$$

Example 28

If 5 painters can paint a building in 24 hours, how long would it take 15 painters to paint the same building?

Solution. This is an inverse proportion: time decreases as the number of painters increase. We then write

$$\frac{5}{15}=\frac{x}{24}$$
$$5(24)=15x \qquad \therefore x=8 \text{ hours}$$

Example 29

It takes Jeffrey 80 minutes to bike between two cities at 16 miles per hour. How long does it take if he travels at 20 miles per hour?

Solution. This is an inverse proportion: as velocity increases, time decreases. The proportion is

$$\frac{80}{x}=\frac{20}{16}$$
$$80(16)=20x \qquad \therefore x=64 \text{ minutes}$$

Inequalities

Inequalities are quite important on the GMAT. Many of the Data Sufficiency questions require that you respond correctly to statements of inequalities.

An inequality is simply a comparison of two quantities or expressions. The following symbols with their meanings are used:

$>$ is greater than

$<$ is less than

$\geq$ is greater than or equal to

$\leq$ is less than or equal to

When two numbers are positive it is quite obvious when one number is greater than or less than the other; for example, $7 > 4$ (7 is greater than 4) and $4 < 7$ (4 is less than 7). If we place all numbers on a number line with negative numbers to the left of zero and positive numbers to the right of zero, then if A is to the right

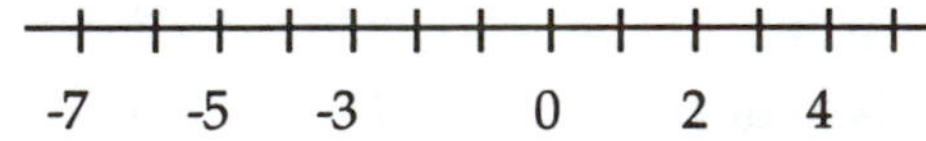

-7 -5 -3 0 2 4

of B we state that $A > B$; if A is to the left of B then $A < B$. Consequently, we conclude that $-5 > -7$ and $-20 < -10$.

We also form inequalities using algebraic symbols. The inequality $3x + 2 > x - 6$ is solved just like an algebraic equation is solved. We subtract 2 from each side of the inequality so that $3x > x - 8$. Then subtract x from each side so that $2x > -8$. Divide by 2 and obtain $x > -4$. This is the solution. Any number greater than -4 satisfies the inequality.

There are several rules that we follow when manipulating inequalities:

- The same number or algebraic expression can be added or subtracted from each side of an inequality.

- The same positive number (or positive algebraic expression) can multiply or divide each side of an inequality.
- Both sides of the same type of inequality can be added and the inequality remains. (If $x < y$ and $w < z$, then $x + w < y + z$.)
- If a negative number (or negative algebraic expression) multiplies or divides each side of an inequality, the inequality sign must be reversed. (Be sure to remember this; it often leads to errors!)

Example 1

Solve the inequality $2x - 2 \geq x - 5$.

Solution. The inequality is treated in much the same manner as an algebraic equation. Add 2 to each side:

$$2x \geq x - 3$$

Subtract x from each side and the solution is

$$x \geq -3$$

NOTE: Retain the same inequality symbol throughout the solution unless an operation reverses the symbol.

Example 2

Solve the inequality $4x < x^2/2$.

Solution. Multiply both sides by 2 and obtain

$$8x < x^2$$

Divide both sides by x (this demands that x is positive) resulting in the solution

$$8 < x$$

For positive x

$$x > 8$$

For negative x

$$x < 8$$

Example 3

Solve the inequality $3r + 5 > 6r - 7$.

Solution. First, subtract 5 from each side:

$$3r > 6r - 12$$

Next, subtract $6r$ from each side:

$$-3r > -12$$

Now divide each side by (-3) and reverse the inequality. The solution is

$$r < 4$$

Rather than working with the negative signs we could have added 7 to each side of the original inequality to obtain:

$$3r + 12 > 6r$$

Then subtract $3r$ from each side and write

$$12 > 3r$$

so that the solution is

$$4 > r$$

This is equivalent to the above solution except that the symbol r is on the right side rather than the more conventional left side.

Example 4

Solve the inequality $x^2 + 4x \geq 12$.

Solution. To solve this inequality we observe that if we add 4 to each side, the left side can be written as $(x + 2)^2$. Do this and obtain

$$x^2 + 4x + 4 \geq 16$$
$$(x+2)^2 \geq 16$$

We must now take the square root, and this leads to a result that can, at first, seem confusing. Remember, if we multiply by (– 1) we must reverse the inequality sign. So

$$\pm(x+2) \geq \pm 4$$

The top signs give

$$(x+2) \geq 4$$

A minus sign on the left and a plus sign on the right results in (multiply by – 1)

$$(x+2) \leq -4$$

The other two combinations do not provide acceptable solutions which a check with the original inequality shows.

The two equations provide the solution

$$x \geq 2$$
$$x \leq -6$$

It is not surprising that a quadratic leads to two different solutions. To check our solutions, substitute 2 and a value greater than 2 (e.g., 4) into the original inequality. Then substitute (– 6) and a value less than (– 6) (e.g., – 8). If our solution is correct, the substituted values should provide acceptable results.

Practice Problems

—Algebra—

Exponents

1. $\left(2xy^2\right)^3 =$

A) $6xy^2$ B) $6x^3y^5$ C) $8x^3y^6$ D) $8x^3y^5$ E) $8x^4y^5$

2. $2^3 \times 2^2 \times 2^4 =$

A) 2^{24} B) 2^9 C) 8^9 D) 8^{24} E) 4^{18}

3. $\left(3a^2b^3\right)\times\left(3ab^2\right)=$

A) $3a^2b^6$ B) $3a^3b^5$ C) $9a^2b^6$ D) $9a^3b^5$ E) $9a^2b^6$

4. $3^2 \times 3^3 \times 3$ can be expressed as

I] 3^6 II] 9^3 III] 27^2

A) I B) II C) III D) I, II E) I, II, III

5. $4x^2y^3 \div 2x^3y^2 =$

A) $2y/x$ B) $2x/y$ C) $8x^5y^5$ D) $\frac{2^3x^5}{y^5}$ E) $\frac{2x^5}{y^5}$

6. $\frac{2x^2}{y^3} \div \frac{2x}{y^4} =$

A) $4x^3y^7$ B) xy C) $\frac{x}{y}$ D) $\frac{y}{x}$ E) $\frac{4x}{y}$

7. Express $\frac{3\cdot 2^2}{5^2\cdot 4^3} \div \frac{2\cdot 3^2}{5^3\cdot 4^2}$ in lowest terms.

A) 2/12 B) 10/12 C) 1/6 D) 5/6 E) 5/3

8. $2\times 10^8 =$

A) 200 billion B) 20 billion C) 2 billion D) 20 million E) 200 million

9. $\left(a^3r^5\right)^3 \times \left(a^2s^3\right)^2 =$

A) $a^{13}r^{15}s^6$ B) $a^{10}r^8s^5$ C) $a^{10}r^{15}s^6$ D) $a^{13}r^8s^6$ E) $a^{10}r^8s^6$

Roots

10. $\sqrt{16x^3} =$

A) $4x^3$ B) $4x^{1/2}$ C) $4x\sqrt{x}$ D) $4x^2$ E) $4x^2\sqrt{x}$

11. $\sqrt[3]{-27a^3/x^6} =$

A) $-3a/x^2$ B) $-3a\sqrt{a}/x^2$ C) $-3a\sqrt{a}/\sqrt{x}$

D) $-3a/x\sqrt{x}$ E) $-3a^2/x^3$

12. $\sqrt[3]{-8x^6y^3} \div \sqrt[4]{16x^8y^2} =$

A) $-\frac{\sqrt{y}}{2}$ B) $-\sqrt{y}$ C) $-\frac{y^2}{2}$ D) $-\frac{\sqrt{y}}{x}$ E) $-\frac{y}{x^2}$

13. $\sqrt{12}+\sqrt{108}-\sqrt{75}=$

A) $3\sqrt{12}$ B) $4\sqrt{5}$ C) $5\sqrt{2}$ D) $3\sqrt{3}$ E) $2\sqrt{6}$

14. $4\sqrt{20}-2\sqrt{48}=$

A) $8\sqrt{2}$ B) $8\sqrt{15}$ C) $8\sqrt{5/3}$
D) $8\sqrt{5}-\sqrt{3}$ E) $8(\sqrt{5}-\sqrt{3})$

15. $(-27)^{1/3}(16)^{1/4}=$

A) $-3\sqrt[4]{2}$ B) $-\sqrt[3]{3}\sqrt[4]{2}$ C) $-3/2$ D) -6 E) -12

Simplify Expressions

16. $3x+\frac{x^2}{x}-y\left(\frac{x}{y}-\frac{2}{y}\right)=$

A) $3x+2y$ B) $2(x-1)$ C) $3x+2$
D) $3x-2$ E) $2x-3$

17. $4-3x+x^2+5x-2x^2-4=$

A) $x(2-x)$ B) $8+2x-x^2$ C) $8+7x-3x^2$
D) $8-7x-x^2$ E) $2x+x^2$

18. Evaluate $[3+x/3+(2-y)/2]$ if $x=6$ and $y=4$.

A) 2 B) 4 C) 3 D) 5 E) 6

19. $2\{a+3(2-a)+2[3(a-2)-2a]\}=$

A) $12a-12$ B) $12a+12$ C) $a+12$
D) -12 E) $10a-12$

20. $3(2x-2(y+3(x-y)))=$

A) $3x-y$ B) $12(x-y)$ C) $12y-9x$
D) $18y-3x$ E) $12(y-x)$

Products of Monomials and Polynomials

21. Multiply $2x(x-2)(x+2)$.

A) $2x^3-8x^2-8x$ B) $2x^3+8x^2-8x$ C) $2x^3$
D) $2x^3-8x$ E) $8x^3$

22. $(x-2y)(x+2y)=$

A) $x^2-4xy+4y^2$ B) $x^2+4xy-4y^2$ C) x^2-4y^2
D) $2x-4y$ E) $2x-4xy+4y$

23. Multiply $(2x-1)(x+2)$.

A) $2x^2-5x-2$ B) $2x^2+3x-2$ C) $2x^2-3x+2$

D) $2x^2-3x-2$ E) $2x^2+5x-2$

24. $(4x+3y)(x-2y)=$

A) $4x^2-5xy-6y^2$ B) $4x^2+5xy+6y^2$ C) $4x^2+5xy-6y^2$

D) $4x^2-11xy+6y^2$ E) $4x^2-11xy-6y^2$

Factoring

25. Factor x^2-16.

A) $(x-8)(x+2)$ B) $(x+8)(x-2)$ C) $(x-8)(x-2)$

D) $(x-4)(x+4)$ E) $(x+8)(x+2)$

26. $3x^2-24x+48=$

A) $(3x-16)(x-3)$ B) $(x-16)(3x-3)$ C) $3(x-4)^2$

D) $3(x-4)(x+4)$ E) $3(x+4)^2$

27. Factor $x^2+4x-12$.

A) $(x+4)(x-3)$ B) $(x-4)(x+3)$ C) $(x-6)(x+2)$

D) $(x+6)(x-2)$ E) $(x-4)(x-3)$

28. $x^2-5x-24=$

A) $(x-8)(x+3)$ B) $(x-12)(x+2)$ C) $(x-6)(x+4)$

D) $(x+6)(x-4)$ E) $(x+8)(x-3)$

29. Factor $2x^2y^2-8x^2y-64x^2$.

A) $2x(y-8)(y-4)$ B) $2xy(y-8)(y+8)$ C) $(2x-y)(x-8y)$

D) $(2y-8x)(y+4x)$ E) $2x^2(y-8)(y+4)$

Division of Algebraic Expressions

30. Divide $\left(x^2-16\right)$ by $(x-4)$.

A) $4x$ B) $x/4$ C) $4(x-4)$ D) $x-4$ E) $x+4$

31. $\left(x^2-6x-16\right)\div(x-8)=$

A) $x-2$ B) $x+2$ C) $x-6$ D $x+6$ E) $x+8$

32. Divide $\left(2x^4+14x^3+24x^2\right)$ by $\left(x^3+4x^2\right)$.

A) $2(x+3)$ B) $2(x+6)$ C) $2(x-3)$
D) $2x^2(x-3)$ E) $2x^2(x+3)$

33. Simplify $\left(a^2-6a+8\right)/\left(a^2+a-20\right)$.

A) $\frac{a-2}{a-5}$ B) $\frac{a-4}{a+4}$ C) $\frac{a-2}{a+5}$ D) $\frac{a-4}{a+5}$ E) $\frac{a-2}{a+4}$

34. $\left(16-x^2\right)/\left(x^2-x-12\right)=$

A) $\frac{4+x}{3+x}$ B) $\frac{4+x}{x-4}$ C) $\frac{4-x}{x+3}$ D) $\frac{x-4}{x+3}$ E) $-\frac{x+4}{x+3}$

Multiplying and Dividing Fractions

35. Simplify $\frac{x-3}{x+4}\,\frac{x^2+5x+4}{x^2-x-6}$.

A) $\frac{x-1}{x-2}$ B) $\frac{x+1}{x+2}$ C) $\frac{x-1}{x+2}$ D) $\frac{x-3}{x+3}$ E) $\frac{x+3}{x-3}$

36. Multiply the fractions $\frac{x^3-2x^2-8x}{x-4}$ and $\frac{2x}{x^2-4}$.

A) $\frac{x+2}{x-2}$ B) $\frac{2x}{x+2}$ C) $\frac{2x^2}{x-2}$ D) $\frac{2x^2}{x+4}$ E) $\frac{x}{x+4}$

37. Divide $\frac{12a^3b^2}{\left(a^2-b^2\right)}$ by $\frac{4ab^2}{(a-b)}$.

A) $\frac{3a^4b^4}{a-b}$ B) $\frac{a+b}{3a^2}$ C) $\frac{a-b}{3a^2}$ D) $\frac{3a^2}{a+b}$ E) $\frac{a-b}{3a^4b^4}$

38. Simplify $\frac{r+s}{r^2-s^2}\div\frac{r^2-2rs-3s^2}{r^4-s^4}$.

A) $\frac{r-s}{r-3s}$ B) $\frac{r+s}{r-3s}$ C) $\frac{r^2+s^2}{r+s}$ D) $\frac{r^2+s^2}{r-3s}$ E) $\frac{r^2-s^2}{r+s}$

Addition of Algebraic Fractions

39. Simplify $\frac{x}{2}-\frac{2x^2}{3x}+\frac{5xy}{6y}$.

A) $\frac{7x}{12}$ B) $\frac{2x}{3}$ C) $\frac{3x}{4}$ D) $\frac{5x}{6}$ E) $\frac{x}{2}$

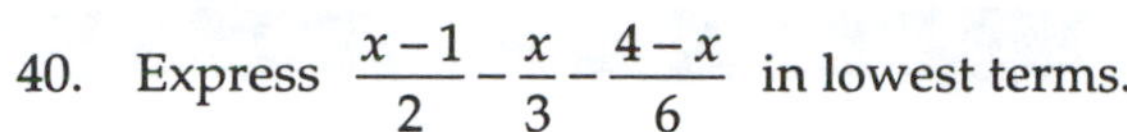

40. Express $\frac{x-1}{2}-\frac{x}{3}-\frac{4-x}{6}$ in lowest terms.

A) $\frac{2x-7}{6}$ B) $\frac{4x-14}{6}$ C) $\frac{4x-14}{12}$ D) $\frac{x-1}{3}$ E) $\frac{5x-18}{12}$

41. Add $\frac{1}{x-1}+\frac{2}{x+1}$.

A) $\frac{2(x+1)}{x-1}$ B) $\frac{3x-1}{x^2-1}$ C) $\frac{x+1}{2(x-1)}$ D) $\frac{2(x-1)}{x+1}$ E) $\frac{2}{x}$

42. Express $(1/a)+(1/b)$ as a single fraction.

A) $\frac{1}{a+b}$ B) $\frac{a+b}{a}$ C) $\frac{a+b}{ab}$ D) $\frac{2}{a+b}$ E) $\frac{ab}{a+b}$

43. Express $(1/a)+(1/b)+1$ as a single fraction.

A) $\frac{3}{a+b}$ B) $\frac{3}{ab}$ C) $\frac{2+ab}{ab}$

D) $\frac{2+ab}{a+b}$ E) $\frac{a+b+ab}{ab}$

Linear Equations

44. Solve $3x+6=x-2$ for x.

A) -3 B) 3 C) -2 D) -4 E) 2

45. If $\frac{x}{2}-\frac{x}{3}=\frac{x}{4}+2$, find x.

A) 2 B) -2 C) 12 D) 24 E) -24

46. Find r if $\frac{4}{5}r=\frac{3}{7}s+10$ and $s=14$.

A) 15 B) 20 C) 24 D) 30 E) 36

47. If $\frac{1}{r}=2s$ and $s=1/r^2$, what is r?

A) 2 B) 1/2 C) 4 D) 1/4 E) 8

48. Find a if $\frac{2a-1}{3}=4+\frac{3a-2}{2}$.

A) $18/5$ B) $-22/5$ C) -4 D) $-5/6$ E) $1/6$

49. Solve $x(b+a)=2ax$ for a.

A) $2bx$ B) bx C) b D) $2b$ E) $1/b$

50. If $\frac{t}{a}+\frac{2t}{3a}=5$, find t.

A) a B) $2a$ C) $3a$ D) $4a$ E) $5a$

Simultaneous Equations

51. Solve $\begin{matrix} x+y=9 \\ 2x-y=-6 \end{matrix}$ for y.

A) 1 B) 3 C) 5 D 6 E) 8

52. Solve $\begin{matrix} 3x+6y=-3 \\ x+5y=2 \end{matrix}$ for xy.

A) -1 B) -2 C) -3 D) 2 E) 3

53. If $5t = 3s$ and $2t = s + 2$, what is t?

A) -6 B) 6 C) -3 D) 3 E) 2

54. If $a - b = 3$ and $a - 2b = 4$, what is $a + b$?

A) 1 B) 2 C) 3 D) 4 E) 5

55. Solve $\frac{a}{2}+\frac{b}{3}=1$ and $\frac{a}{3}-\frac{b}{2}=1$ for a.

A) 5/6 B) $-11/6$ C) $-17/13$ D) -3 E) 30/13

Quadratic Equations

56. Solve for a if $a^2-2a+3=2a^2+\frac{1}{2}(4-4a)$.

A) 2 or -1 B) -2 or 1 C) 1 or 2 D) 1 or -1 E) 0 or 1

57. Find x if $x + (4/x) = 4$.

A) 0 B) 1/2 C) 1 D) 2 E) 4

58. If $x^2-4x+3=0$, what is x?

A) 1 or 3 B) -1 or -3 C) -1 or 3
D) 1 or -3 E) 3 or -4

59. If $x=y-1$ and $y=t^2-t$, find t at $x=5$.

A) 2 or -3 B) 3 or -2 C) 2 or -2
D) 4 or 2 E) -2 or 4

60. If $2x^2-3x-6=x\left(x-4+\frac{6}{x}\right)$ calculate x.

A) 4 or -3 B) -2 or 6 C) 3 or -4
D) -3 or -4 E) 2 or -6

Percentages

61. Convert 36% into a fraction in lowest terms.

A) 18/50 B) 36/100 C) 9/50 D) 9/25 E) 18/25

62. Imports rose from \$300 billion to \$345 billion from 1983 to 1987. What was the percentage increase?

A) 12% B) 15% C) 16% D) 20% E) 22%

63. An auto is purchased and marked up 20% to \$10,000. What was the purchase price?

A) \$8000 B) \$8200 C) $\$8333\frac{1}{3}$ D) \$8500 E) \$12,000

64. A pair of shoes is on sale for \$76. It has been marked down 20%. What was the original price?

A) \$104 B) \$98 C) \$91.20 D) \$90 E) \$95

65. A chair has been marked down from \$800 to \$600. What was the percentage decrease?

A) 0% B) 25% C) 30% D) $33\frac{1}{3}\%$ E) 35%

66. If 2000 people in a city watch baseball (or 25%), how many people do not watch baseball?

A) 4000 B) 5000 C) 6000 D) 6200 E) 6400

67. Four times as many people use natural gas as use oil for heating in a certain area. What percent of the people use oil?

A) 15% B) 20% C) 25% D) 30% E) $33\frac{1}{3}\%$

68. Leonard sells off 10% of the width of his farm and buys a strip adding 20% to the length of his farm. What percent did he gain in acreage?

A) 8% B) 10% C) 12% D) 14% E) 16%

Interest, Discount, and Markup

69. Rodney borrowed \$2500 for 3 months and had to pay \$75 in interest. What rate of interest was he charged?

A) 6% B) 8% C) 10% D) 12% E) 15%

70. Kenny can pay \$200 each month in interest. How much can he borrow if the interest rate is 15%?

A) \$20,000 B) \$16,000 C) \$15,000 D) \$12,000 E) \$10,000

71. Vonda pays \$3,200 for a car that was discounted 20%. What was the original price of the car?

A) \$4,000 B) \$3,840 C) \$3,620 D) \$4,200 E) \$4,400

72. Lindsay bought a \$150 pair of tennis shoes that were discounted 30%. How much did he pay?

A) \$90 B) \$100 C) \$105 D) \$110 E) \$120

73. The markup on an MSU sweatshirt is 200%. If the cost is \$15, what is the selling price?

A) \$50 B) \$45 C) \$30 D) \$25 E) \$23

74. Fred buys a grandfather clock for \$900 and marks it up for resale to \$1500. What is the percent markup?

A) $33\frac{1}{3}\%$ B) 50% C) 60% D) $66\frac{2}{3}\%$ E) 70%

Progressions

75. If 4, 2, 0 are three terms in a progression, what is the 6th term?

A) 6 B) 4 C) 2 D) −4 E) −6

76. The first three terms in a progression are $1\frac{1}{2}, 1\frac{3}{4}, 2$. Find the sum of the first 5 terms.

A) 8 B) $9\frac{1}{2}$ C) $9\frac{3}{4}$ D) 10 E) $10\frac{1}{4}$

77. The first term in an arithmetic progression is 2 and the common difference is – 0.4. Calculate the sum of the first six terms.

A) 5.6 B) 5.4 C) 5.0 D) 6.0 E) 6.2

78. Jana invested \$1000 every January 1 for 4 years at 10% simple interest. What is the accumulated value of her investments December 31 of the fourth year?

A) \$5200 B) \$5000 C) \$4800 D) \$4700 E) \$4600

79. Find the value of x so that $16, x, 4$ forms a geometric progression.

A) 8 B) 10 C) 6 D) 12 E) 9

80. Darla's investment earned her \$15,000 in four years. If it earned her twice as much in each successive year, how much did she earn in the fourth year?

A) \$3000 B) \$4000 C) \$6000 D) \$8000 E) \$15,000

81. A lottery pays \$1 on the first ticket and twice as much on each succeeding ticket. Calculate the total paid on 8 tickets.

A) \$244 B) \$425 C) \$255 D) \$325 E) \$525

Uniform Motion

82. At what rate does an automobile travel if it covers 600 miles in $7\frac{1}{2}$ hours?

A) 80 mph B) 75 mph C) 70 mph D) 65 mph E) 60 mph

83. Jeff and Tim begin a bike ride in opposite directions at 6 a.m. from the same spot, at speeds of 30 kph and 20 kph, respectively. When will they be 120 kilometers apart?

A) 7:30 a.m. B) 7:48 a.m. C) 8:24 a.m.
D) 8:36 a.m. E) 9:12 a.m.

84. How many hours does it take Kelvin to walk x miles if he walks y miles in t minutes?

A) $60x/yt$ B) $xt/60y$ C) $yt/60x$ D) $60xyt$ E) $xy/60t$

85. It takes Sarah as long to paddle 10 miles downstream on a river flowing at 3 mph as it does to paddle 12 miles down a river flowing at 4 mph. How fast does Sarah paddle in still water?

A) 4 mph B) $3\frac{1}{2}$ mph C) 3 mph D) $2\frac{1}{2}$ mph E) 2 mph

86. Ginger leaves home 15 minutes before Anette. If Ginger travels at 50 mph and Anette travels at 60 mph, how many miles pass before Anette catches Ginger?

A) 90 B) 85 C) 80 D) 75 E) 70

87. Alex leaves Atlanta heading directly toward Detroit at 8:00 a.m. traveling at 50 mph. Heidi leaves Detroit, 600 miles away, heading directly for Atlanta at the same time, traveling at 70 mph. When do they meet?

A) 12 noon B) 1 p.m. C) 1:30 p.m. D) 2 p.m. E) 2:30 p.m.

Work

88. It takes Jeanne T hours to type a certain manuscript. How much of the manuscript can she type in n hours?

A) $\frac{n}{T}$ B) $\frac{T}{n}$ C) $\frac{T-n}{n}$ D) $\frac{T-n}{T}$ E) $\frac{nT}{T-n}$

89. It takes Lisa 24 hours to roof a building and Jon 36 hours to roof the same building. How many hours does it take them working together to roof the building?

A) $12\frac{1}{5}$ B) 14 C) $14\frac{2}{5}$ D) 16 E) 18

90. Larry can hoe a garden in 90 minutes and Jim can hoe it in 60 minutes. They work together for 30 minutes then Jim goes fishing and Larry finishes the job. How long did Larry have to work?

A) 15 min. B) 75 min. C) 42 min. D) 45 min. E) 20 min.

91. It takes three fishermen six hours to catch 500 perch on Lake Michigan. How many hours would it take eight fishermen, of equal ability, to catch the 500 perch?

A) $1\frac{3}{4}$ B) $1\frac{7}{8}$ C) 2 D) $2\frac{1}{8}$ E) $2\frac{1}{4}$

92. Anita can do a job in x hours that takes Paul y hours. Find an expression for the number of hours it takes Anita and Paul to do the job together.

A) $\frac{x+y}{x-y}$ B) $\frac{x}{x+y}$ C) $\frac{x+y}{xy}$ D) $\frac{1}{x}+\frac{1}{y}$ E) $\frac{xy}{x+y}$

93. Faye and Greydon pick a berry patch in four hours. Faye can pick the berries alone in six hours. How many hours would it take Greydon to pick the berries?

A) 14 B) 12 C) 10 D) 9 E) 8

Ratio and Proportions

94. The ratio of two numbers is 11 and their sum is 72. One of the numbers is

A) 4 B) 5 C) 6 D) 7 E) 8

95. The ratio of 1 hour and twenty minutes to 2 hours is,

A) 1 : 2 B) 2 : 3 C) 3 : 4 D) 4 : 5 E) 5 : 6

96. The end of a diving board deflects $2\frac{1}{2}$ inches when a 120-pound man stands at its end. How many inches will it deflect if a 192-pound man stands on its end?

A) $3\frac{1}{3}$ B) $3\frac{1}{2}$ C) $3\frac{4}{5}$ D) $3\frac{3}{4}$ E) 4

97. Dale and Rosie purchase 600 and 800 bushels of potatoes, respectively. If they sell them for $11,200 and divide the proceeds proportionately, what is Dale's payoff?

A) $4800 B) $5200 C) $6000 D) $6400 E) $6800

98. Three entrepreneurs are to invest in the ratio of 13 : 6 : 2. If the smallest investment is to be $3000, what is the total investment?

A) $33,000 B) $31,500 C) $30,500 D) $28,000 E) $27,500

99. Larry is six feet tall and casts a ten-foot shadow. He notes that a tree casts a 120-foot shadow. How tall is the tree?

A) 80 B) 72 C) 70 D) 66 E) 60

100. A house plan is drawn on a scale so that 1 inch equals 10 feet. A measurement on the plan of 1/4 inch equals what distance on the house?

A) 1 B) $1\frac{1}{2}$ C) 2 D) $2\frac{1}{2}$ E) 3

Inequalities

101. If $x < -1$, which of the following is the greatest?

A) x^3 B) x C) $\frac{1}{x}$ D) $\frac{1}{x^2}$ E) $\frac{1}{x^3}$

102. Solve the inequality $2 - x < 3 + 2x$.

A) $x < 3$ B) $x > -\frac{1}{3}$ C) $x > 3$ D) $x < -\frac{1}{3}$ E) $x > -\frac{2}{3}$

103. If $r < s$ and $s < t$, then

A) $r < t$ B) $s = 0$ C) $t < r$ D) $t = r$ E) $s > t > r$

104. If $a^2 - 2b^2 > (a - b)(a + 2b)$, then

A) $ab < 0$ B) $a < b$ C) $a > b$
D) $a^2 < b^2$ E) $b^2 < 0$

105. If $x > a$ and $y > b$, then

A) $x > b$ B) $y > a$ C) $x + y > a + b$
D) $xy > ab$ E) $x - y > a - b$

106. One solution to $x^2 + 6x > 7$ is

A) $x > -7$ B) $x < -1$ C) $x > -1$ D) $x > 7$ E) $x < -7$

107. If $x, y,$ and z are the 3 angles of a triangle and $z \geq 100°$, then

A) $x + y < 80°$ B) $x \leq 80°$ C) $x + y \leq 80°$

D) $y \leq 80°$ E) $x - y \leq 80°$

Answers to Practice Problems

—Algebra—

Exponents	Roots	Simplifying Expressions	Multiplying	Factoring	Dividing Expressions
1. C	10. C	16. C	21. D	25. D	30. E
2. B	11. A	17. A	22. C	26. C	31. B
3. D	12. B	18. B	23. B	27. D	32. A
4. E	13. D	19. D	24. A	28. A	33. C
5. A	14. E	20. E		29. E	34. E
6. B	15. D				
7. D					
8. E					
9. A					

Multiplying Fractions	Adding Fractions	Linear Equations	Simult. Equations	Quadratic Equations	Percentages
35. B	39. B	44. D	51. E	56. D	61. D
36. C	40. A	45. E	52. C	57. D	62. B
37. D	41. B	46. B	53. B	58. A	63. C
38. D	42. C	47. A	54. A	59. B	64. E
	43. E	48. C	55. E	60. C	65. B
		49. C			66. C
		50. C			67. B
					68. A

Interest Discount	Progress'ns	Uniform Motion	Work	Ratio Proportion	Inequalities
69. D	75. E	82. A	88. A	94. C	101. D
70. B	76. D	83. C	89. C	95. B	102. B
71. A	77. D	84. B	90. D	96. E	103. A
72. C	78. B	85. E	91. E	97. A	104. A
73. B	79. A	86. D	92. E	98. B	105. C
74. D	80. D	87. B	93. B	99. B	106. E
	81. C			100. D	107. C

Explanations to the Answers
—Algebra—

Exponents

1. C $\left(2xy^2\right)^3 = 2^3 \times x^3 \times \left(y^2\right)^3 = 8x^3y^6$.

2. B $2^3 \times 2^2 \times 2^4 = 2^{(3+2+4)} = 2^9$.

3. D $\left(3a^2b^3\right) \times \left(3ab^2\right) = 3 \times 3 \times a^2 \times a \times b^3 \times b^2 = 9a^3b^5$.

4. E $3^2 \times 3^3 \times 3 = 3^{2+3+1} = 3^6 = \left(3^2\right)^3 = 9^3 = \left(3^3\right)^2 = 27^2$.

5. A $4x^2y^3 \div 2x^3y^2 = \dfrac{4x^2y^3}{2x^3y^2} = \dfrac{4x^2y^2y}{2x^2xy^2} = \dfrac{2y}{x}$.

6. B $2x^2/y^3 \div 2x/y^4 = \dfrac{2x^2}{y^3} \times \dfrac{y^4}{2x} = \dfrac{2xx}{y^3}\dfrac{y^3y}{2x} = xy$.

7. D $3 \cdot 2^2/5^2 \cdot 4^3 \div 2 \cdot 3^2/5^3 \cdot 4^2 = \dfrac{3 \cdot 2^2}{5^2 \cdot 4^3} \times \dfrac{5^3 \cdot 4^2}{2 \cdot 3^2} = \dfrac{3 \cdot 2 \cdot 2}{5^2 \cdot 4^2 \cdot 4}\dfrac{5^2 \cdot 5 \cdot 4^2}{2 \cdot 3 \cdot 3} = \dfrac{5}{6}$.

8. E $2 \times 10^8 = 2 \times 100{,}000{,}000 = 200{,}000{,}000 = 200$ million.

9. A $\left(a^3r^5\right)^3 \times \left(a^2s^3\right)^2 = a^9r^{15}a^4s^6 = a^{9+4}r^{15}s^6 = a^{13}r^{15}s^6$.

Roots

10. C $\sqrt{16x^3} = \sqrt{16}\sqrt{x^2x} = 4\sqrt{x^2}\sqrt{x} = 4x\sqrt{x}$.

11. A $\sqrt[3]{-27a^3/x^6} = \dfrac{\sqrt[3]{(-3)^3a^3}}{\sqrt[3]{\left(x^2\right)^3}} = \dfrac{-3a}{x^2}$.

12. B $\sqrt[3]{-8x^6y^3} \div \sqrt[4]{16x^8y^2} = \dfrac{\sqrt[3]{(-2)^3\left(x^2\right)^3y^3}}{\sqrt[4]{2^4\left(x^2\right)^4y^2}} = \dfrac{-2x^2y}{2x^2y^{1/2}} = \dfrac{-y}{\sqrt{y}} = \dfrac{-\sqrt{y}\sqrt{y}}{\sqrt{y}} = -\sqrt{y}$.

13. D $\sqrt{12} + \sqrt{108} - \sqrt{75} = \sqrt{4 \cdot 3} + \sqrt{36 \cdot 3} - \sqrt{25 \cdot 3} = 2\sqrt{3} + 6\sqrt{3} - 5\sqrt{3} = 3\sqrt{3}$.

14. E $4\sqrt{20}-2\sqrt{48}=4\sqrt{5\cdot 4}-2\sqrt{16\cdot 3}=4\cdot 2\sqrt{5}-2\cdot 4\sqrt{3}$

$$=8\sqrt{5}-8\sqrt{3}=8\left(\sqrt{5}-\sqrt{3}\right).$$

15. D $(-27)^{1/3}(16)^{1/4}=\left[(-3)^3\right]^{1/3}\left(2^4\right)^{1/4}=-3\times 2=-6.$

Simplifying Expressions

16. C $3x+x^2/x-y(x/y-2/y)=3x+x-(x-2)=3x+x-x+2=3x+2.$

17. A $4-3x+x^2+5x-2x^2-4=4-4-3x+5x+x^2-2x^2=2x-x^2=x(2-x).$

18. B $3+\frac{x}{3}+\frac{2-y}{2}=3+\frac{6}{3}+\frac{2-4}{2}=3+2+\frac{-2}{2}=5-1=4.$

19. D $2\{a+3(2-a)+2[3(a-2)-2a]\}=2\{a+6-3a+2[3a-6-2a]\}$
$=2\{6-2a+6a-12-4a\}=2\{-6\}=-12.$

20. E $3(2x-2(y+3(x-y)))=3(2x-2(y+3x-3y))=3(2x-2(3x-2y))$
$=3(2x-6x+4y)$
$=3(4y-4x)=3\cdot 4(y-x)$
$=12(y-x).$

Products of Monomials and Polynomials

21. D $2x(x-2)(x+2)=2x\left(x^2+\cancel{2x}-\cancel{2x}-4\right)=2x\left(x^2-4\right)=2x^3-8x$.

22. C $(x-2y)(x+2y)=x^2+2xy-2xy-4y^2=x^2-4y^2.$

23. B $(2x-1)(x+2)=2x^2+4x-x-2=2x^2+3x-2.$

24. A $(4x+3y)(x-2y)=4x^2-8xy+3xy-6y^2=4x^2-5xy-6y^2.$

Factoring

25. D $x^2-16=x^2-4^2=(x-4)(x+4).$

26. C $3x^2-24x+48=3\left(x^2-8x+16\right)=3(x-4)(x-4)=3(x-4)^2.$
The numbers must add to – 8 and multiply to 16.

27. D $x^2+4x-12=(x+6)(x-2).$
The numbers must add to 4 and multiply to – 12.

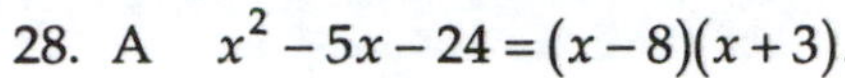

28. A $x^2 - 5x - 24 = (x-8)(x+3)$.
The numbers must add to – 5 and multiply to – 24.

29. E $2x^2y^2 - 8x^2y - 64x^2 = 2x^2\left(y^2 - 4y - 32\right) = 2x^2(y-8)(y+4)$.
The numbers must add to – 4 and multiply to – 32.

Division of Algebraic Expressions

30. E $\dfrac{x^2 - 16}{x - 4} = \dfrac{\cancel{(x-4)}(x+4)}{\cancel{x-4}} = x + 4$.

31. B $\dfrac{x^2 - 6x - 16}{x - 8} = \dfrac{\cancel{(x-8)}(x+2)}{\cancel{x-8}} = x + 2$.

32. A $\dfrac{2x^4 + 14x^3 + 24x^2}{x^3 + 4x^2} = \dfrac{2\cancel{x^2}(x^2 + 7x + 12)}{\cancel{x^2}(x+4)} = \dfrac{2\cancel{(x+4)}(x+3)}{\cancel{x+4}} = 2(x+3)$.

33. C $\dfrac{a^2 - 6a + 8}{a^2 + a - 20} = \dfrac{\cancel{(a-4)}(a-2)}{(a+5)\cancel{(a-4)}} = \dfrac{a-2}{a+5}$.

34. E $\dfrac{16 - x^2}{x^2 - x - 12} = \dfrac{(4-x)(4+x)}{(x-4)(x+3)} = \dfrac{-\cancel{(x-4)}(x+4)}{\cancel{(x-4)}(x+3)} = -\dfrac{x+4}{x+3}$.

Multiplying and Dividing Fractions

35. B $\dfrac{x-3}{x+4}\,\dfrac{x^2+5x+4}{x^2-x-6} = \dfrac{\cancel{x-3}}{\cancel{x+4}}\,\dfrac{\cancel{(x+4)}(x+1)}{\cancel{(x-3)}(x+2)} = \dfrac{x+1}{x+2}$.

36. C $\dfrac{x^3 - 2x^2 - 8x}{x-4}\,\dfrac{2x}{x^2-4} = \dfrac{x(x^2-2x-8)}{x-4}\,\dfrac{2x}{x^2-4} = \dfrac{x\cancel{(x-4)}\cancel{(x+2)}}{\cancel{x-4}}\,\dfrac{2x}{(x-2)\cancel{(x+2)}} = \dfrac{2x^2}{x-2}$.

37. D $\dfrac{12a^3b^2}{a^2-b^2} \div \dfrac{4ab^2}{a-b} = \dfrac{\overset{3}{\cancel{12}}a^3\cancel{b^2}}{\cancel{(a-b)}(a+b)} \times \dfrac{\cancel{a-b}}{\cancel{4ab^2}} = \dfrac{3a^3}{a(a+b)} = \dfrac{3a^2}{a+b}$.

38. D $\dfrac{r+s}{r^2-s^2} \div \dfrac{r^2-2rs-3s^2}{r^4-s^4} = \dfrac{\cancel{r+s}}{\cancel{r^2-s^2}} \times \dfrac{\cancel{(r^2-s^2)}(r^2+s^2)}{(r-3s)\cancel{(r+s)}} = \dfrac{r^2+s^2}{r-3s}$.

Addition of Algebraic Fractions

39. B $\frac{x}{2}-\frac{2x^2}{3x}+\frac{5xy}{6y}=\frac{x}{2}-\frac{2x}{3}+\frac{5x}{6}=\frac{6x}{12}-\frac{8x}{12}+\frac{10x}{12}=\frac{8x}{12}=\frac{2x}{3}.$

40. A $\frac{x-1}{2}-\frac{x}{3}-\frac{4-x}{6}=\frac{6x-6}{12}-\frac{4x}{12}-\frac{8-2x}{12}=\frac{6x-6-4x-8+2x}{12}=\frac{4x-14}{12}=\frac{2x-7}{6}.$

41. B $\frac{1}{x-1}+\frac{2}{x+1}=\frac{x+1}{(x-1)(x+1)}+\frac{2(x-1)}{(x+1)(x-1)}=\frac{x+1+2x-2}{x^2-1}=\frac{3x-1}{x^2-1}.$

42. C $\frac{1}{a}+\frac{1}{b}=\frac{b}{ab}+\frac{a}{ab}=\frac{a+b}{ab}.$

43. E $\frac{1}{a}+\frac{1}{b}+1=\frac{b}{ab}+\frac{a}{ab}+\frac{ab}{ab}=\frac{a+b+ab}{ab}.$

Linear Equations

44. D $3x+6=x-2.$ Subtract x from each side, subtract 6 from each side. $\therefore x=-4$
$2x=-8.$

45. E $\frac{x}{2}-\frac{x}{3}=\frac{x}{4}+2$ or $\frac{6x}{12}-\frac{4x}{12}=\frac{3x}{12}+\frac{24}{12}$ or $\frac{6x-4x}{12}=\frac{3x+24}{12}.$
Then $2x=3x+24.$ $\therefore 0=x+24$ or $x=-24.$

46. B $\frac{4}{5}r=\frac{3}{7}s+10=\frac{3}{7}\times 14+10=6+10=16.$
Then $4r=16\times 5$ or $r=4\times 5.$ $\therefore r=20.$

47. A $\frac{1}{r}=2s=2\frac{1}{r^2}$ or $\frac{1}{r}=\frac{2}{r^2}.$ $\therefore r^2=2r$ and $r=2.$

48. C $\frac{2a-1}{3}=4+\frac{3a-2}{2}$ or $\frac{4a-2}{6}=\frac{24}{6}+\frac{9a-6}{6}$ or $4a-2=24+9a-6.$
Then $-20=5a.$ $\therefore a=-4.$

49. C $x(b+a)=2ax.$ $\therefore b+a=2a$ or $b=a.$

50. C $\frac{t}{a}+\frac{2t}{3a}=5$ or $\frac{3t}{3a}+\frac{2t}{3a}=\frac{15a}{3a}$ or $3t+2t=15a.$ $\therefore t=\frac{15a}{5}=3a.$

Simultaneous Equations

51. E $x+y=9$
$2x-y=-6$

Add the equations: $3x = 3$. $\therefore x = 1$. Substitute back into the first equation: $1 + y = 9$. $\therefore y = 8$.

52. C $3x + 6y = -3$

$x + 5y = 2$

Divide the first equation by – 3 and add:

$$\begin{array}{r} -x - 2y = 1 \\ \underline{x + 5y = 2} \\ 3y = 3 \end{array} \qquad \therefore y = 1.$$

Substitute into the 2nd equation: $x = -3$. $\therefore xy = -3$.

53. B $5t = 3s$

$2t = s + 2$

From the 1st equation, $s = \frac{5t}{3}$. $\therefore 2t = \frac{5t}{3} + 2$.
Multiply all terms by 3: $6t = 5t + 6$. $\therefore t = 6$.

54. A $a - b = 3$

$a - 2b = 4$

Multiply the 2nd equation by – 1 and add:

$$\begin{array}{r} a - b = 3 \\ \underline{-a + 2b = -4} \\ b = -1 \end{array} \qquad \therefore a = 3 - 1 = 2. \qquad \therefore a + b = 2 - 1 = 1.$$

55. E $\frac{a}{2} + \frac{b}{3} = 1$ or $3a + 2b = 6$

$\frac{a}{3} - \frac{b}{2} = 1$ or $2a - 3b = 6$

Multiply 1st equation by 3, and 2nd equation by 2 and add:

$$\begin{array}{r} 9a + 6b = 18 \\ \underline{4a - 6b = 12} \\ 13a = 30 \end{array} \qquad \therefore a = \frac{30}{13}.$$

Quadratic Equations

56. D $a^2 - 2a + 3 = 2a^2 + \frac{1}{2}(4 - 4a)$ or $a^2 - 2a + 3 = 2a^2 + 2 - 2a$

or $0 = a^2 - 1$. $\therefore a^2 = 1$ $\therefore a = \pm 1$.

57. D $x+\frac{4}{x}=4$ or $\frac{x^2+4}{x}=4$ or $x^2+4=4x$
or $x^2-4x+4=0$. $\therefore (x-2)(x-2)=0$. $\therefore x=2$.

58. A $x^2-4x+3=0 = (x-3)(x-1)$. $\therefore x=3,1$.

59. B $x=y-1$, $y=t^2-t$ or $x=t^2-t-1=5$. $\therefore t^2-t-6=0$.
This is factored: $(t-3)(t+2)=0$. $\therefore t=3,-2$.

60. C $2x^2-3x-6=x\left(x-4+\frac{6}{x}\right)$ or $2x^2-3x-6=x^2-4x+6$ or $x^2+x-12=0$.
This is factored: $(x+4)(x-3)=0$. $\therefore x=3,-4$.

Percentages

61. D $36\%=0.36=\frac{36}{100}=\frac{4\times 9}{4\times 25}=\frac{9}{25}$.

62. B $\%\text{ increase}=\frac{345-300}{300}\times 100=\frac{45}{300}\times 100=15\%$.

63. C $\%\text{ markup}=\frac{10{,}000-x}{x}\times 100=20$. $\therefore \frac{10{,}000-x}{x}=0.2$
or $10{,}000-x=0.2x$ or $10{,}000=1.2x$. $\therefore x=\$8{,}333\frac{1}{3}$.

64. E $\%\text{ discount}=\frac{x-76}{x}\times 100=20$. $\therefore \frac{x-76}{x}=0.2$
or $x-76=0.2x$ or $0.8x=76$. $\therefore x=\$95$.

65. B $\%\text{ discount}=\frac{800-600}{800}\times 100=\frac{200}{800}\times 100=25\%$.

66. C No. of people in city $=\frac{2000}{0.25}=8000$. $\therefore 8000-2000=6000$.

67. B x = No. of people who use oil. $4x+x=5x$ = total number of people.

% people who use oil $=\frac{x}{5x}\times 100=20\%$.

68. A Area = length × width = lw. New area = $(l + .2\,l)(w-.1w) = 1.2\,l(.9w) = 1.08\,lw$.
$\frac{1.08\,lw-lw}{lw}\times 100=\frac{0.08\,lw}{lw}\times 100=8\%$. Or, we could just pick a 100 × 100 farm. The new dimensions are 120 × 90. Then
$\%\text{ increase}=\frac{120\times 90-100\times 100}{100\times 100}\times 100=\frac{10{,}800-10{,}000}{10{,}000}\times 100=\frac{800}{10{,}000}\times 100=8\%$.

Interest, Discount and Markup

69. D $I = PiT$. $75 = 2500i \times \frac{3}{12}$. $\therefore i = \frac{300}{2500} = .12$ or 12%.
Interest is always based on one year, unless otherwise stated. So, $T = \frac{3}{12} = \frac{1}{4}$ of a year.

70. B $I = PiT$. $200 = P \times .15 \times \frac{1}{12}$. $\therefore P = \frac{200 \times 12}{.15} = \frac{200 \times 12 \times 100}{15}$
$= 200 \times 4 \times 20 = \$16{,}000$.
Here, we used $T = 1/12$ of a year.

71. A % discount $= \frac{x - 3200}{x} = 0.2$. $\therefore x - 3200 = .2x$ or $0.8x = 3200$. $\therefore x = \$4000$.

72. C % discount $= \frac{150 - x}{150} = 0.3$. $\therefore 150 - x = 45$ or $x = \$105$.

73. B % markup $= \frac{x - 15}{15} = 2.00$. $\therefore x - 15 = 2 \times 15$ or $x = \$45$.

74. D % markup $= \frac{1500 - 900}{900} \times 100 = \frac{600}{900} \times 100 = \frac{60}{9} = 66\frac{2}{3}\%$.

Progressions

75. E This must be an arithmetic progression. The common difference is – 2. The 6 terms of the progression are 4, 2, 0, – 2, – 4, – 6. The 6th term is – 6.

76. D The common difference of this arithmetic progression is 1/4. The five terms are $1\frac{1}{2}, 1\frac{3}{4}, 2, 2\frac{1}{4}, 2\frac{1}{2}$. The sum is $1\frac{1}{2} + 1\frac{3}{4} + 2 + 2\frac{1}{4} + 2\frac{1}{2} = 10$.

77. D Six terms of the progression are 2, 1.6, 1.2, .8, .4, 0. The sum is
2 + 1.6 + 1.2 + .8 + .4 = 6.

78. B The interest on the first \$1000 is 1000 × .1 × 4 = \$400, on the second \$1000 it is \$300, the third, \$200, and the fourth, \$100. The interest alone is 400 + 300 + 200 + 100 = \$1000. She invested \$4000 in principal so the total value is 4000 + 1000 = \$5000.

79. A We look for a multiplying factor. Divide by 2: 16, 8, 4. The element is 8.

80. D Let x be the first element. Then $x, 2x, 4x, 8x$ represent the 4 years. The sum is $x + 2x + 4x + 8x = 15{,}000$ or $15x = 15{,}000$. $\therefore x = \$1000$. In the 4th year Darla earned $8x = 8 \times 1000 = \$8000$.

81. C The geometric progression is 1, 2, 4, 8, 16, 32, 64, 128. The sum is 1 + 2 + 4 + 8 + 16 + 32 + 64 + 128 = \$255.

Uniform Motion

82. A $D = VT$. $600 = V \times 7.5$. $\therefore V = \dfrac{600}{7.5} = 80$ mph.

83. C

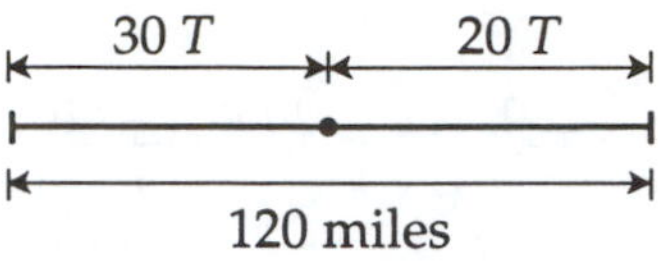

30 T | 20 T

120 miles

$50T = 120$. $\therefore T = 2\frac{2}{5}$ hours $= 2 + \frac{2}{5} \times 60 = 2$ hr $+ 24$ min.

6 a.m. + 2 hr + 24 min = 8:24 a.m.

84. B Kelvin's velocity is $\dfrac{y}{t/60}$ where the time in hours is $t/60$. Using $D = VT$ we have $x = \dfrac{60y}{t}T$. $\therefore T = \dfrac{xt}{60y}$.

85. E Sarah's velocity on a river flowing at 3 mph is $x + 3$, where x is her velocity in still water. Time is D/V so that $T = \dfrac{10}{x+3} = \dfrac{12}{x+4}$, or $10(x+4) = 12(x+3)$, or $10x + 40 = 12x + 36$. $\therefore 4 = 2x$ or $x = 2$ mph.

86. D If Ginger's time is T hours, Anette's time is $\left(T - \frac{15}{60}\right)$ hours. Then, using $D = VT$, $50T = 60\left(T - \frac{15}{60}\right)$ or $50T = 60T - 15$. $\therefore 10T = 15$ and $T = 1.5$ hours.

$D = 1.5 \times 50 = 75$ miles.

87. B

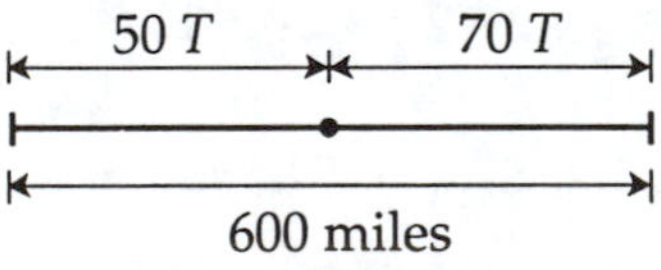

50 T | 70 T

600 miles

$50T + 70T = 600$. $\therefore 120T = 600$.

$T = 5$ hours. 8:00 a.m. + 5 hrs = 1 p.m.

Work

88. A Jeanne's typing rate is $1/T$ manuscripts/hr. In n hrs she can type a fraction of the manuscript equal to n/T.

89. C Lisa's rate is $1/24$ and Jon's is $1/36$. Together, using $W = 1$ job $= RT$,

$1 = \left(\dfrac{1}{24} + \dfrac{1}{36}\right)T$. That is $1 = \dfrac{36+24}{36 \times 24}T$ or $T = \dfrac{36 \times 24}{36+24}$

$= \dfrac{36 \times 2 \times 12}{12 \times 5} = \dfrac{72}{5} = 14\frac{2}{5}$ hrs.

90. D Larry's rate is 1/90 and Jim's is 1/60. They accomplished $\left(\frac{1}{90}+\frac{1}{60}\right)30=\frac{60+90}{60\times 90}\times 30=\frac{150}{2\times 90}=\frac{15}{18}$ of the job; 3/18 of the job remains. It takes Larry $\frac{3/18}{1/90}$ minutes longer, or 15 minutes. In all Larry works 30 + 15 = 45 minutes.

91. E Each fisherman can catch $\frac{500}{3\times 6}=\frac{500}{18}$ perch each hour. To catch 500 perch with 8 fisherman: $500=\left(\frac{500}{18}\times 8\right)T$. $\therefore T=\frac{18}{8}=2\frac{2}{8}$ hrs or $2\frac{1}{4}$ hrs.

92. E Anita's rate is $1/x$ and Paul's is $1/y$. Together their rate is $(1/x)+(1/y)$. Using $W=RT$ we have $1=\left(\frac{1}{x}+\frac{1}{y}\right)T$ or $1=\frac{y+x}{xy}T$. $\therefore T=\frac{xy}{x+y}$.

93. B Faye's rate is 1/6 and Greydon's is $1/x$. Together their rate is $(1/6)+(1/x)$. Using $W=RT$,

$$1=\left(\frac{1}{6}+\frac{1}{x}\right)4 \quad \text{or} \quad 1=\left(\frac{x+6}{6x}\right)4 \quad \text{or} \quad 6x=4x+24. \quad \therefore 2x=24 \quad \text{or} \quad x=12 \text{ hrs.}$$

Ratio and Proportion

94. C $\frac{x}{y}=11,\ \ x+y=72.\quad \therefore 11y+y=72 \ \text{ or } \ 12y=72.\quad \therefore y=6, x=66.$

95. B $\frac{1\frac{20}{60}}{2}=\frac{1\frac{1}{3}}{2}=\frac{\frac{4}{3}}{2}=\frac{4}{6}=\frac{2}{3}.$

96. E $\frac{120}{2\frac{1}{2}}=\frac{192}{x}.\quad \therefore x=\frac{192}{120}\times 2\frac{1}{2}=\frac{32}{20}\times 2\frac{1}{2}=\frac{8}{5}\times\frac{5}{2}=4.$

97. A $\frac{600}{600+800}\times 11{,}200=\frac{3}{7}\times 11{,}200=\frac{3}{1}\times 1{,}600=\$4800.$

98. B The investments are \$3000 : 9000 : (13/2) × 3000. The sum is

3000 + 9000 + 19,500 = \$31,500

99. B $\frac{6}{10}=\frac{x}{120}.\quad \therefore x=\frac{120\times 6}{10}=72$ feet.

100. D $\frac{1}{10}=\frac{1/4}{x}.\quad \therefore x=\frac{1}{4}\times 10=2.5$ feet.

Inequalities

101. D Try $x=-2$; which is greatest, $-8, -2, -1/2, 1/4, -1/8$? The positive value is greatest, i.e., 1/4 is greatest.

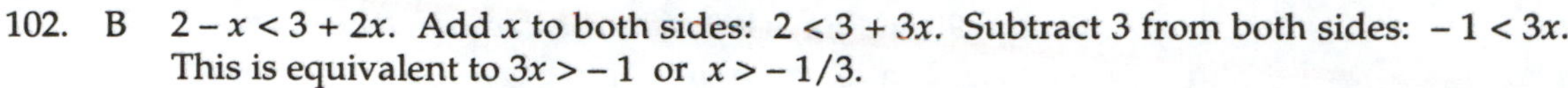

102. B $2 - x < 3 + 2x$. Add x to both sides: $2 < 3 + 3x$. Subtract 3 from both sides: $-1 < 3x$. This is equivalent to $3x > -1$ or $x > -1/3$.

103. A $r < s < t$. $\therefore r < t$.

104. A $a^2 - 2b^2 > (a - b)(a + 2b)$ or $a^2 - 2b^2 > a^2 + 2ab - ab - 2b^2$. Then $0 > ab$ or $ab < 0$.

105. C Add the two inequalities

$$\begin{array}{r} x > a \\ \underline{y > b} \\ x + y > a + b \end{array}$$

106. E $x^2 + 6x > 7$ is equivalent to $x^2 + 6x - 7 > 0$ or $(x + 7)(x - 1) > 0$. $\therefore x > 1$ or $x < -7$. The appropriate signs are determined by substituting into the original inequality.

Or, complete the square:

$$x^2 + 6x + 9 > 7 + 9$$

$$(x + 3)^2 > 16. \qquad \therefore x + 3 > +4 \quad \therefore x > 1$$

$$x + 3 < -4 \quad \therefore x < -7$$

107. C $x + y + z = 180°$. If $z \geq 100°$, then $x + y = 180 - z \leq 180 - 100$ or $x + y \leq 80°$.

7.3 Geometry

Geometry is the study of points, lines and planes; it allows us to calculate angles, lengths, areas and volumes. You may recall that you were required to prove theorems in your study of geometry. In this review, the proof of a theorem will not be considered; it is not included in the GMAT. We will focus our attention on angles, lengths and areas of triangles, rectangles and circles—and areas and volumes of rectangular solids and circular cylinders.

Angles and Lines

An *angle* is formed when two line segments intersect. The point of intersection is the *vertex* and the two lines form the *sides* of the angle. The angle is designated in a number of ways. It is $\angle BAC$ where the middle letter is the vertex, $\angle A$ where A is the vertex, or $\angle x$ where x is located inside the angle.

There are special kinds of angles. *Acute angles* are less than 90°, *obtuse angles* are greater than 90°, and *right angles* are exactly 90°. *Complementary angles* are two angles that sum to 90°; *supplementary angles* are two angles that sum to 180° (or a straight line).

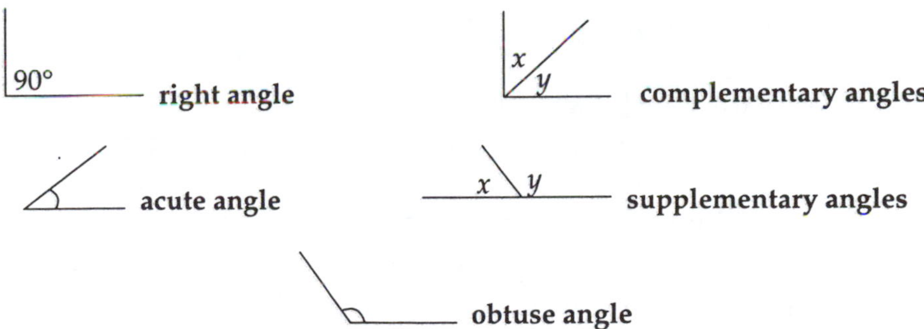

When two lines intersect, they form four angles: angles next to each other are supplementary angles, and angles opposite each other are *vertical angles*. Vertical angles are equal to each other. *Adjacent angles* have the same vertex and a common side. Note that in the following diagram angles 1 and 4, 2 and 4, 2 and 3, and 1 and 3 are adjacent angles.

4 1
2 3

$$\angle 1 = \angle 2$$
$$\angle 3 = \angle 4$$
$$\angle 1 + \angle 4 = 180°$$
$$\angle 2 + \angle 4 = 180°$$

Two parallel lines never intersect. If a third line, a *transversal,* intersects two parallel lines eight angles are formed. *Corresponding angles* are equal: 1 and 5, 2 and 6, 3 and 7, and 4 and 8. *Alternate interior angles* are equal: 3 and 6, and 4 and 5. The symbol $\|$ means *is parallel to*: $m \| n$.

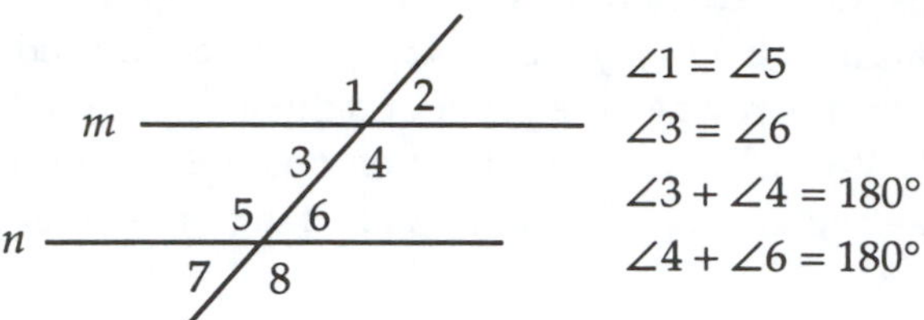

Two lines that intersect such that all four angles are equal are *perpendicular* and all four angles are right angles. A small box in a corner indicates an angle of 90°, a right angle. The symbol $\perp$ means *is perpendicular to* : $m \perp n$.

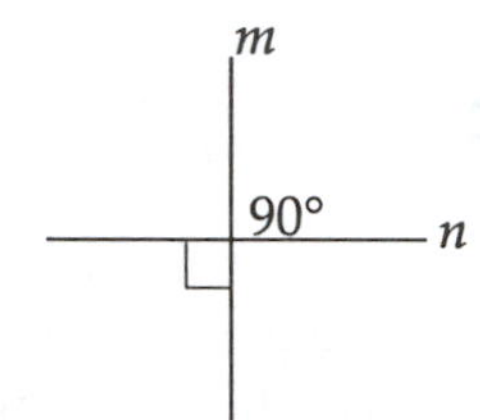

Example 1

An incident ray strikes a flat surface and is reflected at the same angle. If the angle between the reflected ray and the incident ray is three times the angle of incidence, what is the angle of incidence?

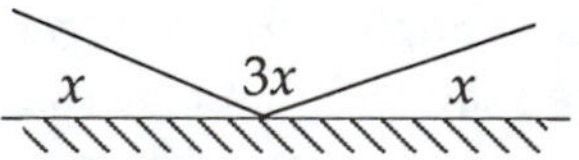

Solution. The above sketch of the incident ray and the reflected ray is helpful. If x is the angle of incidence, then

$$x + x + 3x = 180°$$

since a flat surface is a straight line of 180°. This is

$$5x = 180°. \qquad \therefore x = 36°$$

Example 2

If the complement of an angle is one quarter of its supplement, what is the angle?

Solution. Let x be the angle. Its complement y is

$$y = 90 - x$$

Its supplement z is

$$z = 180 - x$$

If $y = z/4$, we have

$$90 - x = \frac{180 - x}{4}$$

This is solved as follows:

$$360 - 4x = 180 - x$$

$$180 = 3x. \qquad \therefore x = 60°$$

Triangles

A triangle has three sides and three angles; the sum of its three angles is 180°. There are three triangles that are particularly important to us. An *isosceles triangle* has two equal sides; the angles opposite the equal sides are also equal. All three sides of an *equilateral triangle* are equal; each of its three angles are 60°. A *right triangle* is a triangle that has a 90° angle; the *Pythagorean Theorem* states that $c^2 = a^2 + b^2$, where c is its *hypotenuse* and a and b are its *legs*. The hypotenuse is always opposite the 90° angle and the legs are always shorter than the hypotenuse.

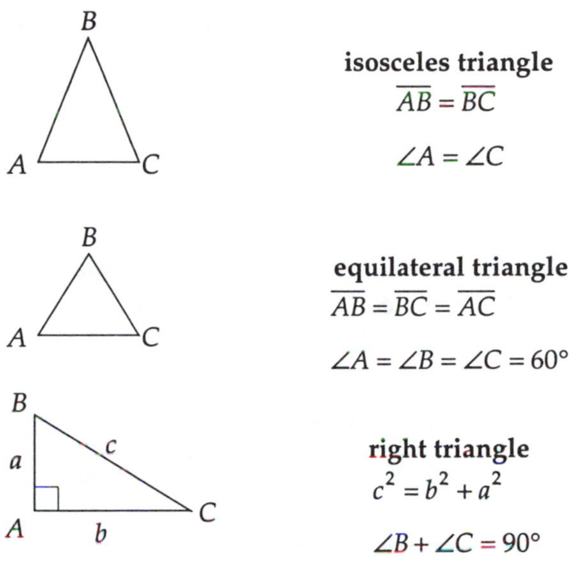

There are several special right triangles that show up often on the GMAT. The 3-4-5 triangle may be the most popular; note that the Pythagorean theorem is satisfied since $5^2 = 3^2 + 4^2$. The 5-12-13 triangle surfaces occasionally, also. The second most popular triangle is the 30°-60°-90° triangle because the ratio of its short leg to its hypotenuse is 1 : 2. The 45°-45°-90° triangle has equal legs and is also encountered quite often.

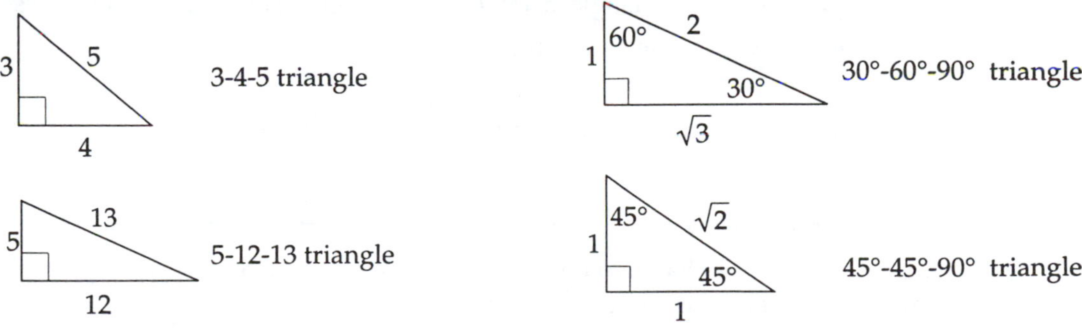

A triangle may not have the actual dimensions shown above, but may have a multiple of the dimensions. For example, if two legs of a right triangle have dimensions of 9 and 12, their ratio is 3 : 4 so the triangle is a 3-4-5 triangle and the hypotenuse is 3 × 5 = 15, as shown below.

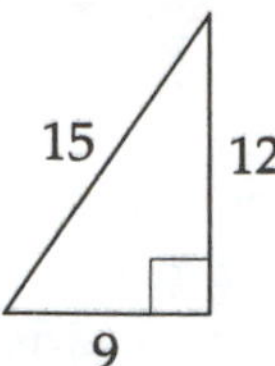

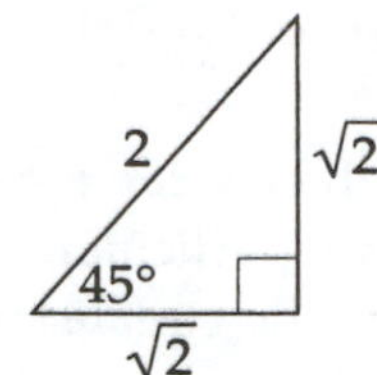

If the hypotenuse of a 45°-45°-90° triangle has dimension 2 then the legs have dimension $\sqrt{2}$ larger than the base 45°-45°-90° triangle, as shown above.

Example 1

For the triangle shown, find L.

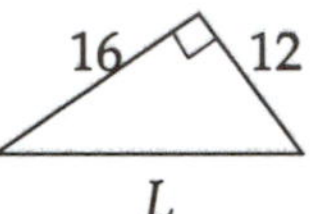

Solution. The small box in the corner signifies a right triangle. The ratio of the two legs is $12/16 = 3/4$. It is a 3-4-5 triangle. It is 4 times the base 3-4-5 triangle; consequently, its hypotenuse L is

$$L = 4 \times 5 = 20$$

Or, we could have used the Pythagorean Theorem to obtain

$$L = \sqrt{12^2 + 16^2} = \sqrt{144 + 256} = \sqrt{400} = 20$$

Example 2

Calculate the length L for the triangle shown.

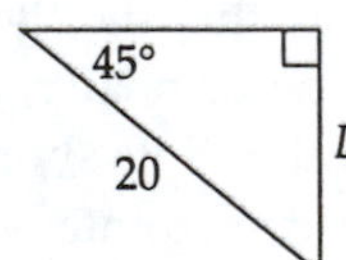

Solution. This is a right triangle, a 45°-45°-90° triangle. The length of a leg of such a triangle is $\frac{1}{\sqrt{2}}$ times the hypotenuse. This gives

$$L = \frac{1}{\sqrt{2}} \times 20 = \frac{20\sqrt{2}}{\sqrt{2}\sqrt{2}} = \frac{20\sqrt{2}}{2} = 10\sqrt{2}$$

Example 3

An isosceles triangle has two equal angles of 30°. The side connecting the 30° angles has length 4. How long are the equal sides?

Solution. A sketch of the triangle is always helpful. Let x be the unknown length. Divide the isosceles triangle into 2 right triangles. The ratio of the side adjacent to the 30° angle and

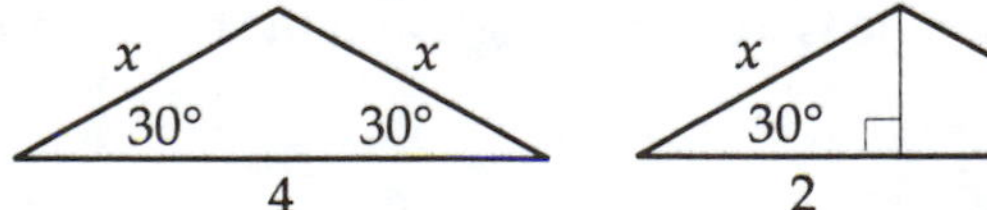

the hypotenuse is $\sqrt{3} : 2$. Hence,

$$\frac{\sqrt{3}}{2} = \frac{2}{x}, \qquad x = \frac{4}{\sqrt{3}} \quad \text{or} \quad x = \frac{4\sqrt{3}}{3}.$$

Example 4

A triangle has two angles of 45° and 75°. The side opposite the 45° angle has length 6. What is the length of the side opposite the 75° angle?

Solution. Sketch the triangle. The remaining angle is 180 – (75 + 45) = 60°. Form two right triangles and label the unknowns x, y, z. The side adjacent to the 60° angle is 1/2 the hypotenuse.

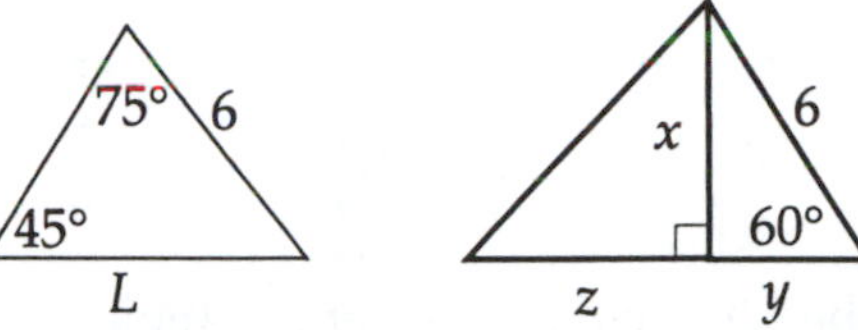

Hence, $y = 3$. The side opposite the 60° angle is $x = 3\sqrt{3}$ (the triangle is 3 times as big as the base 30°-60°-90° triangle). Since the legs of a 45°-45°-90° triangle are equal, $z = x = 3\sqrt{3}$. The length L is then

$$L = z + y = 3\sqrt{3} + 3 = 3\left(\sqrt{3} + 1\right)$$

Circles

The diameter d of a circle is twice the radius r. Its circumference is πd or $2\pi r$. A *central angle* has its vertex at the center of a circle and its measure equals the measure of the arc it intercepts (in degrees). For example, if $\angle AOB = 60°$,

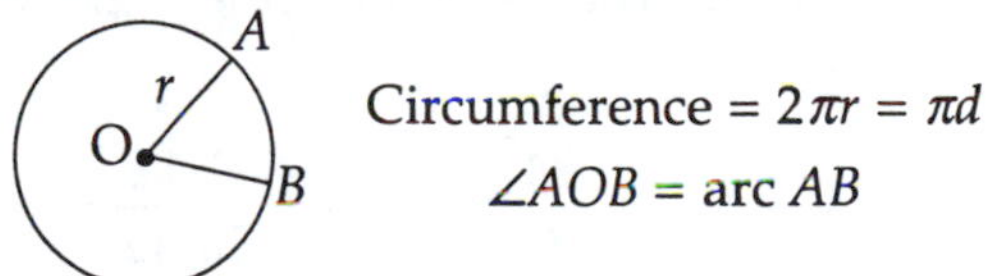

then the measure of arc AB is 60°, or $\frac{60}{360} = \frac{1}{6}$ of the circle's circumference. An *inscribed angle* has its vertex on the circle itself; and its measure is $\frac{1}{2}$ of the measure of the arc it intercepts, that is, in the diagram below, $\angle ACB = \frac{1}{2}\,\text{arc}AB$. A line that just touches a circle is called a *tangent*. It is perpendicular to the radius drawn to the point of touching.

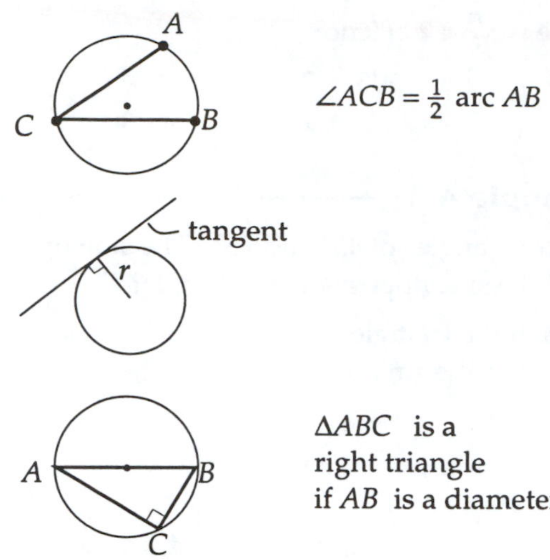

A triangle inscribed in a circle is a right triangle if one of its sides is a diameter. Obviously, $\angle C$ has its vertex on the circle, and it intercepts half of the circle so that $\angle C = \frac{180}{2}^\circ = 90°$.

Example 1

What arc length is intercepted by a central angle of 42° on a circle of radius = 12?

Solution. The 42° central angle intercepts $\frac{42}{360}$ of the circle. The circumference is $2\pi r = 2\pi \times 12 = 24\pi$. The arc length is

$$\text{arc length} = \frac{42}{360} \times 24\pi = \frac{7 \cdot 6}{12 \cdot 30} \times 12 \cdot 2 \times \frac{22}{7} = \frac{44}{5} = 8.8$$

where $\pi = 3.14 \cong \frac{22}{7}$.

Example 2

What arc length is intercepted by an inscribed angle of 42° on a circle with $r = 12$?

Solution. The 42° inscribed angle intercepts $\frac{1}{2}(\text{arc}°)$ or arc° = 84°, that is, $\frac{84}{360}$ of the circle is intercepted by the angle. The circumference is $2\pi r = 24\pi$ so that the arc length is, using $\pi = \frac{22}{7}$,

$$\text{arc length} = \frac{84}{360} \times 24\pi = \frac{7 \cdot 12}{30 \cdot 12} \times 6 \times 4 \times \frac{22}{7} = \frac{88}{5} = 17.6$$

Example 3

A triangle is inscribed in a circle with shorter sides 6 and 8 units long. If the longer side is a diameter, find the length of the diameter.

Solution. A triangle so inscribed (with one side a diameter) is a right triangle. Consequently,

$$d^2 = 6^2 + 8^2 = 36 + 64 = 100$$
$$\therefore d = 10$$

Perimeters and Areas

The *perimeter* of a figure is the distance around the figure. The perimeter P and area A of common figures are shown.

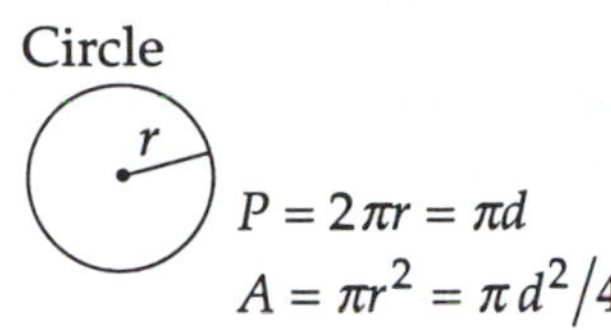

$P = 2\pi r = \pi d$
$A = \pi r^2 = \pi d^2/4$

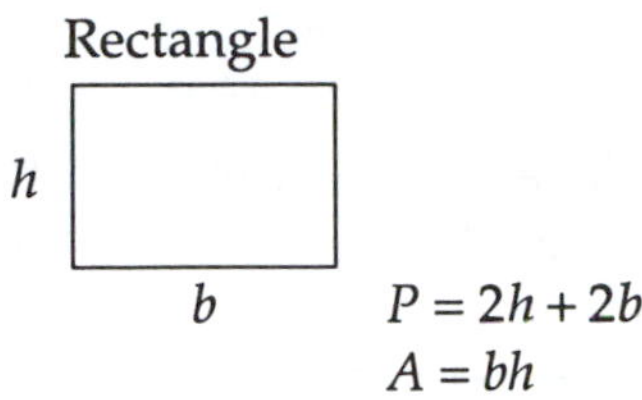

$P = 2h + 2b$
$A = bh$

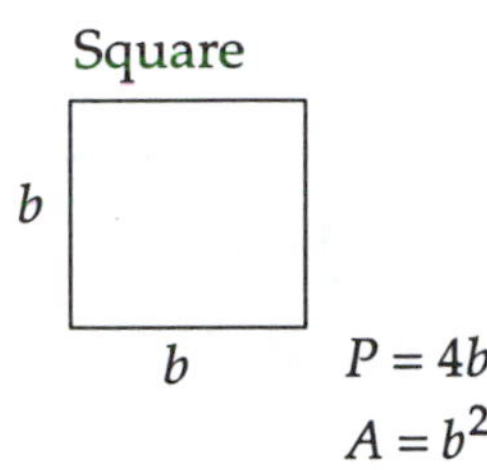

$P = 4b$
$A = b^2$

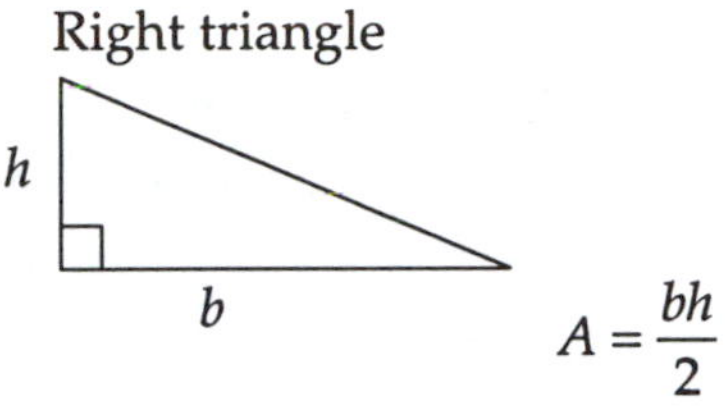

$A = \frac{bh}{2}$

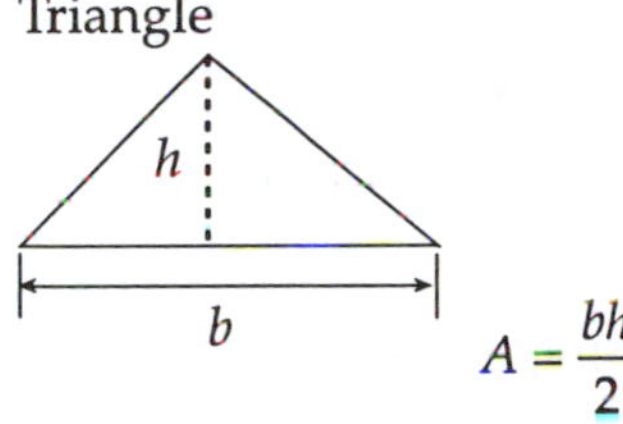

$A = \frac{bh}{2}$

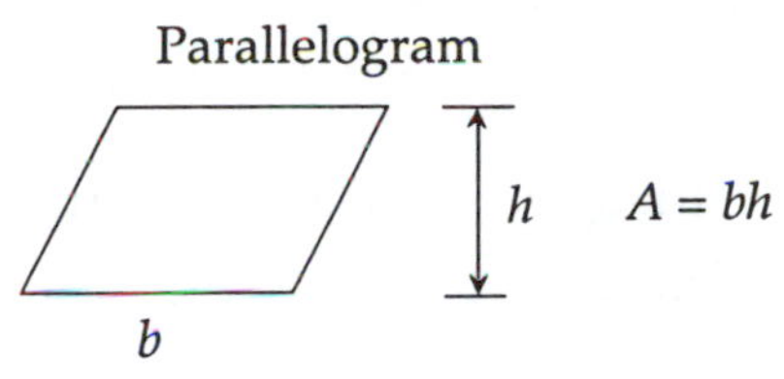

$A = bh$

Example 1

What is the radius of a circle if its perimeter is numerically equal to twice its area?

Solution. The perimeter is the same as the circumference = $2\pi r$. The area is πr^2, so that

$$2\pi r = 2\pi r^2. \qquad \therefore r = 1$$

Example 2

A gallon of paint covers 400 ft² of wall area. How many gallons are required to paint a building with perimeter 200 ft and height 10 ft?

Solution. The perimeter is the distance around the building, that is, the length of the rectangles that makes up its sides. Since each rectangular side is assumed to be 10 ft high, the total area is

$$A = bh = 200 \times 10 = 2000 \text{ ft}^2$$

The number of gallons is

$$\text{No. of gallons} = \frac{2000}{400} = 5$$

Example 3

An automobile travels 2 miles. How many rotations does a 15-inch radius tire make?

Solution. The circumference of a tire is $2\pi r = 2\pi \times 15 = 30\pi$ inches or $\frac{30\pi}{12}$ feet.

$$\text{No. of rotations} = \frac{2 \times 5280}{30\pi/12} = \frac{2 \times 5280 \times 12}{30\pi} = \frac{5280 \times 12 \times 7}{15 \times 22} = \frac{1056 \times 2 \times 7}{11} = 1344$$

In the above, first we simplified by canceling out common factors and then multiplied and divided. It is important to first simplify to save time in the final step.

Example 4

A square is inscribed in a circle of radius 10. Determine the ratio of the area of the circle to the area of the square.

Solution. First, sketch the figure. The area of the circle is $\pi r^2 = 100\pi$. The diameter is 20, which is also equal to the diagonal of the square, which is also the hypotenuse of a right

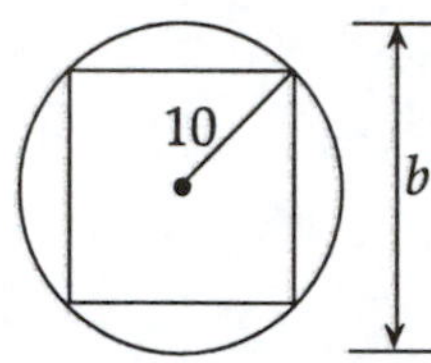

triangle. The legs of the triangle are equal so that $b = \frac{20}{\sqrt{2}}$ (or $b^2 + b^2 = 20^2$). The area of the square is $b^2 = \frac{20^2}{2} = 200$. The ratio of the areas is

$$\frac{\text{Area circle}}{\text{Area square}} = \frac{100\pi}{200} = \frac{\pi}{2}.$$

Solids

There are two solids that interest us in preparing for the GMAT. They are the rectangular solid (a box) and a circular cylinder. A *cube* is a special rectangular box whose sides are all equal. The volume of a box is the product of its three sides: $V = bwh$. The volume of a circular cylinder is the area of the base times the height: $V = \pi r^2 h$.

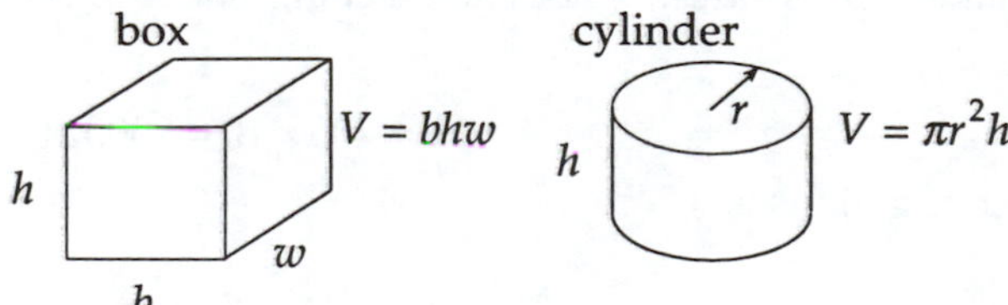

Example 1

How many liters does it take to fill a box that is 2 m by 20 cm by 20 mm?

Solution. There are 1000 liters in a cubic meter. Hence, we find the volume in cubic meters and multiply by 1000. The volume is

$$V = bwh$$
$$= 2 \times 0.2 \times 0.02 = 0.008 \text{ m}^3$$
$$1000 \frac{\text{liters}}{\text{m}^3} \times 0.008 \text{ m}^3 = 8 \text{ liters}$$

Example 2

A large box measuring 20 ft $\times$ 10 ft and 8 ft high is to be painted, including the top. If one quart covers 100 ft^2 of area, how many quarts are required?

Solution. The surface area includes 5 rectangles: top—20 × 10, 2 sides—20 × 8, and 2 more sides—10 × 8. The total area is

$$\text{Area} = 20 \times 10 + 2 \times 20 \times 8 + 2 \times 10 \times 8 = 680 \text{ ft}^2$$

The required number of quarts is

$$\text{No. of quarts} = \frac{680}{100} = 6.8 \quad \text{or} \quad 7 \text{ quarts}$$

Note: it is assumed that the bottom of the box is not painted.

Example 3

It takes about $7\frac{1}{2}$ gallons to fill a volume of one cubic foot. How many gallons are needed to fill a cylinder 2 ft high and 28 inches in radius?

Solution. The volume of a cylinder is the area of its circular base times its height:

$$V = \pi r^2 h$$
$$= \frac{22}{7} \times \left(\frac{28}{12}\right)^2 \times 2 = \frac{11}{1} \times \frac{4}{6} \times \frac{4 \times 7}{4 \times 3} \times 2 = \frac{308}{9}$$

The number of gallons is

$$\text{No. of gallons} = \frac{308}{9} \div 7\frac{1}{2} = \frac{308}{9} \div \frac{15}{2}$$
$$= \frac{308}{9} \times \frac{2}{15} = \frac{616}{135} = 4.56$$

Rectangular Coordinates

A point P is positioned relative to two perpendicular lines, called the *coordinate axes*. The perpendicular distance from the y-axis to point P is the x-coordinate of P called the *abscissa;* the perpendicular distance from the x-axis to point P is the y-coordinate of P called the *ordinate*. The abscissa x and ordinate y form an ordered pair (x, y). Usually the unit of length for the x-coordinate and y-coordinate are the same.

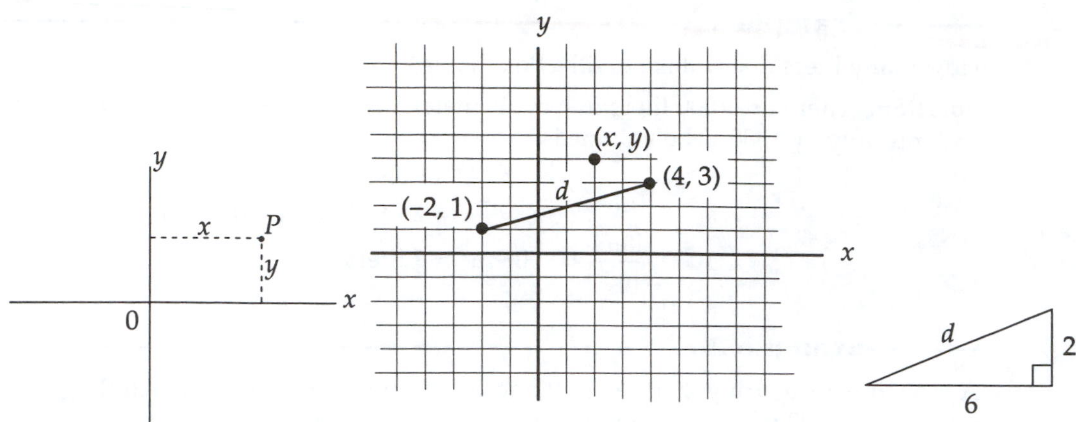

Often, a grid is used to display points relative to the coordinate axes. The point (4, 3) is located 4 units from the y-axis to the right, and 3 units above the x-axis; the point (– 2, 1) is 2 units to the left of the y-axis and 1 unit above the x-axis. The distance d between the two points can be found by the Pythagorean Theorem. The horizontal leg is the total distance in the x-direction: $4 - (-2) = 6$; the vertical leg is the distance in the y-direction: $3 - 1 = 2$. The distance d is then $\sqrt{6^2 + 2^2} = \sqrt{40} = 2\sqrt{10}$.

Example 1

Three corners of a rectangle are at (3, 4), (– 5, 4), and (3, – 2). What are the coordinates of the fourth corner? What is the length of a diagonal?

Solution. A sketch of the three points is quite helpful. The coordinates of the fourth corner are obvious: (–5, –2).

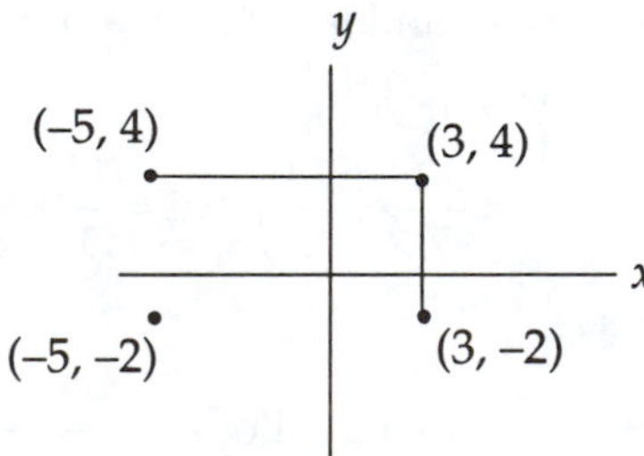

The diagonal connects (– 5, – 2) and (3, 4). Its legs are of length $3 - (-5) = 8$ and $4 - (-2) = 6$. The length of the diagonal is

$$\text{length of diagonal} = \sqrt{8^2 + 6^2} = \sqrt{100} = 10$$

Example 2

A square has two corners of a diagonal at (6, 8) and (2, 4). What is its area?

Solution. The difference in the x-direction is $6 - 2 = 4$ and in the y-direction $8 - 4 = 4$. The sides are both of length 4 so that the area is

$$A = 4 \times 4 = 16$$

Practice Problems

—Geometry—

Angles and Lines

1. If the supplement of an angle is 3 times its complement, what is the angle?

   A) 45° B) 50° C) 60° D) 40° E) 30°

2. Find the angle whose supplement minus twice its complement is 60°?

   A) 30° B) 40° C) 45° D) 50° E) 60°

3. Compute the value of $x - y$.

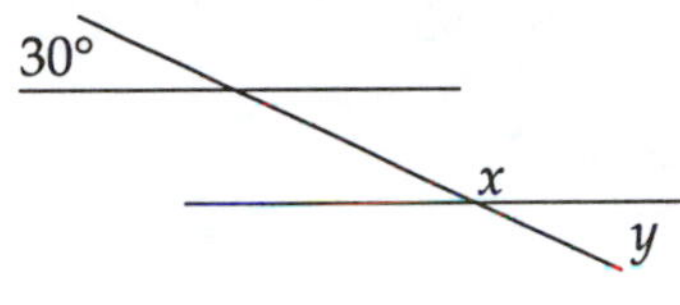

   A) 60° B) 90° C) 100° D) 120° E) 135°

4. What is the value of x?

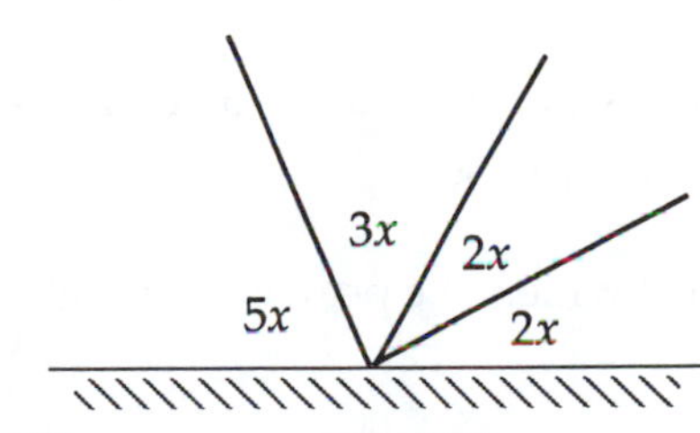

   A) 30° B) 25° C) 20° D) 15° E) 10°

5. If line $m \perp$ line n, what is x?

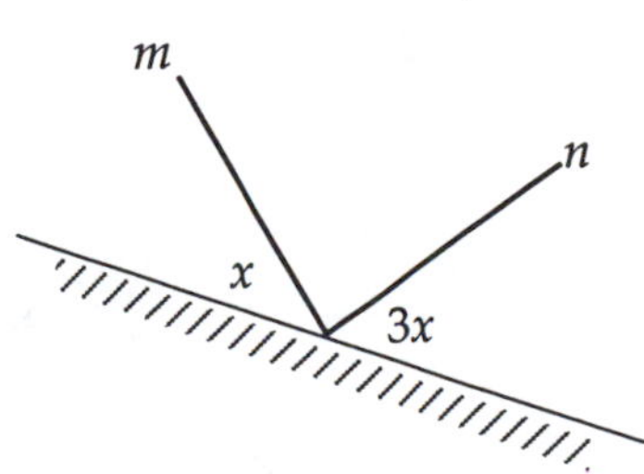

   A) 10° B) $15\frac{1}{2}$° C) 20° D) $22\frac{1}{2}$° E) 30°

6. Given line $m \perp$ line n. Find x.

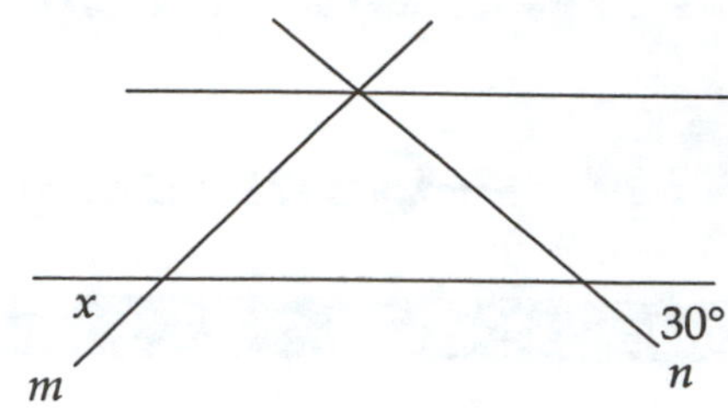

A) 60° B) 50° C) 45° D) 40° E) 30°

7. What is the angle x?

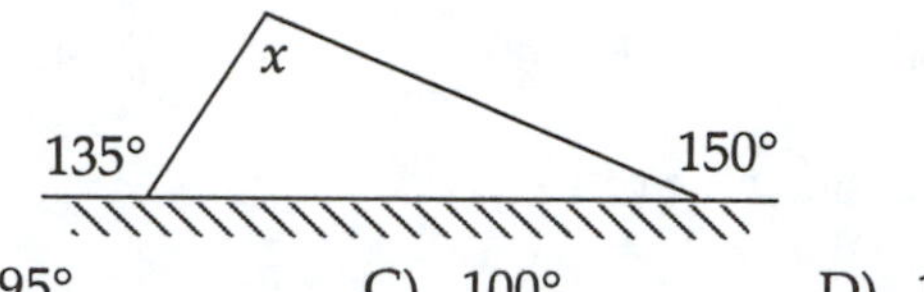

A) 90° B) 95° C) 100° D) 105° E) 110°

8. What is the value of x?

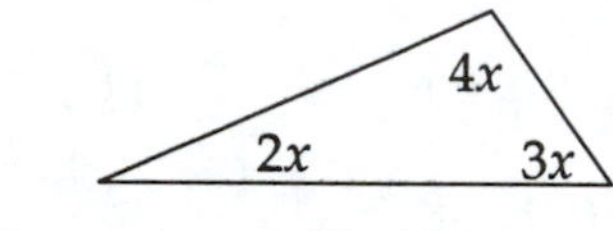

A) 10° B) 15° C) 20° D) 25° E) 30°

9. In a triangle ABC, sides AB and BC are equal. Also, $\angle B = 100°$. Find $\angle A$.

A) 40° B) 50° C) 60° D) 70° E) 80°

10. A house is 40 feet wide. The peak is 15 feet above the base. Find L.

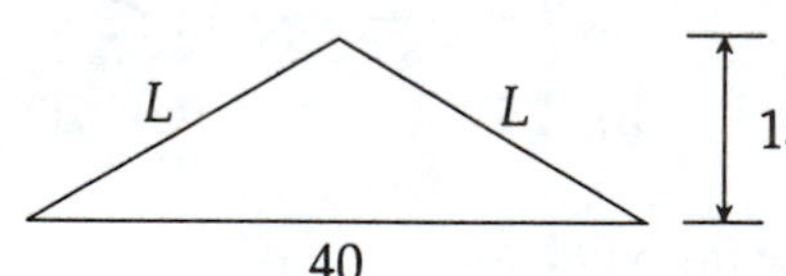

A) 20 B) $22\frac{1}{2}$ C) 25 D) $27\frac{1}{2}$ E) 30

11. Find L.

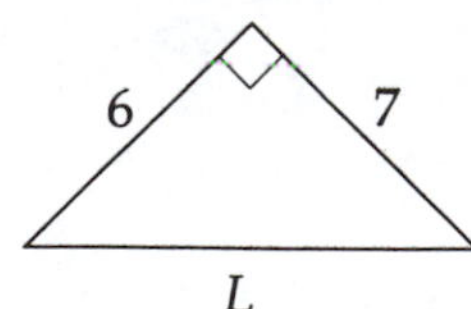

A) $\sqrt{13}$ B) $\sqrt{90}$ C) $\sqrt{85}$ D) 8 E) 9

12. What is the distance AC across the lake?

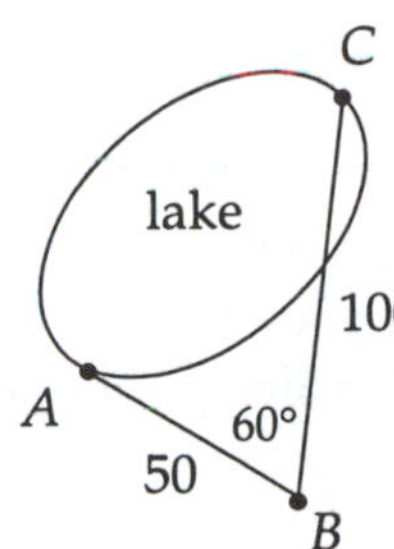

A) 85 B) $50\sqrt{2}$ C) $60\sqrt{2}$ D) $50\sqrt{3}$ E) 80

13. The sides of a rectangle are 6 feet and 8 feet. How long is a diagonal?

A) $8\frac{1}{2}$ B) 9 C) $9\frac{1}{2}$ D) 10 E) $10\frac{1}{2}$

14. A 40-foot rope, taut and fastened to the ground, is attached to the top of a 32-foot vertical wall. How far from the base is the rope fastened to the ground?

A) 22 B) 24 C) 26 D) 28 E) 30

15. The hypotenuse of an isosceles, right triangle measures 10 feet. How long is one of the legs?

A) 8 B) $5\sqrt{3}$ C) $6\sqrt{2}$ D) 7 E) $5\sqrt{2}$

16. Calculate the distance x.

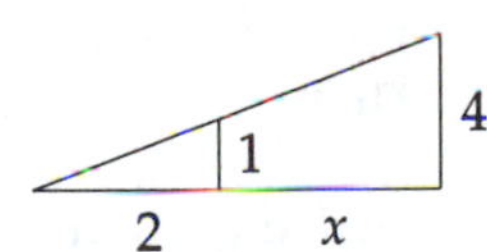

A) 2 B) 3 C) 4 D) 5 E) 6

17. A boy rides a bike 3 miles north from his house, then 2 miles east, then 5 miles north, then 4 miles east. How far is he from his house (the way the crow flies)?

A) 8 B) 9 C) 10 D) 11 E) 12

Circles

18. A central angle intercepts an arc length of 11 inches on a 14-inch-diameter circle. What is the measure of the angle?

A) 30° B) 45° C) 60° D) 90° E) 120°

19. A central angle in a circle is 60°. If the radius is 6, what is the length of the arc opposite the 60° angle?

A) π B) 2π C) 3π D) 4π E) 5π

20. A straight cut 8 inches long is made by a chain saw in an 8-inch-radius tree. What is the measure of the arc, in degrees, cut by the saw?

A) 30° B) 45° C) 60° D) 90° E) 120°

21. Find one of the angles made by the hands of a clock at 5:00.

A) 120° B) 130° C) 140° D) 145° E) 150°

22. Find one of the angles made by the hands of a clock at 1:40.

A) 200° B) 190° C) 185° D) 180° E) 160°

23. A square is inscribed in a 20-inch-diameter circle. What is the length of a side?

A) $10\sqrt{2}$ B) 10 C) $9\sqrt{2}$ D) 9 E) $8\sqrt{2}$

24. A square with diagonal length 20 circumscribes a circle. What is the diameter of the circle?

A) $10\sqrt{2}$ B) 10 C) $5\sqrt{2}$ D) 9 E) $8\sqrt{2}$

Perimeters and Areas

25. If a rectangle has a diagonal of length 10 and a side of length 6, what is the area of the rectangle?

A) 60 B) 56 C) 50 D) 48 E) 40

26. If the isosceles triangle has a height of 10, what is its area?

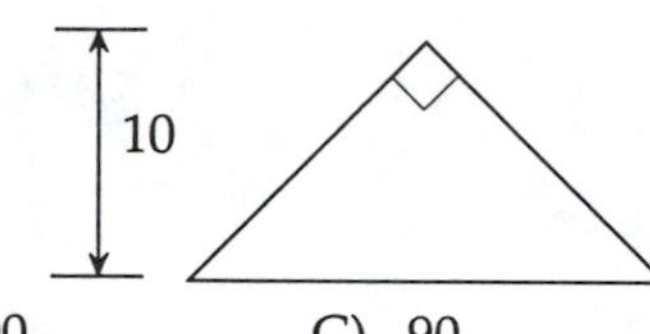

A) 120 B) 100 C) 90 D) 80 E) 60

27. What is the area of the shaded portion?

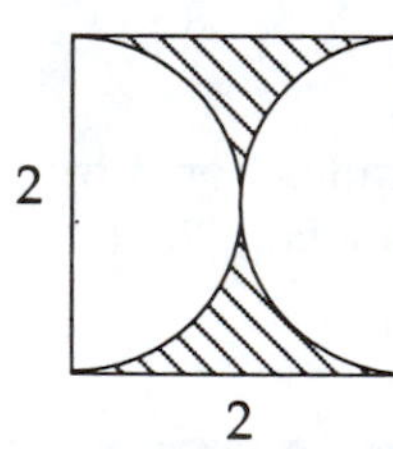

A) $2 - \pi$ B) $4 - 2\pi$ C) $4 - 4\pi$ D) $4 - \pi$ E) π

28. Find the area of the shaded portion.

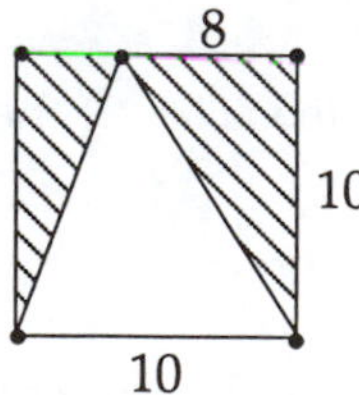

A) 70 B) 65 C) 60 D) 5 E) 50

29. How many 9-inch × 9-inch tiles are needed to tile the room? Dimensions are in feet.

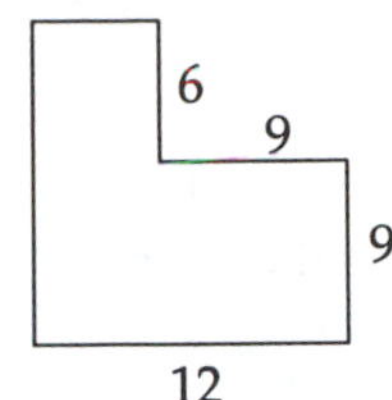

A) 224 B) 240 C) 250 D) 265 E) 270

30. A circle of radius r circumscribes a square. What is the area inside the circle but outside the square?

A) $r^2(\pi - 1)$ B) $r^2(\pi - 2)$ C) $r^2(\pi - 3)$
D) $r^2(\pi - 4)$ E) $r^2(\pi - 8)$

31. The area of a circle of radius r is twice the area of a square with side length b. What is the ratio r/b?

A) $\sqrt{\pi/2}$ B) $2/\sqrt{\pi}$ C) $\sqrt{\pi}/2$ D) $2/\pi$ E) $\sqrt{2/\pi}$

32. How many times could a 22-foot-long string wrap around a 1-foot-diameter tree?

A) 3 B) 4 C) 5 D) 6 E) 7

Solids

33. The surface area of a cube is 24 square feet. What is its volume in cubic feet?

A) 4 B) 6 C) 8 D) 10 E) 12

34. The end of a box is a 2 ft × 2 ft square. If the volume of the box is numerically equal to $\frac{1}{4}$ of its surface area, what is its length?

A) $\frac{1}{2}$ B) 1 C) $1\frac{1}{2}$ D) 2 E) 4

35. A box has dimensions w by w by h. The ratio of its volume to the volume of a box with dimensions $2w$ by $3w$ by $2h$ is

A) 1 : 7 B) 2 : 15 C) 3 : 4 D) 1 : 12 E) 1 : 15

36. A dump truck has a cubical box trailer. If each dimension is doubled on a new truck, what is the ratio of the volume of the new truck to the volume of the truck?

A) 2 B) 4 C) 6 D) 8 E) 10

37. A cube 10 inches on a side is composed of smaller cubes 1 inch on each side. How many small cubes do not have at least one side on the exterior of the large cube?

A) 488 B) 512 C) 600 D) 640 E) 720

38. The lateral surface area (exclude the end areas) of a cylinder is numerically equal to twice the volume. What is its diameter?

A) 1 B) 2 C) 3 D) 4 E) 5

39. A cylinder of diameter 1 and height 1 is inserted into a box with dimensions $1\times1\times1$. What volume is outside the cylinder but inside the box?

A) $1-\pi$ B) $1-\frac{\pi}{2}$ C) $1-\frac{\pi}{4}$ D) $1-\frac{\pi}{6}$ E) $1-\frac{\pi}{8}$

Rectangular Coordinates

40. What kind of triangle connects the three points (3, 4), (– 6, 4), (3, – 4)?

A) right B) isosceles C) scalene D) equilateral E) 3-4-5

41. How long is the line that connects the two points (8, 4) and (– 4, – 5)?

A) 10 B) 12 C) 13 D) 14 E) 15

42. What are the coordinates of the midpoint of the line segment?

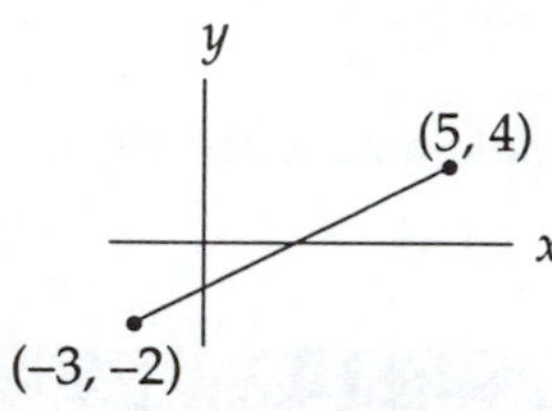

A) (2, 0) B) (1, 1) C) (0, 2) D) (2, 2) E) (1, 2)

43. The area of the triangle is 20. What are the coordinates of *P*?

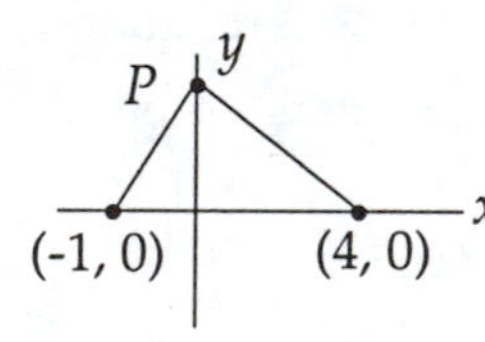

A) (0, 8) B) (0, 4) C) (4, 0) D) (8, 0) E) (0, 6)

44. Calculate the area of the circle with center at (3,1).

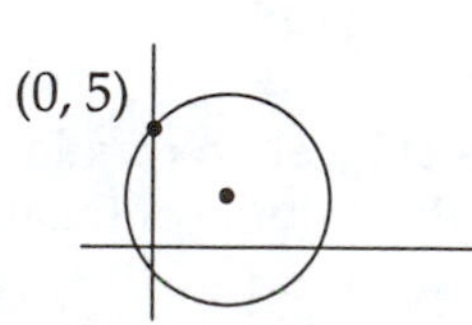

A) 16π B) 18π C) 20π D) 21π E) 25π

45. The area of the figure formed by connecting the four points (4, 6), (– 6, 6), (– 6, – 4), and (4, – 4) is

A) 40 B) 60 C) 80 D) 100 E) 120

Answers to Practice Problems

—Geometry—

Angles, Lines	Triangles	Circles	Perimeter and Areas	Solids	Rectangular Coordinates
1. A	**7.** D	**18.** D	**25.** D	**33.** C	**40.** A
2. E	**8.** C	**19.** B	**26.** B	**34.** B	**41.** E
3. D	**9.** A	**20.** C	**27.** D	**35.** D	**42.** B
4. D	**10.** C	**21.** E	**28.** E	**36.** D	**43.** A
5. D	**11.** C	**22.** B	**29.** A	**37.** B	**44.** E
6. A	**12.** D	**23.** A	**30.** B	**38.** B	**45.** D
	13. D	**24.** A	**31.** E	**39.** C	
	14. B		**32.** E		
	15. E				
	16. E				
	17. C				

Explanations to the Answers

—Geometry—

Angles and Lines

1. A Let x be the angle. Then its supplement is $(180 - x)$ and its complement is $(90 - x)$:
$180 - x = 3(90 - x)$. $\therefore 180 - x = 270 - 3x$ or $2x = 90$. $\therefore x = 45°$.

2. E Let x be the angle. Then its supplement is $(180 - x)$ and its complement is $(90 - x)$:
$180 - x - 2(90 - x) = 60$. $\therefore 180 - x - 180 + 2x = 60$ or $x = 60°$.

3. D $z = 30°$ (vertical angles), $x + z = 180°$ (supplementary angles).
$y = z = 30°$ (corresponding angles), $\therefore x = 180 - 30 = 150°$.
$\therefore x - y = 150 - 30 = 120°$.

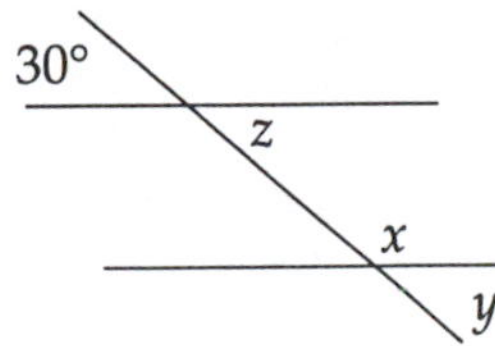

4. D $5x + 3x + 2x + 2x = 180$. $\therefore 12x = 180$. $x = 15°$.

5. D The $\angle$ between m and n is 90°. $\therefore x + 90 + 3x = 180$. $\therefore 4x = 90$, and $x = 22\frac{1}{2}°$.

6. A 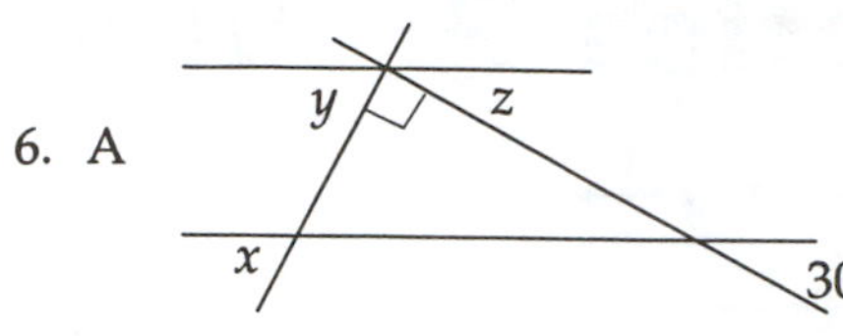

$z = 30°$ (corresponding angles). $y + 90 + 30 = 180$. $\therefore y = 60°$. $x = y = 60°$ (corresponding angles).

Triangles

7. D 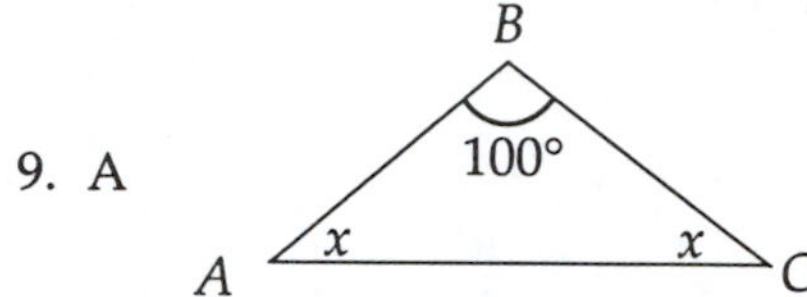

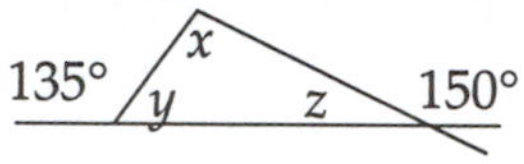

$y + 135 = 180$. $\therefore y = 45°$
$z + 150 = 180$. $\therefore z = 30°$
$x + y + z = 180°$ $\therefore x = 180 - 45 - 30 = 105°$.

8. C $2x + 3x + 4x = 180$. $\therefore 9x = 180$. $x = 20°$.

9. A 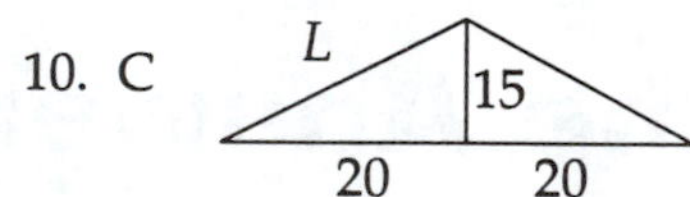

Since the triangle is isosceles, $\angle A = \angle C = x$. $x + x + 100 = 180$. $\therefore 2x = 80$. $x = 40°$.

10. C 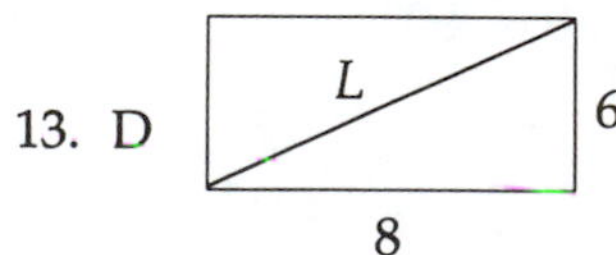

Drop a perpendicular from the peak. This is a 3-4-5 triangle which is 5 times bigger than the base triangle. Hence, the hypotenuse is $5 \times 5 = 25$. Alternatively, the Pythagorean Theorem gives $\sqrt{20^2 + 15^2} = \sqrt{400 + 225} = \sqrt{625} = 25$.

11. C The Pythagorean Theorem: $L^2 = \sqrt{6^2 + 7^2} = \sqrt{36 + 49} = \sqrt{85}$.

12. D Since the sides on either side of the 60° angle are 50 and 100 (one is 1/2 the other), the line AC completes a right triangle, a 30°-60°-90° triangle. It is 50 times bigger than the base triangle with sides 1, $\sqrt{3}$, and 2. Hence, the hypotenuse is $50\sqrt{3}$.

13. D

L (diagonal)	6
8	

The diagonal forms a 3-4-5 triangle with the sides, which is twice as big as the base triangle. Hence, $L = 2 \times 5 = 10$.

14. B

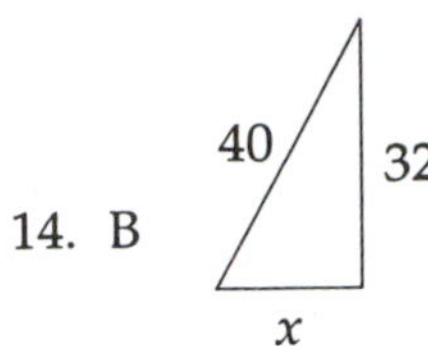

This is a 3-4-5 triangle, 8 times as large as the base triangle. Hence $x = 3 \times 8 = 24$.

15. E The legs are equal in length x. Hence, $x^2 + x^2 = 10^2$ or $2x^2 = 100$. $\therefore x^2 = 50$ and $x = \sqrt{50} = 5\sqrt{2}$.

16. E The sides in similar triangles are proportional: $\frac{1}{2} = \frac{4}{2+x}$. Cross multiply: $2 + x = 8$. $\therefore x = 6$.

17. C

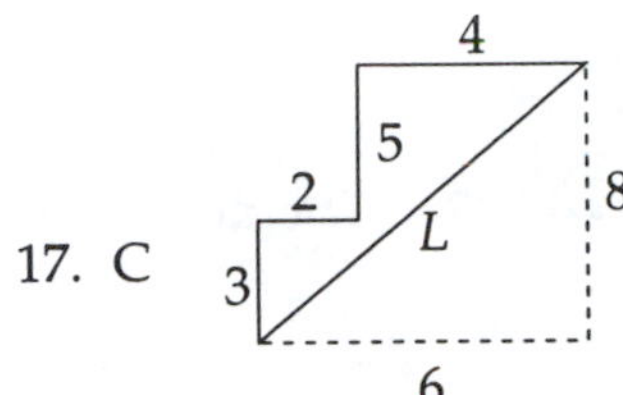

This is a 3-4-5 triangle, twice the size of the base triangle. $\therefore L = 2 \times 5 = 10$.

Circles

18. D The circumference is $\pi D = \pi \times 14 = \frac{22}{7} \times 14 = 44$. The arc length is 11, or $\frac{11}{44} = \frac{1}{4}$ of the circle. The angle is then $\frac{1}{4} \times 360° = 90°$.

19. B The circumference is $2\pi r = 2\pi \times 6 = 12\pi$. A 60° angle includes $\frac{60}{360} = \frac{1}{6}$ of the circumference or $\frac{12\pi}{6} = 2\pi$.

20. C

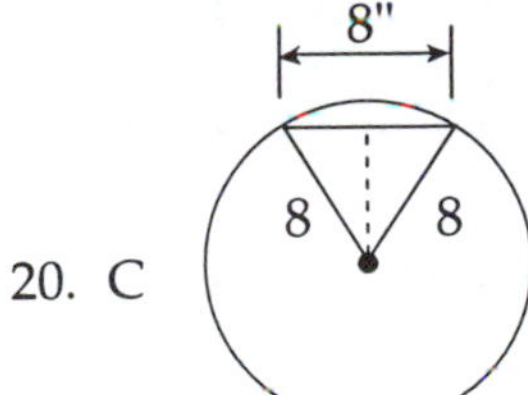

The cut with the two radii form an equilateral triangle. Thus, the angle is 60°, as in all equilateral triangles.

21. E

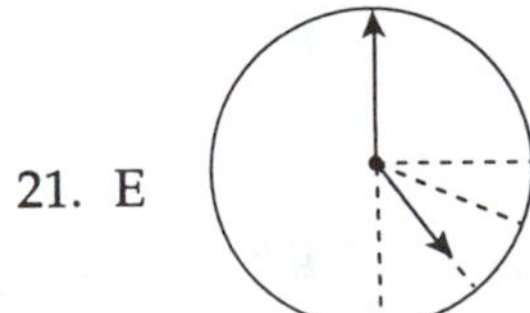

The angle between each number on a clock is 30° (12 numbers in 360°). Hence, $180 - 30 = 150°$. (An angle of 210° would also be correct.)

22. B

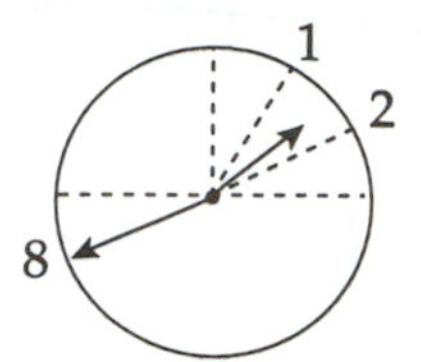

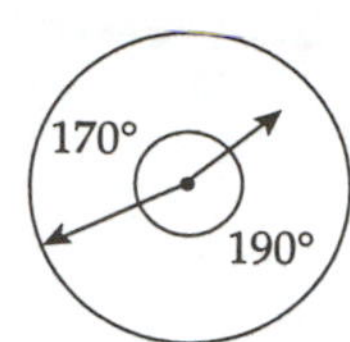

There are 30° between the numbers 1 and 2. The large hand has gone 240° around the clock from 12 and points to 8. The small hand has gone 30° to 1 and $\frac{240}{360} \times 30 =$ 20° further toward 2. Hence, the angle is 240 – (30 + 20) = 190°. (An angle of 170° would also be correct.)

23. A

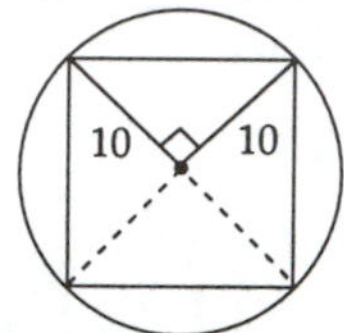

The radius is 10 so a side is $\sqrt{10^2 + 10^2} = \sqrt{200} = 10\sqrt{2}$. (The diagonals are perpendicular.)

24. A

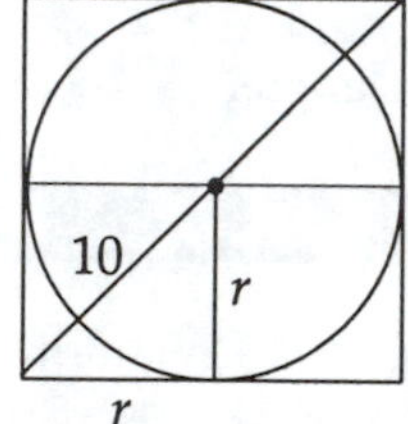

Half of the diagonal is 10. Hence, $r^2 + r^2 = 100$ or $2r^2 = 100$. $\therefore r^2 = 50$ and $r = \sqrt{50} = 5\sqrt{2}$. $\therefore d = 10\sqrt{2}$.

Perimeters and Areas

25. D

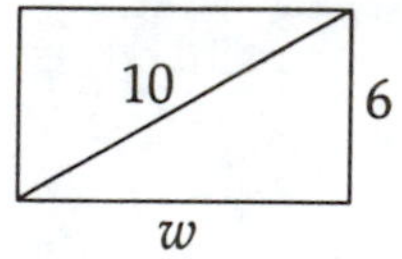

The diagonal and sides form a 3-4-5 triangle, twice the base size. Hence, $w = 8$ and the area = $6w$ = 48.

26. B

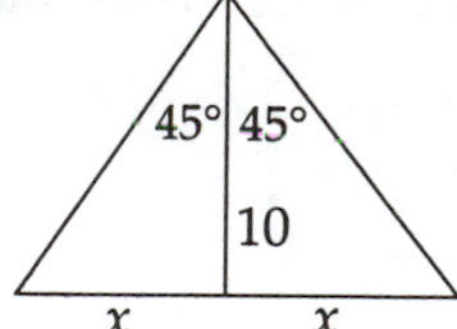

Since the bisector splits the 90° angle, the triangle is a 45°-45°-90° triangle. Hence, $x = 10$ and the base is 20. The area = $\frac{1}{2}$ (height × base) = $\frac{1}{2} \times 10 \times 20 = 100$.

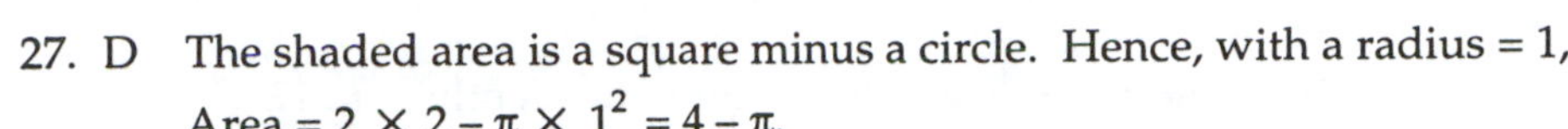

27. D The shaded area is a square minus a circle. Hence, with a radius = 1,
Area = $2 \times 2 - \pi \times 1^2 = 4 - \pi$.

28. E The area of the triangle = 1/2 (height × base) = (1/2) × 10 × 10 = 50. The area of the shaded area is: Area = 10 × 10 – 50 = 100 – 50 = 50.

29. A The 12-foot length takes $\frac{12 \times 12}{9} = 16$ tiles. The 9-foot length takes $\frac{9 \times 12}{9} = 12$ tiles. Hence, the 9 × 12 foot rectangle takes 12 × 16 = 192 tiles. This leaves a 3 × 6 foot rectangle. The 3-foot length takes $\frac{3 \times 12}{9} = 4$ tiles and the 6-foot length, 8 tiles. This rectangle takes 4 × 8 = 32 tiles giving a total of 192 + 32 = 224.

30. B

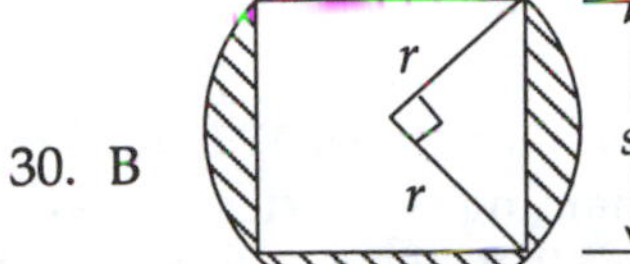

The side of a square is $s = \sqrt{r^2 + r^2} = \sqrt{2r^2} = r\sqrt{2}$. The area of the square is $\left(r\sqrt{2}\right)^2 = 2r^2$. The area of the circle is πr^2. The shaded area is

$$\text{Area} = \pi r^2 - 2r^2 = r^2(\pi - 2).$$

31. E Area of circle = πr^2. Area of square $= b^2$.

$$\pi r^2 = 2b^2. \quad \therefore \frac{r^2}{b^2} = \frac{2}{\pi}. \quad \frac{r}{b} = \sqrt{\frac{2}{\pi}}.$$

32. E The circumference = $\pi d = \pi \cong \frac{22}{7}$.

$$22 \div \frac{22}{7} = 22 \times \frac{7}{22} = 7.$$

Solids

33. C There are six squares that make up the surface. ∴ $6A = 24$ and $A = 4$ ft². $4 = s^2$.
∴ $s = 2$ feet. (s = length of a side.) Volume = $s \times s \times s = 2 \times 2 \times 2 = 8$.

34. B Volume = $2 \times 2 \times L = 4L$. Surface area = 2 ends + 4 sides
$= 2(2 \times 2) + 4(2 \times L) = 8 + 8L$. $\therefore 4L = \frac{1}{4}[8 + 8L] = 2 + 2L$.
∴ $2L = 2$ and $L = 1$.

35. D The first box has Volume = $w \times w \times h = w^2h$. The second box has
Volume = $2w \times 3w \times 2h = 12w^2h$. The ratio is

$$\text{ratio} = \frac{w^2h}{12w^2h} = \frac{1}{12} \qquad \text{or equivalently,} \quad 1:12.$$

36. D Volume of old truck = $w \times b \times h$.
Volume of new truck = $2w \times 2b \times 2h = 8wbh$. The ratio is

$$\text{ratio} = \frac{8wbh}{wbh} = 8.$$

37. B

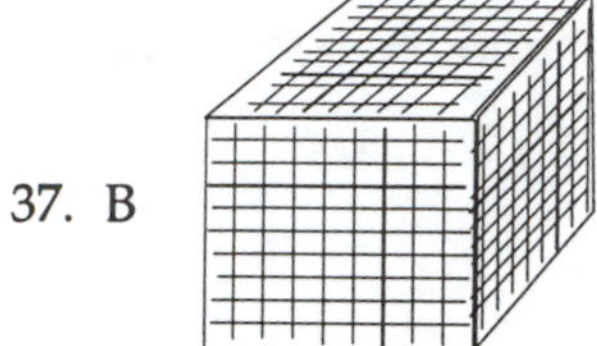

There are 10 × 10 = 100 cubes on each end. Then there are 8 × 10 = 80 cubes on 2 of the sides that have an exterior side. On the remaining two sides there are 8 ×8 = 64 cubes that have an exterior side. In all there are 2 × 100 + 2 × 80 + 2 × 64 = 488 cubes with an exterior side. Hence, there are 1000 – 488 = 512 interior cubes. Alternatively, a cube 8 × 8 × 8 = 512 makes up the interior.

38. B The lateral surface area of a cylinder (excluding the ends) is $\pi d \times h$. Its volume is $\frac{\pi d^2}{4} \times h$ (the area of the base times the height). Hence, $\pi d \times h = 2\frac{\pi d^2}{4} \times h$, or, canceling like quantities, $d = 2$.

39. C The volume of the box is 1 × 1 × 1 = 1. The volume of a cylinder with diameter 1 and height 1 is $\frac{\pi \times 1^2}{4} \times 1 = \frac{\pi}{4}$. The difference is $1 - \frac{\pi}{4}$.

Rectangular Coordinates

40. A

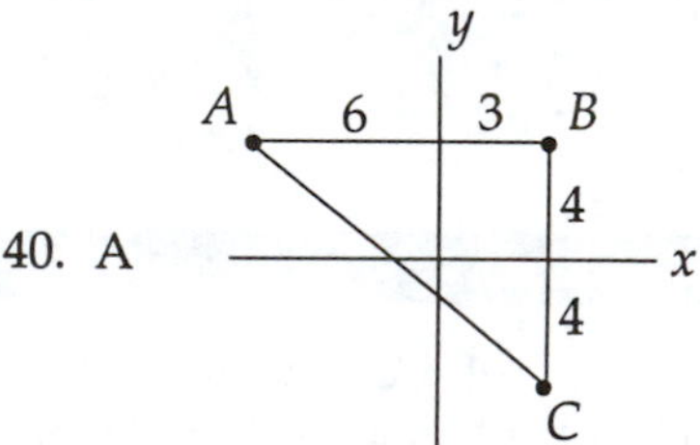

Plot the points: the y-coordinates of A and B are equal. Also, the x-coordinates of B and C are equal. Hence, $\angle B$ is a right angle and the triangle is a right triangle.

41. E To find the length L of a line connecting two points, find the difference in the x-coordinates: 8 – (– 4) = 12, and the y-coordinates: 4 – (– 5) = 9. This is a 3-4-5 triangle, triple the base triangle. Thus, $L = 3 \times 5 = 15$. Or,
$\sqrt{9^2 + 12^2} = \sqrt{81 + 144} = \sqrt{225} = 15$.

42. B The difference in the x-coordinates is 5 – (– 3) = 8. 1/2 (8) = 4. Add 4 to (– 3) and the x-coordinate of the midpoint is 1. The difference in the y-coordinates is

$4 - (-2) = 6$. $1/2\ (6) = 3$. Add 3 to (-2) and the y-coordinate of the midpoint is also 1. The midpoint is at (1, 1).

43. A Area $= \frac{1}{2}bh = \frac{1}{2}(5)h$. $\therefore 20 = \frac{5}{2}h$ or $h = 8$. This is the y-coordinate of P. Its x-coordinate is observed from the plot to be 0. Hence, (0, 8) are the coordinates of P.

44. E

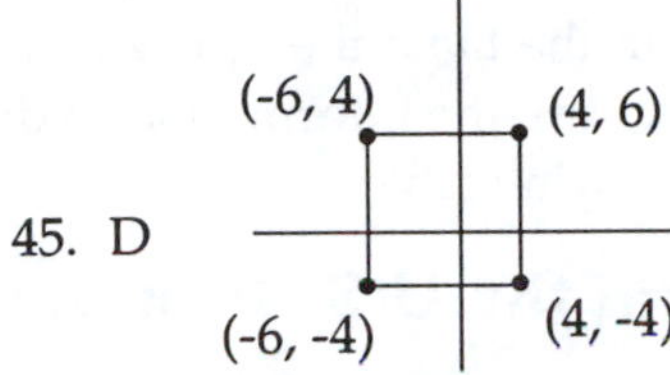

The height of the left leg of the triangle is $5 - 1 = 4$. The triangle is a 3-4-5 triangle so that $r = 5$. The area of the circle is $A = \pi r^2 = \pi 5^2 = 25\pi$.

45. D

(-6, 4) (4, 6)

(-6, -4) (4, -4)

The points form the corners of a rectangle whose height is $6 - (-4) = 10$ and whose base is $4 - (-6) = 10$. Its area is $A = bh = 10 \times 10 = 100$.

7.4 Data Interpretation

Questions that require the proper interpretation of data included in tables and graphs are often included on the GMAT. Make sure you read the questions carefully. This article describes the various techniques used to present data.

Tables

Much data can be presented in the systematic and concise format of a table. Tables are used to provide information in newspapers and magazines as well as many of your college texts, so you should be quite familiar with them. The questions on the GMAT assess your ability to accurately interpret the information provided.

Each table has a title and each column in the table has a heading indicating the specific type of information presented in that column. Each row in the table then provides the same information for a particular subgroup. The problem is to use the information to draw accurate conclusions. Examples are illustrated by using the following table.

Table 1. Deaths and Death Rates in the U.S. from Accidents

TYPE OF ACCIDENT	DEATHS (number)					RATE PER 100,000 POPULATION				
	1970	1980	1985	1987	1988	1970	1980	1985	1987	1988
Accident and adverse effects	**114,638**	**105,718**	**93,457**	**95,020**	**97,100**	**56.4**	**46.7**	**39.1**	**39.0**	**39.5**
Motor-vehicle accidents	54,633	53,172	45,901	48,290	49,078	26.9	23.5	19.2	19.8	20.0
Traffic	53,493	51,930	44,822	47,297	48,024	26.3	22.9	18.8	19.4	19.5
Non-traffic	1,140	1,242	1,079	993	1,054	0.6	0.5	0.5	0.4	0.4
Water-transport accidents	1,651	1,429	1,111	949	979	0.8	0.6	0.5	0.4	0.4
Air and space transport accidents	1,612	1,494	1,428	1,263	1,012	0.8	0.7	0.6	0.5	0.4
Railway accidents	852	632	551	624	571	0.4	0.3	0.2	0.3	0.2
Accidental falls	16,926	13,294	12,001	11,733	12,096	8.3	5.9	5.0	4.8	4.9
Fall from one level to another	4,798	3,743	3,365	3,362	3,317	2.4	1.7	1.4	1.4	1.3
Fall on the same level	828	415	411	404	433	0.4	0.2	0.2	0.2	0.2
Fracture, cause unspecified, and other and unspecified falls	11,300	9,136	8,225	7,967	8,346	5.6	4.0	3.4	3.3	3.4
Accidental drowning	6,391	6,043	4,407	4,360	4,199	3.1	2.7	1.8	1.8	1.7
Accidents caused by—										
Fires and flames	6,718	5,822	4,938	4,710	4,965	3.3	2.6	2.1	1.9	2.0
Firearms	2,406	1,955	1,649	1,440	1,501	1.2	0.9	0.7	0.6	0.6
Electric current	1,140	1,095	802	760	714	0.6	0.5	0.3	0.3	0.3
Accidental poisoning by—										
Drugs and medicines	2,505	2,492	3,612	3,907	4,865	1.2	1.1	1.5	1.6	2.0
Other solid and liquid substances	1,174	597	479	508	488	0.6	0.3	0.2	0.2	0.2
Gases and vapors	1,620	1,242	1,079	900	873	0.8	0.5	0.5	0.4	0.4
Complications due to medical procedures	3,581	2,437	2,852	3,032	3,038	1.8	1.1	1.2	1.3	1.2
Inhalation and ingestion of objects	2,753	3,249	3,551	3,688	3,805	1.4	1.4	1.5	1.5	1.5
All other accidents	10,676	10,765	9,096	8,856	8,916	5.2	4.7	3.8	3.6-	3.6

Source: ***Statistical Abstract of the United States,*** **1991. Data from** ***International Classification of Diseases.***

Example 1

What percent of the population died as a result of accidents in 1970?

Solution. There were 56.4 deaths for every 100,000 people. The percent of the population that died was

$$\frac{56.4}{100,000} \times 100 = \frac{56.4}{1000} = 0.0564\%$$

To use the number 114,638 from the first column to solve the problem, we would have had to divide by the total population!

Example 2

How many state lottery tickets would you have to buy so that the odds of being killed in an accident in 1988 are equal to the odds of winning the lottery? (Assume the odds of winning a state lottery with one ticket to be 1 in 7 million.)

Solution. The odds of being killed in an accident in 1988 are 39.5 in 100,000 people. That is

$$\frac{39.5}{100,000} = \frac{395}{1,000,000} = \frac{7 \times 395}{7,000,000} = \frac{2765}{7,000,000}.$$

You would have to buy 2765 tickets to even the odds.

Example 3

What percent decrease occurred in accidental drownings between 1980 and 1988?

Solution. Use the data from the first set of columns:

$$\frac{6043 - 4199}{6043} \times 100 = \frac{1844}{6043} \times 100 \cong \frac{1800}{6000} \times 100 = 30\%$$

Note that we rounded off the numbers (we decreased the numbers in both numerator and denominator) to get an easy calculation. The long calculation required by the numbers before we rounded off would provide greater accuracy, but that is not required to get the correct answer for most GMAT problems.

Example 4

Select any of the following statements that can be inferred from the tabulated data.

I. The greatest decrease in deaths between 1970 and 1988 occurred in motor-vehicle accidents.

II. The death rate for every accident type decreased or remained constant between 1970 and 1980.

III. Accidental deaths due to drugs and medicines increased from 1970 to 1980.

Solution. The question requires that we select the correct responses based on the data. **I** is true; it is based on the first set of columns (*number* of deaths). **II** is also true, based on the second set of columns. **III** is false; there was a drop between 1970 and 1980.

Example 5

Infer the total population in 1970 by using the data from Railway accidents.

Solution. In 1970, the death rate per 100,000 was 0.4 and the total deaths was 852. If we let P represent the total population, we have

$$\frac{0.4}{100,000} P = 852. \qquad \therefore P = \frac{852 \times 100,000}{0.4} = 213,000,000$$

The number 0.4 is only one significant number. Consequently, the answer is accurate to only one significant number (a chain is only as strong as its weakest link!) so $P = 200,000,000$.

Bar Graphs

Certain data is best presented in a bar graph, in which a quantity is proportional to the length of a bar. The bars can be either horizontal or vertical, although vertical bars are the most common. Bars on the same graph always represent the same type of quantity: bushels of grain, dollars, or number of people. We could form a bar graph of the death rates from the various types of accidents, presented in Table 1.

A bar graph will have a title stating the quantity being presented. There will be a scale along one of the two axes from which the quantity of a given bar can be inferred. The other axis will present what each bar represents: the type of grain, the year, or the type of accident. This is illustrated with examples based on the following bar graph.

Figure 1. Federal and State Prisoners.

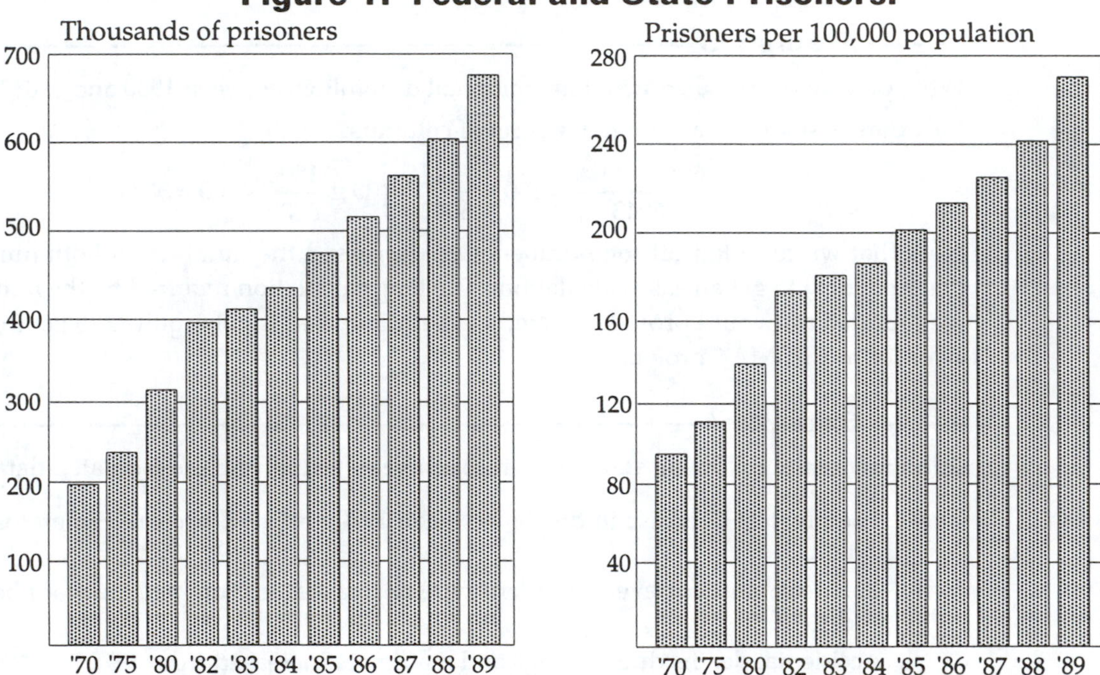

Source: ***Statistical Abstract of the United States*, 1991, Data from U.S. Bureau of the Census.**

Example 1

For every million people, what was the increase in the number of federal and state prisoners between 1980 and 1988?

Solution. The number of prisoners per 100,000 in 1980 is approximated from the second bar graph to be 140 (the bar is half way between 120 and 160). In 1988 it is about 240 (maybe 245, but 240 is close enough). The difference is 240 − 140 = 100 per 100,000 population. Per 1,000,000 people we must multiply by 10:

$$\text{increase} = 1000 \text{ prisoners}$$

Example 2

What was the increase in federal and state prison population from 1970 to 1989? Also, calculate the percent increase.

Solution. For this problem, we use the first bar graph. In 1970 the bar reads about 200 (a little less), and in 1989 it reads about 675 (place a mark with your pencil half way between 600 and 700 - that is 650. Another bisecting mark suggests about 675). The difference is 675 – 200 = 475. This is thousands of prisoners, so that

$$\text{increase} = 475 \times 1000 = 475{,}000$$

The percent increase is

$$\%\ \text{increase} = \frac{675-200}{200} \times 100 = \frac{475}{200} \times 100 = 237.5\%$$

The numbers we read were accurate to about 2 significant numbers, so we report this as a 240% increase.

Example 3

What was the approximate number of people in the U.S. in 1988?

Solution. The number of prisoners per 100,000 people in 1988 was 240. If we let P be the total population, then the number of prisoners was

$$\text{No. of prisoners} = \frac{P}{100{,}000} \times 240\ .$$

From the first bar graph, the number of prisoners was 600,000 in 1988. Hence,

$$600{,}000 = \frac{P}{100{,}000} \times 240\ . \qquad \therefore P = \frac{600{,}000 \times 100{,}000}{240} = 250{,}000{,}000.$$

There were 250 million people.

Example 4

What was the average percent increase per year in the number of prisoners between 1980 and 1989?

Solution. We use data from the first bar graph since it is the number we desire, not the number per 100,000 population. In 1988 there were about 600 and in 1980 there were about 320. The percent increase was

$$\frac{600-320}{320} \times 100 = \frac{280}{320} \times 100 = \frac{700}{8} = 87.5\%\ .$$

This is over a period of 10 years (not 9—count them if you need to). The average percent increase is found by dividing by 10:

$$\text{average}\ \%\ \text{increase} = \frac{87.5}{10} = 8.8\%$$

Cumulative Bar Graphs

If several quantities of a similar type are to be presented in a single figure, it may be that the use of a cumulative bar graph is best. Such a graph presents the quantities in a single bar, with each section of the bar proportional to the quantity being graphed.

Figure 2. Retail sales of farm machinery.

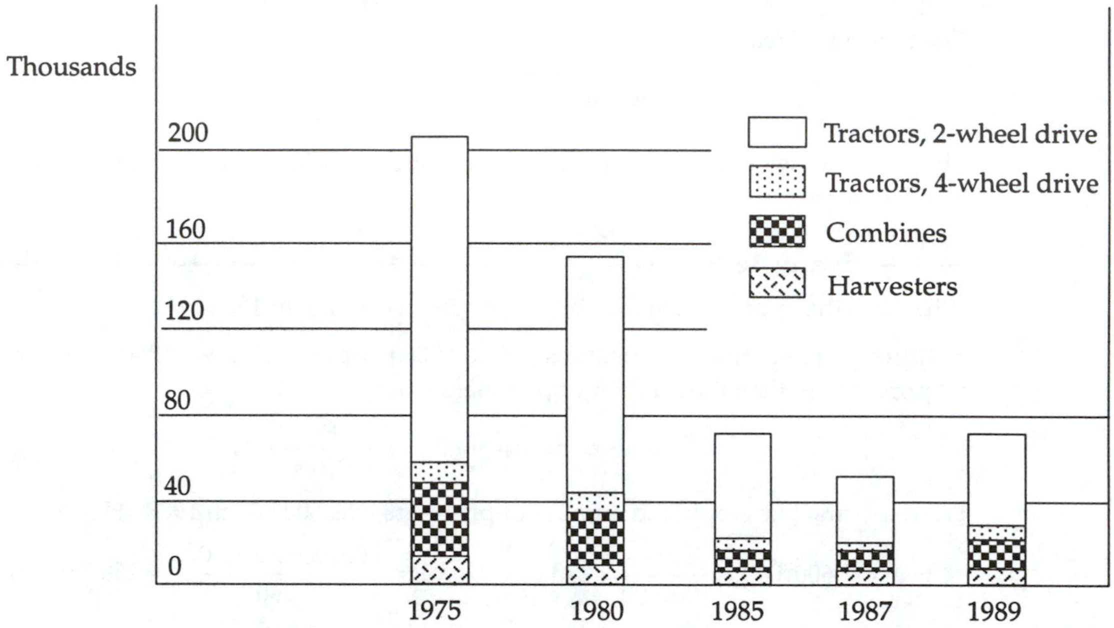

Thousands

200
160
120
80
40
0

Tractors, 2-wheel drive
Tractors, 4-wheel drive
Combines
Harvesters

1975 1980 1985 1987 1989

Source: ***Statistical Abstract of the United States*, 1991, Data from U.S. Department of Agriculture.**

Example 1

What percentage of the farm machinery sold in 1980 was 2-wheel drive tractors?

Solution. The total number of units sold in 1980 was about 155 thousand. Of that, the bar indicates that about 110 thousand units were 2-wheel drive tractors. The percent is

$$\text{\% 2-wheel drive tractors} = \frac{110}{155} \times 100 = 71\%$$

(To obtain the number of 2-wheel drive tractors sold, use the side of your answer sheet and mark the top and bottom of the section that represents the 2-wheel drive tractors. Then slide the two marks over to the vertical axis and read about 110 thousand units.)

Example 2

What was the total number of combines sold in 1975, 1980 and 1985?

Solution. Estimate, as accurately as possible, the number of combines sold in each year, then add the three numbers:

total sold = 65,000 combines.

This is done by marking, on the edge of your answer sheet, the top and bottom of the combine section of the bar for 1975. Then place the top mark on the bottom of the combine section of the bar for 1980 and mark the top of that section. Then repeat for 1985. Now, slide the edge of the sheet over to the vertical axis and estimate the answer.

Example 3

What was the percent decrease in the sale of 2-wheel drive tractors between 1975 and 1985?

Solution. The number of 2-wheel drive tractors sold in 1975 was 145,000. In 1985 there were 50,000 sold. The percent decrease is

$$\% \text{ decrease} = \frac{145-50}{145} \times 100 = \frac{95}{145} \times 100 = \frac{1900}{29} = 66\%.$$

Circle Graphs

A circle graph, or pie chart, is sometimes the chosen mechanism to present data. The angle of the sector is directly proportional to the quantity being graphed. Each sector of a circle graph most often presents the percent contribution that the sector contributes to the whole. Since there are 360° in a circle, 90° degrees would represent 1/4 of the circle or a 25% contribution.

Figure 3. Percentage of persons receiving Social Security benefits, 1989.

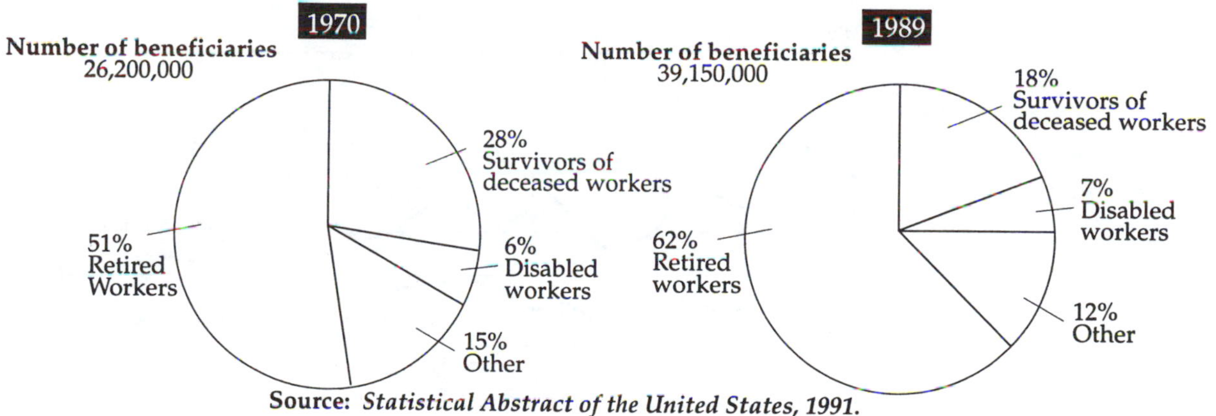

Source: *Statistical Abstract of the United States, 1991.*

Example 1

If the total number of persons receiving social security benefits in 1989 were 39 million, how many were disabled workers receiving benefits?

Solution. The percentage of disabled workers receiving benefits was 7%. The number of disabled workers was

$$39{,}000{,}000 \times 0.07 = 2{,}730{,}000 \text{ workers.}$$

Example 2

Calculate the percent decrease in the ratio of the survivors of deceased workers to disabled workers from 1970 to 1989.

Solution. The ratio of the survivors of deceased workers to disabled workers in 1970 is

$$\text{ratio} = \frac{28}{6} = 4.7\,.$$

In 1989 the ratio is

$$\text{ratio} = \frac{18}{7} = 2.6.$$

The percent decrease is

$$\%\ \text{decrease} = \frac{4.7 - 2.6}{4.7} \times 100 = 45\%.$$

We retain only two significant numbers in the calculations because the percentages are obviously given to only two significant numbers.

Line Graphs

If the top of the bars in a bar graph were replaced with a single point in the middle of the bar and then the points connected, a line graph would result. Most commonly, line graphs are plots of quantities with time. A glance can tell if a quantity is increasing or decreasing. You may find it more difficult to interpret a line graph than a bar graph.

Figure 4. Domestic consumption of timber products.

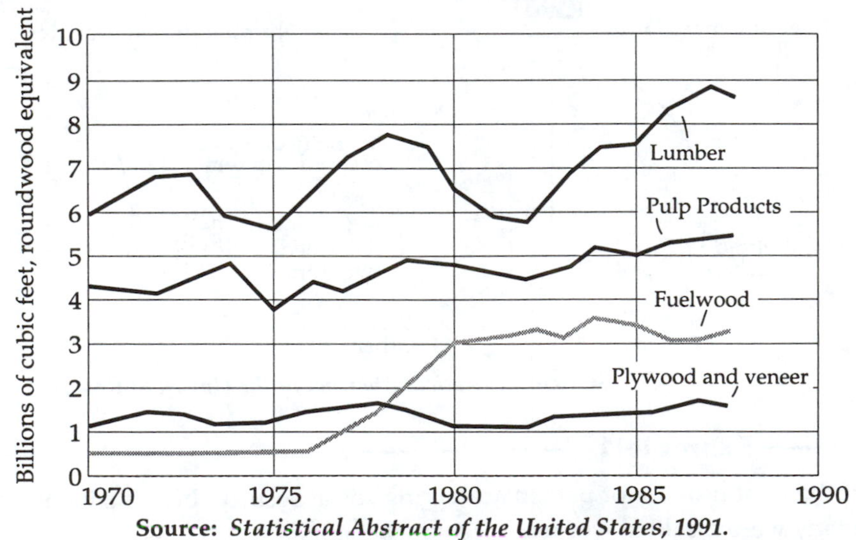

Source: ***Statistical Abstract of the United States, 1991.***

Example 1

In what year did the minimum consumption of pulp products occur? In what year did the maximum consumption of fuelwood occur?

Solution. From the line graph, we see that the consumption of pulp products reached a minimum in 1975. The consumption of fuelwood peaked out in 1984. This, of course, only covers the years on the graph. There may have been a different minimum or maximum from 1975 and 1984 in previous years not shown on the graph.

Example 2

The consumption of what timber product was about 400% greater than the consumption of plywood and veneer in 1980?

Solution. The consumption of plywood and veneer in 1980 was about 1.2. Multiply this by 4 and obtain 4.8. The product with a consumption of 4.8 was *pulp products*.

Example 3

The total consumption of the timber products graphed in Fig. 4 increased by what percentage between 1970 and 1985?

Solution. The total consumption in 1970 was 0.5 + 1.1 + 4.4 + 5.9 = 11.9 billion cubic feet. In 1985 the total consumption was 1.5 + 3.4 + 5.0 + 7.7 = 17.6 . We round these off to 12 and 18. The increase is

$$\% \text{ increase} = \frac{18-12}{12} \times 100 = \frac{600}{12} = 50\%.$$

Practice Problems

—Data Interpretation—

Tables

Questions 1-5 refer to the following table taken from *Statistical Abstract of the U.S., 1991*.

Estimated number of legal abortions, by race

YEAR	ALL RACES				WHITE				BLACK AND OTHER			
	Women 15-44 years old (1,000)	Abortions			Women 15-44 years old (1,000)	Abortions			Women 15-44 years old (1,000)	Abortions		
		Number (1,000)	Rate per 1,000 women	Ratio per 1,000 live births		Number (1,000)	Rate per 1,000 women	Ratio per 1,000 live births		Number (1,000)	Rate per 1,000 women	Ratio per 1,000 live births
1972 . .	44,588	586.8	13.2	184	38,532	455.3	11.8	175	6,056	131.5	21.7	223
1975 . .	47,606	1,034.2	21.7	331	40,857	701.2	17.2	276	6,749	333.0	49.3	565
1976 . .	48,721	1,179.3	24.2	361	41,721	784.9	18.8	296	7,000	394.4	56.3	638
1977 . .	49,814	1,316.7	26.4	400	42,567	888.8	20.9	333	7,247	427.9	59.0	679
1978 . .	50,920	1,409.6	27.7	413	43,427	969.4	22.3	356	7,493	440.2	58.7	665
1979 . .	52,016	1,497.7	28.8	420	44,266	1,062.4	24.0	373	7,750	435.3	56.2	625
1980 . .	53,048	1,553.9	29.3	428	44,942	1,093.6	24.3	376	8,106	460.3	56.5	642
1981 . .	53,901	1,577.3	29.3	430	45,494	1,107.8	24.3	377	8,407	469.6	55.9	645
1982 . .	54,679	1,573.9	28.8	428	46,049	1,095.2	23.8	373	8,630	478.7	55.5	646
1983 . .	55,340	1,575.0	28.5	436	46,506	1,084.4	23.3	376	8,834	490.6	55.5	670
1984 . .	56,061	1,577.2	28.1	423	47,023	1,086.6	23.1	366	9,038	490.6	54.3	646
1985 . .	56,754	1,588.6	28.0	422	47,512	1,075.6	22.6	360	9,242	512.9	55.5	659
1986 . .	57,483	1,574.0	27.4	416	48,010	1,044.7	21.8	350	9,473	529.3	55.9	661
1987 . .	57,964	1,559.1	27.1	406	48,288	1,017.3	21.1	338	9,676	541.8	56.0	648

1. What year had the maximum number of legal abortions?

A) 1987 B) 1986 C) 1985 D) 1983 E) 1980

2. If a typical state had 10,000 live births in 1980, about how many legal abortions were performed in that state?

   A) 1550 B) 2930 C) 4300 D) 5310 E) 8100

3. What approximate percentage of legal abortions in 1975 were performed for white women?

   A) 90% B) 85% C) 80% D) 70% E) 60%

4. Calculate the approximate increase in legal abortions between 1975 and 1980.

   A) 60% B) 50% C) 40% D) 35% E) 30%

5. The population of the United States in 1987 was about 250 million. What percentage were women aged 15-44?

   A) 23% B) 20% C) 18% D) 16% E) 15%

Bar Graphs

Questions 6-10 refer to the following bar graph from *Statistical Abstract of the U.S., 1991.*

Percentage of persons 25 years old and over completing 4 years of college or more.

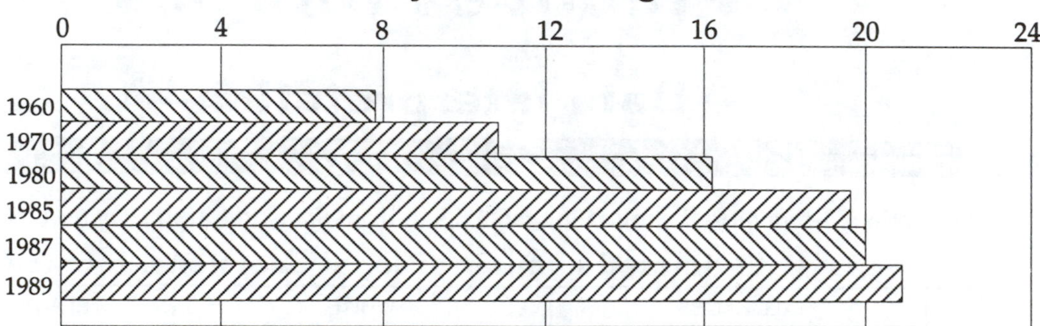

6. What percentage of persons 25 and over completed 4 years of college or more in 1970?

   A) 10.2% B) 10.4% C) 10.7% D) 11% E) 11.2%

7. What was the average percentage increase per year from 1970 to 1980?

   A) 0.5% B) 0.7% C) 1.0% D) 2% E) 5%

8. If in 1987 a typical state had 125,000 persons 25 and over with 4 years of college or more, what population of the state was 25 and over?

   A) 375,000 B) 475,000 C) 525,000
   D) 500,000 E) 625,000

9. What was the percent increase in the percentage of persons 25 and over completing 4 years of college or more between 1960 and 1989?

   A) 80% B) 100% C) 120% D) 160% E) 200%

10. If some other country had three times as many people 25 and over in 1989 as the U.S. with the same number of persons completing 4 years of college or more, what percentage of that country's people 25 and over would complete college?

A) 5% B) 7% C) 9% D) 10% E) 12%

Cumulative Bar Graphs

Questions 11-15 refer to the following graph.

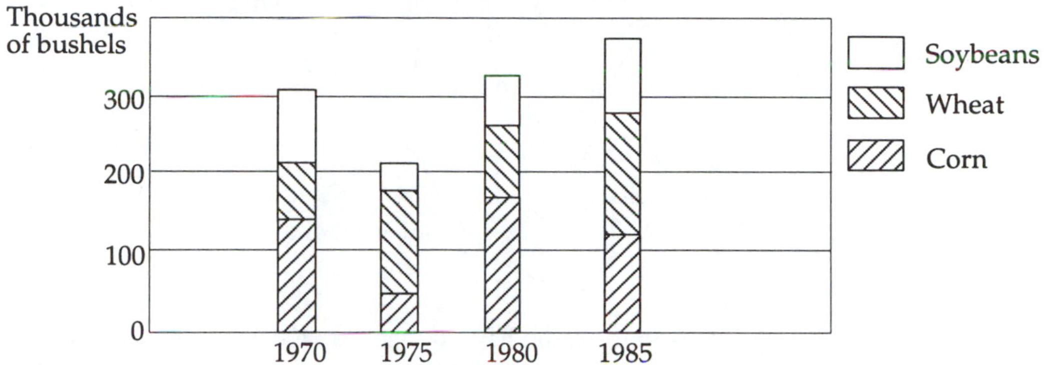

11. How many more bushels of wheat did the farmer grow in 1980 than in 1970?

A) 30,000 B) 50,000 C) 60,000
D) 70,000 E) 80,000

12. In what year was the soybean production greatest?

A) 1970 B) 1975 C) 1980
D) 1985 E) Cannot determine

13. Calculate the percentage increase in wheat production from 1975 to 1985.

A) 120% B) 80% C) 65% D) 50% E) 30%

14. In what year was wheat the highest percentage of the total crop?

A) 1970 B) 1975 C) 1980 D) 1985 E) Can't tell

15. If a bushel of corn sells for \$3, soybeans for \$8, and wheat for \$5, what percentage did wheat contribute to the gross sales in 1985?

A) 60% B) 50% C) 40% D) 30% E) 20%

Circle Graphs

Questions 16-20 refer to the following graph and table.

The average budget for a store in a chain of stores

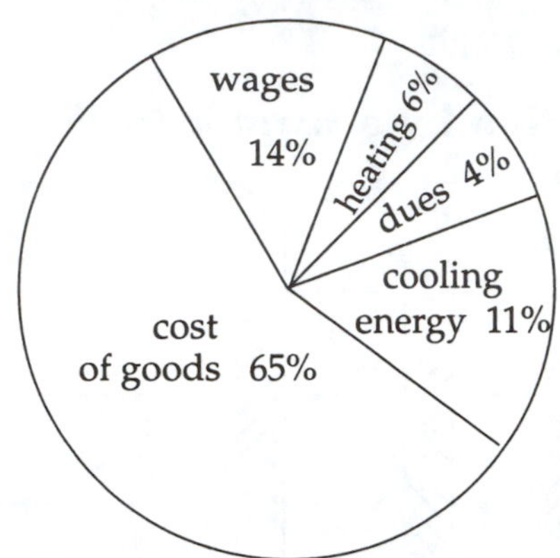

The budget of store A

cost of goods	—	$200,000
wages	—	50,000
cooling energy	—	20,000
heating	—	20,000
dues	—	10,000

16. An average store in the chain has a budget of $400,000. How much should be budgeted for heating?

    A) $2400 B) $4000 C) $6000 D) $16,000 E) $24,000

17. What is the ratio of wages paid by store A to its total budget?

    A) $\frac{1}{3}$ B) $\frac{1}{4}$ C) $\frac{1}{5}$ D) $\frac{1}{6}$ E) $\frac{1}{7}$

18. What percentage more does store A spend for heating than the average store in the chain?

    A) 7% B) 10% C) 14% D 18% E) 20%

19. Calculate the ratio of the percentage store A spends on wages to the percentage the average store spends on wages.

    A) $\frac{3}{2}$ B) $\frac{4}{3}$ C) $\frac{5}{4}$ D) $\frac{6}{5}$ E) $\frac{25}{21}$

20. If there are 15 stores in the chain and the average budget for each store is $400,000, how much should be budgeted for the total chain for cooling energy?

    A) $110,000 B) $220,000 C) $600,000 D) $660,000 E) $820,000

Line Graphs

Questions 21-25 refer to the following graph.

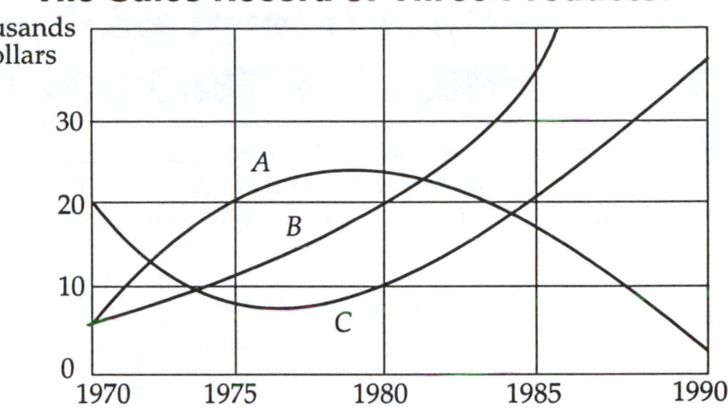

21. Estimate the total sales of the three products in 1980.

    A) $10,000 B) $20,000 C) $34,000
    D) $44,000 E) $54,000

22. The ratio of the best sales of product *A* to the worst sales of product *C* is about

    A) 5 : 2 B) 2 : 1 C) 10 : 3 D) 4 : 1 E) 3 : 2

23. In what year were the sales of product *B* 150% better than in 1975?

    A) 1978 B) 1980 C) 1983 D) 1985 E) 1986

24. The percent increase in total sales from 1975 to 1985 was about

    A) 80% B) 90% C) 120% D) 150% E) 180%

25. If the sales total for the three products accounted for 4% of the total sales of the company in 1980, what were the company's total sales that year?

    A) $640,000 B) $720,000 C) $840,000
    D) $1,400,000 E) $2,200,000

Answers to Practice Problems

—Data Interpretation—

Tables	Bar Graphs	Cumulative Bar Graphs	Circle Graphs	Line Graphs
1. C	6. C	11. A	16. E	21. E
2. C	7. E	12. D	17. D	22. C
3. D	8. E	13. D	18. B	23. C
4. B	9. D	14. B	19. E	24. B
5. A	10. B	15. C	20. D	25. D

Explanations to the Answers

—Data Interpretation—

Tables

1. C The first column is the number of women in the U.S., not the number of abortions. The third column is the rate of abortions, not the number of abortions. The maximum number of legal abortions (1,588,600) occurred in 1985.

2. C The ratio of abortions to live births is $\frac{428}{1000}$. If there were 10,000 live births, the number of abortions would be $10 \times 428 = 4280$, or about 4300.

3. D There were 701.2 thousand abortions for white women out of a total number of 1034.2 thousand. Hence,

$$\% = \frac{701}{1034} \times 100 \cong \frac{700}{1000} \times 100 = 70\%.$$

Note that we decrease both numerator and denominator just a little to simplify the calculation.

4. B The percentage increase is found by using data from the 2nd column:

$$\% \text{ increase} = \frac{1553.9 - 1034.2}{1034.2} \times 100 = \frac{519.7}{1034.2} \times 100 \cong 50\%.$$

5. A The first column provides the needed data:

$$\% \text{ women 15-44} = \frac{57{,}964{,}000}{250{,}000{,}000} \times 100 \cong \frac{58}{250} \times 100 = 23.2\%.$$

Bar Graphs

6. C This requires an accurate reading of the graph. Use the edge of a paper and estimate the center between 8 and 12. It is obviously more than 10, but is it 11 or more? You can see it is slightly less than 11. It is about 10.7!

7. E In 1970 it is 10.7. In 1980 it is about 16.2. The percentage increase is

$$\% \text{ increase} = \frac{16.2 - 10.7}{10.7} \times 100 = \frac{5.5}{10.7} \times 100 \cong 51\%.$$

This is for 10 years. For each year we divide by 10 to obtain the average per year to be about 5%.

8. E 20% of the population over 25 had 4 years of college. This means that

$$\frac{125{,}000}{P} = 0.2 \quad \text{or} \quad P = \frac{125{,}000}{0.2} = 625{,}000.$$

9. D In 1989 there was 21% completing 4 years and in 1960 it was about 8%. The percent increase in the percentages was

$$\% \text{ increase} = \frac{21-8}{8} \times 100 = \frac{13}{8} \times 100 = 162\%.$$

10. B The number N of people completing 4 years of college was 21% of P, the population. This is written as

$$N = 0.21P.$$

If N is the same for both countries but the population of the other country is $3P$, then if x is that country's percentage we have

$$0.21P = x(3P). \quad \therefore x = \frac{0.21}{3} = 0.07 \qquad \text{or } 7\%.$$

Cumulative Bar Graphs

11. A Two marks on a piece of paper for the wheat (the middle section) in 1980, followed by another mark (use one of the two marks from 1980) for 1970 provides approximately 30,000 more bushels.

12. D The section for soybeans is greatest in 1985. It is just under 100,000 bushels, whereas in 1970 it is about 75,000 bushels.

13. D In 1985 the wheat production is 165,000 and in 1975 it is 110,000. The percentage increase is

$$\% \text{ increase} = \frac{165-110}{110} \times 100 = \frac{55}{110} \times 100 = 50\%.$$

Careful estimating is important in this kind of problem. Your answer could be slightly different, maybe 45% or 55%, but (D) would still be your selection.

14. B The choice appears to be between 1975 and 1985. Wheat production is greater in 1985, but so is the total crop production, so we must compare the two. In 1975 the wheat crop was 110 out of 200 for a percentage of $\frac{110}{200} \times 100 = 55\%$. In 1985 the wheat crop was 165 out of 375 for a percentage of $\frac{165}{375} \times 100 = \frac{33}{75} \times 100 = 44\%$. Therefore, 1975 is selected.

15. C Corn + soybeans + wheat = $125 \times 3 + 95 \times 8 + 165 \times 5 = 375 + 760 + 825 = 1960$. The percentage contribution by wheat was

$$\frac{825}{1960} \times 100 \cong \frac{850}{2000} \times 100 = 42.5\%.$$

Note: To make the division easier, we notched the numerator and denominator up a bit! We are not looking for accuracy, just a good approximation.

Circle Graphs

16. E Heating is 6%. Hence, $0.06 \times 400{,}000 = \$24{,}000$.

17. D The total budget is the sum of the components: \$300,000. This gives

$$\frac{50{,}000}{300{,}000} = \frac{5}{30} = \frac{1}{6}.$$

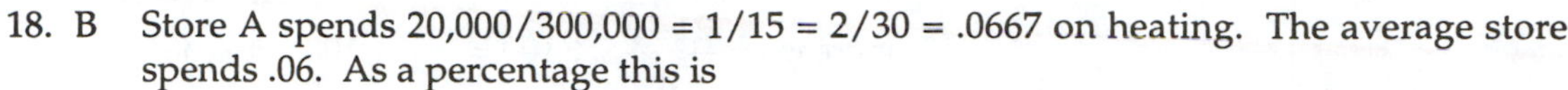

18. B Store A spends 20,000/300,000 = 1/15 = 2/30 = .0667 on heating. The average store spends .06. As a percentage this is

$$\frac{.0667-.06}{.06}\times 100=\frac{66}{6}=11\,\%\,.$$

19. E Store A spends 50,000/300,000 = $\frac{1}{6}$ on wages. The average store spends 14% or 14/100 on wages. The ratio is

$$\frac{1}{6}\div\frac{14}{100}=\frac{1}{6}\times\frac{\overset{50}{\cancel{100}}}{\underset{7}{\cancel{14}}}=\frac{25}{21}\,.$$

20. D The total chain budget is 15 × 400,000 = \$6,000,000. Cooling energy requires 11% of the budget or

Cooling energy costs = 0.11 × 6,000,000 = \$660,000.

Line Graphs

21. E The total sales is the sum: (10 + 20 + 24) × 1000 = \$54,000.

22. C The best sales of *A* was \$25,000. The worst sales of *C* was \$7500. The ratio is

$$\text{ratio}=\frac{25{,}000}{7500}=\frac{250}{75}=\frac{50}{15}=\frac{10}{3}\,.$$

23. C In 1975 the sales of *B* were \$11,000. Sales 150% better than this is 11,000 × 1.5 + 11,000 = \$27,500. This is represented by 27.5 on the graph. It occurred in about 1983. (Do not make the mistake of assuming the sales to be 1.5 × 11,000 = \$16,500. This is only 50% better.)

24. B Total sales in 1985 were (17 + 21 + 36) × 1000 = \$74,000. In 1975 total sales were (8+ 11 + 20) × 1000 = \$39,000. The percent increase was

$$\%\text{ increase}=\frac{74-39}{39}\times 100=\frac{35}{39}\times 100\cong\frac{36}{40}\times 100=90\%.$$

Note: To make the calculation relatively simple, we increased the numerator and denominator just a little; the approximate value does not change much!

25. D The total sales in 1980 were (10 + 20 + 24) × 1000 = \$54,000. This is 4% of the total sales *S*, that is

$$54{,}000=0.04S \qquad \therefore S=\frac{54{,}000}{0.04}=\$1{,}350{,}000.$$

7.5 Data Sufficiency

The Data Sufficiency questions on the GMAT often give college students the most trouble in the mathematics sections of the exam. Students are least familiar with this rather unusual type of question; they simply have not encountered it before. It is often difficult to understand what is being asked and consequently how to respond. The content is the same as that of the Problem Solving questions: arithmetic, algebra, and geometry. After you understand what is being asked, and then practice with a number of questions, you will be better able to respond correctly. Since you took the Diagnostic Test you should know if you have to spend additional time with this type of question. If you are like most other students, you better practice!

Remember, you never have to solve a problem for a numerical answer in the Data Sufficiency Section; you must simply decide when sufficient information is given so that a solution is possible. In fact, if you do solve the problems you are simply wasting time and you probably will not be able to finish the section. Make sketches and write out equations that may be given with words to help you in deciding if there is sufficient information.

Study the following examples and practice with the following problems to become familiar with this type of question. After a number of practice problems you should find these Data Sufficiency questions much easier. Remember, if you know that a problem can be worked with the information given, then respond accordingly; you do not have to be able to actually work the problem, only know that the problem can be solved.

Each Data Sufficiency problem has a QUESTION followed by two additional STATEMENTS. The question can never be answered using the data contained in the question alone. You must first make two decisions: *Decision 1*: Can the question be answered using only the data contained in STATEMENT 1? *Decision 2*: Can the question be answered using only the data contained in STATEMENT 2? If decision 1 is "YES" and decision 2 is "NO", then the correct response is A. If decision 1 is "NO" and decision 2 is "YES", then the correct response is B. If both decisions are "YES", then the correct response is D. If both answers are "NO", then we arrive at *Decision 3*: Can the question be answered using the data contained in STATEMENT 1 *AND* STATEMENT 2? If the answer is "YES", then the correct response is C. If there is not sufficient data in STATEMENT 1 and STATEMENT 2 together, then the correct response is E.

The following examples illustrate this unusual type of problem.

Example 1

What is the length of the hypotenuse?

1) $\overline{AC} = 4$
2) $x = 30°$

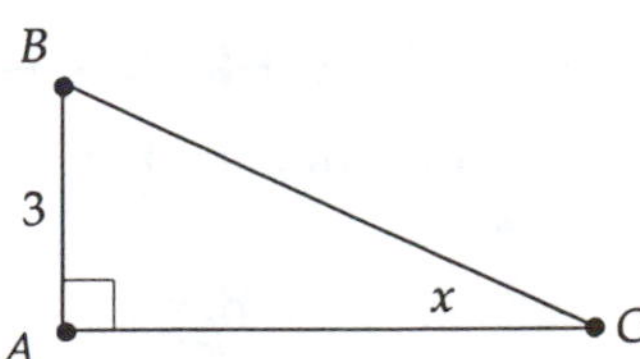

Solution. The little square in the corner implies a right triangle. First, we must determine if (1) provides sufficient information. We see that (1) is sufficient since $3^2 + 4^2 = \overline{BC}^2$. So $\overline{BC}$, the hypotenuse, is known. It is $\overline{BC} = 5$, but it is not necessary to actually make the calculation, just make the decision that the calculation can be made.

Now, ignore (1) and determine if (2) by itself provides sufficient information to answer the question. If $x = 30°$, we see that $\overline{BC}$ sin 30° = 3, or $\overline{BC}$ = 3/sin 30°. (2) is also sufficient. The correct selection is D since (1) and (2) are each sufficient to answer the question. Even if we forget that if we need sin 30° or cos 30°, we know that (2) is sufficient!

Example 2

Is $x > 4$?

1) $x^2 = 9$

2) $x^2 = 25$

Solution. (1) implies that $x = \pm 3$. Both +3 and –3 are less than 4 so the answer is "NO" and (1) is sufficient. A "NO" answer is equally acceptable as a "YES" answer. It is only necessary that there is sufficient information to answer the question.

(2) implies $x = \pm 5$. –5 is less than 4 and +5 is greater than 4 so the question cannot be answered with the information given in (2). The correct response is A.

Example 3

What is $x - y$?

1) $x + y = 8$
2) $x - 2y = 2$

Solution. (1) is not sufficient since $(x-y)$ is the quantity desired. Likewise, (2) is not sufficient. But (1) and (2) together provide us with 2 equations and two unknowns from which $x - y$ can be determined. The correct response is C. (We can solve the problem by subtracting (2) from (1): $3y = 6$, $\therefore y = 2$ and $x = 6$, so that $x - y = 6 - 2 = 4$. This calculation is, however, unnecessary.)

Example 4

How old is Gloria?

1) Gloria's age is four times Alex's age plus Becky's age.
2) Becky was Alex's age fifteen years ago.

Solution. (1) is obviously not sufficient as is (2). Can the question be answered with (1) and (2)? Let x be Gloria's age, y be Alex's age, and z be Becky's age. (1) states that $x = 4y + z$. (2) states that $z - 15 = y$. These two equations contain three unknowns; consequently, we cannot determine x. More information is needed and the correct response is E.

Example 5

A student group sold only donuts and GMAT books to raise funds. How many GMAT books were sold?

1) 30% of the 90 items sold were GMAT books.
2) 63 donuts were sold.

Solution. (1) is sufficient since 30% of 90 is $0.3 \times 90 = 27$. (2) is not sufficient since we do not know the total number of items sold. So the correct response is A. A note of caution: Never let information in (1) influence your decision regarding the information in (2). In this example we cannot assume that 90 items were sold when deciding if (2) provides sufficient information.

Example 6

Is $x^{3.67} > y$?

1) $x = 1, y = 2$

2) $x = 6.95, y = 2065$

Solution. (1) is sufficient since $1^{3.67} = 1$ and the answer is "NO", 1 is not larger than 2. (2) is also sufficient since if we had a calculator we could evaluate $6.95^{3.67}$ and compare it to 2065. The answer can be determined. The correct response is D. Remember, it is not necessary that we make the calculation, or that we have the ability to make the calculation; it is only necessary that we decide if there is sufficient data to answer the question.

Practice Problems

—Data Sufficiency—

Directions: Each data sufficiency problem includes a question followed by two statements, labeled (1) and (2), that contain certain information. Using your knowledge of mathematics and common facts, you must determine if the information in the statements is sufficient to solve the problem. Select:

A if (1) alone is sufficient, but (2) alone is not sufficient;

B if (2) alone is sufficient, but (1) alone is not sufficient;

C if (1) and (2) together are sufficient, but neither alone is sufficient;

D if each statement alone is sufficient;

E if you cannot solve the problem with the information given.

Numbers: Only real numbers are used; no imaginary numbers are used or implied.

Diagrams: Diagrams reflect the information contained in the question, not necessarily the information contained in the two statements.

1. What is the least common multiple of m and n? A B C D E

   (1) n is a factor of m.

   (2) n is not a factor of m.

2. What is the numerical value of a fraction? A B C D E
   (1) Its numerator is its denominator minus 2.
   (2) Its numerator is twice its denominator.

3. Is ab odd or even? A B C D E
   (1) a is odd.
   (2) b is even.

4. Can n/m be written as a mixed number? n and m are integers. A B C D E
   (1) $n > m$
   (2) m is not a factor of n.

5. Is the ratio $\frac{x}{y} \div \frac{n}{m}$ a whole number? x, y, n, and m are integers. A B C D E
   (1) y is a factor of x.
   (2) m is a factor of n.

6. What is the least common denominator of $\frac{1}{x} + \frac{2}{y} + \frac{3}{z}$? x, y, and z are integers. A B C D E
   (1) x and y are factors of z.
   (2) x, y, and z are prime numbers.

7. The average of n and m is 30. What are n and m? A B C D E
   (1) n is twice m.
   (2) n is $m + 6$.

8. Is the set of numbers . . . $w, x, y, z,$ . . . a consecutive set? A B C D E
   (1) w, x, y, z are even numbers.
   (2) w, x, y, z are prime numbers.

9. y workers receive x dollars per week. What is the average wage per worker? A B C D E
   (1) The number of all workers is 7.
   (2) The median wage of the workers is $240.

10. Evaluate $2^x 2^y$. A B C D E
   (1) $x + y = 4$
   (2) $xy = 3$

11. Calculate $6^x/6^y$. A B C D E
   (1) $x/y = 2$
   (2) $x - y = 2$

12. Is xy greater than x^2y^2? A B C D E
    (1) $x = 2$
    (2) $y = 1/3$

13. Is x^2 greater than x^3? $x \neq 0$. A B C D E
    (1) x is less than 1.
    (2) x is positive.

14. Is x^2/y^2 greater than 1? A B C D E
    (1) $x > y$
    (2) y is positive.

15. Is $x = 2$? A B C D E
    (1) $x^2 = 4$
    (2) x is positive.

16. Is $x - y$ greater than $x^2 - y^2$? A B C D E
    (1) $x + y < 1$
    (2) $x > y$

17. What is $\frac{1}{x} + \frac{2}{y}$? A B C D E
    (1) $2x + y = 2$
    (2) $x + y = 4$

18. What is $x/2y$? A B C D E
    (1) $x - y = 2$
    (2) $x/y = 4$

19. Is $(r - y)^2$ greater than $r^2 + y^2$? A B C D E
    (1) $r > y$
    (2) $r > 0$

20. Are the integers l, m, and n consecutive? A B C D E
    (1) The sum of the three integers is 30.
    (2) l is 1 less than m and n is 1 greater than m.

21. Evaluate a fraction if its numerator is x and its denominator is y. A B C D E
    (1) $x = 2y$
    (2) $x + y = 4$

22. What is the value of a fraction if its numerator plus 3 is equal to its denominator minus 2? A B C D E
    (1) Its numerator is 5.
    (2) Its denominator plus its numerator is 6.

23. Calculate $x - 2y$. A B C D E
    (1) $x + y = -6$
    (2) $2x = y + 3$

24. Solve $x^2 - 10ax + 24a^2 = 0$ for a. A B C D E
    (1) $x = -4$
    (2) $x + a = 2$

25. How many people live in a city if 20% of them ride bikes? A B C D E
    (1) 5000 people ride bikes.
    (2) 20,000 people do not ride bikes.

26. Michelle bought a hat on a special sale for $20. How much was it marked down? A B C D E
    (1) It cost the store $40.
    (2) It cost $30 to make the hat.

27. A store owner marks a piece of jewelry up 120%. What is the selling price? A B C D E
    (1) It cost $60 to make the piece.
    (2) It cost the owner $100.

28. A stock falls in price from when it was purchased. What was the percentage loss? A B C D E
    (1) It was purchased for $109.31.
    (2) It sold for $79.62.

29. Write the 3rd term of a geometric progression. A B C D E
    (1) The sixth term is 24.
    (2) The common ratio is 1.25.

30. What is the sum of the first six terms of an arithmetic progression that starts at zero? A B C D E
    (1) The 8th term is 84.
    (2) The common difference is 4.

31. Is t greater than zero? A B C D E
    (1) $t = t^2$
    (2) t is not negative.

32. Is x greater than y? A B C D E
    (1) $xy = 1$
    (2) $y > 1$

33. Is $\frac{x-2}{x+1} \div \frac{x^2-4}{x^2-1}$ greater than y? A B C D E
    (1) $y = -1$
    (2) $x > 0$

34. Is 2^{n+5} equal to y? A B C D E
    (1) $y = 16$
    (2) $n = -2$

35. Is $\frac{1}{x} - \frac{1}{y}$ greater than $y - x$? A B C D E
    (1) $x > 0$
    (2) $y > 0$

36. Is 2, x, y, 54 a progression? A B C D E
    (1) $x = 6$
    (2) $y = 16$

37. How long does it take to walk from A to B to C and back to A if one walks 3 miles per hour? A B C D E
    (1) It's 6 miles from A to C passing through B.
    (2) It's 3 miles from C back to A.

38. A train goes 40 mph from A to B. How far is A from B? A B C D E
    (1) The train leaves at 2 p.m.
    (2) The travel time is $2\frac{1}{2}$ hours.

39. A tree casts a 30-foot shadow. How long is Adam's shadow? A B C D E
    (1) Adam's height is one quarter the tree's height.
    (2) Adam is 10 feet from the tree.

40. What angle do the hands of a clock make? A B C D E
    (1) It's 4:32 p.m.
    (2) The angle is acute.

41. It takes Sheldon's 3 horses 15 hours to plow a field. How long does it take Caleb's horses to plow the same field? A B C D E
    (1) The field is 44 acres.
    (2) Caleb has 5 horses.

42. Hans earned 10% on his investment in 1990. How much money did Hans have invested? A B C D E
    (1) Hans earned $150 in the first six months of 1990.
    (2) Hans earned 10% more in 1990 than he did in 1989.

43. There are 500 items on an assembly line at 11:00. How many are on the line at 11:30? A B C D E
    (1) 10 items leave the assembly line each minute.
    (2) The assembly line holds 800 items.

44. Joe buries 6% of his earnings in his back yard. How much does he have buried? A B C D E
    (1) Joe has worked for 20 years with raises of 5% each year.
    (2) Joe started working for $5000 per year.

45. Angles x and y are acute angles. What is $\angle x$? A B C D E
    (1) $x + y = 120°$
    (2) $\angle x = 2\angle y$

46. Angles A and B are part of a triangle but angle A is acute. What is $\angle A$? A B C D E
    (1) Angle B is obtuse.
    (2) $A + B = 120°$

47. Lines m and n are parallel. What are the acute alternate interior angles cut by a transversal? A B C D E
    (1) The corresponding angles are equal.
    (2) The obtuse alternate interior angles are 112°.

48. What are the two equal angles in an isosceles triangle? A B C D E
    (1) The sum of all three angles is 180°.
    (2) The third angle is 82°.

49. Calculate the length of the hypotenuse of a right triangle. A B C D E
    (1) The angle opposite the hypotenuse is 90°.
    (2) The adjacent leg has a length of 2.6.

50. A pool ball strikes a side rail and departs. What is the angle between the line of approach and the line of departure? A B C D E
    (1) The angle of approach with the side rail is 30°.
    (2) The angle of departure with the side rail is 40°.

51. On the next page, is triangle ABC similar to triangle DEF? A B C D E
    (1) Angle x = Angle y
    (2) $AC = EF$

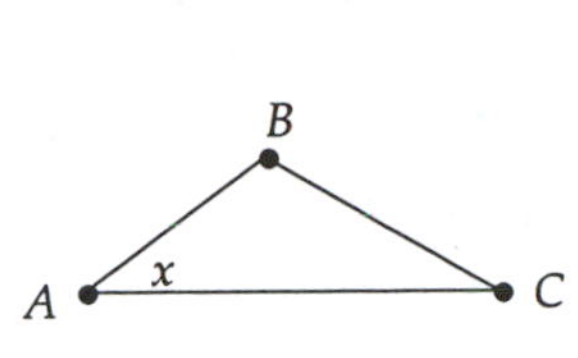

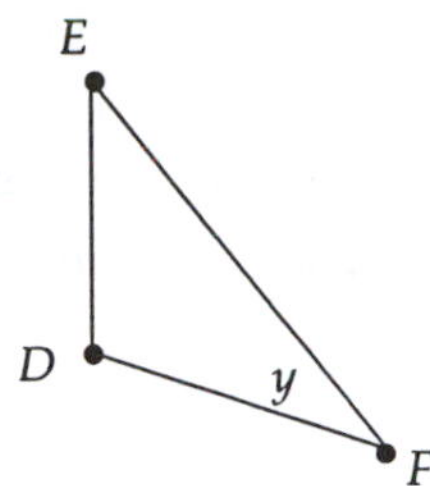

52. What is the value of a central angle of a circle? A B C D E
    (1) It intercepts an arc length of 12.
    (2) The circle radius is 6.

53. Calculate the length of one side of a square that is inscribed in a circle. A B C D E
    (1) The circle diameter is 10.
    (2) The circle circumference is 20.

54. A chain saw makes a 10-inch straight cut in a tree. What is the tree's diameter? A B C D E
    (1) The arc angle is 80°.
    (2) The arc length is 12 inches.

55. What is the area of a rectangle? A B C D E
    (1) Its diagonal is 12 inches long.
    (2) One side is 4 inches long.

56. The volume of a box is numerically equal to one quarter of its surface area. What is the length of the box? A B C D E
    (1) An end of the box is 2 ft by 2 ft.
    (2) The box is upright.

57. What is the length of a line that connects points (8, 4) and (x, y)? A B C D E
    (1) $x = 2y$
    (2) $y = 3$

58. What is the area of a circle with center at (2, 3)? A B C D E
    (1) Point (5, 7) lies on the circle.
    (2) The circumference of the circle is 20.

59. A bar graph presents the annual production of grain in 1990 in a certain county. How much wheat was grown in 1990? A B C D E
    (1) The total grain production in 1990 was 682,070 bushels.
    (2) Wheat made up 12% of the grain crop.

60. A circle graph presents a state's budget. What percentage of the budget goes to education? A B C D E
    (1) The education sector is 115°.
    (2) The state's total budget is $6,321,692.

Answers to Practice Problems

—Data Sufficiency—

1.	A	**13.**	A	**25.**	D	**37.**	C	**49.**	E
2.	C	**14.**	C	**26.**	E	**38.**	B	**50.**	C
3.	B	**15.**	C	**27.**	B	**39.**	A	**51.**	E
4.	C	**16.**	C	**28.**	C	**40.**	C	**52.**	C
5.	E	**17.**	C	**29.**	C	**41.**	B	**53.**	D
6.	D	**18.**	B	**30.**	D	**42.**	E	**54.**	D
7.	D	**19.**	E	**31.**	E	**43.**	E	**55.**	C
8.	E	**20.**	B	**32.**	C	**44.**	C	**56.**	C
9.	E	**21.**	A	**33.**	C	**45.**	C	**57.**	C
10.	A	**22.**	D	**34.**	C	**46.**	E	**58.**	D
11.	B	**23.**	C	**35.**	E	**47.**	B	**59.**	C
12.	C	**24.**	E	**36.**	C	**48.**	B	**60.**	A

Explanations to the Answers

—Data Sufficiency—

1. A The LCM is the smallest integer which is a common multiple of m and n. (1) alone is sufficient since if n is a factor of m (e.g., $m = 12$, $n = 3$), m is the LCM. (2) alone is not sufficient since if n is not a factor of m, m could be a factor of n (e.g., $n = 12$, $m = 3$).

2. C Let x be the numerator and y be the denominator. Then (1) states that $x = y - 2$ and (2) states that $x = 2y$. Both are required for a solution. (There are two unknowns so two equations are needed.)

3. B (1) is not sufficient since an odd times an even is even and an odd times an odd is odd; b could be even or odd. (2) is sufficient since an even times an odd or an even is even.

4. C A mixed number is an integer plus a fraction (e.g., $2\frac{1}{5}$). (1) is not sufficient since m could be a factor of n (e.g., $n = 12$, $m = 3$). (2) is not sufficient since n could be less than m. Both (1) and (2) together are sufficient.

5. E Invert the divisor and multiply giving $\frac{xm}{yn}$. (1) is not sufficient since information on m and n is required. (2) is not sufficient since information on x and y is required. If n were a factor of m (e.g., $m = 12$, $n = 3$) then n could be divided into m, but if m is a factor of n this is not true. Thus, the problem cannot be solved.

6. D (1) is sufficient since z is the LCD (e.g., $x = 3, y = 4, z = 12$). (2) is sufficient since the product xyz is the LCD (e.g., $x = 3, y = 5, z = 7$).

7. D The question is represented by $\frac{n+m}{2} = 30$. (1) is sufficient since $n = 2m$. (2) is sufficient since $n = m + 20$.

8. E A set is consecutive if each member is a successor of its predecessor. The numbers 2, 10, 4, 8 are even but are not consecutive. And 3, 7, 5, 13 are prime but not consecutive. More information is needed for both (1) and (2).

9. E To calculate an average z, we must know the total x and the number of workers y, i.e., $z = \frac{x}{y}$. (1) is not sufficient and (2) is unrelated to the average.

10. A To evaluate $2^x 2^y = 2^{x+y}$, (1) alone is sufficient since $x + y = 4$. (2) is not sufficient.

11. B To evaluate $6^x/6^y = 6^{x-y}$, (2) alone is sufficient since $x - y = 2$. (1) is not sufficient.

12. C If xy is less than 1, then $(xy)^2 < xy$. If xy is greater than 1 then $(xy)^2 > xy$. Both (1) and (2) are needed and neither alone is sufficient.

13. A A negative number is less than 1 (e.g., $-2 < 1$). Is $(2)^2 > (-2)^3$? Yes, since $(-2)^2$ is positive and $(-2)^3$ is negative; a positive is always greater than a negative. Suppose $x = \frac{1}{2}$: Is $\left(\frac{1}{2}\right)^2 > \left(\frac{1}{2}\right)^3$? Yes, since $\frac{1}{4} > \frac{1}{8}$. Hence, (1) is sufficient since x cannot be zero. Statement (2) is not sufficient since x could equal 4.

14. C (1) is not sufficient since, for negative numbers, x^2/y^2 is less than one if $x > y$ (e.g., $x = -2, y = -3$). If y is positive, then $x^2/y^2 > 1$ if $x > y$. (2) alone is obviously not sufficient.

15. C (1) implies $x = +2$ or -2. So (2) is also necessary.

16. C $x^2 - y^2$ is factored as $x^2 - y^2 = (x - y)(x + y)$. So $x - y > x^2 - y^2$ if $(x + y) < 1$ and $x - y$ is positive. $x - y$ is positive if $x > y$. (An example is $x = \frac{1}{2}$, $y = \frac{1}{4}$.)

17. C $\frac{1}{x}+\frac{2}{y}=\frac{2x+y}{xy}$. If $(2x + y)$ is known that is not sufficient. Since (1) and (2) can be solved to yield x and y, $\frac{2x+y}{xy}$ can be determined.

18. B (1) alone is not sufficient. (2) alone is sufficient since $x/2y = 2$ by dividing both sides by 2.

19. E If r is positive and y is negative (e.g., $r = 2$, $y = -4$) then $r > y$ and $(r - y)^2 = 36$ and $r^2 + y^2 = 4 + 16 = 20$. If r and y are both positive (e.g., $r = 4$, $y = 2$) then $(r - y)^2 = 4$ and $r^2 + y^2 = 20$. Hence, there is insufficient information.

20. B (1) is obviously not sufficient. (2) is sufficient (e.g., 9, 10, 11 or –9, –8, –7). Their sum is not of interest.

21. A Evaluate x/y. (1) alone is sufficient since $x/y = 2$. (2) alone is not sufficient.

22. D Evaluate x/y if $x + 3 = y - 2$. (1) alone is sufficient; if $x = 5$ we can calculate y and evaluate x/y. (2) alone is sufficient; if $x + y = 6$ and $x + 3 = y - 2$, calculate x and y and evaluate x/y. (Add and find $x = 1/2$. Then $y = 11/2$ and $x/y = 1/11$. A solution is not needed, however!)

23. C (1) is not sufficient and (2) is not sufficient. But, (1) and (2) can be solved simultaneously to determine x and y and consequently $x - 2y$.

24. E If $x = -4$, can we solve $16 + 40a + 24a^2 = 0$? This quadratic can be solved. If $x = 2 - a$, the given quadratic can be written as $(a - 2)^2 - 10a(2 - a) + 24a^2 = 0$; this is obviously another quadratic that can be solved. But, both quadratics provide two answers and sufficient information to select one of the two does not exist.

25. D Let x be the number of people. Then $0.2x$ ride bikes. (1) states that $5000 = 0.2x$ so we can determine x; (1) is sufficient. If 20% ride bikes then 80% do not ride bikes. (2) states that $0.8x = 20{,}000$ so (2) is also sufficient.

26. E To determine how much the hat was marked down we must know the original sale price of the hat. Neither (1) nor (2) provide the original sale price.

27. B The selling price is $(x + 1.2x)$ where x is the owner's cost. The cost to make the piece is not of interest so (1) is not sufficient. (2) is sufficient since it provides $x = \$100$.

28. C To calculate the percentage loss we must know the original purchase price and the selling price. Both (1) and (2) are required.

29. C To write the terms in a geometric progression we must know the ratio of two successive terms (the common ratio) and the value of one of the terms. (1) and (2) provide the required information.

30. D We can find the terms in an arithmetic progression if we know the first term and the 8th term, since the common difference could be calculated. The sum of the first six terms could then be determined. Hence (1) is sufficient. If we know the first term and the common difference, the progression can also be written; hence (2) is also sufficient.

31. E $t = t^2$ can be written as $t^2 - t = 0$ or $t(t-1) = 0$. This has 2 solutions: $t = 0$ and $t = 1$. To answer the question, (1) is not sufficient. Since 0 and 1 are not negative, (2) does not help. Hence, more information is needed.

32. C If $xy = 1$ and $y = -2$, then $x = -\frac{1}{2}$ so that $x > y$. If $y = 2$, $x = \frac{1}{2}$ then $x < y$. So (1) is not sufficient. If in addition to $xy = 1$ we require $y > 1$, then $x < y$ and the answer is "No".

33. C Invert the dividend and factor: $\frac{x-2}{x+1}\frac{x^2-1}{x^2-4} = \frac{x-2}{x+1}\frac{(x-1)(x+1)}{(x-2)(x+2)} = \frac{x-1}{x+2}$.

Is $\frac{x-1}{x+2} > -1$? This can be rewritten as $x-1 > -x-2$ or $2x > -1$. So the answer is "Yes" if $x > -\frac{1}{2}$. Consequently, both (1) and (2) are needed.

34. C Using (1) we have $2^{n+5} = 16 = 2^4$. Hence, $n + 5 = 4$ so that $n = -1$. (2) specifies n and with $n = -2$ the answer is "No". The question is answered using both (1) and (2).

35. E Write $\frac{1}{x} - \frac{1}{y} = \frac{y-x}{xy}$. The question is then, is $\frac{y-x}{xy} > y - x$? If $x > 0$, then $y - x$ is positive if $y > x$ or negative if $y < x$. If both x and y are greater than zero we are left with the same result: $y - x > 0$ if $y > x$ and $y - x < 0$ if $y < x$. Since a negative flips the "greater than" sign we cannot answer the questions; i.e., we must have additional information.

36. C We must know both terms x and y to determine if the numbers form a progression. With the two numbers specified the answer can be determined. (It's either "Yes" or "No"; we do not care which!)

37. C Using (1) we can determine how long it takes to walk from A to C (time = $\frac{6 \text{ miles}}{3 \text{ miles/hr}}$ = 2 hrs). But we do not know if we take the same route back to A. Hence, (2) is needed to determine the time to return to A (time = $\frac{9 \text{ miles}}{3 \text{ miles/hr}}$ = 3 hrs).

38. B (1) is obviously not sufficient since we do not know how long it takes. (2) provides the time of travel which is sufficient to calculate the distance (D = $2\frac{1}{2} \times 40$ = 100 miles).

39. A The tree's height and shadow and Adam's height and shadow form similar triangles so that $\frac{H}{L} = \frac{h}{l}$. If $h = \frac{1}{4}H$ then we can solve for l. $\left(l = \frac{h}{H}L = \frac{1}{4} \times 30.\right)$ (1) is sufficient and (2) is of no interest.

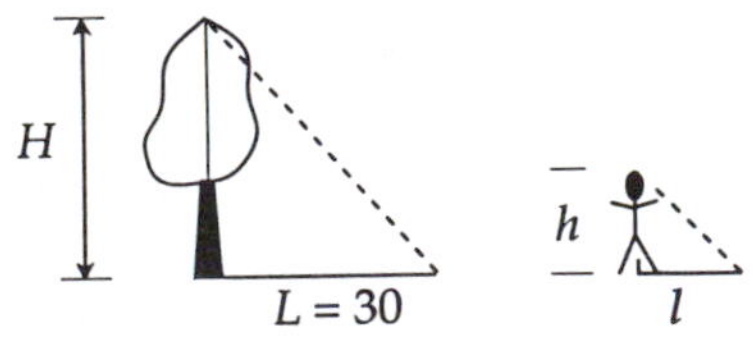

40. C The hands of a clock form two angles, one acute and the other obtuse. With (1) alone we cannot determine which of the two angles is desired. (2) allows us to make that determination. (To actually calculate the angle is not our objective—so let's not do it!)

41. B The size of the field is of no interest. Caleb's 5 horses will take $\frac{3}{5}$ of the time that Sheldon's horses take $\left(\frac{3}{5}\times 15 = 9 \text{ hrs}\right)$. Only (2) is needed. The size of the field given by (1) is not of interest.

42. E (1) is not sufficient since we do not know how much Hans earned in the last six months. (2) does not indicate how much he earned in 1989 so we cannot determine how much he earned in 1990. More information is needed. (If Hans earned an additional \$150 in the last six months, we could determine the amount P invested from $0.10P = 300$, so that $P = \$3000$; but we cannot make that assumption.)

43. E (1) is not sufficient since we must know how many leave the assembly line each minute. (2) does not give the needed information so more information is needed. (The number N of items on the line would be $N = 500 - 10(30) + n(30)$ where n is the number added each minute.)

44. C (1) is not sufficient since we do not know his earnings per year. (2) provides that information so we could make the calculation.

45. C Acute angles are less than 90°. To find x we must solve the two equations given by (1) and (2) simultaneously. So both are needed. ($2y + y = 120$. $\therefore$ $3y = 120$. $\therefore$ $y = 40$ and $x = 80$.)

46. E Let the three angles of the triangle be A, B, and C. Then $A + B + C = 180$. If $A + B = 120$, then $C = 180 - 120 = 60$. We know that $A < 90$ and $B > 90$, but that is not sufficient to solve for A. So, more information is needed.

47. B Corresponding angles are always equal, so (1) does not provide useful information. The acute alternate interior angles are the angles shown as x. Since $x + 112 = 180$ we can find x with statement (2). ($x = 68°$.)

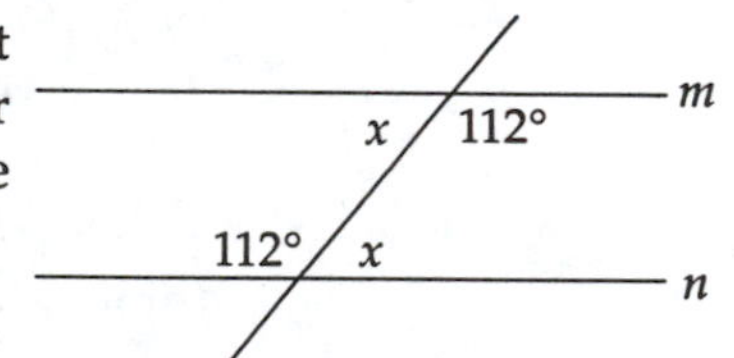

48. B In an isosceles triangle two angles (and two sides) are equal. Let each of the angles be x and the third angle be y. Then (1) states that $2x + y = 180$ and (2) states that $y = 82$. So we find that $2x = 180 - 82 = 98$ so that $x = 49°$. But the information in (1) is generally true for all triangles, a fact that is assumed known. Consequently, only (2) is needed. (1) is redundant and not needed.

49. E The angle opposite the hypotenuse of a right triangle is always 90° so (1) is not of interest. We must know both legs to calculate the hypotenuse (or one leg and one of the acute angles). So (2) does not provide sufficient information.

50. C The approach angle and the departing angle are not, in general, equal. But the side rail is a straight line so the sum of the approach angle x, the angle of departure y, and the third angle z must equal 180° (i.e., $x + y + z = 180$). If $x = 30°$ and $y = 40°$, (1) and (2) allow us to calculate z ($z = 180 - 70 = 110°$).

51. E For two triangles to be similar, they must have two angles equal, not just one. An additional requirement that two sides be equal is insufficient. Additional information is needed.

52. C The central angle is the angle formed by the two radii that connect each end of the arc. To calculate the central angle we must know the arc length and the radius, as provided by (1) and (2). (In this problem the central angle = 12/6 = 2 radians, or $2\left(\frac{180}{\pi}\right) = \frac{360}{\pi}$ degrees.)

53. D If $r = \frac{d}{2} = 5$, then we can calculate l, so (1) is sufficient. If the circumference is 20, then $20 = 2\pi r$ and $r = \frac{10}{\pi}$, so (2) is also sufficient to calculate l.

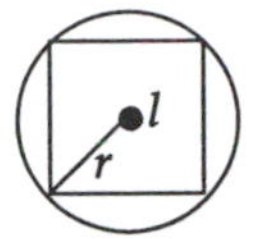

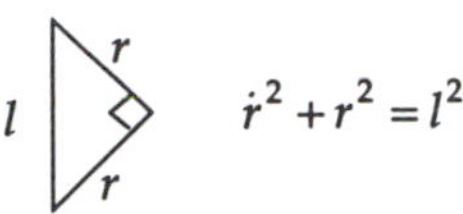

$r^2 + r^2 = l^2$

The diagonals of a square are ⊥ each other.

54. D If the arc angle is 80°, then the other two angles of the isosceles triangle can be determined. With one side specified, the other two can be determined so that (1) is sufficient. If the arc length is 12, and the cut length is 10, then two equations could be written to find the diameter, so (2) is also sufficient. One could also visualize only one circle passing through the ends of a 10-inch line with arc length 12 inches; therefore, its diameter must be determinable.

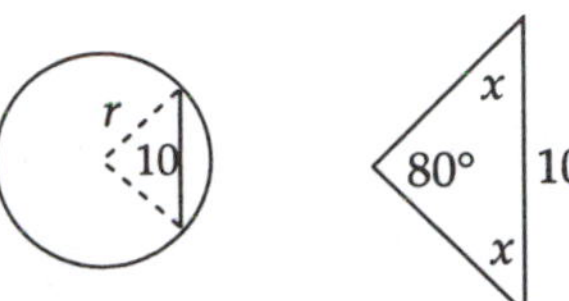

55. C The length of a diagonal is not sufficient to determine the sides of a rectangle. If one side and a diagonal are known, the other side can be determined ($4^2 + x^2 = 12^2$). Hence, (1) and (2) are required.

56. C The volume of a box is the product of its three sides, providing it is upright; so (2) is needed. If it is upright, its volume is xyz and its surface area is $2xy + 2xz + 2yz$. If $xyz = \frac{1}{4}(2xy + 2xz + 2yz)$ and $x = 2, y = 2,$ then z can be calculated so (1) and (2) are necessary.

57. C The length L is given by solving the equation $L^2 = (x-8)^2 + (y-4)^2$. We must know both x and y before we can determine L. The fact is $x = 2y$ is not sufficient to find L, but with the additional information, $y = 3$, L can be determined.

58. D If (2, 3) is the center of the circle and (5, 7) lies on the circle, the radius is the distance between the points; this can be found, so (1) is sufficient $\left(r = \sqrt{(5-2)^2 + (7-3)^2} = \sqrt{9+16} = \sqrt{25} = 5. \quad \therefore A = \pi r^2 = 25\pi\right)$.
If the circumference is 20 then the radius is known $\left(C = 2\pi r. \quad \therefore r = \frac{20}{2\pi} = \frac{10}{\pi}\right)$ and the area is known $\left(A = \pi r^2 = \pi \frac{100}{\pi^2} = \frac{100}{\pi}\right)$; so (2) is also sufficient.

59. C Both (1) and (2) are needed to determine how much wheat was grown. ($0.12 \times 682{,}070 =$ bushels of wheat.)

60. A There are 360° degrees in a circle graph. The percentage of the budget that goes to education is $\frac{115}{360} \times 100$, so (1) is sufficient. (2) is not sufficient since we do not know the total budget.

Test No. 1

Sections:

1. Reading Comprehension
2. Sentence Correction
3. Critical Reasoning
4. Problem Solving
5. Analysis of an Issue
6. Data Sufficiency
7. Critical Reasoning
8. Data Sufficiency
9. Analysis of an Argument

Followed by:

Score Analysis Charts
Explanations To All Answers

Practice these suggestions for Test #1:

1. Write your answers next to the questions on each page. Then transfer your answers to the answer sheet a block at a time.

2. On a difficult question, if you cannot eliminate at least two choices, leave the question blank and do not guess.

3. Put a circle around a question number if you are uncertain of the correct answer and think you may return to it if time permits. Before moving on to the next question, guess an answer if you can eliminate at least two choices; you may not have time to return.

4. Construct diagrams, draw sketches, and write equations in the empty space on the exam. Such aids are often helpful in your thought process.

5. Try to simulate actual exam conditions and time yourself very carefully. Do not exceed the allotted 25 or 30 minutes per section. Take a break after the fifth section to simulate the actual exam.

6. Do not worry if you leave some questions unanswered. The GMAT is quite difficult and students often leave questions unanswered. If you cannot eliminate at least two choices on a question, do not guess.

7. Write each of your Analytical Writing exercises on the front sides of three of the six unlined 8.5"x11" sheets that you should have at hand for this exam. Practice writing legibly, with a #2 pencil. Try to fill all three front sides, but leave an inch or so margins all around and don't write too small or too large. We recommend that you write 4-8 paragraphs of 4-8 sentences each. [To have your essays graded professionally by a team coordinated by our Writing section author, mail them to: GLP, POB 483, Okemos MI 48805, or fax to: 517-339-4455. Your writing will be graded and returned within 2 weeks. The fee is $20.00. Include your Visa/MC number with expiration date or a check or money order.]

How to handle the answer sheet:

- Each section begins with number 1.
- If a section has fewer than 25 questions, ignore the extra answer blanks.
- If you change an answer, erase it completely.
- Do not make any extraneous marks on the answer sheet.

SIGNATURE:

ANSWER SHEET

(simulated GMAT form)

BE SURE EACH MARK IS DARK AND COMPLETELY FILLS THE INTENDED SPACE AS ILLUSTRATED HERE: ●.
YOU MAY FIND MORE RESPONSE SPACES THAN YOU NEED. IF SO, PLEASE LEAVE THEM BLANK.

	SECTION 1	SECTION 2	SECTION 3	SECTION 4	SECTION 6	SECTION 7	SECTION 8
1.	ⒶⒷⒸⒹⒺ	ⒶⒷⒸⒹⒺ	ⒶⒷⒸⒹⒺ	ⒶⒷⒸⒹⒺ	ⒶⒷⒸⒹⒺ	ⒶⒷⒸⒹⒺ	ⒶⒷⒸⒹⒺ
2.	ⒶⒷⒸⒹⒺ	ⒶⒷⒸⒹⒺ	ⒶⒷⒸⒹⒺ	ⒶⒷⒸⒹⒺ	ⒶⒷⒸⒹⒺ	ⒶⒷⒸⒹⒺ	ⒶⒷⒸⒹⒺ
3.	ⒶⒷⒸⒹⒺ	ⒶⒷⒸⒹⒺ	ⒶⒷⒸⒹⒺ	ⒶⒷⒸⒹⒺ	ⒶⒷⒸⒹⒺ	ⒶⒷⒸⒹⒺ	ⒶⒷⒸⒹⒺ
4.	ⒶⒷⒸⒹⒺ	ⒶⒷⒸⒹⒺ	ⒶⒷⒸⒹⒺ	ⒶⒷⒸⒹⒺ	ⒶⒷⒸⒹⒺ	ⒶⒷⒸⒹⒺ	ⒶⒷⒸⒹⒺ
5.	ⒶⒷⒸⒹⒺ	ⒶⒷⒸⒹⒺ	ⒶⒷⒸⒹⒺ	ⒶⒷⒸⒹⒺ	ⒶⒷⒸⒹⒺ	ⒶⒷⒸⒹⒺ	ⒶⒷⒸⒹⒺ
6.	ⒶⒷⒸⒹⒺ	ⒶⒷⒸⒹⒺ	ⒶⒷⒸⒹⒺ	ⒶⒷⒸⒹⒺ	ⒶⒷⒸⒹⒺ	ⒶⒷⒸⒹⒺ	ⒶⒷⒸⒹⒺ
7.	ⒶⒷⒸⒹⒺ	ⒶⒷⒸⒹⒺ	ⒶⒷⒸⒹⒺ	ⒶⒷⒸⒹⒺ	ⒶⒷⒸⒹⒺ	ⒶⒷⒸⒹⒺ	ⒶⒷⒸⒹⒺ
8.	ⒶⒷⒸⒹⒺ	ⒶⒷⒸⒹⒺ	ⒶⒷⒸⒹⒺ	ⒶⒷⒸⒹⒺ	ⒶⒷⒸⒹⒺ	ⒶⒷⒸⒹⒺ	ⒶⒷⒸⒹⒺ
9.	ⒶⒷⒸⒹⒺ	ⒶⒷⒸⒹⒺ	ⒶⒷⒸⒹⒺ	ⒶⒷⒸⒹⒺ	ⒶⒷⒸⒹⒺ	ⒶⒷⒸⒹⒺ	ⒶⒷⒸⒹⒺ
10.	ⒶⒷⒸⒹⒺ	ⒶⒷⒸⒹⒺ	ⒶⒷⒸⒹⒺ	ⒶⒷⒸⒹⒺ	ⒶⒷⒸⒹⒺ	ⒶⒷⒸⒹⒺ	ⒶⒷⒸⒹⒺ
11.	ⒶⒷⒸⒹⒺ	ⒶⒷⒸⒹⒺ	ⒶⒷⒸⒹⒺ	ⒶⒷⒸⒹⒺ	ⒶⒷⒸⒹⒺ	ⒶⒷⒸⒹⒺ	ⒶⒷⒸⒹⒺ
12.	ⒶⒷⒸⒹⒺ	ⒶⒷⒸⒹⒺ	ⒶⒷⒸⒹⒺ	ⒶⒷⒸⒹⒺ	ⒶⒷⒸⒹⒺ	ⒶⒷⒸⒹⒺ	ⒶⒷⒸⒹⒺ
13.	ⒶⒷⒸⒹⒺ	ⒶⒷⒸⒹⒺ	ⒶⒷⒸⒹⒺ	ⒶⒷⒸⒹⒺ	ⒶⒷⒸⒹⒺ	ⒶⒷⒸⒹⒺ	ⒶⒷⒸⒹⒺ
14.	ⒶⒷⒸⒹⒺ	ⒶⒷⒸⒹⒺ	ⒶⒷⒸⒹⒺ	ⒶⒷⒸⒹⒺ	ⒶⒷⒸⒹⒺ	ⒶⒷⒸⒹⒺ	ⒶⒷⒸⒹⒺ
15.	ⒶⒷⒸⒹⒺ	ⒶⒷⒸⒹⒺ	ⒶⒷⒸⒹⒺ	ⒶⒷⒸⒹⒺ	ⒶⒷⒸⒹⒺ	ⒶⒷⒸⒹⒺ	ⒶⒷⒸⒹⒺ
16.	ⒶⒷⒸⒹⒺ	ⒶⒷⒸⒹⒺ	ⒶⒷⒸⒹⒺ	ⒶⒷⒸⒹⒺ	ⒶⒷⒸⒹⒺ	ⒶⒷⒸⒹⒺ	ⒶⒷⒸⒹⒺ
17.	ⒶⒷⒸⒹⒺ	ⒶⒷⒸⒹⒺ	ⒶⒷⒸⒹⒺ	ⒶⒷⒸⒹⒺ	ⒶⒷⒸⒹⒺ	ⒶⒷⒸⒹⒺ	ⒶⒷⒸⒹⒺ
18.	ⒶⒷⒸⒹⒺ	ⒶⒷⒸⒹⒺ	ⒶⒷⒸⒹⒺ	ⒶⒷⒸⒹⒺ	ⒶⒷⒸⒹⒺ	ⒶⒷⒸⒹⒺ	ⒶⒷⒸⒹⒺ
19.	ⒶⒷⒸⒹⒺ	ⒶⒷⒸⒹⒺ	ⒶⒷⒸⒹⒺ	ⒶⒷⒸⒹⒺ	ⒶⒷⒸⒹⒺ	ⒶⒷⒸⒹⒺ	ⒶⒷⒸⒹⒺ
20.	ⒶⒷⒸⒹⒺ	ⒶⒷⒸⒹⒺ	ⒶⒷⒸⒹⒺ	ⒶⒷⒸⒹⒺ	ⒶⒷⒸⒹⒺ	ⒶⒷⒸⒹⒺ	ⒶⒷⒸⒹⒺ
21.	ⒶⒷⒸⒹⒺ	ⒶⒷⒸⒹⒺ	ⒶⒷⒸⒹⒺ	ⒶⒷⒸⒹⒺ	ⒶⒷⒸⒹⒺ	ⒶⒷⒸⒹⒺ	ⒶⒷⒸⒹⒺ
22.	ⒶⒷⒸⒹⒺ	ⒶⒷⒸⒹⒺ	ⒶⒷⒸⒹⒺ	ⒶⒷⒸⒹⒺ	ⒶⒷⒸⒹⒺ	ⒶⒷⒸⒹⒺ	ⒶⒷⒸⒹⒺ
23.	ⒶⒷⒸⒹⒺ	ⒶⒷⒸⒹⒺ	ⒶⒷⒸⒹⒺ	ⒶⒷⒸⒹⒺ	ⒶⒷⒸⒹⒺ	ⒶⒷⒸⒹⒺ	ⒶⒷⒸⒹⒺ
24.	ⒶⒷⒸⒹⒺ	ⒶⒷⒸⒹⒺ	ⒶⒷⒸⒹⒺ	ⒶⒷⒸⒹⒺ	ⒶⒷⒸⒹⒺ	ⒶⒷⒸⒹⒺ	ⒶⒷⒸⒹⒺ
25.	ⒶⒷⒸⒹⒺ	ⒶⒷⒸⒹⒺ	ⒶⒷⒸⒹⒺ	ⒶⒷⒸⒹⒺ	ⒶⒷⒸⒹⒺ	ⒶⒷⒸⒹⒺ	ⒶⒷⒸⒹⒺ

SECTIONS 5 & 9 ARE "WRITING ANALYSIS"
—TO BE COMPLETED ON 6 SEPARATE SHEETS
OF PAPER THAT YOU SHOULD HAVE READY.

SECTION 1 Reading Comprehension

23 Questions
Time: 30 minutes

Directions: In this group, each passage is followed by questions based on its content. On the basis of what is stated or implicit in the passage, please select the best answer to each question.

Passage 1:

In a large number of cases the incentive for acquisition or merger of enterprises producing competitive products was to gain more effective control of output, price, and markets. Such horizontal combination increased organizational capabilities and productivity *only* if a single, centralized administrative control was quickly established over the merged or acquired companies and then the facilities and personnel were rationalized to exploit more fully the economies of scale and scope. . . . But if the companies acquired or those coming into the merger were not administratively centralized and rationalized but instead continued to operate autonomously much as they had before the change, the enlarged enterprise remained little more than a federation of firms. The resulting cost advantages were minimal.

The reasons for vertical integration—growth through obtaining facilities along the chain of production—were more complex. Faster throughput and with it significant cost reductions and increased productivity in terms of output per worker or unit of equipment rarely resulted from vertical integration unless the additional processes were directed to the firm's existing ones by its own rails, conveyors, or pipes. Such integration was particularly successful in the production of chemicals, metals, and machinery. Where the facilities to make related processes were located at a distance, increased throughput was less feasible.

The motive for such investments in growth by vertical integration was primarily defensive, but not in the same way as through horizontal combination. Sometimes the aim was to withhold supplies from competitors and so create barriers to entry in the industry. Far more often, however, the motive for such vertical integration was to assure a steady supply of materials into the enterprise's production processes, which was essential if the cost advantages of scale and scope were to be maintained. It provided insurance against great cost increases resulting from fluctuating production or even shutdown. It reduced the cost of high inventory storage and other carrying costs. It lowered the risk that suppliers would fail to carry out contractual agreements—risks economists and organizational theorists have termed "bounded rationality" (human fallibility) and "opportunism" (self-interest with guile). The greater the investment in capital-intensive facilities and the greater the optimal size of these facilities, the greater the incentive for insurance against such transaction costs. Thus the more concentrated the facilities of production and the more concentrated the sources of supply, the more likely was the integration of the two within a single enterprise.

Alfred D. Chandler, Jr. Scale and Scope: The Dynamics of Industrial Capitalism. Cambridge, Massachusetts: The Belknap Press of Harvard University Press, 1990. pp. 37-38.

1. The purpose of this passage is to
   A) analyze reasons for and effects of vertical integration and horizontal combination.
   B) analyze cost reductions and increased productivity as incentives in mergers.
   C) analyze feasibility of increased throughput.
   D) analyze defensive motive for investment in growth.
   E) analyze bounded fallibility and opportunism.

2. What is the more frequent motive for vertical integration?
   A) to gain control of output, price, and market
   B) to establish administrative control over acquired companies
   C) to assure a steady supply of materials into production processes
   D) to federate acquired firms
   E) to increase organizational capabilities

3. The passage identifies risks that derive from which two kinds of behavior identified by economists and organizational theorists?
   A) vertical integration and horizontal combination
   B) administrative centralization and rationalization
   C) fluctuating production and shutdown
   D) bounded rationality and opportunism
   E) withholding supplies from competitors and creating barriers to entry in the industry

4. Vertical integration is associated with control of the chain of production; horizontal combination is associated with control of
   A) investment.
   B) cost advantage.
   C) administration.
   D) increased throughput.
   E) insurance against great cost increases.

5. Which of the following is not an effect of vertical integration cited in this passage?
   A) increased control of output, price, and market
   B) insurance against great cost increases resulting from fluctuating production or shutdown
   C) lowered risk that suppliers might default on contracts
   D) reduction in cost of high inventory storage
   E) reduction in other carrying costs

6. Which two conditions promote incentive for insurance against transaction costs?
   A) more concentrated production facilities and sources of supply
   B) greater investment in and optimal size of capital-intensive facilities
   C) reduced costs of inventory storage and other carrying costs
   D) fuller exploitation of economies of scale and scope
   E) fluctuating production and shutdown

Passage 2:

In the half century before the coming of the railroad and the telegraph, . . . nearly all [business enterprises] remained partnerships, and the partners managed as well as owned the business. As a result, the number of salaried managers in 1850, except for plantation overseers, was still tiny. Owners managed and managers owned.

The railroad provided the technology . . . to move an unprecedented volume of goods at unprecedented speed. . . . And the telegraph made possible . . . almost instantaneous communication between distant points.

Yet this new continental transportation and communication system could not be created overnight. The construction of the new nationwide networks, the development of the organizational capabilities of the enterprises that provided such transportation and communication, and the working out of the essential inter-company arrangements required more than half a century.

. . . The efficient operation of this transportation and communication infrastructure required a series of organizational as well as technological innovations. Most critical was the creation of managerial hierarchies for the individual roads, to schedule—and to coordinate administratively with utmost precision—the flow of trains and traffic across the railroad's different operating units or "divisions."

Thus during the 1850s American railroads became the pioneers in modern management. Because of the complexities of their operations they formed almost overnight the nation's first managerial enterprises. In the larger railroads . . . managers with almost no equity in the enterprise made the operating decisions. And as the roads grew, these managers came to play a critical role in determining the strategy of their growth and competition.

These managers subdivided their operations into smaller operating groups and then appointed middle managers to supervise, monitor, and coordinate the different functional activities on each division: the movement of trains; the handling of traffic . . .; the maintenance of motive power, equipment, and roadbed; and the handling of and accounting for the thousands of daily financial transactions. To operate such an organization, railroad managers devised a line-and-staff system of administration. The managers responsible for the movement of trains were the line officers, acting on the line of authority running from the president to the general manager, to the general superintendent, to the division superintendent. The managers responsible for the other functions—the movement of freight and passengers, maintenance, and finances—were designated staff executives. Line officers ordered the movement of men and trains; the staff executives set the standards and policies for their functional departments. Railroad executives . . . devised the accounting and informational systems needed to control the movement of trains and traffic, to account for the funds handled, and to determine profit and loss for the several operating units and for the enterprise as a whole. These systems provided basic techniques used by the founders of early multi-unit industrial enterprises to create their internal control and accounting systems.

Alfred D. Chandler, Jr. **Scale and Scope: The Dynamics of Industrial Capitalism. Cambridge, Massachusetts: The Belknap Press of Harvard University Press, 1990. pp. 53-55**

7. The purpose of this passage is to
   A) analyze the formation of early railroad and telegraph companies.
   B) identify the origin of modern management systems in the organization of early railroad companies.
   C) describe operations of the railroads.
   D) analyze coordination of routes and schedules.
   E) analyze working out of essential inter-company relationships.

8. Which of the following is the central idea of this passage?
   A) Managers of railroads determined competitive strategies of railroad companies.
   B) Managers of railroads appointed middle managers to supervise divisions.
   C) Managers of railroads formed the nation's first managerial enterprise.
   D) Managers with no equity in railroads made operating decisions.
   E) Managers of railroads created early internal control and accounting systems.

9. What innovation was most critical to the effective operation of the early infrastructure discussed in this passage?
   A) the declining number of enterprises managed by partner-owners
   B) the invention of the telegraph
   C) early information systems to control movement of trains
   D) creation of managerial hierarchies for individual roads
   E) construction of new nationwide networks

10. What induced officers of railroads to devise managerial hierarchies and techniques?
    A) the complexity of railroad operations
    B) the need to control movement of trains and traffic
    C) the need to determine profit/loss for several operating units
    D) the need to account for funds handled
    E) the incentive of ownership

11. Concerning the transportation and communication infrastructure discussed in this passage, it may be inferred from information given that
    A) the new continental system was created by managers with considerable investment in the enterprise.
    B) organizational and technological innovations were made only by larger railroads that could afford them.
    C) its organizational and technological innovations transformed certain features of American business.
    D) the seeds of managerial techniques for American business were planted by 1800.
    E) the subdivision of operations tended to weaken the line of managerial authority.

12. According to the passage, what is the central fact about the origin of the inter-company arrangements in the infrastructure?
    A) its immediate efficiency
    B) its development over more than one-half century
    C) the precision of coordination required
    D) the unprecedented speed of the railroads
    E) the instantaneous triumph over distance provided by the telegraph

Passage 3:

In most respects dissatisfaction with market processes in their broad impacts on society has developed more sharply in the twentieth than in the nineteenth century. Concentration on the immediate interests of the bargainers, emphasis on interests measurable in money . . .[,] these features of market processes were not felt as sources of major strain in a relatively simple economy and in a culture which valued the means the market provided for expressing prized initiatives of individual will. It took the rapid growth of closer social interdependence and belated perception of postponed costs of market-borne change after 1900 to generate pronounced worry over products of these aspects of market operations. In contrast, however, substantial controversy marched with the course of affairs from 1790 on regarding market influences on unequal distribution of wealth and income and the political and social alignments which contributed to and were shaped by inequalities.

Criticism might pursue two counts: one, that the market contributes materially to creating economic inequality; second, that where it does not create inequality it does not provide a reliable means for redressing inequality, but is more likely to entrench it. In fact the record is mixed—mixed enough so that realistic appraisal cannot simply label the market an instrument or a bulwark of oppression.

The Anglo-American tradition has valued the private market and the law's protection of its relative autonomy as contributors to civil liberty. This doctrine has taught that assets acquired in market dealing . . . and livelihood gained from occupations that require no official license to serve private customers nerve and arm individuals to play roles in public affairs and if necessary to oppose mistakes or abuse of official power. Healthy dispersion of power in public policy making also derives largely from diverse private associations. . . . The Supreme Court has in effect recognized this civil liberties contribution of the market in the breadth of First Amendment protection it has cast about private political contributions and private lobbying activity.

. . . [A]ggressive private operators have used market gains to build preeminent practical power for themselves in markets and in public arenas. From such vantage points they have pursued profit according to their own criteria of propriety. In its administrative flexibility and reach the market has offered great leverage for accumulating and concentrating wealth or control of wealth. Moreover, the focus of the private market is on allocating resources to produce and distribute goods and services for sale, not on determining suitable standards for distributing ultimate life satisfactions. Thus, pursuing its ordinary working goals, insofar as it has not fostered growth of inequality of wealth or incomes, market activity has tended to support enjoyment of superior economic power wherever superior power already existed.

James Willard Hurst. Law and Markets in United States History: Different Modes of Bargaining Among Interests. Madison, Wisconsin: The University of Wisconsin Press, 1982. pp. 64-66

13. The subject of this passage is
    A) prevention of abuse of official power.
    B) opposition to economic oppression.
    C) impacts of market processes on society.
    D) judicial protection of civil liberty.
    E) dispersion of power in public policy making.

14. What aspect of the autonomy of the private market does the Anglo-American tradition value?
    A) its concentration of power
    B) its administrative flexibility and reach
    C) its opposition to mistakes of official power
    D) the practical power it confers upon private operators
    E) its contributions to civil liberty

15. According to the passage, market processes were not a source of worry in
    A) a simple economy.
    B) a complex economy.
    C) a culture that devalues individual will.
    D) a culture that values collective will.
    E) legal commentary on the private market.

16. Since 1790, controversy has attended what market influence?
    A) its provision of a means for redressing inequality
    B) its emphasis on interests measurable in money
    C) its concentration on the immediate interests of bargainers
    D) its contributions to inequality
    E) its belated perception of costs of change

17. According to this passage, the ordinary working goals of the private market are
    A) the pursuit of profit according to standards of propriety.
    B) the allocation of resources to produce and distribute goods and services for sale.
    C) interests measurable in money.
    D) expression of initiatives of reformist zeal.
    E) fixing of standards for distributing life satisfactions.

18. The administrative flexibility and reach of the market enable it to
    A) allocate resources to produce goods and services.
    B) pursue profit without impediment.
    C) accumulate, concentrate, or control wealth.
    D) concentrate on the interests of bargainers.
    E) emphasize interests measurable in money.

19. Which statement below best expresses the central idea of this passage?
    A) The market contributes unequivocally to economic inequality.
    B) The market provides no reliable means of redressing inequality.
    C) Dispersion of power in public policy making promotes democracy.
    D) Market activity tends to support superior economic power wherever superior power already exists.
    E) Social interdependence stimulates worry over effects of market operations.

<u>Passage 4</u>:

Until recently, the generation and tabulation of [toxicological and environmental] data in the United States has been carried out in an unsystematic fashion by several federal and state government agencies, industry, and the medical profession. . . . Generally, chemicals were considered to be harmless unless proven otherwise. It was not until the 1960s that Americans began to believe that systematic investigation and regulation of the toxicological and environmental impact of chemicals was necessary. By this time, however, DuPont had been doing research on the toxic effects of chemicals for thirty years at its Haskell Laboratory for Toxicology and Industrial Medicine.

. . . DuPont encountered its first toxicological problems when it began to manufacture dynamite in the 1880s. Nitric acid fumes destroyed lung tissue and caused numerous fatalities; nitroglycerin absorbed through the skin caused headaches. . . .

[B]enzene caused immediate problems for DuPont. Because it was a cheap and effective solvent for rubber, DuPont used benzene to make coated fabrics. . . . In the spring of 1920, two workers in the plant died from benzene poisoning, prompting an investigation by the company's safety division. Dr. A. K. Smith discovered that all the workers had cotton plugs in their noses to stop chronic nose bleeds caused by benzene fumes. At this time, the proportion of benzene in the solvent was cut from 60 to 45 percent and the ventilation improved. Two years later, however, another worker died, and DuPont abandoned the use of benzene.

. . . Not long after the benzene crisis, DuPont experienced the tetraethyl-lead (TEL) poisonings. . . . The episode received nationwide attention . . . because of the wild behavior of the victims. . . . Although not required to by any regulatory or legislative body, DuPont designed and installed a completely closed process to protect the lives of its employees. . . .

In the 1920s, DuPont's need for toxicological data increased, in part to ensure that the company's products posed no risks for consumers. Before introducing moisture-proof cellophane for food packaging, in 1927, DuPont commissioned Henry Field Smith to carry out guinea pig feeding studies in his private laboratory. . . . Smith concluded that the cellophane coating was "absolutely harmless." However, a few years later, one of the principal ingredients, tricresyl phosphate (TCP), was implicated in a major public health disaster. [An alcoholic] drink called "ginger jake," which had been laced with TCP, caused thousands of cases of paralysis and numerous deaths in 1930 and 1931. After learning that moisture-proof cellophane contained TCP, the National Institute of Health undertook experiments with chickens and discovered that the birds developed . . . paralysis at a dosage of 10 milligrams of TCP per day. DuPont replaced TCP in the coating after learning of these results.

David A. Hounshell and John Kenley Smith, Jr. Science and Corporate Strategy: DuPont R & D, 1902-1980. Cambridge: Cambridge University Press, 1988. pp. 555-558

20. According to the passage, after testing or use showed that a chemical was toxic, DuPont generally followed which course of action?
    A) continued testing
    B) modified use
    C) continued use
    D) reduced proportion of harmful chemical
    E) abandoned use or installed closed manufacturing process

21. DuPont's experience with toxicological problems dates to
    A) its manufacture of cellophane.
    B) its manufacture of dynamite.
    C) its manufacture of tetraethyllead.
    D) its manufacture of benzene.
    E) routine regulation of toxic chemicals in the 1960s.

22. In general, DuPont has acted to protect workers and consumers
    A) under public pressure.
    B) under legal directive.
    C) when required by regulatory agency or legislative body.
    D) at the discretion of its executives.
    E) in response to practical experience and research evidence.

23. Against a background of unsystematic gathering of data on toxicity of chemicals by federal and state agencies, industry, and the medical profession, DuPont
    A) took the initiative and established a record of testing.
    B) adhered to slowly evolving government regulation.
    C) followed the dictum that chemicals were harmless unless proven otherwise.
    D) dealt slowly and reluctantly with the threat of toxicity to employees.
    E) moved only in order to ensure favorable consumer relations.

STOP!

If you finish before time is up (30 minutes), you may return to any of the questions in Section 1. Do not turn to any other section of the test.

SECTION 2 Sentence Correction

22 Questions
Time: 25 minutes

Directions: Some part of the following sentences, or the entire sentence, is underlined. The first of the five versions beneath each sentence is identical to the underlined portion. If you think the text is most correct as written in the problem, select (A); otherwise, choose the best sentence correction from the four remaining choices. Follow the requirements of written English when making your selection. Pay attention to grammar, word choice, and general sentence construction. Select the version that expresses most effectively and accu-rately what is contained in the original sentence.

1. Coming in from the rain, a gust of wind hit them with the ferocity of a small tornado.
   A) Coming in from the rain, a gust of wind hit them
   B) Coming in from the rain, they were hit by a gust of wind
   C) After they had come in from the rain, they were hit by a gust of wind
   D) After coming in from the rain, a gust of wind hit them
   E) As they had come in from the rain, a gust of wind hit them

2. Over the objections of Jenny and I, the committee passed the resolution before it adjourned.
   A) Jenny and I, the committee passed
   B) Jenny and I, the committee had passed
   C) Jenny and me, the committee passed
   D) Jenny and me, the committee had passed
   E) Jenny and me the committee passed

3. John was not ready to move to the new company because they had not rated it highly by any investment company.
   A) John was not ready to move to the new company because they had not rated it highly by any investment company.
   B) Because of its low investment rating, John was not ready to move to the new company.
   C) Because of it's low investment rating, John was not ready to move to the new company.
   D) John was not ready to move to the new company because no investment company rated it highly.
   E) John was not ready to move to the new company since it was not rated highly by any investment company.

4. Neither his frequent attempts at humor or his numerous attempts to cooperate with both his roommates together seemed to change his standing with them.
   A) Neither his frequent attempts at humor or his numerous attempts to cooperate with both his roommates together
   B) Neither his frequent attempts to be funny nor his numerous attempts to cooperate with both his roommates
   C) Neither his frequent attempts at humor nor his numerous attempts to cooperate with both his roommates
   D) Neither his frequent attempts to be funny or his numerous attempts to cooperate with both his roommates
   E) Neither his frequent tries at humor or his numerous attempts to cooperate with his roommates

5. Many people like sitting by the fireplace, trying to be different from each other and to quaff a mug of beer when they are in a ski lodge.
   A) like sitting by the fireplace, trying to be different from each other and to quaff a mug of beer
   B) like sitting by the fireplace, trying to be different from each other and quaffing a mug of beer
   C) like having sat by the fireplace, trying to being different from each other and having quaffed a mug of beer
   D) like sitting by the fireplace, trying to be different than each other and quaffing a mug of beer
   E) like sitting by the fireplace, being different than each other and to quaff a mug of beer

6. If Americans take stock of their values, they will come to understand that they are quite philanthropic.
   A) their values, they will come to understand that they are quite philanthropic
   B) their values, we will come to understand that they are quite philanthropic
   C) their values, we have come to understand that they are quite philanthropic
   D) their values, they have come to understand that they are quite philanthropic
   E) their values, we have been coming to understand that they are quite philanthropic

7. First put on your skis, and then you should adjust the binders.
   A) First put on your skis, and then you should adjust the binders.
   B) First put on your skis and then adjust the binders.
   C) First put on your skis and then your binders should be adjusted.
   D) First put on your skis, and then adjust the binders.
   E) First you should put on your skis and then adjust the binders.

8. Jacques who is obviously one of the best marksmen in France although few people like his brusque manner or undisciplined life style.
   A) Jacques who is obviously one of the best marksmen in France although few people like his brusque manner or undisciplined life style.
   B) Although few people like his brusque manner or undisciplined life style, Jacques is obviously one of the best marksmen in France.
   C) Jacques, obviously one of the best marksmen in France, has an undisciplined life style which few people like together with his brusque manner.
   D) Although Jacques is obviously one of the best marksmen in France, few people like his brusque manner or undisciplined life style.
   E) Jacques is obviously one of the best marksmen in France liking neither his brusque manner nor his undisciplined life style.

9. Every person feels that their needs are more crucial than that of other human beings.
   A) Every person feels that their needs are more crucial than that of other human beings.
   B) Every person feels that his needs are more crucial than that of other human beings.
   C) Every person feels that his needs are more crucial than those of other human beings.
   D) Every person feels that his needs are more crucial from that of other human beings.
   E) Every person feels that his needs are more crucial from those of other human beings.

10. A big raise has not only been given, at the beginning of the year, to the janitors but to the maintenance workers also.
   A) A big raise has not only been given, at the beginning of the year, to the janitors but to the maintenance workers also.
   B) At the beginning of the year, a big raise has been given, not only to the janitors but to the maintenance workers also.
   C) A big raise has not only been given, at the beginning of the year, to the janitors but also to the maintenance workers.
   D) A big raise has not only been given, at the beginning of the year, to the janitors but to the maintenance workers also.
   E) At the beginning of the year, a big raise was given, not only to the janitors but also to the maintenance workers.

11. Irregardless of the complaints of his troops, they were led into dangerous circumstances by the general.
   A) Irregardless of the complaints of his troops, they were led into dangerous circumstances by the general.
   B) Regardless of the complaints of his troops, the general led them into dangerous circumstances.
   C) Irregardless of the complaints of his troops, the general led them into dangerous circumstances.
   D) Regardless of the complaints of his troops, they were led into dangerous circumstances by the general.
   E) Regardless of the complaints of his troops, they had been led into dangerous circumstances by the general.

12. The concert having been finished and the audience having filtered out, the maestro relaxed in the dressing room with the impresario.
   A) The concert having been finished and the audience having filtered out, the maestro relaxed in the dressing room with the impresario.
   B) Because the maestro had finished the concert and because the audience had been filtered out, he relaxed in the dressing room with the impresario.
   C) Since the concert had been finished and the audience had filtered out, the maestro relaxed in the dressing room with the impresario.
   D) Since the concert had finished and the audience had filtered out, the maestro relaxed in the dressing room with the impresario.
   E) The concert having been finished and the audience having filtered out, the maestro had relaxed in the dressing room with the impresario.

13. When a married couple has discovered that they are incompatible, they should divorce and marry someone quite different than their first mate.
   A) discovered that they are incompatible, they should divorce and marry someone quite different than
   B) discovered that they were incompatible, they should divorce and marry someone quite different than
   C) discovered that they are incompatible, they should divorce and marry someone quite different from
   D) discovered that they were incompatible, they should divorce and marry someone quite different from
   E) discovered that they were incompatible, they divorce and marry someone quite different from

14. Jimmy, who ate sardines from the officer's mess, became quite ill.
   A) Jimmy, who ate sardines from the officer's mess, became quite ill.
   B) Jimmy, that ate sardines from the officers mess, became quite ill.
   C) Jimmy that ate sardines from the officer's mess became quite ill.
   D) Jimmy, who has eaten sardines from the officers mess, became quite ill.
   E) Jimmy who has eaten sardines from the officer's mess became quite ill.

15. The minister of justice wants to try a fix of the country's very unique court system.
   A) wants to try a fix of the country's very unique court system
   B) wants to try to fix the country's most unique court system
   C) wants to try and fix the country's unique court system
   D) wants to try to fix the country's unique court system
   E) wants to try and fix the country's very unique court system

16. She is the lady who baked a cake for whomever would come.
   A) who baked a cake for whomever would come
   B) whom baked a cake for whoever would come
   C) who baked a cake for whoever would come
   D) whom baked a cake for whomever would come
   E) , who baked a cake for whoever would come

17. For years the Ptolemaic view of a geocentric universe had held sway before the Copernican view became dominant.
    A) had held sway before the Copernican view became dominant
    B) held sway before the Copernican view became dominant
    C) was held by a lot of people before the Copernican view became dominant
    D) held its own before the Copernican view became dominant
    E) held sway before the Copernican view was adopted by the society

18. In Newtonian laws of motion, there is a condition and it's converse regarding bodies at rest and bodies in motion.
    A) there is a condition and it's converse regarding bodies at rest and bodies in motion
    B) there is a condition and its converse regarding bodies at rest and bodies in motion
    C) there are a condition and its converse regarding bodies at rest and bodies in motion
    D) there are a condition and it's converse regarding bodies at rest and bodies in motion
    E) there has been a condition and its converse regarding bodies at rest and bodies in motion

19. Some people have very clear opinions about capital punishment, the incarceration of child abusers and what should be done to common, ordinary thieves.
    A) child abusers and what should be done to common, ordinary thieves
    B) child abusers and what the police should do to thieves
    C) child abusers and what should be done to common, ordinary thieves
    D) child abusers and the length of jail terms for thieves
    E) child abusers and the length of jail terms for common, ordinary thieves

20. When the policeman said "It's them all right", the teacher thought "Oh, no, who would say such a sentence?"
    A) "It's them all right", the teacher thought "Oh, no, who would say
    B) "It's they all right", the teacher thought "Oh, no, who would say
    C) "It's them all right", the teacher thought "Oh, no, whom would say
    D) "It's they all right", the teacher thought "Oh, no, whom would have been saying
    E) "It's them all right", the teacher thought "Oh, no, who would have been saying

21. A good time was had by all at the Halloween party and the next day was spent recovering.
    A) A good time was had by all at the Halloween party and the next day was spent recovering.
    B) A good time was had by all at the Halloween party but the next day was spent recovering.
    C) Everybody had a good time at the Halloween party but they spent the next day recovering.
    D) At the Halloween party, everybody had a good time but the next day was spent recovering.
    E) All the partygoers had a good time at the Halloween party but they spent the next day recovering.

22. After he lay down, having finished a hard day's work, sleep descended on him like a soft, velvet blanket.

A) having finished a hard day's work, sleep descended on him
B) having finished a hard day's work, he felt sleep descend on him
C) sleep descended on him having finished a hard day's work
D) having finished a hard day's work, sleep had descended on him
E) having completed a hard day's work, sleep descended on him

STOP!

If you finish before time is up (25 minutes), you may return to any of the questions in Section 2.
Do not turn to any other section of the test.

SECTION 3 Critical Reasoning

16 Questions
Time: 25 minutes

Directions: Select the best answer for each of the following questions.

1. A researcher announces that a survey of a sample of dentists specializing in children's dentistry showed that 71% of them bought for their own children toothpaste which was fortified with the new poly-carbonate additive. He adds that this confirms the claim that poly-carbonate toothpaste is an effective aid in dental hygiene.

   A critic responds by pointing out that the research was commissioned and paid for by the manufacturer of the poly-carbonate additive, and that this manufacturer has just contracted with the same researcher to do another project.

   The critic's observation, if true,

   A) casts some substantial doubt on the connection between the survey results and the conclusion drawn from them.
   B) casts some substantial doubt on the accuracy of the reported survey results.
   C) casts some substantial doubt on the expertise of practicing dentists.
   D) casts some substantial doubt on the care with which dentists treat their own families.
   E) has no real bearing on the claims made by the researcher.

Questions 2 and 3 refer to following scenario.

The Academic Dean of Sunset College has proposed a sweeping revision of the pre-med curriculum. As evidence of the comparatively poor quality of the present program (relative to other pre-med programs) he cites the fact that, over the past ten years, Sunset students who have taken the Medical College Admissions Test (MCAT) have on the average scored more than ten points below the national average. Some professors, however, are resisting the Dean's proposal, maintaining that the pre-med program is quite satisfactory as it stands.

2. Which of the following, if it is a fact, will best support the professors' case against the Dean?

   A) Sunset students also score below the average in other nationally administered tests, such as the GRE and the GMAT.
   B) The average scores of Sunset students in the MCAT have risen consistently over the past ten years.
   C) The average GPA for Sunset students in the pre-med program is higher than that for any other major in the college.
   D) Impending changes in the system of health care delivery will probably soon make medicine less attractive as a profession.
   E) Academic counselors at Sunset have long been encouraging any student with an interest in medicine to take the MCAT, saying that "You can't lose much by trying."

3. The Dean's case would be weakened if it could be shown that
   A) several other colleges which are roughly similar to Sunset in size and resources have higher average scores on the MCAT than does Sunset.
   B) the top ten percent of Sunset scores on the MCAT are consistently well below the top ten percent of scores nationally.
   C) Sunset seems to attract a comparatively small number of the very best high school graduates who express an interest in medicine.
   D) at Sunset a surprisingly high number of students who begin the pre-med program drop out of it before taking the MCAT.
   E) demographic data indicates that a serious shortage of primary-care physicians is likely to develop within the next 15 years.

4. Many common proverbs have an "opposite" proverb which seems to make more-or-less the opposite point. Of the following proverbs, which one fits least well with "Nothing ventured, nothing gained."?
   A) A stitch in time saves nine.
   B) He who laughs last laughs loudest.
   C) A penny saved is a penny earned.
   D) A bird in the hand is worth two in the bush.
   E) Penny wise, pound foolish.

5. Mrs. Jones: "My daughter Barbara recently graduated from college and has just taken a good job in Chicago."

   Mrs. Smith: "That's wonderful! I hope she enjoys the work."

   Mrs. Jones: "I think she will. She has had summer jobs for the past four years, and she enjoyed all of them."

   Which of the following, if they are facts, would strengthen our confidence in Mrs. Jones' conclusion?

   i. The four summer jobs were all with advertising agencies, and the new job is also in advertising.
   ii. The four summer jobs were in advertising, manufacturing, direct sales, and entertainment.
   iii. The four summer jobs were all in advertising.

   A) i
   B) i and ii
   C) ii
   D) i, ii, and iii
   E) i and iii

6. American roulette wheels are divided into 38 equal spaces, numbered 1 through 36, 0, and 00. Henry, an avid gambler, has calculated that the "average" number of times for any given number to come up in 988 spins of the wheel is exactly 26. He has also recorded the last 988 spins of a particular wheel, and he notices that the number 7 has come up only 16 times, while 19 came up 27 times. Which of the following conclusions is most strongly supported by this data?
   A) In the next 988 spins of that wheel, the number 7 will probably come up more than 26 times.
   B) In the next 988 spins of that wheel, the number 7 will probably come up less than 26 times.
   C) In the next 988 spins of that wheel, the number 7 will probably come up exactly 26 times.
   D) In the last 988 spins of that wheel, at least one number came up 36 times or more.
   E) In the next spin of that wheel, 7 is slightly more likely to come up than is 19.

7. A statistics professor greets his new class by saying, "Of course, all of you are strangers to me, and I don't really know anything about your personal lives. But I'm sure that at least three of you celebrate your birthdays in the same month."

   What is the smallest size of class for which the professor is bound to be right?

   A) 25
   B) 3
   C) 36
   D) 35
   E) 23

8. Joe and Barbara Fisher, walking into the Golden Glitter Hotel and Casino, are greeted by the manager, along with some photographers, and others. The manager explains that Barbara is the one-millionth customer to visit this year, and she will receive a nice assortment of gifts. One of these is a completely free shot at a special game. Barbara will be allowed to roll a single (ordinary, six-sided) die one time. Before she rolls she must choose one of two payoff options. The first option will pay her $7,200 if she rolls a six, and nothing otherwise. The other option will pay nothing if she rolls a six, and $1,200 otherwise.

   Joe quickly does some mental arithmetic. He argues that a 1/6 chance of winning $7,200 is worth $1,200, while a 5/6 chance of winning $1,200 is worth only $1,000. He therefore urges Barbara to choose the first option. But she is somewhat skeptical of his advice, and is inclined toward the other option.

   Which of the following, if it is a known fact, would properly re-enforce Barbara's skepticism?

   A) A $7,000 windfall now would enable the Fishers to have a nice European trip for their 25th anniversary, but they have nothing special in mind which could be done for $1,200.
   B) Barbara still remembers her first trip to Las Vegas, when she stayed up all night playing slot machines and lost almost $400.
   C) Barbara has a strong moral aversion to gambling.

D) An extra $1,200 now would make it possible for the Fishers to close the deal on a boat they'd love to have, and at a very good price. $7,200 would, of course, also make that possible, and the extra money would go into the bank.
E) If Barbara wins in this game, then the hotel will probably use her picture in its publicity.

9. It is said that Louis Pasteur was interested in the fact that chickens are very resistant to anthrax infection. He also knew that chickens have a higher body temperature than the common animals which are susceptible to anthrax. He formed the hypothesis that it was this higher temperature which conferred the resistance.

To test his hypothesis, he inoculated some chickens with the anthrax bacillus. He then placed them in a cool-water bath which reduced their body temperature by a few degrees. The next day all of these chickens were dead. Pasteur took this as a confirmation of his hypothesis.

The experiment, as described above, would be strengthened considerably by the inclusion of a control group of chickens. Which of the following control groups could be expected to contribute the most to the decisiveness of the experiment?

A) A group of infected chickens which were kept in normal conditions—i.e., without the cooling bath.
B) A group of chickens previously inoculated with Pasteur's anthrax vaccine, now infected and kept in normal conditions.
C) A group of non-infected chickens placed in the cooling bath.
D) A group of chickens previously inoculated with Pasteur's anthrax vaccine and kept in normal conditions.
E) A group of chickens previously inoculated with Pasteur's anthrax vaccine, now infected and placed in the cooling bath.

10. Lou observes that if flight 409 is canceled, then the manager could not possibly arrive in time for the meeting. But flight 409 was not canceled. Therefore, Lou concludes, the manager will certainly be on time. Evelyn replies that even if Lou's premises are true, his argument is fallacious. And therefore, she adds, the manager will not arrive on time after all.

Which of the following is the strongest thing that we can properly say about this interchange?

A) Evelyn is mistaken in thinking Lou's argument to be fallacious, and so her own conclusion is unwarranted.
B) Evelyn is right about Lou's argument, but nevertheless her own conclusion is unwarranted.
C) Since Evelyn is right about Lou's argument, her own conclusion is well-supported.
D) Since Evelyn is mistaken about Lou's argument, her own conclusion must be false.
E) Evelyn is right about Lou's argument, but nevertheless her own conclusion is false.

11. There has been a sharp increase in the subscription prices of many professional and scholarly journals in the past seven years. Many publishers ascribe the necessity for these increases to the easy availability of photo-copying facilities, which enable people simply to copy the articles they want rather than buying the journal.

Which of the following, if it is a fact, would make this explanation more plausible?

A) The great majority of professional and scholarly journals have a massive backlog of papers awaiting publication.
B) Over the past five years there has been a substantial decline in the number of individual subscriptions to professional and scholarly journals, while library subscriptions have remained fairly stable.
C) In the five years immediately preceding the price surge, there was a substantial decline in the number of individual subscriptions to professional and scholarly journals, while library subscriptions remained fairly stable.
D) Many libraries have recently begun cutting back on subscriptions to professional and scholarly journals.
E) In almost every field, several new professional and scholarly journals have begun publication in the past few years.

12. The U.S. is not one of the world's large gold producers. Most of the known U.S. gold deposits—those sites which could be mined primarily for their gold yield—are profitable only when the price of gold is rather high. However, much U.S. copper ore is associated with small amounts of gold. This gold is routinely recovered, at very little additional expense, during copper smelting, and it adds a little to the profitability of copper production.

Which of the following conclusions could be reasonably inferred from this data?

i. When the price of gold is low, then U.S. gold production will probably fluctuate up and down, following the price of copper.
ii. When gold prices rise, then copper prices will probably also soon increase.
iii. When copper prices rise, then gold prices will probably soon decline significantly.

A) i
B) ii
C) iii
D) i and ii
E) i and iii

13. In Sunset College, a small liberal-arts institution, the faculty have long complained that their offices are uncomfortably hot during much of the year. Recently, the trustees have voted to allow faculty members to install window air-conditioners in their own offices, but they must buy the units themselves. An enterprising salesman immediately mailed brochures to all of the faculty, describing a new energy-efficient unit. The brochure explains that while the unit may cost a little more than the competition, the savings in electric power over a period of three years will completely cover that increased cost. These units will then generate a significant net saving over the remaining seven to ten years of their estimated useful life.

    Despite the attractiveness of this argument, and the statistical data which supported it in the brochure, most Sunset faculty members chose one of the cheaper competing makes. Which of the following would be a plausible explanation of this fact?

    A) Many of the faculty fear that the costs of electrical energy will rise steadily for the foreseeable future, and consequently the calculations in the brochure will soon be outdated.
    B) Most of the faculty believe that competing manufacturers will soon introduce new models of their own which will match the efficiency of the make described in the brochure.
    C) Academicians are generally skeptical of advertising and commercial claims.
    D) The faculty members must pay for the unit, but the college pays for the power to operate it.
    E) Most faculty members believe that the cost of air-conditioning units, like that of most consumer goods, will soon rise significantly, and that consequently they should buy as soon as possible (if they intend to buy at all).

14. Officials of Kosmos Importing are planning a massive direct-mail operation to sell a new imported hand-tool to home craftsmen. They expect to mail to about 5,000,000 addresses, at a cost of about 28 cents per mailing. And they expect to import the tool at a net cost of $7.00 per unit.

    They have conducted a preliminary price test, involving three randomly selected groups of one thousand people from their mailing lists. One group was offered the tool at $9.95, the second group at $14.95, and third group at $19.95. An additional charge of $3.00 for shipping and handling is added to each price, and Kosmos estimates that the actual cost of shipping and handling a unit will be $2.45.

    At the highest price, they received 30 orders for a response rate of 3%. At $14.95, the response was approximately 5%; and at $9.95, 9% made the purchase.

    Several executives now argue for another test mailing, to test two new prices. If their suggestion is heeded, which of the following pair of prices would be the most useful to test?

    A) $8.95 and $21.95
    B) $8.95 and $13.95
    C) $10.95 and $13.95
    D) $12.95 and $17.95
    E) $16.95 and $21.95

15. A recent editorial in a London newspaper laments the fact that no senior minister in the British government (roughly equivalent to a cabinet member in the U.S.) has a university degree in science or has been a working scientist. This was thought to be especially distressing in view of the fact that many questions of public policy, from abortion to nuclear power, involve responses to opportunities or problems generated by science and technology.

    A promising response to this concern, arguing that things are not as bad as they might seem, could involve which of the following claims?

    A) Most of the public policy questions in this area are really about the morality and value of scientific and technological developments. They do not require much technical understanding of the sort which scientists have and other people do not have.
    B) Scientists, by and large, have little interest in politics and public policy. It would be difficult to find scientists with the degree of commitment required for a serious contribution at the highest governmental level.
    C) British science, more than any other segment of British intellectual life, has suffered from the "brain drain" to the United States.
    D) There is very little opportunity for, and indeed little need for, scientific expertise in the lower levels of government. There is therefore almost no way for a scientist to rise through the ranks to a top-level position in government.
    E) The rewards of a life of public service in politics, in terms of both money and prestige, are not high enough to attract top-flight scientists to this area.

16. During the past year, Bottle & Capp, a corporation manufacturing vitamin supplements and other health-related products, has engaged in a rather expensive campaign of "corporate image" advertising. One of the vice-presidents now urges that the contract for such advertising be extended for another year. He argues that it has been a good investment, citing the fact that in the last three quarters of the fiscal year just ended, sales increased by 29% over the comparable part of the previous year, and profits were up by 22%.

    Another vice-president, however, is skeptical, and would prefer a different advertising strategy. She observes that the cited increases are typical for the industry as a whole over the past year, although none of their competitors have used corporate image advertising.

    The most accurate way of summarizing the second officer's point would be

    A) She argues that the effect may not really be due to its supposed cause, because there has not been a sufficient lapse of time between the cause and the effect.
    B) She argues that the assignment of a cause for this effect is premature, because there is as yet no well-established theory of such interactions.
    C) She argues that corporate image advertising is unprofitable, since it has evidently benefited competitors as much as the corporation which paid for it.
    D) She knows that effective advertising requires a constant influx of new ideas and approaches, and she argues that one year of corporate image advertising is enough for awhile.
    E) She argues that the effect may not be due to its alleged cause, since the same effect is found elsewhere without that cause.

STOP!

If you finish before time is up (25 minutes), you may return to any of the questions in Section 3. Do not turn to any other section of the test.

SECTION 4 Problem Solving

16 Questions
Time: 25 minutes

Directions: Solve each problem and mark the best answer on the Answer Marking Sheet provided. You may use the open space on the test paper for scratch work (in the actual exam no scratch paper is permitted). Figures are drawn to scale unless otherwise noted. All numbers are real numbers (no imaginary numbers).

1. Evaluate $1\frac{1}{3}+5\frac{1}{6}-6\frac{1}{2}$.
   A) 2/3 B) 1/2 C) 1/3 D) 5/6 E) 0

2. If $x+3=y$ and $x-y=4$, find x.
   A) 1 B) 2 C) 3 D) 4 E) none of the above

3. A pool ball strikes a table edge at 20° and leaves at 30°. What is the angle between the line of impact and the line of reflection?
   A) 90° B) 110° C) 120° D) 130° E) 150°

4. What type of triangle connects the points (0, 0), (8, 0), and (4, 5)?
   A) Isosceles B) Equilateral C) Right D) Scalene E) 3-4-5

5. If $x \otimes y = -\frac{x}{y}$ defines the operator $\otimes$, calculate x if $x \otimes 4 = 16 \otimes x$.
   A) – 2 B) – 4 C) – 6 D) 6 E) 8

Questions 6 and 7 refer to this diagram

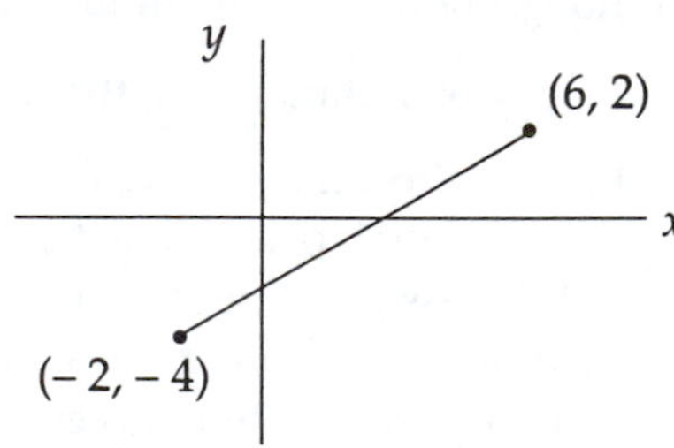

6. If the line segment shown above is the hypotenuse of a triangle which is a multiple of a 3-4-5 right triangle, select the coordinates of the missing vertex.
   A) (6, – 2) B) (– 2, 4) C) (4, – 4) D) (– 2, 2) E) (2, – 4)

7. If the line segment shown above is the diameter of a circle, what is the circle's area?
   A) 25π B) 36π C) 49π D) 64π E) 100π
   D) $(x-y)/xy$ E) none of the above

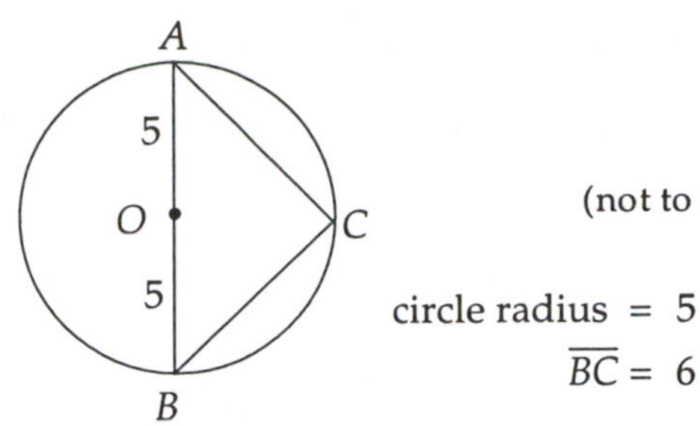

8. Calculate the area of the above triangle *ABC*.
   A) 20 B) 24 C) 28 D) 32 E) 36

9. Evaluate $(-2)^3 + 3^{-1} + 4\frac{2}{3}$.
   A) $8\frac{1}{3}$ B) $-1\frac{2}{3}$ C) 13 D) -3 E) -5

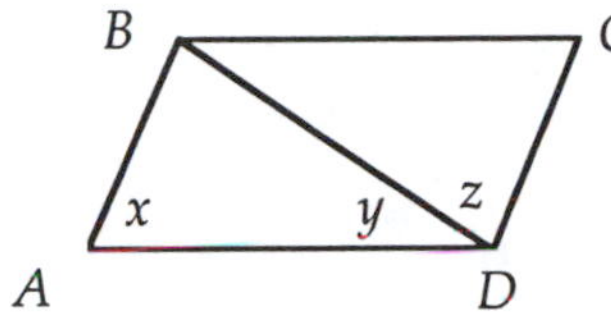

Parallelogram *ABCD*
(not to scale)

10. If angle $x = 60°$ and angle $y = 50°$ in the diagram above, calculate angle *z*.
    A) 75° B) 70° C) 65° D) 60° E) 55°

11. An investment yields an interest payment of \$200 each month. If the interest rate is 8%, what is the amount of the investment?
    A) \$16,000 B) \$24,000 C) \$28,000 D) \$30,000 E) \$32,000

12. If $a^2 + 3 = 2a^2 - a - 3$ find *a*.
    A) 3 and -2 B) 3 and 2 C) -3 and -2
    D) -3 and 2 E) none of the above

13. A farmer has a field that measures 1000 ft by 2000 ft. An untillable strip 20 ft wide surrounds the field, and a 30 ft wide untillable strip bisects the field into two squares. What percentage of the field is tillable?
    A) 95% B) 93% C) 91% D) 90% E) 88%

14. In a group of 15 students, 7 play baseball, 5 play basketball, and 4 are not involved in either sport. How many play both baseball and basketball?
    A) 0 B) 1 C) 2 D) 3 E) 4

15. If $x = y + \frac{x}{t}$ select the correct expression for t.

A) $\frac{x}{x-y}$ B) $\frac{y-x}{x}$ C) $\frac{xy}{x-y}$ D) $x(x-y)$ E) $y(x-y)$

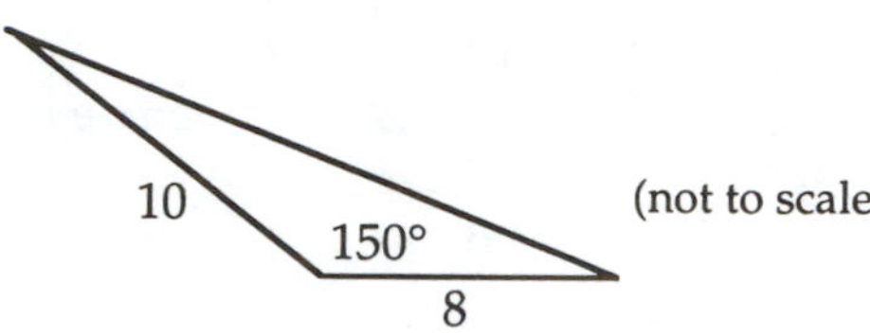

16. Calculate the area of the above triangle.

A) 20 B) 25 C) 30 D) 35 E) 40

STOP!

If you finish before time is up (25 minutes), you may return to any of the questions in Section 4.
Do not turn to any other section of the test.

SECTION 5 Analysis of an Issue

Directions: In this section you are asked to analyze and explain your views on the issue presented below. The question has no 'correct' answer. Instead, you should consider various perspectives as you develop your own position on the issue.

Read the statement and directions, and then make any notes in your test booklet that will help you plan a response. Begin writing your response on the separate answer document. Make sure that you use the answer document that goes with this writing task.

(The instructions above are as they will be for the real exam. For your own informal test essay—to be graded by us or your own service—use three unlined 8.5"x11" sheets of paper which you must provide, writing on the front side only.)

> Because mass hysteria is always incipient in human cultures, the contemporary system of justice in America is no more or less prone to convict innocent people of crimes than it was 400 years ago. Ideas which sweep through American culture captivate juries and often causes them to make mistakes.

STOP!

If you finish before time is up (30 minutes), do not turn to any other section of the test.

SECTION 6 Data Sufficiency

20 Question
Time: 25 minutes

Directions: Each data sufficiency problem includes a question followed by two statements, labeled (1) and (2), that contain certain information. Using your knowledge of mathematics and common facts, you must determine if the information in the statements is sufficient to solve the problem. Select:

A if (1) alone is sufficient, but (2) alone is not sufficient;

B if (2) alone is sufficient, but (1) alone is not sufficient;

C if (1) and (2) together are sufficient, but neither alone is sufficient;

D if each statement alone is sufficient;

E if you cannot solve the problem with the information given.

Numbers: Only real numbers are used; no imaginary numbers are used or implied.

Diagrams: Diagrams reflect the information contained in the question, not necessarily the information contained in the two statements.

1. Is k odd?
   (1) k^2 is even.
   (2) $k+k$ is even.

2. Is x^2 less than x^{13}?
   (1) $x > 0$
   (2) $x < 0$

3. Find the area of the triangle.
   (1) $x = 40°$
   (2) $\overline{AC} = 8$

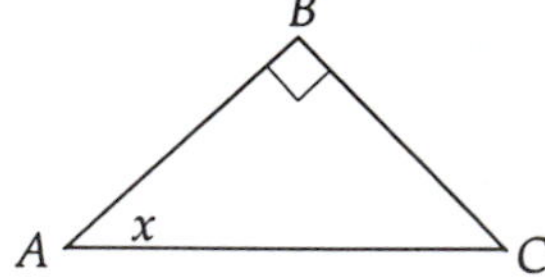

4. If $5s = 3t$ what is $s - t$?
   (1) $s + t = 8$
   (2) $t^{1/3} = \sqrt[3]{5}$

5. A store sells a pair of shoes on a special sale for \$50. What did the store owner pay for the shoes?
   (1) The shoes were marked down 30%.
   (2) The shoes had a markup of 100% before the sale.

6. What is the perimeter of the parallelogram?
   (1) $x = 60°$
   (2) $\overline{AB} = 10$

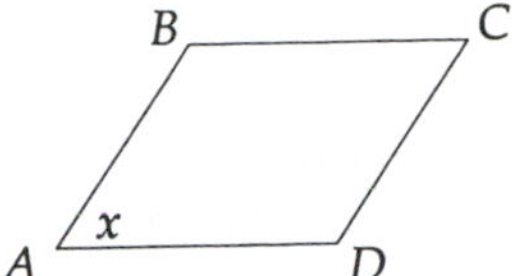

7. What is the average wage for a small city of 500 workers?
   (1) The median wage is \$22,000.
   (2) The top 250 workers average \$26,000.

8. What is angle x?
   (1) $m \perp n$
   (2) $y = 30°$

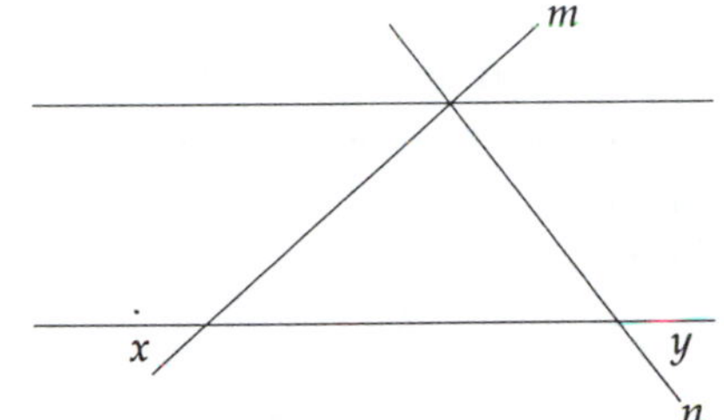

9. Is $\frac{1}{x + x^3}$ greater than $\frac{1}{x^2 + x^4}$?
   (1) $x > 0$
   (2) $x < 0$

10. What is the ratio of the volume of a cube with sides d to the volume of a cylinder with height h and radius r?
   (1) $d = 2r$
   (2) $h = d$

11. How long does it take to travel from A to B if you can travel from B to C in 10 hours? The speed is constant.
   (1) It is 30 miles from A to B.
   (2) It is 40 miles from A to C.

12. Is $x^2 - x + 6 > 0$?
   (1) $x > -2$
   (2) $x < -2$

13. Is the two-digit integer, with digits ℓ and m, a multiple of 7?
   (1) $\ell + m = 13$
   (2) ℓ is divisible by 3.

14. What is the sum of the first six terms of a geometric progression?
   (1) The first two terms are 1 and 2.
   (2) The sum of terms five and six is 48.

15. Is $\frac{1}{x}+\frac{1}{y}$ greater than $x+y$?

(1) $x<0$

(2) $y<x$

16. Is angle A a supplement of angle B?

(1) Angle A plus angle B equals 90°.

(2) Angle A plus angle B equals 180°.

17. Michelle and John can type a manuscript in 60 hours. How long does it take Martha and Jeff to type the same manuscript?

(1) Michelle types 60 words per minute and John types 40 words per minute.

(2) Martha types 30 words per minute and Jeff types 80 words per minute.

18. What is the maximum radius of a circle that can just fit in the triangle?

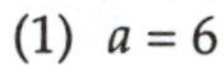

(1) $a=6$

(2) $x=30°$

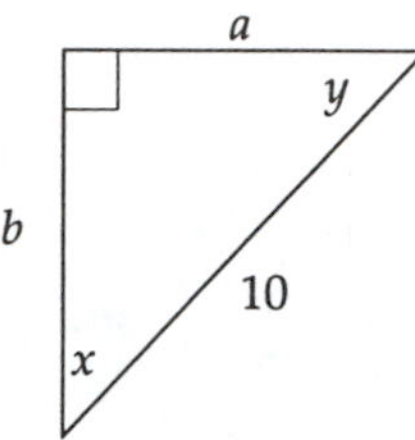

19. What is x/y?

(1) $x^2+2x-8=0$

(2) $x=2y$

20. What is the area of a circle with center at (3, 4)?

(1) The circle intercepts the x-axis at $x=6$.

(2) The circle intercepts the y-axis at $y=8$.

STOP!

If you finish before time is up (25 minutes), you may return to any of the questions in Section 6. Do not turn to any other section of the test.

SECTION 7 Critical Reasoning

16 Questions
Time: 25 minutes

Directions: Select the best answer for each of the following questions.

1. Jeremy, a student, maintains that the correct spelling of "umbrageous" is U-M-B-R-A-G-E-O-U-S. He supports this claim by appealing to two premises: (i) The *ABC Dictionary* is highly reliable, and (ii) The *ABC Dictionary* gives the spelling as U-M-B-R-A-G-E-O-U-S. Mrs. Clarke, his teacher, agrees that the dictionary is very reliable, but she says that it does not, in fact, give that spelling for the word. If Mrs. Clarke is correct, then
   A) her argument undermines the idea that there can be such a thing as the "correct" spelling of a word.
   B) her argument in fact shows that the *ABC Dictionary* is unreliable, though she does not claim that herself.
   C) her claims have very little relevance to Jeremy's argument, since the spelling can be checked in several other dictionaries.
   D) the evidential force of Jeremy's argument is completely eroded.
   E) the evidential force of Jeremy's argument is reduced by about 50%.

2. Visiting a bustling city in the developing world, Mrs. Inouyoke notices that nearly all business buildings, and most residences, have water tanks on the roof. Water from the municipal water supply is piped directly into the tank, and from the tank it goes into the plumbing system of the building. The most likely explanation of this arrangement is that
   A) the municipal water supply is contaminated by amoeba and coliform bacteria.
   B) the municipal water supply is frequently interrupted.
   C) because of the rapid growth of the city, the municipal water supply has not yet been extended to the entire urban area.
   D) the municipal system is supplied from deep wells.
   E) municipal water is supplied to various classes of users at flat rates, rather than being metered.

3. An engineer claims that solar cells for the generation of electrical power can never supply a large part of our need for such energy. He points out that such cells are made largely of silicon, and that silicon is extracted and refined by the use of electrical energy. He says that the amount of energy required to produce the silicon in a solar cell is greater than the energy that cell will produce during its useful working life. The engineer's conclusion seems to depend on which of the following assumptions?
   A) We will not continue to produce large amounts of electrical energy by burning fossil fuels.
   B) Our overall need for electrical energy cannot be reduced.
   C) We will not find more efficient ways of extracting and refining silicon.
   D) Electrical energy, since it does not decay, can be recycled indefinitely.
   E) It will soon become economically feasible to harness solar energy by other means—e.g., by heating water and using the water to power "minimum gradient" engines.

4. A European doctor who directed a mission hospital in West Africa for many years reported that he never saw a case of appendicitis in the Black African population which the hospital served. However, European personnel who came to work in the hospital sometimes developed appendicitis, as did their children, born and brought up in that area. The doctor also knew that Black Africans who immigrated to Europe from that area sometimes developed appendicitis in Europe, at rates comparable to those for native Europeans. Of the following hypotheses, which seems the most promising as an explanation of this curious state of affairs?
   A) The climate of Europe is much more conducive to appendicitis than is that of West Africa.
   B) There are genetic differences which make Europeans much more susceptible to appendicitis than Black Africans.
   C) Because western-style medicine has been introduced into this part of Africa only recently, the indigenous population has long ago developed a natural resistance to appendicitis.
   D) The very high temperatures in the African environment tend to suppress the bacteria which cause appendicitis.
   E) Some feature of the common diet of Europeans, something not normally present in the diet of indigenous Africans, is conducive to appendicitis.

5. A small boy is reported to have expressed the view that the moon is much more important than the sun, at least for human beings. When asked by his teacher why he thought so, he replied that the moon shines at night, when things are rather dark and we need the light. The sun, however, shines in the daytime when there is usually plenty of light. The boy's argument is defective because
   A) it is false that there is normally enough light for human activities in the daytime.
   B) the moon can often be seen in the sky during daylight hours.
   C) light is not very important for human activities.
   D) the fact that there is a lot of light in the daytime is due to the sun.
   E) it is false that moonlight significantly decreases the darkness of nighttime hours.

6. Quality control managers often concern themselves with the "failure rate" of a manufacturing process—the proportion of defective units in the output of the process. The converse of this—the "reliability rate"— is the proportion of satisfactory units in the output. In a certain factory, a line foreman urges a change in the assembly process, and he cites data and calculations which he says show that the change can be expected to cut the failure rate by at least one-half. The general manager opposes the change, which he says is not worth making. He produces facts and figures which he claims show that the change will probably increase the reliability rate by scarcely more than 1%, and could not possibly increase it by as much as 3%. What can we conclude about this disagreement?

   A) At least one of these managers must be seriously mistaken in his data or calculations, and the disagreement over policy probably cannot be resolved until that mistake is corrected.
   B) It is quite possible that both of these managers are correct in their calculations and data, and so their real disagreement (if they have one) may lie elsewhere.
   C) While of course at least one of these managers must be seriously mistaken in his data or calculations, it is possible that this mistake does not contribute much to their disagreement about policy.
   D) The dispute illustrates the fact that there is no reliable way of predicting the effect of a change in manufacturing processes.
   E) While of course at least one of these managers must be seriously mistaken in his data or calculations, there may be no feasible way of determining which one is mistaken, short of actually trying the new method of assembly.

7. Horticultural researchers have recently announced the development of a new variety of grapes. While the overall yield is comparable to that of many other varieties, the special feature of these grapes is that some bunches mature much earlier than others, with the ripening of the entire crop spread out fairly evenly over a period of 8 to 10 weeks. Some have expressed hopes that this new variety will be attractive to large commercial users, such as wineries and preserve-makers, since it will enable them to spread out their industrial operations more evenly over a period of time. That would be economically attractive, since it would allow for more efficient use of facilities and labor. Some skeptics, however, respond that the cost of harvesting these grapes, requiring hand-pickers to make repeated passes over the same vines week after week, will be so high as to offset any increased efficiency in the manufacturing processes. In this interchange, the skeptics

   A) challenge the original argument by trying to show that one or more of its premises are false.
   B) challenge the original conclusion by presenting a new argument with the opposite conclusion.
   C) challenge the original argument by trying to show that its premises are irrelevant to its conclusion.
   D) invert the original argument by assuming that its conclusion is false, and then inferring that one of its premises is also false.
   E) challenge the original argument by trying to show that its premises are incompatible with its conclusion.

8. Sir Fred Hoyle, a noted astronomer, holds that a substantial amount of organic life—bacteria and viruses—passes through inter-planetary space, and that there is a significant "rain" of such organisms into the terrestrial environment. One piece of evidence which he cites is that many species of bacteria are known to be resistant to very high levels of radiation, levels much higher than any which they encounter in their terrestrial habitat. Hoyle argues that it is difficult to see how such an adaptation could have evolved on earth, where there is no need for it, but it is not hard to understand if these strains of bacteria are adapted to inter-planetary space, where high radiation levels may be encountered. We might say that Hoyle believes that some species of bacteria are resistant to radiation because they have had a long extra-terrestrial habitat, and also that he believes that some species of bacteria are of extra-terrestrial origin because they are highly resistant to radiation. In its most sympathetic plausible interpretation, when we describe Hoyle's view in this way, we are

A) ascribing to Hoyle an explanation of the extra-terrestrial origin of some bacterial species.
B) ascribing to Hoyle a non-circular argument for the extra-terrestrial origin of some bacterial species, and an explanation of those species' high resistance to radiation.
C) ascribing to Hoyle a circular argument about the cause of a bacterial resistance to radiation.
D) ascribing to Hoyle a non-circular argument for the conclusion that some species of bacteria are highly resistant to radiation.
E) ascribing to Hoyle a circular argument for the conclusion that certain species of bacteria have an extra-terrestrial origin.

9. Another of Hoyle's arguments can be summarized as follows: On Earth, all the natural occurrences of methane that we know of are associated with "methanogens"—methane-producing bacteria. But there is evidence that methane is also present in some inter-planetary material—in comets, for example. Therefore, it is likely that methanogens are present in these materials also. Which of the following is true of this argument?

A) Since this argument appeals to an analogy or similarity between terrestrial and extra-terrestrial phenomena, it would be strengthened by the discovery of other compounds which occur both on earth and in comets, and whose terrestrial occurrence is strongly correlated with bacterial action.
B) Since this argument appeals to no analogies between terrestrial and extra-terrestrial phenomena, it does not need any explanation of how methanogens synthesize methane.
C) This argument has no evidential force with respect to the extra-terrestrial existence of bacteria unless it can be supplemented with an explanation of the process by which terrestrial bacteria synthesize methane.
D) The plausibility of Hoyle's conclusion would be seriously weakened if on-site explorations of other planets in our solar system were to reveal the existence of methanogenic bacteria there.
E) Since Hoyle's argument appeals to a similarity or analogy between what happens on earth and in comets, it would be strengthened if it were discovered that methane is generated in Antarctica, without bacterial action, at low temperatures, which approximate those of comets far out in the solar system.

10. Some philosophers of science claim that no serious scientific theory can be tested experimentally without taking for granted some other body of scientific beliefs—e.g., the operation of the instruments—for we cannot interpret the experimental results without appealing to such beliefs. If this is true, then which of the following conclusions seems most likely?

A) Any particular scientific theory can be consistently retained, even in the face of apparently incompatible evidence, if we are willing to give up certain other scientific beliefs.
B) Experimental evidence is really irrelevant to scientific theorizing.
C) Experimental evidence is more relevant to the testing of scientific theories than to their initial formulation.
D) Experimental evidence is more relevant to the initial formulation of scientific theories than to their testing.
E) The best scientific theories are those which are formulated in such a way as to be subject to conclusive experimental refutation.

11. Steve and JoAnne are both members of a certain club, though they are not speaking to each other. Cecily, the club president, is appointing members to the fund-raising committee, but she has resolved that she will not appoint anyone without his or her explicit consent. Steve tells Cecily, "I will not consent to appointment on that committee unless I know whether JoAnne is to be a member of it." And JoAnne says, "I will not consent to be a member of that committee unless I know whether Steve will be appointed to it." If all three of these people stick by these resolutions, then

A) neither of them can be appointed to the committee.
B) the situation described in the scenario cannot arise, because it is inherently incoherent.
C) they must either both be appointed or both be left out.
D) the committee may finally have one of them, both of them, or neither of them as members.
E) either one of them can be appointed, but not both.

12. In a typical year, most visitors to Wyoming's Yellowstone National Park are not residents of Wyoming. But most of the visitors are residents of the U.S. From this it follows that

A) most residents of the U.S. are not residents of Wyoming.
B) some residents of Wyoming are not visitors to Yellowstone Park.
C) most residents of Wyoming are residents of the U.S.
D) some residents of the U.S. are not residents of Wyoming.
E) some residents of the U.S. are not visitors to Yellowstone Park.

13. If a given argument is deductively valid, then it is not possible for all of its premises to be true unless its conclusion is also true. Which of the following claims follows from that fact about validity?

A) If a certain argument is deductively valid and its conclusion is false, then all of its premises are false also.
B) If a certain argument has a false conclusion, then it is not deductively valid.
C) If a certain argument is deductively valid and all of its premises are false, then its conclusion is also false.
D) If a certain argument is deductively valid, then it has at least one true premise.
E) None of the above claims follows from the given fact about validity.

14. The football coach at Sunset College would like to run a three-week "football camp" for high-school students in July on the college campus. This would be a private, for-profit operation of his own, but he would rent the playing field and locker rooms from the college. In addition, the "campers" would be housed in college dormitories, and would pay for their room and board there. The coach points out that this arrangement would be advantageous for the college, since it would generate some income from facilities which would normally be unused during the summer. Several trustees have advanced arguments against this proposal. Which of the following considerations is addressed most directly to the positive argument given in the preceding paragraph?

A) The professional staff of the college library is unavailable during the summer months.
B) There is little reason to believe that the most talented athletes who attend the football camp will enroll at Sunset when they graduate from high-school.
C) The dormitories and other facilities may be damaged by the high-school students, living away from home for the first time.
D) Hosting such a camp will give Sunset College an undesirable reputation as a football school.
E) Sunset College has traditionally had a stronger program in basketball than in football.

15. Pedro Hernandez, a management trainee, casually mentions to a senior officer of his company that Jamaica is one of the world's largest producers of bauxite. When pressed for some evidence of this alleged fact, Pedro replies that this information is included in the article on Jamaica in the highly reliable *Encyclopedia Britannica*. The officer later verifies this by looking in the encyclopedia, and is highly impressed by the breadth of Pedro's knowledge.

Pedro, however, admits to a fellow trainee that he has never read the article in the *Britannica*. Instead, he recalled his father's telling him about Jamaica, including the information about bauxite mining. He had quickly inferred that the article in the usually thorough *Britannica* would include this information, and thought this would be more impressive to the senior official than a reference to his father. Which of the following can properly be said of Pedro's statements?

A) Pedro has committed the fallacy of circular argumentation, but his argument is nevertheless valid.
B) Pedro's argument is logically defective because he had not read the article himself, and therefore it provides no reason at all for believing that Jamaica is a major producer of bauxite.
C) Pedro's strategy may be risky and ill-advised, but the argument he gave the company officer is itself a respectable argument appealing to a reliable authority.
D) Because Pedro's argument is circular, it cannot be either a valid deductive argument or a strong inductive argument.
E) If Pedro's father is in fact knowledgeable about Jamaica, and a reliable truth-teller, then the argument Pedro gave the officer is OK, and otherwise not.

16. It is sometimes argued that U.S. income-tax laws must have some large "loop-holes" because some very wealthy individuals pay very little income tax in a given year. Which of the following, if it is a fact, most strongly refutes this argument?
A) Wealthy individuals, unlike the average taxpayer, usually employ specialized tax lawyers and accountants to prepare their returns.
B) It is quite possible for an individual to be wealthy and yet to have very little net income in a given year.
C) Wealthy people, in comparison with the average taxpayer, tend to spend a larger proportion of their income on services rather than on commodities.
D) Wealthy people, even if they earn their income in the U.S., tend to spend a larger part of their income abroad.
E) Highly paid people, on the average, do more worthwhile work per dollar earned than do those who are less highly paid.

STOP!

If you finish before time is up (25 minutes), you may return to any of the questions in Section 7. Do not turn to any other section of the test.

SECTION 8 Data Sufficiency

20 Questions
Time: 25 minutes

Directions: Each data sufficiency problem includes a question followed by two statements, labeled (1) and (2), that contain certain information. Using your knowledge of mathematics and common facts, you must determine if the information in the statements is sufficient to solve the problem. Select:

A if (1) alone is sufficient, but (2) alone is not sufficient;

B if (2) alone is sufficient, but (1) alone is not sufficient;

C if (1) and (2) together are sufficient, but neither alone is sufficient;

D if each statement alone is sufficient;

E if you cannot solve the problem with the information given.

Numbers: Only real numbers are used; no imaginary numbers are used or implied.

Diagrams: Diagrams reflect the information contained in the question, not necessarily the information contained in the two statements.

1. Is x^2 greater than x^{10}?
   (1) $x < 0$
   (2) $x > 0$

2. What is the perimeter of the triangle?
   (1) $\angle A = 37°$
   (2) $\overline{AB} = 1.6\,\overline{BC}$

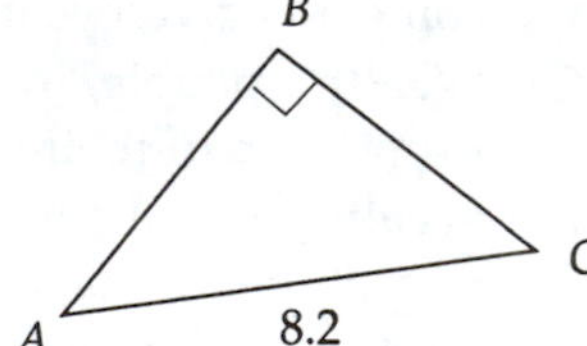

3. What is x^y?
   (1) $x = 4y$
   (2) $x + 2y = 12$

4. The average of r and s is 26. What are r and s?
   (1) r is three times as large as s.
   (2) r and s are both positive.

5. What is $x + y + z$?
   (1) $x = 2 - y$
   (2) $z = 3$

6. What is x?
   (1) $x^2 = 2x$
   (2) $x > 0$

7. What is the diameter of the circle inscribed in the triangle?
   (1) $\angle C = 60°$
   (2) $\angle C = 2\angle B$

8. Is $x > 1$?
   (1) $x^2 > 1$
   (2) $x^{1/2} = 1$

9. Does Chris earn more than Darla?
   (1) Chris has worked for 10 years and has averaged 5% raises.
   (2) Darla has worked for 8 years and has averaged 8% raises.

10. Was the enrollment of Ivy League University greater than twice the enrollment of Midwest University in 1990?
    (1) Ivy League University raised $10 million by charging each student $5,000 tuition and Midwest University raised $6 million by charging each student $8,000 tuition in 1990.
    (2) Ivy League University enrolled 300 more students than Midwest University in 1990.

11. How many adults ride bicycles in city A if all adults either ride bicycles or drive cars?
    (1) 85% of the 10,000 adults in city A drive cars.
    (2) 1500 adults in city A drive cars.

12. What is area of the triangle if its perimeter is 12?
    (1) $\overline{AC} = 4$
    (2) $\angle C = 30°$

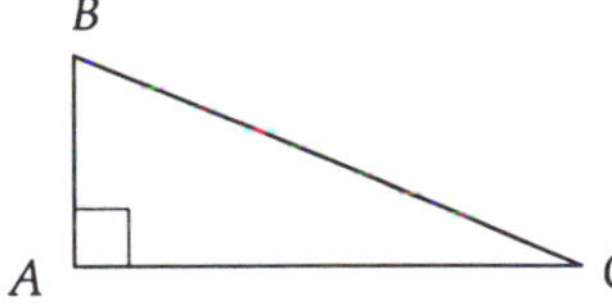

13. Is m a factor of n?
    (1) $n > m$
    (2) m^2 is even and n^2 is odd.

14. Is the distance from the origin to the point (x, y) greater than the shortest distance from (x, y) to the y-axis?
    (1) $y > 0$
    (2) $y = 0$

15. Is x greater than the average of y and z?
    (1) $3x = y + z$
    (2) $x = y - z$

16. Three squares are oriented as shown. What is the area of the small square?

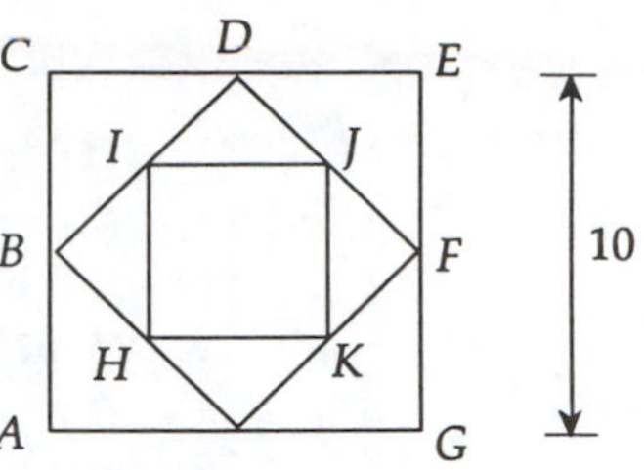

(1) $\overline{AB} = \overline{DE}, \quad \angle BHI = \angle FJK$

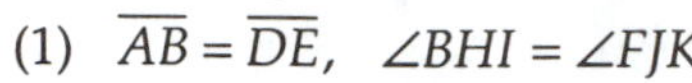

(2) $\overline{AB} = \overline{DE}, \quad IJ \parallel CE$

17. Joe sells twice as many \$10 tickets as Sue and Sue sells three times as many \$5 tickets as Joe. How many tickets did Joe sell?
   (1) Sue sold a total of 35 tickets.
   (2) Together Joe and Sue sold 70 tickets for \$500.

18. Is $x^{3.25} \geq y$?
   (1) $y = 2x$
   (2) $x = 3.67, y = 43.2$

19. Is $x + y > z$?
   (1) $x - y + z = 2$
   (2) $x = 4$

20. What is the cross-hatched area inside the larger circle of radius r_1 and outside the smaller circle of radius r_2?

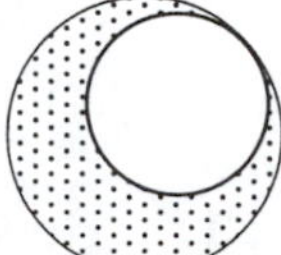

   (1) $3r_2 = 2r_1$
   (2) The perimeter of the larger circle exceeds that of the smaller circle by 20.

STOP!

If you finish before time is up (25 minutes), you may return to any of the questions in Section 8. Do not turn to any other section of the test. This is the last section of Test 1.

SECTION 9 Analysis of an Argument

Directions: In this section you will write a critique of the argument presented below. You may, for example, consider what questionable assumptions underlie the thinking, what alternative explanations or counter examples might weaken the conclusion, or what sort of evidence could help strengthen or refute the argument. Read the argument and directions, and then make any notes in your test booklet that will help you plan a response. Begin writing your response on the separate answer document. Make sure that you use the answer document that goes with this writing task. (For your own informal test essay—to be graded by us or your own service—use three unlined 8.5"x11" pages, writing on front and back sides.)

The USA is a prosperous nation, surrounded by impoverished nations to the south and to the east. The peoples of these nations are within relatively easy traveling distance of the continental USA. As a result, illegal immigration to the USA will persist at unacceptable rates, and the USA will be forced to intervene militarily in the affairs of these nations from time to time, regardless of the legality or illegality of such intervention.

STOP!

If you finish before time is up (30 minutes), you may return to any of the questions in Section 9. Do not turn to any other section of the test. This is the last section of Test 1.

Answer Key to Test No. 1

Section 1 *Reading*	Section 2 *Sentences*	Section 3 *Reasoning*	Section 4 *Problems*	Section 6 *Data*	Section 7 *Reasoning*	Section 8 *Data*
1. A	1. B	1. B	1. E	1. A	1. D	1. E
2. C	2. D	2. E	2. E	2. B	2. B	2. D
3. D	3. D	3. C	3. D	3. C	3. C	3. C
4. C	4. B	4. D	4. A	4. D	4. E	4. A
5. A	5. B	5. B	5. E	5. C	5. D	5. C
6. B	6. A	6. B	6. D	6. E	6. B	6. C
7. B	7. B	7. A	7. A	7. E	7. B	7. D
8. C	8. B	8. D	8. B	8. C	8. B	8. B
9. D	9. C	9. C	9. D	9. B	9. A	9. E
10. A	10. E	10. B	10. B	10. C	10. A	10. A
11. C	11. B	11. C	11. D	11. E	11. E	11. A
12. B	12. C	12. A	12. A	12. B	12. D	12. D
13. C	13. C	13. D	13. B	13. E	13. E	13. B
14. E	14. A	14. D	14. B	14. A	14. C	14. D
15. A	15. D	15. A	15. A	15. E	15. C	15. E
16. D	16. C	16. E	16. A	16. D	16. B	16. B
17. B	17. A			17. C		17. B
18. C	18. C			18. D		18. B
19. D	19. D			19. B		19. C
20. E	20. B			20. D		20. C
21. B	21. E					
22. E	22. B					
23. A						

Note: Sections 5 & 9 are "Writing Analysis," to be completed on 6 separate sheets.

Self-Grading & Score Conversion

Upon completing this Practice Test, it is extremely beneficial for you to grade yourself. This will enable you to identify your weak areas so that you can organize a review that will give you the greatest improvement.

Using the Answer Sheet, determine your Raw Score using the following formula for each of the seven sections of the test and fill in the following table:

$$\text{Raw Score} = \#\text{ Correct} - \tfrac{1}{4}\,(\#\text{ Incorrect})$$

Your Rating (Poor to Excellent) in each section is determined using the second table.

Self-Grading Table

Section	Correct	Incorrect	Blank	Raw Score	Rating
1					
2					
3					
4					
6					
7					
8					

Rating Determination (use Raw Scores)

Section	Poor	Fair	Good	Excellent
1	0-9	10-14	15-19	20-23
2	0-8	9-13	14-18	19-22
3	0-6	7-9	10-13	14-16
4	0-6	7-9	10-13	14-16
6	0-8	9-12	13-17	18-20
7	0-6	7-9	10-13	14-16
8	0-8	9-12	13-17	18-20

Your Verbal and Quantitative scores and your total score can be converted to approximate percentile rankings using the following formulas:

Verbal Raw Score = Sum of Raw Scores from Sections 1, 2, and 3
Quantitative Raw Score = Sum of Raw Scores from Sections 4, 6, and 8
Total Score = Sum of Verbal and Quantitative Raw Scores

Top Quarter Percentile	Middle Half Percentile	Bottom Quarter Percentile
Verbal > 40	40 > Verbal > 20	Verbal < 20
Quantitative > 36	36 > Quantitative > 18	Quantitative < 18
Total > 74	74 > Total > 40	Total < 40

Explanations to the Answers

SECTION 1 Reading Comprehension

1. A Clearly, the passage compares in detail motives and effects of vertical integration and horizontal combination. (B) is incorrect, for incentives in mergers are mentioned only with respect to horizontal combination. The answer is too narrow to accurately reflect the coverage of the passage. (C) is likewise incorrect since increased throughput is a likely effect of vertical integration. The answer is too narrow. (D) is incorrect, since it explains one motive for vertical integration.

2. C (A), (C), and (E) are motives of horizontal combination. (D) is an aim of neither vertical integration nor horizontal combination.

3. D (A), (B), (C), and (E) are incorrect. They name considered procedures rather than kinds of behavior.

4. C (A) is incorrect, for investment is associated with both vertical integration and horizontal combination. (B) is incorrect, since cost advantage may be associated with both. (D) is incorrect, because it is associated solely with vertical integration. (E) is incorrect, for it is associated narrowly with vertical integration.

5. A (B), (C), (D), and (E) are all clearly associated with vertical integration.

6. B (A) is associated with integration of two facilities within a single enterprise. (C) names effects of vertical integration, not incentives for insurance against transaction costs. (D) is incorrect, for it names a motive for vertical integration. (E) is incorrect, since it names events that vertical integration aims to prevent, motives that are not mentioned in the passage as incentives.

7. B Clearly (B) is the most comprehensive statement describing the purpose of this passage. (A), (B), (C), and (D) are incorrect, for each describes a small, contributing aspect of the need for complex managerial systems during the formation of the railroads.

8. C (A), (B), (D), and (E) are accurate, but each is a supporting idea, not a comprehensively stated central idea.

9. D This passage explicitly declares that the creation of managerial hierarchies was the "most critical" innovation.

10. A (B), (C), and (D) are correct as far as they go, but each is a contributing factor to complexity, the broadly correct answer, "Because of the complexities of their operations they formed almost overnight the nation's first managerial enterprises." (E) is incorrect, for the passage clearly declares the contrary.

11. C (A) is untrue, according to the information given in the passage. (B) is unsupported by evidence from the passage—larger railraods were the key players, but their better ability to afford managers cannot be inferred. (D) is flatly untrue, according to the information given in the passage. (E) is not supported by evidence from the passage.

12. B (A), (C), (D), and (E) are all accurate but not the central fact about the inter-company arrangements in the infrastructure argued by the passage. Several times, the passage mentions the great amount of time it took for managerial principles to be devised.

13. C The passage connects market activity with social effects. (A), (B), and (E) are incorrect, since they name only effects of the private market. (D) is incorrect, for the passage says nothing of judicial protection of civil liberty.

14. E (A), (B), (C), and (D) are all accurate insofar as they describe characteristics of the private market, but the only aspect of the market that the Anglo-American tradition is said to value is its contributions to civil liberty.

15. A (B) is flatly untrue. (C) is incorrect, for the passage clearly declares the contrary. (D) is incorrect, for the passage has nothing to say about a culture that values collective will. (E) is incorrect, for the passage says nothing about legal commentary on the private market.

16. D (A) is incorrect, because the passage declares the contrary. (B), (C), and (D) are accurate descriptions of the features of the market but do not answer the question concerning controversy.

17. B The ordinary working goals are economic. (A) is incorrect, since standards of propriety have nothing to do with an economic definition of market processes. (C) is incorrect, for it does not name goals. (D) is incorrect, for nowhere is reformist zeal mentioned in the passage. (E) is incorrect, since the passage flatly declares the contrary.

18. C (A), (B), (D), and (E) are features of the market but not a consequence of "administrative flexibility and reach of the market."

19. D (A) is incorrect, because it is too grandly overstated and inaccurate. (B), (C), and (E) are justified by the information given in the passage, but none are the central idea of the passage.

20. E (A), (B), (C), and (D) are incomplete or untrue.

21. B (A), (C), (D), and (E) are inaccurate as clearly indicated by the passage.

22. E (A), (B), (C), and (D) are untrue and unsupported by evidence in the passage. The whole point of the passage is to assert that in each case DuPont has taken the initiative to protect workers during manufacture and consumers during use.

23. A (B), (C), (D), and (E) are contributory risks and study criteria, but they are not the research subjects mentioned in the question.

SECTION 2 Sentence Correction

1. B The basic problem is the dangling participial phrase at the beginning of the sentence. It has a different subject, *they* (understood), from the main clause, *a gust* (A) and (D). (C) and (E) are implausible because the gust of wind does not enter the house.

2. D The first person pronoun follows the preposition *of* and must be in the objective case. The action in the main clause, *pass*, is anterior to the action in the adverb clause, *adjourn*. Therefore, the perfect is necessary, (D).

3. D The first answer has a pronoun with no antecedent, *they*. In addition, the sentence is ungrammatical having a *by*-phrase from a passive without the required form of *be* in the verb. Answers (A) and (E) have passives. In (C) *it's* is incorrectly used for *its*.

4. B *Neither* must be used with nor since it is a correlative conjunction. *Together* is re-dundant when used with *cooperate*. *Humor* is not parallel in form with *to cooperate*. Only (B) could be correct.

5. B The basic problem is two verb forms with *-ing* connected to one with an infinitive *to quaff*. Also, *different than* in (D) and (E) is not correct; it must be *different from*. The perfect tense is not called for because the subordinate clause is in the present, (C). The answer can only be (B).

6. A One of the problems here is that the subject of the *if*-clause, *Americans*, is different from the subject of the main clause, *we*. This is remedied by (A) and (D). The other problem is the tense. The time in the main clause is not anterior to the time in the *if*-clause; therefore the perfect tense is incorrect.

7. B The problem here is that the verb forms are not parallel. One has *should* in the verb phrase; the other does not. In (D) there is no need for a comma.

8. B (A) is an incomplete sentence. (C) has a misplaced modifier. In (D) the main idea is in a subordinate clause. (E) has a dangling modifier. Only (B) is correct.

9. C The basic problem with the sentence is number agreement —*person* is singular, *their* is plural and so is *human beings*. Besides this, *needs* is plural and *that* is singular. Only (C) corrects both.

10. E There are three problems here. The passive in the first clause, the unnecessary use of the perfect, and the breaking up of the correlative conjunction *not only* and *but also*. These problems are corrected in (E).

11. B The use of *irregardless* (not regardless) constitutes the use of a cliché. The main clause has a passive, *were led*. Answer (B) corrects both of these.

12. C The subjects in the first part of the sentence, *concert* and *audience*, are different from the subject in the second part of the sentence, *maestro*. Consequently, the *-ing* phrase, a participial phrase, is dangling. There is also a problem with the perfect tense; the present perfect is anterior to a time in the present. Here, *relaxed* signals a time in the past.

13. C There are two problems with this sentence: (l) the use of the perfect tense, and (2) the use of *different than*. The time in the main clause, *should discover*, is not in the past tense; hence, it does not qualify for past perfect in the subordinate clause.

14. A *That* introduces only restrictive relative clauses and thus cannot be used with proper nouns such as *Jimmy*, (B) and (C). Only non-restrictive clauses can be used with proper nouns, eliminating (E). The present perfect tense is used only with present time; thus (D) is eliminated.

15. D *Very unique* is a cliché based on an absurdity. Unique is one of a kind; it cannot be 'intensified' with *most* or *very*. *Try and* is grammatically incorrect.

16. C Since *who baked a cake* is a restrictive relative clause, no commas are permitted (E). Both *who* and *whoever* are subjects of their respective clauses; therefore, only (C) can be correct.

17. A There is nothing wrong with *held sway*. Further, the passive is not to be used, as in (C). The past tense in *became dominant* requires the past perfect in the main clause.

18. C The subject after *there, condition* and *converse* is plural since it deals with two entities. The verb must also be plural (*are*). The possessive pronoun is *its*. As a result, (C) is correct.

19. D The basic problem in this sentence is the lack of parallelism in the noun phrases joined by *and*. A smaller problem is the wordiness involved with the expression *common, ordinary thieves*. Both of these can be remedied as in (D).

20. B The subjective case is always required after a form of *be*—in this case, the contracted form, *'s*. *Who* is the subject of *say*.

21. E The original sentence (A) does not have the same subject on both sides of *and*. It also has a cliché with the passive voice, *a good time was had by all*. One attempt at remedying these problems introduces the problem of number agreement, *everybody—they*, (C). Only (E) is correct.

22. B As in other participial phrases, the subject of the phrase *finished* must be the subject of the verb in the main clause. This problem is corrected by (B).

SECTION 3 Critical Reasoning

1. B Ordinary observers of an interchange like this probably have some independent way of judging the connection between the actions of dentists and their judgments about matters of dental health. They can also judge independently about the concerns which parents are likely to have for their children. They don't have to take the researcher's word for things like that. But they probably do not have an independent way of judging whether the survey results really were as the researcher said—whether the sample was fairly selected. For those parts of the argument, they have only the researcher's word. In that case, observations which tend to show that the researcher may well be biased, that he has a motive for deception, for shaving the facts a little, are relevant. And that is just the place where (B) locates the relevance of the critic's remarks.

2. E (E) would seem to be the strongest support for the professors' side of the controversy. (E) suggests that the low average scores may be due to the fact that advisors have encouraged many marginal students, with no realistic chance of success, to take the test.

(A) might be taken to show that the pre-med program is no worse than others at Sunset, but they might all be unsatisfactory and in need of revision. If (B) is true, then, given the sustained shortfall in Sunset average scores, the national average for the MCAT must also have risen over the past ten years, so the truth of (B) would leave the dean's argument unanswered. (C) might show either that pre-med students were, on the average, the best in the college, or that there was more grade inflation in the pre-med program than elsewhere in the college. But it would do little to refute the suggestion that, compared with other colleges, Sunset was giving its pre-med students an inferior preparation for medical school. (D) is simply irrelevant to the point at issue in the controversy.

3. C (C) is the strongest response. The question in 3 is pretty much the same as that in 2, but there is a new set of possibilities. Again, the point at issue is that of whether the low MCAT score averages show that the pre-med curriculum is in need of revision. (C) addresses that point, suggesting an alternative explanation for the low average scores. That explanation is that the average ability of the incoming pre-med students is lower than that in many other colleges—Sunset does not attract many of the very best high school graduates with an interest in medicine—rather than any deficiency in the pre-med curriculum.

(A) would, if anything, strengthen the dean's position by eliminating still another alternative explanation, one dependent on size or resources. (B) would also strengthen the dean's case by tending to show that the problem is not generated only by excessively low grades at the bottom of the scale, and (D) would also seem to strengthen it for a similar reason. (E) is simply irrelevant to the point at issue.

4. D (D) is the best response. The point of the proverb is that it is desirable to risk something for the sake of a possibly greater gain. But (D) seems to defend the contrary view that a sure thing is more valuable than a risky possibility, even if the latter has a larger promise.

None of the other proverbs really addresses the comparative values of risk and safety. (A) is about the cost of procrastination, not about risk. (B) advises us not to judge a course of action until all the facts and consequences are in, but it doesn't seem to opt for safety over risk. (C) extols the virtue of care and frugality, even in small things, and (E) suggests (in contrast) that there is a danger of being excessively careful about small matters and careless about more important things, but none of them address the elements of safety and risk.

5. B (B) is the best response, claiming that (i) and (ii) strengthen the inference, but (iii) does not. Mrs. Jones apparently draws an analogy between, on the one hand, the four summer jobs, and, on the other hand, the new job in Chicago. The first four items resemble the fifth in that they are all jobs which Barbara has held or will hold. The first four share a known property—Barbara enjoyed them. Mrs. Jones infers that the fifth will also have that property—Barbara will also enjoy it.

(i) stipulates a further known property which the summer jobs share with the new job—they are all advertising jobs. This increased similarity between the premise analogues and the conclusion analogue strengthens the inference to a further similarity.

If Barbara liked the first jobs because they were in advertising, then she will probably also like the new job, since it is also in that field. If she liked the first jobs for other reasons, maybe even despite their being in advertising, then again it seems probable that she will also like the new job, even though it also is in advertising.

We might initially think that if (i) strengthens the inference, then (ii) should weaken it. But in fact (ii) would also strengthen the inference. (ii) does not tell us what the field of the new job is (and the original statement does not tell us that either), though presumably the new job cannot share its field with all of the summer jobs. Nevertheless, if we combine (ii) with the original information we can see that Barbara has enjoyed many jobs despite the different sorts of work involved. She is apparently the kind of person who can enjoy many different tasks, who has the knack of making the best of a job. And that augurs well for her enjoyment of the new job, regardless of its field. In general, diversity in the premise analogues strengthens an analogical argument.

(iii) perhaps weakens the argument, and at least does not strengthen it, because it introduces the possibility that the reason Barbara enjoyed the summer jobs was because they were in advertising. But (iii), unlike (i), does not stipulate that the new job is in advertising. So (iii) reduces the diversity among the premise analogues without compensating by increasing their similarity to the conclusion analogue.

6. B (B) is the best response, though it is not clear that it is strongly supported by the data. All of the other responses are worse. The low frequency of 7's in Henry's record may be simply a chance effect, or it may be due to some systematic cause. If it is the latter, then the most likely thing is that the wheel is biased against 7. And in that case, 7 will probably continue to come up with a frequency below that of its chance expectancy. And then, of course, (A), (C), and (E) would be false.

If, on the other hand, it is merely a chance effect, then (B) is not true. But neither is (A). (The supposition that (A) must be true "to balance out the law of averages" is the "gambler's fallacy.") The wheel doesn't remember how many times 7 came up, and so it has no systematic way of compensating later for this low frequency. For the same reason, (E) is false.

(C) is also false. 26 is indeed more likely than any other single frequency for 7 (and for any other particular number), assuming that the wheel is unbiased. But it is nevertheless far more likely that 7 will come up some number of times other than 26. 7 is, for example, slightly more likely to come up 26 times rather than 25, but it is almost twice as likely to come up either 25 or 27 times than exactly 26 times.

(E) is also false. Of course, if some number turns up less than 26 times in 988 spins, then some other number must come up more than 26 times. But the shortfall of one number need not be matched by an exactly equal surplus for any one other number.

7. A 25 students is correct. Problems about the minimal circumstances in which something is necessary or bound to happen, require us to think about worst-case scenarios. (Problems about the circumstances in which something is possible, in contrast, involve best-case scenarios.) In this problem, it would be possible for the professor to be right in a class with only three students. But he is not bound to be right in such a small group, for the birthdays might be spread out over different months. Even in a class of 24 students he might be wrong, since the birthdays might be spread exactly evenly, two in each month (that is the worst case). But if one additional student were

to join the class, then that person's birthday is bound to make a triple, no matter in what month it falls. 25 students, therefore, is the minimum number which guarantees that the professor is right.

8. D (D), if it expresses a known fact, would properly re-enforce Barbara's skepticism. The problem of choosing between risky alternatives can often be clarified by calculating the "expected value" of each alternative. In this case Joe seems to make that calculation correctly, simply multiplying each prize by the probability of winning it. If Barbara could play this game many times, then she would probably win more by choosing the first option, and thus winning a few big prizes, than with the second option—winning five times as many small prizes. But in fact, she can play the game only once.

In addition, we must remember that the value of money may not be proportional to the amount of money, and in many cases it is not. We may assume that, for almost anyone, $7,200 is worth more than $1,200. But it may not be worth six times as much. (B) describes just such a situation. Because of the special opportunity for the boat, it would be worth a lot to the Fishers to get an extra $1,200 now. Of course, $7,200 would be even better, but maybe only four or five times as good. And if one calculates the real expected values using those proportions, then the second option turns out to be preferable. Perhaps Barbara understands that in an informal way.

The situation described in (A) would, if anything, strengthen Joe's advice, for (A) suggests that the larger prize may really be worth more than six times as much as the smaller prize, given the Fishers' circumstances. (C) and (E) might be reasons for Barbara to decline this opportunity altogether, but they do not distinguish between Joe's advice and its alternative. (B) might make Barbara skittish about choosing the riskier option, or perhaps it will attract her to the large risk, but it does not seem to provide any proper reason for a choice one way or the other.

9. C (C) describes the most relevant control group. Remember that the purpose of the experiment is to test the hypothesis that the higher body temperature accounts for the chickens' normal resistance to anthrax. In the experiment as originally described, infected chickens whose temperature was reduced soon died. Perhaps they died of anthrax. But another possibility would seem to be that they died from the effects of the lowered temperature, pretty much independently of the anthrax infection. The control group described in (C) is directly relevant to that possibility, since it tests the effect of lowered temperature without the infection.

The group described in (A) could not be expected to contribute, since it is presumably already known what will happen to them. They will survive, since chickens in normal conditions are highly resistant to anthrax. Groups (B), (D), and (E) introduce a new factor, the anthrax vaccine. But the experiment is not intended to test for the effects of the vaccine, and its introduction in this way would only detract from the decisiveness of the test for the effect of lowered temperature.

10. B It is useful to notice that all of the alternatives have at least two parts—one is about Lou's argument and the other is about Evelyn's conclusion, so we might try to evaluate Lou's argument first. It is certainly fallacious. (Logicians sometimes call this fallacy "Denying the Antecedent.") We can see that it is fallacious because there are many other factors that might keep the manager from arriving on time—he may have missed the flight because of traffic delays, or he may have felt ill and canceled his

trip, and so on. So Evelyn is right in saying that Lou's argument is fallacious. That eliminates responses (A) and (D).

From the fact that Lou's argument is fallacious, Evelyn apparently infers that its conclusion is false, and so she asserts the opposite conclusion. But that is also a fallacy. Except in rather special cases, the fact that a certain argument is fallacious does not show anything at all about the truth of its conclusion. Truths, just as well as falsehoods, can be the conclusions of faulty arguments. So we can eliminate (C).

If we were to choose response (E), we would ourselves be committing the same fallacy we just ascribed to Evelyn. The fact that Evelyn's argument is fallacious does not give us any reason for supposing that her conclusion is false. And nothing else in the problem gives us a reason for thinking that the manager will not arrive on time. So (E) is not correct. (B) is correct. Evelyn is right about Lou's argument. And her own conclusion, even if it happens to be true, is unsupported by anything she has said in this interchange.

11. C (C) describes a development which would severely curtail publishers' revenues prior to the price increases. Furthermore, it is a development which can be plausibly connected with easy photo-copying. Individuals were dropping their personal subscriptions, and simply going to the library to copy the articles they wanted.

(B) describes a similar development, but after the price increases had begun. That development would more likely be a result of the price increases, rather than an explanation of them. So also with (D). (A) and (E) may well be true, but they do not seem to have any relevance to the question of explaining the necessity for the recent price increases.

12. A (A), which chooses the first option by itself, is the best response. When the gold price is low, then most U.S. gold production will be a by-product of copper mining. We can reasonably expect copper mining to fluctuate in response to the price of copper, and gold production will consequently have the same fluctuations.

If gold prices rise enough, then probably some gold mines will come back into operation. Gold production will then be less sensitive to the price of copper. But nothing in the given data suggests that high gold prices will either cause or signal high copper prices, and so (ii) is unwarranted.

As we already noted, high copper prices will probably result in an increased U.S. production of gold. If the U.S. were a major world supplier of gold, this might cause a decline in the price of gold. But since the U.S. is only a minor producer, it would be rather implausible to expect a significant decline in gold prices from this development. So (iii) is unlikely to be true.

13. D (D) contains the most plausible explanation. The argument in the brochure will appeal to people who must pay both for the unit and the power to run it. They will reap the power savings to recompense them for the increased initial cost, and then they will benefit from the further future savings. But if some other entity, the college, for example, pays for the power, then an individual faculty member is unlikely to think of a saving there as much of a benefit to him or her. But the increased initial expense is borne by the individual. It would not be surprising, therefore, if they generally opted for the cheaper and less efficient makes.

(A) may well be true, but if it is, then it increases the attractiveness of the energy-efficient units since they will realize even more than the anticipated savings. (A) is unlikely, therefore, to explain the actual choices. (B) is irrelevant since the faculty members have chosen among the presently available units, not future developments. (C) does not explain why the faculty members accepted the claims of competing manufacturers rather than those in the brochure. (E) also fails to make the required distinction, since those who wished to buy quickly could have bought the energy-efficient model as readily as any other.

14. D Of the given responses, (D) is the most attractive. The idea, presumably, is to select the price which generates the greatest overall profit in this operation. The initial test generated some relevant data. Of course, gross profit per unit is highest at the highest price ($13.50 gross profit, including the padding in the S & H charge). But sales are low. Comparing the gross profit for each price in the original test is simply a matter of multiplying the profit per unit by the indicated number of sales in some fixed number of prospects. You can simplify the arithmetic by choosing 100 prospects as the base. Then 3% amounts to 3 sales. This calculation shows that $14.95 is the most profitable of the three tested prices. The test also shows that profitability drops off on each side of $14.95. (Incidentally, the cost of the mailing is irrelevant to this comparison. It will be the same whatever price is chosen.)

The optimum price is therefore probably in the vicinity of $14.95, higher than the lowest tested price and lower than the highest. And that suggests that the most useful pair to try in a further test will be a pair which brackets $14.95. (D) is the only pair like that among the alternatives.

If you didn't have time to do the calculations, you might have guessed anyway that the best strategy would be to bracket the best tested price. That would enable you to quickly eliminate (A) and (C).

15. A (A) describes the strongest claim which would tend to support the view that things are not as bad as the editorial suggests. For if (A) is true, then the sort of knowledge and understanding which is the special province of scientists is not really needed very much in making public policy decisions. So the scarcity of scientists at the highest levels may not be a serious failure.

All of the other responses suggest possible reasons for the scarcity of scientists in the government, but they do not address the question of whether that lack is a matter for serious concern.

16. E (E) seems to be the best response. Presumably the dispute in the boardroom is about whether the increases in sales and profits are due to the advertising campaign. When the second officer cites the fact that other companies in the same field have experienced similar increases, but without such advertising, she can be taken to suggest that these increases may well be due to some other cause, such as an increased public concern over health. That is the point summarized in (E).

A case might be made for (C), especially if you know what corporate image advertising is. (But generally questions in this test should not appeal to special knowledge.) But as it is put here, (C) does not seem to be true. If the effect really is due to the advertising, then even if it has benefited competitors, it has been profitable for Bottle & Capp—a 22% increase in profits. (A), (B), and (D) might be true, but they do not seem to connect well with anything in the scenario. They could quickly be eliminated, leaving at worst a guess between (C) and (E).

SECTION 4 Problem Solving

1. E $1\frac{1}{3}+5\frac{1}{6}-6\frac{1}{2}=\frac{4}{3}+\frac{31}{6}-\frac{13}{2}=\frac{8}{6}+\frac{31}{6}-\frac{39}{6}=\frac{8+31-39}{6}=0.$

2. E $\left.\begin{array}{l}x-y=-3\\x-y=4\end{array}\right\}$ Subtract equations and find $0=-7$ which is impossible.

3. D The straight line is 180°. $\therefore 20+x+30=180.$ $\therefore x=180-50=130°.$

4. A Make a sketch: 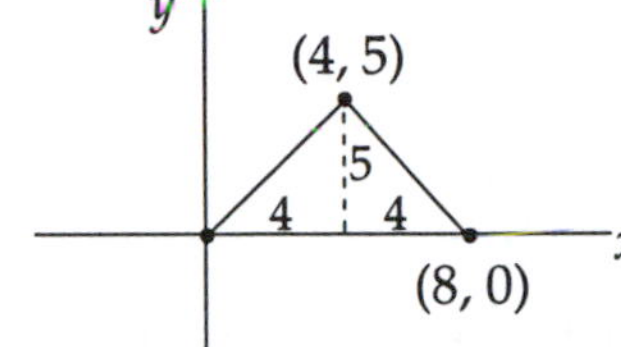

It is isosceles.

5. E $x \otimes y=-\frac{x}{y}.$ $x\otimes 4=-\frac{x}{4}$ and $16\otimes x=-\frac{16}{x}.$

$\therefore -\frac{x}{4}=-\frac{16}{x}$ or $x^2=64$ and $x=\pm 8.$

6. D Complete the sketch:

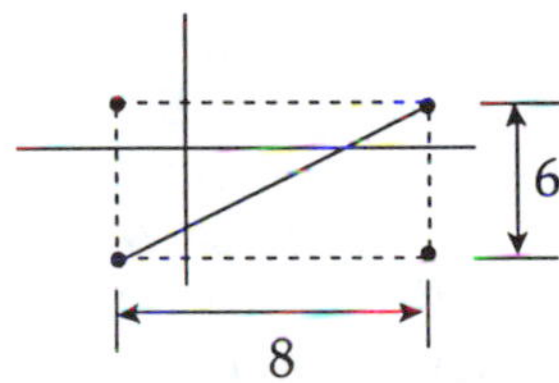

Either (6, – 4) or (– 2, 2) are possible corner points.

7. A The length is 10 since it is twice a 3-4-5 triangle. The radius is 5. Area $=\pi r^2=25\pi.$

8. B An inscribed triangle with the hypotenuse the diameter is a right triangle. Hence, if the radius is 5, the triangle is twice a 3-4-5 triangle and the area of the triangle is $\frac{1}{2}bh=\frac{1}{2}6\times 8=\frac{48}{2}=24.$

9. D $(-2)^3=-8=-\frac{24}{3}.$ $3^{-1}=\frac{1}{3}.$ $4\frac{2}{3}=\frac{14}{3}.$

$-\frac{24}{3}+\frac{1}{3}+\frac{14}{3}=\frac{-24+1+14}{3}=-\frac{9}{3}=-3.$

10. B Angle z is equal to the third angle in the triangle ABD. Hence, $x+y+z=180$ or $60+50+z=180.$ $\therefore z=180-110=70°.$

11. D $P \times 0.08 = 200 \times 12. \quad \therefore P = \frac{200 \times 12}{0.08} = \frac{200 \times 12 \times 100}{8} = \$30,000.$
Note: $P \times i$ is the interest per year. Hence, 200 is multiplied by 12.

12. A $0 = 2a^2 - a^2 - a - 3 - 3 = a^2 - a - 6 = (a-3)(a+2). \quad \therefore a = 3, -2.$

13. B Ignore the corners and overlapping area—they are relatively small.
$1000 \times 2000 - 20(2000 + 4000) - 30 \times 1000 = 2,000,000 - 120,000 - 30,000$
$= 1,850,000$ tillable area. % tillable $= \frac{1.85}{2} \times 100 = 92.5\%.$
The correct answer would be a little greater than this.

14. B 15 – 4 = 11 students who participate in the two sports. Seven play baseball so the remaining four must play basketball. That means that only 1 plays both sports.

15. A $x - y = \frac{x}{t}. \quad \therefore t = \frac{x}{x-y}.$

16. A Since there are 180° in a straight line, the angle next to the 150° angle must be 30°. The leg opposite a 30° angle is 1/2 the hypotenuse, so the vertical distance is $\frac{1}{2}(10) = 5$. The area is then $\frac{1}{2}bh = \frac{1}{2} \times 8 \times 5 = \frac{40}{2} = 20.$

SECTION 5 Analysis of an Issue

You may wish to have a friend or colleague grade your writing using the scoring guidelines presented on page 136 in 'Analytical Writing.' Or, should you desire a pro- fessional assessment of your writings, you may send the two essays to: Great Lakes Press, POB 483, Okemos, MI 48805-0483. Or fax to (517) 339-4455. You must also provide your Visa/MC # and expiration date (or a check or money order). Within 2 weeks, we will return a well-informed GMAT-type score, an evaluation of your writing and some suggestions for improvement for $20. Essays will be graded through an expertly-staffed program managed by Dr. James Ney, the author of this chapter.

SECTION 6 Data Sufficiency

1. A (1) is sufficient since, if k^2 is even then k must be even and the answer is "No". (2) is not sufficient since $k + k$ is even for an odd or even k.

2. B (1) is not sufficient since $x^2 > x^{13}$ if $x < 1$ and $x^2 < x^{13}$ if $x > 1.2$. (2) is sufficient since x^2 is positive and x^{13} is negative for all $x < 0$; a positive is always greater than a negative so the answer is "No".

3. C The small square in the corner implies a right triangle. If we know the angle x and one of the lengths, then all angles and lengths can be determined and subsequently the area.

   (Area $= \frac{1}{2}\overline{BC} \times \overline{AB}$. $\overline{AB} = 8 \cos 40°$ and $\overline{BC} = 8 \sin 40°$. $\therefore$ Area $= 32 \cos 40° \sin 40°$.)

4. D (1) is sufficient since two equations can be solved for s and t and then ($\frac{3t}{5} + t = 8$ or $\frac{8t}{5} = 8$ so $t = 5$. $\therefore s = 3$ and $s - t = 3 - 5 = -2$.) (2) is also sufficient since $t = \left(5^{1/3}\right)^3 = 5$ and again $s = 3$.

5. C (1) is not sufficient. With (2) sufficient information is provided. Let x be the cost of the shoes. Then $x + x = 2x$ is the price before the sale, and $2x - 0.3\,(2x) = 50$. this provides x, the original cost. ($2x - .6x = 50$ so that $1.4x = 50$.)

6. E (1) is not sufficient. (2) is not sufficient. Together (1) and (2) are not sufficient since $\overline{AD} = \overline{BC}$ must also be known. $\left(\text{Area} = \left(\overline{AB}\right)\left(\overline{AD}\right)\sin x°.\right)$

7. E (1) is not sufficient since the median is not related to the average. (2) is not sufficient since we'd need the average wage of both groups of 250. More information is needed.

8. C If $m \perp n$ and $y = 30°$, then corresponding angles allow $30 + 90 + x = 180$ so that $x = 60°$. Both (1) and (2) are needed.

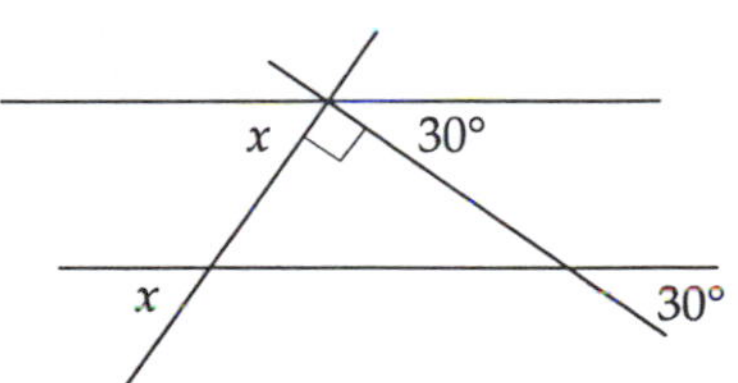

9. B (1) is not sufficient since if $x < 1$ (say $x = \frac{1}{2}$) then $\frac{1}{x + x^3} < \frac{1}{x^2 + x^4}$, and if $x > 1$ (say $x = 2$) then $\frac{1}{x + x^3} > \frac{1}{x^2 + x^4}$. (2) is sufficient since a negative $\left(\frac{1}{x + x^3}\right)$ is always less than a positive $\left(\frac{1}{x^2 + x^4}\right)$ so the answer is "No".

10. C The volume of a cube is d^3. the volume of a cylinder is $\pi r^2 h$. (1) is not sufficient. With (2) the question becomes: What is $\frac{(2r)^3}{\pi r^2(2r)} = \frac{8r^3}{2\pi r^3} = \frac{8}{2\pi}$? With a calculator this is obviously known so both (1) and (2) are needed.

11. E (1) is not sufficient since we do not know the speed. Both (1) and (2) are not sufficient since we cannot infer the distance from B to C.

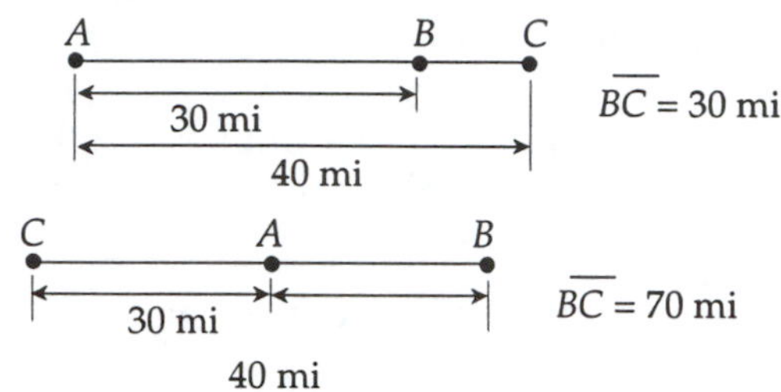

12. B Factor the quadratic: $(x - 3)(x + 2) > 0$? If $x > -2$ but less than 3 (e.g., $x = 0$) then $(x - 3)(x + 2)$ is negative; if x is greater than 3 then $(x - 3)(x + 2)$ is positive so the question cannot be answered with (1) alone. (2) is sufficient, since if $x < -2$ then $(x - 3)$ is negative and $(x + 2)$ is negative so the product is positive.

13. E (1) is not sufficient. Let's try (1) and (2) together. If ℓ is divisible by 3, it is 3, 6, or 9 (each digit in a two-digit number is less than 10). It can't be 3 since m would then be 10. If it's 6, $m = 7$ and if it's 9, $m = 4$. The possibilities are 67, 76, 94, and 49. More information is needed.

14. A (1) is sufficient since the factor is 2 and the subsequent terms are known: 1, 2, 4, 8, 16, 32, . . . The sum can be found. Let the first term be x and the common factor be y. Then the terms are $x, xy, \ldots$. Thus $xy^4 + xy^5 = 48$. To find these two unknowns, more information is needed.

15. E (1) is not sufficient since we must have information about y. (2) states that y is also negative; Then $\frac{1}{x} + \frac{1}{y}$ and $x + y$ are both negative. If x and y are negative but greater than -1 (e.g., $x = -\frac{1}{4}, y = -\frac{1}{2}$) then $\frac{1}{x} + \frac{1}{y}$ is greater than $x + y$. so more information is needed.

16. D If angle A plus angle B is 180°, the angles are supplements of each other so (1) is sufficient and the answer is "No." (2) is also sufficient and the answer is "Yes."

17. C It is assumed that Michelle and John work at the same time; they type at 100 words per minute. Martha and Jeff type 110 words per minute so they can type the manuscript in $\frac{100}{110} \times 60$ hours. Both (1) and (2) are needed.

18. D The small box implies a right triangle. If $a = 6$, then $6^2 + b^2 = 10^2$ so that $b = 8$. the triangle is fixed and the largest circle that can fit in the triangle is obviously fixed. Given the correct analysis it could be determined. It is not necessary to calculate the radius, only determine that (1) is sufficient. If $x = 30°$, a and b are both known ($a = 1 -$ sin 30°, $b = 10$ cos 30°) and again, the triangle is fixed. (2) is also sufficient.

19. B Factor the quadratic: $(x + 4)(x - 2) = 0$. $\therefore x = 2, - 4$. Obviously, (1) is not sufficient since y is not known. (2) is sufficient since $x/y = 2y/y = 2$.

20. D (1) states that the circle passes through the point (6, 0). The distance from (3, 4) to (6, 0) can be determined; it is the radius, so the area is known. $(r = \sqrt{(3-0)^2 + (4-0)^2} = \sqrt{9+16} = 5)$. (2) states that the circle passes through the point (0, 8) so that the radius is known: $r = \sqrt{(3-0)^2 + (4-0)^2} = \sqrt{9+16} = 5$. The area is $\pi r^2 = 25\pi$.

SECTION 7 Critical Reasoning

1. D Jeremy's argument needs both premises: either one without the other has no force at all in establishing his conclusion. In particular, the fact that the dictionary is reliable tells us nothing about the proper spelling of the word, without some information about what spelling the dictionary gives. So if Mrs. Clarke is correct, then Jeremy's argument fails entirely.

   Sometimes two separate lines of evidence converge independently on a single conclusion. In such a case the refutation of one line may leave the other one untouched, and something like (E) would be correct. But that is not the case here. Mrs. Clarke's claim about what the dictionary says does not itself show that the dictionary is unreliable (that would need the additional premise that some given spellings were incorrect), nor that there is no correct spelling. So (A) and (B) are not right. And what can be discovered in other dictionaries cannot affect the relevance of Mrs. Clarke's claim to the propriety of Jeremy's argument, which appeals to one dictionary and not to others.

2. B (B) expresses the most likely explanation. If the water supply is often interrupted, people will naturally try to find a way to store water and have it available during the interruptions. Roof water tanks provide just such a method.

Since there is no evidence that the tanks are used as part of any purification system, (A) is an unlikely explanation. And (C), (D), and (E), though possibly true, have no obvious relevance to the use of individual storage tanks.

3. C The engineer's conclusion is that solar cells will *never* supply a large part of our electrical power. But his premise refers to present methods of extracting silicon. So his argument needs the assumption that no more efficient means will be found. The other proposed assumptions are irrelevant to the conclusion actually attributed to the engineer.

4. E (E) seems to express the most promising explanation of those suggested. But the curious fact described in the scenario may in fact have some other explanation not suggested here. (E) is the most promising of these because it fits the described facts better than do the others.

   (A) seems unlikely because Europeans in Africa, especially including children born and brought up there, get appendicitis there. (B) seems unlikely because Black Africans who immigrate to Europe get appendicitis there. (C) appears to be just a special case of (B), and (D) is a special case of (A), and they are unlikely for the reasons already cited. (A) is left (given the plausible assumption that Europeans in Africa probably keep to their traditional diet more closely than do Africans in Europe).

5. D What is crucial to the sun's importance is the hypothetical (or "counter-factual") statement, "If it were not for the sun, the earth would be dark." The boy in effect argues that because the effect actually occurs, the cause is not needed. But it may well be that if the cause had not operated, the effect would not have occurred.

   (A) , (C), and (E) cannot be what is wrong with the argument, because they are themselves false. (B) is true, but irrelevant.

6. B (B) is the best we can say about this exchange. We can notice immediately that three of the alternatives include the claim that one of the managers is mistaken. So a useful first step is determining whether that is true. The crucial fact here is that both managers can be correct in their data and calculations, and such a situation would not even be unusual. If, for example, the current production system yields, on the average, about 98 satisfactory items and 2 defective items in every 100, then its failure rate is 2% and its reliability rate is 98%. Cutting the failure rate by one-half would yield 1 defective item and 99 satisfactory items. But that would increase the reliability rate by only a little over 1%. Whether such an improvement is worth the cost of the change might be a legitimate matter of disagreement, but it should not be obscured by the two ways of figuring essentially the same thing.

   Since neither manager need be mistaken, (A), (C), and (E) are ruled out. And the dispute has no obvious relevance to the claim that the effects of changes in production methods are unpredictable. So (D) is also excluded.

7. B The original conclusion is that the new variety will be economically attractive for commercial users. The critics present a new argument whose conclusion is that the new variety will be economically unattractive. But they do not attempt to show that the original premise, about spreading out the time for the industrial operations, is false, nor that it is irrelevant. They try to show, instead, that its significance is over-

balanced by another consideration, the cost of harvesting. That strategy is summarized in (B), and not in the other alternatives.

8. B There is an appearance of circularity, especially in the summary in the final paragraph of the scenario. But that is superficial, generated by the use of the word "because" twice. The possible circularity disappears when we recognize that the first "because" is that of causation and explanation, while the second is that of inference and serves to identify a premise. For better or worse, then, Hoyle presents a non-circular argument in favor of the claim that some species of bacteria are inter-stellar immigrants to the earth. And this argument involves two premises: (i) these bacteria are highly resistant, and (ii) this high resistance can best be explained by an extra-terrestrial origin. Neither of these premises is identical with Hoyle's conclusion. There is also an argument in favor of (ii), which appeals to claims about the circumstance under which such a resistance would be beneficial to the organism. That argument, too, is non-circular.

   As described, the Hoyle argument does not explain how, or why, these bacteria developed in the extra-terrestrial environment. So (A) cannot be correct. As we have seen, (C) is not true. Hoyle's argument assumes as a premise that we know (presumably from tests) that some bacteria are highly resistant. He does not present an argument for that claim. So (D) is ruled out. (E) is right about the conclusion of Hoyle's argument, but wrong about the circularity.

9. A (A) is the only alternative which fits the description given of Hoyle's argument. The argument clearly does appeal to a similarity between terrestrial and extra-terrestrial phenomena—that methane occurs both on earth and in comets. And it concludes that there (probably) is a further similarity—that the methane in comets is the product of bacteria, just as it invariably is on earth. This line of argument would, of course, be strengthened by the discovery of further similarities of the first kind—i.e., other compounds which occur in both places, and whose terrestrial occurrence is, like that of methane, strongly linked to bacterial action. (B) cannot be correct, since it denies that the original argument appeals to an analogy. Concerning (C), the argument might be strengthened if we had some good account of the process of bacterial production of methane. But we might know that this production is a fact, and even that it is, so far as we can tell, the only source of terrestrial methane, without knowing that process. And in that case the analogy would still have some evidential force with respect to what happens extraterrestrially. The scenario in (D) would *strengthen* the plausibility of Hoyle's conclusion; indeed, it is hard to think of anything which would strengthen it more. The events described in (E) would weaken it by revealing an analogy which suggests a non-organic source of methane in comets.

10. A (A) is the conclusion which follows most directly from the philosophical thesis. For if an experimental result is in conflict with some theory, but only in conjunction with some other scientific beliefs, then we can consistently retain both the experiment and the theory. What we need to do in that case is to abandon some of those other beliefs. And that is just what (A) says.

    It doesn't follow, however, that experimentation is wholly irrelevant to scientific theorizing—just that it is not conclusive. And it has no clear relevance to the question of just where the greatest relevance of experimentation lies.

11. E Because of the resolutions of Steve and JoAnne, neither of them can be appointed before a decision is made about the other one. That rules out making a positive deci-

sion to appoint in either case, because no such decision could be the <u>first</u> decision. But nothing in the scenario rules out Cecily's first making a negative decision—the decision, say, not to appoint Steve. Then she could inform JoAnne of that fact, JoAnne might then consent to the appointment, and thus be appointed. Or, of course, the first negative decision might have been made about JoAnne, resulting in the possible appointment of Steve.

12. D (D) is correct. More generally, if most X's are Y's, and most X's are Z's, then some Y's must be Z's. You can visualize X as being a circle which is overlapped by two others, Y and Z. Y laps over more than half of X (<u>most</u> of X), and Z also overlaps more than half of X. In that case, there must be <u>some</u> overlap belonging to both Y and Z. In this problem, the visitors to the park constitute X, the "middle" class. Y is the class of people who are <u>not</u> residents of Wyoming, and Z is the class of residents of the U.S. Since each of them takes up more than half of the park's visitors, there have to be some people who belong to both Y and Z. Therefore, there are some people who are residents of the U.S. and not residents of Wyoming. None of the other suggestions, though of course some of them are in fact true, <u>follow</u> from the facts stated in the scenario.

13. E None of the stated alternatives follow from the stated fact about validity. That fact guarantees that one combination of truth and falsity is impossible in a valid deductive argument—a set of true premises and a false conclusion. But it leaves open the possibility of any other combination. Therefore, it is quite possible for a valid argument to have a false conclusion, contrary to (B), and for a valid argument to have a true conclusion even if all of its premises are false, contrary to (C) and (D). It does follow from the stated fact that if a valid argument has a false conclusion, then it has <u>some</u> false premise, but it need not be the case that <u>all</u> of its premises are false. So (A) is not correct either.

14. C (C) is best. More than one of these suggestions may be a good reason for the trustees not to approve this arrangement. But the question asks for the consideration which most directly addresses the argument put forward by the coach. That argument concerns the financial benefit which the college will reap from renting the otherwise unused facilities. (C), which cites possible financial losses from the operation, seems to directly address that argument. The other alternatives either cite other sorts of undesirable consequences, or else are more or less irrelevant to the proposal.

15. C (C) seems to be the best response. This is a fairly difficult problem, and a good candidate for being postponed until the end. It may strike you that the decision about the best response is not as clear as in many other problems. But actual GMAT tests sometimes have problems with that feature. Do the best you can with them. For this one, work out your own answer and see how it compares with ours.

More than one argument is described in this scenario. Clearly there is the argument which Pedro gave the company officer, one with premises about the *Britannica* and what it said, and a conclusion about Jamaica. Then there is the inference which Pedro says he himself made, starting with a premise about Jamaica and drawing a conclusion about what the *Britannica* said. And perhaps there is a third argument with premises about Pedro's father, and a conclusion about Jamaica. None of those arguments is circular—none of them even looks like it has a premise which is the same as its conclusion. If the first and second argument were combined into one, then that one argument *would be* circular. But nothing in the scenario suggests that Pedro (or anyone else) combined those arguments into one, or ever intended to do so. So it seems that there is no circular argument here, so we rule out (A) and (D).

Both (B) and (E) seem to confuse speculations about Pedro's own reasons for his beliefs with the logical features and evidential force of the argument which he gave to the officer. But that latter argument appeals to a respected and reliable authority, and is typical of probabilistic arguments which we rely on all the time. And, in fact, though Pedro had not read the article, he did have a plausible reason for his belief about what it said. So (C) seems to be the best of the suggested responses.

16. B This question is about how a certain fact, low taxes paid by certain wealthy people, is related to the possibility of loop-holes in the income tax laws. (B) tends to undermine that link by reminding us that income and wealth are not the same thing, and that income taxes are presumably intended to tax incomes, and not necessarily wealth.

(A) does not tend to refute the original argument, because of the possibility that the wealthy employ lawyers precisely in order to find and exploit loop-holes in the tax laws. (C) and (D) are irrelevant to the original argument, since it is about taxes on incomes, and not on the spending of those incomes. (E) might involve a consideration which would support the propriety of lower taxes for high incomes, but as it stands it does not seem to address the question of whether the cited apparent anomaly (inconsistency) is indicative of the prevalence of loop-holes.

SECTION 8 Data Sufficiency

1. E (1) is not sufficient since $x^2 > x^{10}$ if $x = -\frac{1}{2}$, and $x^2 < x^{10}$ if $x = -2$. (2) is not sufficient since $x^2 > x^{10}$ if $x = \frac{1}{2}$, and $x^2 < x^{10}$ if $x = 2$. Using (1) and (2) together does not help.

2. D If we know a side and an angle for a right triangle, then the other two sides and the other angle can be found. (1) is sufficient since the other sides can be found. ($\overline{BC} = 8.2 \sin 37°$ and $\overline{AB} = 8.2 \cos 37°$. $\therefore$ Perimeter $= \overline{AB} + \overline{BC} + 8.2$). (2) is also sufficient since $\overline{AB}^2 + \overline{BC}^2 = 8.2^2$ or $1.6^2\overline{BC}^2 + \overline{BC}^2 = 8.2^2$ from which $\overline{BC}$ can be found and then $\overline{AB} = 1.6\overline{BC}^2 + \overline{BC}$.

3. C (1) is not sufficient. Neither is (2). But (1) and (2) together can be solved and x^y determined. (Substitute (1) into (2): $4y + 2y = 12$. $\therefore 6y = 12$ and $y = 2$ so that $x = 8$. Then $8^2 = 64$.)

4. A $\frac{r+s}{2} = 26$. (1) is sufficient since it states that $r = 3s$. ($\frac{3s+s}{2} = 26$, $\therefore 45 = 52$ and $s = 13$, $r = 39$). (2) is not sufficient.

5. C (1) is not sufficient since it states that $x + y = 2$. (2) is obviously not sufficient. Together $x + y + z = 2 + 3 = 5$.

6. C (1) is not sufficient since x can be either 0 or 2. (0 satisfies the equation since $0 = 0$; also 2 satisfies the equation since $4 = 4$. Don't just divide out the x since the solution $x = 0$ will be lost!) With (2) the $x = 0$ solution is not acceptable and the answer is $x = 2$.

7. D (1) is sufficient since a right triangle with one side and an acute angle specified is completely known. Obviously, only one circle will then just fit (the meaning of "inscribed") into the space and its diameter can be determined (it may not be easy!). (2) is also sufficient since $\angle C + \angle B = 90°$ so that $3\angle B = 90°$ and $\angle B = 30°, \angle C = 60°$; again the triangle is completely known and the diameter of the circle can be found (with the clever use of trig!).

8. B (1) is not sufficient since $x = +1$ or $x = -1$ and we cannot state that $x > 1$. (2) is sufficient since $\sqrt{x} = 1$ means that $x = 1$ and the answer is "No."

9. E (1) is not sufficient; neither is (2). If they both started at the same salary we could answer the question with some calculations, but the starting salaries are not given so more information is needed.

10. A (1) is sufficient since Ivy League University enrolled 10 million/5,000 = 2,000 students and Midwest University enrolled 6 million/5,000 = 750. (2) is not sufficient since we do not know the enrollment of either school.

11. A (1) is sufficient since if 8,500 drive cars then 1,500 ride bicycles. (2) is not sufficient since we do not know the total population; it cannot be assumed from (1).

12. D (1) is sufficient since if its perimeter is 12 and one leg is 4 and we let the hypotenuse be x and the other leg be y, we have $12 = x + y + 4$ and $x^2 = 4^2 + y^2$: two equations and two unknowns. ($x + y = 8$ and $x^2 - y^2 = 16$ or $(x - y)(x + y) = 16$. $\therefore (x - y)9 = 16$ or $x - y = 2$. $\therefore 2x = 10$ and $x = 5, y = 3$.) (2) is also sufficient since if we let x, y and z be the hypotenuse and two legs: $x + y + z = 12$, $y = x \sin 30°$ and $z = x \cos 30°$ so that $x + x \sin 30° = 12$ and x is known as is y and z. (Perhaps an easier way to answer the question is to visualize $\overline{AB} \perp \overline{AC}$ with $\overline{AC} = 4$—sketch it; there is only one placement of point B so that the perimeter is 12. Also, if $\angle C = 30°$, there is only one unique triangle that would give a perimeter of 12.)

13. B (1) is not sufficient. If m^2 is even then m is even; if n^2 is odd then n is odd. An even number cannot be a factor of an odd number, e.g., 4 cannot be a factor of 21. So, (2) is sufficient to provide a "No" answer to the question.

14. D The shortest distance from (x, y) to the y-axis is x. The question is: Is $\sqrt{x^2 + y^2} > x$? If $y > 0$ then the answer is "Yes" and (1) is sufficient. If $y = 0$ then $x = x$ and the answer is "No" (it is "equal to" not "greater than") so (2) is also sufficient.

15. E The average of y and z is $\frac{y+z}{2}$. The question is: Is $x > \frac{y+z}{2}$? If $y + z = 3x$, as required by (1), then the question is: Is $x > \frac{3x}{2}$? If x is negative (say, $y + z = -6$), the answer is "Yes" $(-2 > -3)$; if x is positive (say $y + z = 6$), the answer is "No" $(2 < 3)$ and (1) is not sufficient. (2) also is not sufficient. (1) and (2) can be solved simultaneously (add them together) to yield $y = 2x$ and $z = x$. The question is: Is $x > \frac{2x + x}{2} = \frac{3}{2}x$? More information is needed.

16. B If $\overline{AB} = \overline{DE}$, the second square is symmetrically oriented in the large square. Angle *BHI* is equal to angle *FJK* regardless of the orientation of the small square. Hence, (1) is not sufficient. If *IJ* is parallel to *CE*, then the small square is half the area of the large square—Area $= \frac{1}{2}(10 \times 10) = 50$. (2) is sufficient.

17. B (1) is not sufficient. Let x = the number of \$10 tickets sold by Sue and y = the number of \$5 tickets sold by Joe. Then Joe sold $2x$ \$10 tickets and Sue sold $3y$ \$5 tickets. (2) implies $70 = x + 2x + y + 3y$ and $500 = 10(x + 2x) + 5(y+3y)$. These two equations ($70 = 3x + 4y$ and $50 = 3x + 2y$) can be solved for x and y and subsequently $2x + y$. ($y = 10$ and $x = 10$ so Joe sold $2(10) + 10 = 30$ tickets.)

18. B If $y = 2x$, the question is $x^{3.25} > 2x$? x cannot be negative since $x^{3.25}$ is not defined if x is negative. So, divide both sides by x: Is $x^{2.25} > 2$? (1) is not sufficient since if $x = 1$, the answer is "No," and if $x = 2$ the answer is "Yes." With (2) the question is: Is $3.67^{3.25} > 43.2$? Obviously, with a calculator the answer can be determined; there is sufficient information.

19. C The question is equivalent to : Is $x > z - y$? (1) implies $z - y = 2 - x$. Is $x > 2 - x$, or $2x > 2$. (1) is not sufficient. (2) is not sufficient, but (1) and (2) together asks: Is $8 > 2$? The answer is "Yes."

20. C The cross-hatched area is $\pi r_1^2 - \pi r_2^2 = \pi(r_1^2 - r_2^2)$. If $r_1 = \frac{3}{2} r_2$ the cross-hatched is $\pi\left(\frac{9}{4} r_2^2 - r_2^2\right) = \frac{5\pi}{4} r_2^2$. (1) is not sufficient. If $\pi r_1 - \pi r_2 = 20$ then $r_1 - r_2 = \frac{20}{\pi}$. Thus, (2) is also not sufficient. (1) and (2) together provide two equations and two unknowns, hence a solution. ($\frac{3}{2} r_2 - r_2 = \frac{20}{\pi}$. $\therefore r_2 = \frac{40}{\pi}$. Then $Area = \frac{5\pi}{4}\left(\frac{40}{\pi}\right)^2 = \frac{2000}{\pi}$.)

SECTION 9 Analysis of an Argument

You may wish to have a friend or colleague grade your writing using the scoring guidelines presented on page 136 in 'Analytical Writing.' Or, should you desire a professional assessment of your writings, you may send the two essays to: Great Lakes Press, POB 483, Okemos, MI 48805-0483. Or fax to (517) 339-4455. You must also provide your Visa/MC # and expiration date (or a check or money order). Within 2 weeks, we will return a well-informed GMAT-type score, an evaluation of your writing and some suggestions for improvement for \$20. Essays will be graded through an expertly-staffed program managed by Dr. James Ney, the author of this chapter.

Test No. 2

Sections:

1. Reading Comprehension
2. Sentence Correction
3. Critical Reasoning
4. Problem Solving
5. Analysis of an Issue
6. Data Sufficiency
7. Problem Solving
8. Sentence Correction
9. Analysis of an Argument

Followed by:

Score Analysis Charts
Explanations To All Answers

Practice these suggestions for Test #2:

1. Write your answers next to the questions on each page. Then transfer your answers to the answer sheet a block at a time.

2. On a difficult question, if you cannot eliminate at least two choices, leave the question blank and do not guess.

3. Put a circle around a question number if you are uncertain of the correct answer and think you may return to it if time permits. Before moving on to the next question, guess an answer if you can eliminate at least two choices; you may not have time to return.

4. Construct diagrams, draw sketches, and write equations in the empty space on the exam. Such aids are often helpful in your thought process.

5. Try to simulate actual exam conditions and time yourself very carefully. Do not exceed the allotted 25 or 30 minutes per section. Take a break after the fifth section to simulate the actual exam.

6. Do not worry if you leave some questions unanswered. The GMAT is quite difficult and students often leave questions unanswered. If you cannot eliminate at least two choices on a question, do not guess.

7. Write each of your Analytical Writing exercises on the front sides of three of the six unlined 8.5″x11″ sheets that you should have at hand for this exam. Practice writing legibly, with a #2 pencil. Try to fill all three front sides, but leave an inch or so margins all around and don't write too small or too large. We recommend that you write 4-8 paragraphs of 4-8 sentences each. [To have your essays graded professionally by a team coordinated by our Writing section author, mail them to: GLP, POB 483, Okemos MI 48805, or fax to: 517-339-4455. Your writing will be graded and returned within 2 weeks. The fee is $20.00. Include your Visa/MC number with expiration date or a check or money order.]

How to handle the answer sheet:

- Each section begins with number 1.
- If a section has fewer than 25 questions, ignore the extra answer blanks.
- If you change an answer, erase it completely.
- Do not make any extraneous marks on the answer sheet.

SIGNATURE:

ANSWER SHEET

(simulated GMAT form)

BE SURE EACH MARK IS DARK AND COMPLETELY FILLS THE INTENDED SPACE AS ILLUSTRATED HERE: ●.
YOU MAY FIND MORE RESPONSE SPACES THAN YOU NEED. IF SO, PLEASE LEAVE THEM BLANK.

SECTION 1	SECTION 2	SECTION 3	SECTION 4	SECTION 6	SECTION 7	SECTION 8
1. ⒶⒷⒸⒹⒺ	1. ⒶⒷⒸⒹⒺ	1. ⒶⒷⒸⒹⒺ	1. ⒶⒷⒸⒹⒺ	1. ⒶⒷⒸⒹⒺ	1. ⒶⒷⒸⒹⒺ	1. ⒶⒷⒸⒹⒺ
2. ⒶⒷⒸⒹⒺ	2. ⒶⒷⒸⒹⒺ	2. ⒶⒷⒸⒹⒺ	2. ⒶⒷⒸⒹⒺ	2. ⒶⒷⒸⒹⒺ	2. ⒶⒷⒸⒹⒺ	2. ⒶⒷⒸⒹⒺ
3. ⒶⒷⒸⒹⒺ	3. ⒶⒷⒸⒹⒺ	3. ⒶⒷⒸⒹⒺ	3. ⒶⒷⒸⒹⒺ	3. ⒶⒷⒸⒹⒺ	3. ⒶⒷⒸⒹⒺ	3. ⒶⒷⒸⒹⒺ
4. ⒶⒷⒸⒹⒺ	4. ⒶⒷⒸⒹⒺ	4. ⒶⒷⒸⒹⒺ	4. ⒶⒷⒸⒹⒺ	4. ⒶⒷⒸⒹⒺ	4. ⒶⒷⒸⒹⒺ	4. ⒶⒷⒸⒹⒺ
5. ⒶⒷⒸⒹⒺ	5. ⒶⒷⒸⒹⒺ	5. ⒶⒷⒸⒹⒺ	5. ⒶⒷⒸⒹⒺ	5. ⒶⒷⒸⒹⒺ	5. ⒶⒷⒸⒹⒺ	5. ⒶⒷⒸⒹⒺ
6. ⒶⒷⒸⒹⒺ	6. ⒶⒷⒸⒹⒺ	6. ⒶⒷⒸⒹⒺ	6. ⒶⒷⒸⒹⒺ	6. ⒶⒷⒸⒹⒺ	6. ⒶⒷⒸⒹⒺ	6. ⒶⒷⒸⒹⒺ
7. ⒶⒷⒸⒹⒺ	7. ⒶⒷⒸⒹⒺ	7. ⒶⒷⒸⒹⒺ	7. ⒶⒷⒸⒹⒺ	7. ⒶⒷⒸⒹⒺ	7. ⒶⒷⒸⒹⒺ	7. ⒶⒷⒸⒹⒺ
8. ⒶⒷⒸⒹⒺ	8. ⒶⒷⒸⒹⒺ	8. ⒶⒷⒸⒹⒺ	8. ⒶⒷⒸⒹⒺ	8. ⒶⒷⒸⒹⒺ	8. ⒶⒷⒸⒹⒺ	8. ⒶⒷⒸⒹⒺ
9. ⒶⒷⒸⒹⒺ	9. ⒶⒷⒸⒹⒺ	9. ⒶⒷⒸⒹⒺ	9. ⒶⒷⒸⒹⒺ	9. ⒶⒷⒸⒹⒺ	9. ⒶⒷⒸⒹⒺ	9. ⒶⒷⒸⒹⒺ
10. ⒶⒷⒸⒹⒺ	10. ⒶⒷⒸⒹⒺ	10. ⒶⒷⒸⒹⒺ	10. ⒶⒷⒸⒹⒺ	10. ⒶⒷⒸⒹⒺ	10. ⒶⒷⒸⒹⒺ	10. ⒶⒷⒸⒹⒺ
11. ⒶⒷⒸⒹⒺ	11. ⒶⒷⒸⒹⒺ	11. ⒶⒷⒸⒹⒺ	11. ⒶⒷⒸⒹⒺ	11. ⒶⒷⒸⒹⒺ	11. ⒶⒷⒸⒹⒺ	11. ⒶⒷⒸⒹⒺ
12. ⒶⒷⒸⒹⒺ	12. ⒶⒷⒸⒹⒺ	12. ⒶⒷⒸⒹⒺ	12. ⒶⒷⒸⒹⒺ	12. ⒶⒷⒸⒹⒺ	12. ⒶⒷⒸⒹⒺ	12. ⒶⒷⒸⒹⒺ
13. ⒶⒷⒸⒹⒺ	13. ⒶⒷⒸⒹⒺ	13. ⒶⒷⒸⒹⒺ	13. ⒶⒷⒸⒹⒺ	13. ⒶⒷⒸⒹⒺ	13. ⒶⒷⒸⒹⒺ	13. ⒶⒷⒸⒹⒺ
14. ⒶⒷⒸⒹⒺ	14. ⒶⒷⒸⒹⒺ	14. ⒶⒷⒸⒹⒺ	14. ⒶⒷⒸⒹⒺ	14. ⒶⒷⒸⒹⒺ	14. ⒶⒷⒸⒹⒺ	14. ⒶⒷⒸⒹⒺ
15. ⒶⒷⒸⒹⒺ	15. ⒶⒷⒸⒹⒺ	15. ⒶⒷⒸⒹⒺ	15. ⒶⒷⒸⒹⒺ	15. ⒶⒷⒸⒹⒺ	15. ⒶⒷⒸⒹⒺ	15. ⒶⒷⒸⒹⒺ
16. ⒶⒷⒸⒹⒺ	16. ⒶⒷⒸⒹⒺ	16. ⒶⒷⒸⒹⒺ	16. ⒶⒷⒸⒹⒺ	16. ⒶⒷⒸⒹⒺ	16. ⒶⒷⒸⒹⒺ	16. ⒶⒷⒸⒹⒺ
17. ⒶⒷⒸⒹⒺ	17. ⒶⒷⒸⒹⒺ	17. ⒶⒷⒸⒹⒺ	17. ⒶⒷⒸⒹⒺ	17. ⒶⒷⒸⒹⒺ	17. ⒶⒷⒸⒹⒺ	17. ⒶⒷⒸⒹⒺ
18. ⒶⒷⒸⒹⒺ	18. ⒶⒷⒸⒹⒺ	18. ⒶⒷⒸⒹⒺ	18. ⒶⒷⒸⒹⒺ	18. ⒶⒷⒸⒹⒺ	18. ⒶⒷⒸⒹⒺ	18. ⒶⒷⒸⒹⒺ
19. ⒶⒷⒸⒹⒺ	19. ⒶⒷⒸⒹⒺ	19. ⒶⒷⒸⒹⒺ	19. ⒶⒷⒸⒹⒺ	19. ⒶⒷⒸⒹⒺ	19. ⒶⒷⒸⒹⒺ	19. ⒶⒷⒸⒹⒺ
20. ⒶⒷⒸⒹⒺ	20. ⒶⒷⒸⒹⒺ	20. ⒶⒷⒸⒹⒺ	20. ⒶⒷⒸⒹⒺ	20. ⒶⒷⒸⒹⒺ	20. ⒶⒷⒸⒹⒺ	20. ⒶⒷⒸⒹⒺ
21. ⒶⒷⒸⒹⒺ	21. ⒶⒷⒸⒹⒺ	21. ⒶⒷⒸⒹⒺ	21. ⒶⒷⒸⒹⒺ	21. ⒶⒷⒸⒹⒺ	21. ⒶⒷⒸⒹⒺ	21. ⒶⒷⒸⒹⒺ
22. ⒶⒷⒸⒹⒺ	22. ⒶⒷⒸⒹⒺ	22. ⒶⒷⒸⒹⒺ	22. ⒶⒷⒸⒹⒺ	22. ⒶⒷⒸⒹⒺ	22. ⒶⒷⒸⒹⒺ	22. ⒶⒷⒸⒹⒺ
23. ⒶⒷⒸⒹⒺ	23. ⒶⒷⒸⒹⒺ	23. ⒶⒷⒸⒹⒺ	23. ⒶⒷⒸⒹⒺ	23. ⒶⒷⒸⒹⒺ	23. ⒶⒷⒸⒹⒺ	23. ⒶⒷⒸⒹⒺ
24. ⒶⒷⒸⒹⒺ	24. ⒶⒷⒸⒹⒺ	24. ⒶⒷⒸⒹⒺ	24. ⒶⒷⒸⒹⒺ	24. ⒶⒷⒸⒹⒺ	24. ⒶⒷⒸⒹⒺ	24. ⒶⒷⒸⒹⒺ
25. ⒶⒷⒸⒹⒺ	25. ⒶⒷⒸⒹⒺ	25. ⒶⒷⒸⒹⒺ	25. ⒶⒷⒸⒹⒺ	25. ⒶⒷⒸⒹⒺ	25. ⒶⒷⒸⒹⒺ	25. ⒶⒷⒸⒹⒺ

SECTIONS 5 & 9 ARE "WRITING ANALYSIS"
—TO BE COMPLETED ON 6 SEPARATE SHEETS
OF PAPER THAT YOU SHOULD HAVE READY.

SECTION 1 Reading Comprehension

18 Questions
Time: 25 minutes

Directions: In this group, each passage is followed by questions based on its content. On the basis of what is stated or implicit in the passage, please select the best answer to each question.

Passage 1:

In the late 1930s, the Chemical Department's liberal, though unwritten, publication policy on fundamental research experienced a major reversal, largely in response to the damage done to DuPont's proprietary position on nylon by one of Carothers' early papers. Carothers had published in 1931 a paper in which he stated categorically that caprolactam could not be polymerized either with or without a catalyst. In the spring of 1937, while negotiating on another matter, DuPont (believing its patent position impregnable) informed I.G. Farben that it had succeeded with a major development of a polyamide fiber—what would soon be named nylon 66. Once informed about nylon, I.G. Farben's researchers went over every inch of DuPont research looking for a place to drive a wedge in the U.S. company's patent position. They shrewdly found Carothers' statement on caprolactam and by January 1938 had succeeded in polymerizing it into nylon 6. To DuPont's research managers, who thought they had built a perfect patent position, I.G.'s nylon 6 was a low blow. A witch-hunt must have followed; the Chemical Department's liberal publication policy was quickly identified as the culprit. For a period of years after 1938, managers in the Chemical Department severely restricted publication of research results.

. . . In the industrial departments, researchers could expect a far tighter, though still unwritten, publication policy. Because research work in the industrial departments was usually of a much shorter range and hence more likely to have an immediate effect on the commercial position of the department, publication was more problematic and more apt to be prohibited.

In . . . reporting, procedures differed greatly among departments. Moreover, from the decentralization of 1921 until the 1950s, the company maintained no central index or access system to all the company's research reports. Some departmental research divisions wrote few reports while others barred their circulation to other industrial departments. L.G. Wise, head of the Chemical Department's intelligence division, sought unsuccessfully in the mid-1930s to create a central indexing and filing system at DuPont. He pointed out that it was difficult, if not impossible, to be sure that all research information generated in the company could be recovered, and he stressed that "if research is worth doing, the results should be worth keeping." In 1935, Wise argued research was more or less "being thrown away" because of the way reports were being handled. He cautioned that "as time goes on and more and more data are collected, the difficulty in making such data available and useful will be greater and greater. The difficulty in correlating and codifying such a mass of information will be greater and greater and after a time may become impossible. . ." Chemical department researchers and research managers who were active in the 1930s and 1940s have argued that industrial department autonomy precluded the creation of any report indexing system. Industrial department research divisions often did not want their counterparts in other departments to know what research they were doing.

David A. Hounshell and John Kenley Smith, Jr. Science and Corporate Strategy: DuPont R & D, 1902-1980. Cambridge: Cambridge University Press, 1988. pp. 302 and 307

1. What is the subject of this passage?
   A) recovery of research information at DuPont
   B) autonomy of central indexing and filing system at DuPont
   C) commercial position of the Chemical Department at DuPont
   D) DuPont's proprietary position on nylon
   E) development of publication policy at DuPont

2. Which statement below best expresses the central idea of this passage?
   A) Publication policy of industrial departments was far tighter than that of the Chemical Department.
   B) Publication policy of the Chemical Department was for years too liberal.
   C) For varying reasons, the publication policies of departments within DuPont were not uniform.
   D) In one case, managers in the Chemical Department tardily restricted publication of research results.
   E) Industrial department researchers preserved secrecy of research even from other departments within DuPont.

3. According to the passage, which event reversed the Chemical Department's liberal publication policy on research?
   A) the failed attempt to centralize indexing and filing of reports
   B) the mishandling of reports within all departments
   C) the destruction of DuPont's patent position on nylon by I.G. Farben
   D) the difficulty of correlating and codifying a mass of information
   E) the autonomy of research divisions of the industrial departments

4. Why was publication in the industrial departments likely to be prohibited?
   A) Competition between departments was especially vigorous.
   B) Research was of short range and had immediate commercial effect on the departments.
   C) Making data available and useful among departments was very difficult.
   D) Work in the Chemical Department was not of immediate commercial importance to the company.
   E) The industrial departments did not want other departments to negotiate patent positions for industrial department findings.

5. According to the passage, what was the greatest impediment to the development of a centralized report indexing system?
   A) decentralization of reporting procedure
   B) industrial department autonomy
   C) difficulty of correlating and codifying information
   D) mass of research information generated in the company
   E) differences in reporting procedures among departments

6. Which inference below may be drawn from the information given in this passage?
   A) Publication policy of DuPont from the late 1930s until the 1950s, however internally inefficient, was largely self-protective.
   B) Publication policy ensured that all research information generated in the company would be recovered.
   C) The Chemical Department's liberal publication policy had no effect on company-wide publication of research results.
   D) Correlating and cataloging information will become more feasible over time.
   E) Because reporting among departments differed dramatically, much research was thrown away.

Passage 2:

National and state legislative powers cluster under four principal heads. All four took root within the first fifty years of the nation's independence, but their full demonstration waited on the years from about 1880 to 1940. (1) The legislative branch holds the broadest authority of any agency short of the constitution-makers to define standards and rules of official and private conduct. By the early twentieth century the chapter headings and subject-matter indexes of federal and state statute books attested how far legislation had preempted from older, judge-made (common) law the governance of market transactions . . . as well as of such non-market fields of policy concern as protection of public health and conservation of natural resources. (2) Its powers to tax, borrow, and spend provide the legislative branch a role in allocating economic resources in substantial competition with the allocations function of the private market. . . . The taxing power proved potent not simply to finance government operations but also as an instrument of economic planning. Especially in the twentieth century, tax laws have pervaded entrepreneurial decision-making and operated as forms of economic regulation by defining taxable income, setting terms of depreciation allowances, or providing investment tax credits. (3) Legislatures hold plenary power to create new forms of organization for public or private collective action. They can create and finance executive and administrative agencies to pursue ends or programs outlined by statute. They may create public-function corporations, such as the Tennessee Valley Authority. They may set terms for chartering private corporations for business or for nonprofit enterprises. They may command or influence creation of procedures to govern relations among public and private institutions, groups, and individuals. . . . (4) Legislatures have authority to investigate matters of fact and of fact-involved values which they judge to be of public concern and relevant to possible legislation. In some respects the power of investigation is potentially the broadest, most significant legislative power. The investigatory power has come to bear on all other legal agencies and on the general community over a wide range of social concerns. It offers means for building and informing public opinion. It provides the chief practical procedure for legislative review of executive and administrative activity, especially when appropriations committees examine budgets.

James Willard Hurst. Law and Markets in United States History: Different Modes of Bargaining Among Interests. Madison, Wisconsin: The University of Wisconsin Press, 1982. pp. 122-123

7. What is the subject of this passage?
   A) four major legislative powers as they affect the private market
   B) four legislative powers, created in the early 1800s and fully expressed from 1880 to 1940
   C) the extent to which legislative power has superseded judicial power in the governance of market transactions
   D) the predominance of the taxing power over other powers of the legislature
   E) the broad authority to define standards and rules of official and private conduct

8. According to the passage, what is the broadest, most significant legislative power?
   A) power to tax as an instrument of economic planning
   B) power to create agencies and public-function corporations
   C) governance over the charters of private corporations
   D) power to allocate economic resources to compete with the private market
   E) authority to investigate matters of fact and issues of public concern

9. Which of the powers below is not part of the legislative taxing power?
   A) power to finance government operations
   B) power to define taxable income
   C) power to create executive and administrative agencies
   D) power to define taxable income
   E) power to provide investment tax credits

10. What evidence leads the author to generalize that legislatures, more than judge-made law, controlled governance of market transactions and non-market fields of policy concern?
    A) evidence that tax laws have pervaded entrepreneurial decision-making
    B) evidence that tax laws operate as forms of economic regulation
    C) evidence provided by chapter headings and subject-matter indexes of federal and state statute books
    D) evidence that executive and administrative agencies are subject to legislative control
    E) evidence that organizations for public and private collective action are subject to legislative control

11. According to the passage, what body holds broader authority than the legislative branch to define standards and rules of official and private conduct?
    A) administrative agencies B) the judiciary C) the common law
    D) the constitution-makers E) the private market

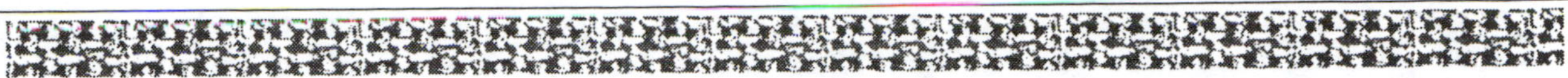

12. Which of the following statements is not true of the investigative power of the legislative branch?
    A) It governs relations among institutions, groups, individuals.
    B) It has come to bear on all legal agencies.
    C) It is concerned with a wide range of general community and social issues.
    D) It provides a procedure for review of executive and administrative activity.
    E) It offers a means for shaping public opinion.

13. Which inference below may be drawn from the information given in the passage?
    A) The investigatory power of the legislature preempts the investigatory power of the judiciary.
    B) The power of the legislative branch wholly supersedes executive and judicial action.
    C) The importance of the legislature in broad economic regulation is disproportionate to its importance in the regulation of private conduct.
    D) The power of the legislative branch is confined solely to the financing of government operations.
    E) The legislative power has broad authority that ventures occasionally even into spheres of judicial and executive action.

<u>Passage 3</u>:

Throughout the immediate prewar and wartime period, DuPont's executives took the position that the company would cooperate fully with the government as requested but that they wished to keep the company on its highly successful track of commercial development as much as possible. . . .

Yet the great press of DuPont's war effort in the immediate aftermath of Pearl Harbor delayed detailed planning for the postwar expansion of DuPont's research and development.

The United States' entry into the war rapidly altered DuPont research. . . . Some of the projects undertaken by the Chemical Department for war agencies included development of protection against war gases (uniforms, masks, antidotes, and decontaminants), synthesis of new war gases, development of new insecticides and antimalarial drugs, studies of anti-icing materials for airplane propellers, and the invention of self-sealing fuel cells for airplanes. Yet most of the Chemical Department's—and the industrial departments'—R & D efforts were directed at adapting and improving existing DuPont products for wartime applications.

. . . Unquestionably, emphasis on the short-range research and development of products for wartime applications forced a significant reduction in . . . fundamental research. . . . "Many attractive problems, [Bolton] noted in 1945, "have been set aside because they could not be pointed to specific war objectives." . . . [T]he section on research in . . . the report to the stockholders, *DuPont's Part in the National Security Program*, concluded, "Although war stimulates applied research and accelerates the utilization of previously determined scientific facts, it brings fundamental research to a virtual standstill. DuPont was able to carry out its wartime assignments largely because of the research carried out in time of peace in the various Company laboratories."

David A. Hounshell and John Kenley Smith, Jr. <u>Science and Corporate Strategy: DuPont R & D, 1902-1980</u>. Cambridge: Cambridge University Press, 1988. pp. 333, 337-339

14. What is the subject of this passage?
    A) delay in detailed planning for postwar expansion of research
    B) conflict between research for war objectives and for commercial development
    C) acceleration of use of previously determined scientific facts
    D) adapting and improving existing DuPont products for wartime application
    E) reduction in fundamental research

15. What forced a significant reduction in fundamental research?
    A) emphasis on short-range research and development for wartime applications
    B) adaptation of DuPont products for wartime applications
    C) improvement of DuPont products for wartime applications
    D) emphasis on applied rather than fundamental research
    E) acceleration of use of already determined scientific facts

16. All of the items below are mentioned as projects undertaken by DuPont for war agencies **except**
    A) development of masks, antidotes, decontaminants
    B) synthesis of new war gases
    C) development of insecticides
    D) improvement of existing weapons
    E) studies of anti-icing materials

17. Which fact below was critical to DuPont's ability to carry out its wartime work?
    A) its delay of detailed planning for postwar commercial research and development
    B) its full cooperation with the government
    C) its adaptation of existing products for wartime applications
    D) its earlier, peacetime research
    E) its halt of fundamental research

18. Which inference below may be drawn from the information given in this passage?
    A) DuPont complied halfheartedly with government requests for research and development for wartime applications.
    B) DuPont's wartime research yielded significant findings applicable to commercial uses.
    C) Fundamental research and development at DuPont were set back significantly by its efforts to achieve war objectives of the government.
    D) DuPont's executives abandoned their goal of successful commercial development until after the war.
    E) Most of the Chemical Department's products for wartime applications were the result of new research and development.

STOP!

If you finish before time is up (25 minutes), you may return to any of the questions in Section 1. Do not turn to any other section of the test.

SECTION 2 Sentence Correction

22 Questions
Time: 25 minutes

Directions: Some part of the following sentences, or the entire sentence, is underlined. The first of the five versions beneath each sentence is identical to the underlined portion. If you think the text is most correct as written in the problem, select (A); otherwise, choose the best sentence correction from the four remaining choices. Follow the requirements of written English when making your selection. Pay attention to grammar, word choice, and general sentence construction. Select the version that expresses most effectively and accurately what is contained in the original sentence.

1. Having completed a series of evasive tactics, the fighter pilot managed to elude his attacker.

   A) Having completed a series of evasive tactics, the fighter pilot managed to elude
   B) Having completed a series of evasive tactics, the fighter pilot managed to allude
   C) Since a series of evasive tactics had completed by the fighter pilot, he managed to elude
   D) As a result of the fact that he completed a series of evasive tactics, the fighter pilot managed to allude
   E) There having been completed a series of evasive tactics, the fighter pilot managed to elude

2. The preacher commanded his parishioners to not only abjure the love for filthy lucre but also to abandon their lavish life styles.

   A) to not only abjure the love for filthy lucre but also to abandon
   B) to not only espouse the love of money but also to abandon
   C) not only to abjure the love of money but also to abandon
   D) not only to espouse the love of money but also to abandon
   E) to not only abjure the love for filthy lucre but to also abandon

3. If I was you, I wouldn't let nobody talk me out of accepting a large raise and a transfer.

   A) was you, I wouldn't let nobody talk me out of
   B) were you, I wouldn't let anybody dissuade me from
   C) were you, I wouldn't let nobody dissuade me from
   D) was you, I wouldn't let anybody dissuade me from
   E) was you, I wouldn't let they talk me out of

4. The painter scarcely brought himself to inform his employer about the most unique furniture that he had only just recently created.
   A) scarcely brought himself to inform his employer about the most unique furniture that he had only just
   B) scarcely did not bring himself to inform his employer about the unique furniture that he had only
   C) scarcely brought himself to inform his employer about the unique furniture that he had just
   D) scarcely did not bring himself to inform his employer about the unique furniture that he had just
   E) scarcely brought himself to inform his employer about the unique furniture that he had only just

5. His psychotherapist told him to drive more fast or more slowly than his brother because it hadn't ought to make any difference to his brother.
   A) more fast or more slowly than his brother because it hadn't ought to
   B) faster or slower than his brother because it shouldn't ought to
   C) faster or more slowly than his brother because it hadn't ought to
   D) faster or more slowly than his brother because it shouldn't
   E) more fastly or more slowly than his brother because it shouldn't

6. For a sculptor, completing a perfect figurine is as satisfying as to finish a life-sized statute.
   A) as satisfying as to finish
   B) more satisfying than to finish
   C) as satisfying as it is finishing
   D) more satisfying then to finish
   E) as satisfying as finishing

7. If they would except the work of his old age, they will find it uniformly brilliant since Van Gogh had mental problems in his old age.
   A) they would except the work of his old age
   B) the critics would except the work of his old age
   C) the critics would accept the work of his old age
   D) they would accept the work of his old age
   E) they would have excepted the work of his old age

8. His impeccable behavior resulted in no kudos for the age-worn sojourner on the barren planet that floated leagues beyond the sun in a separate galaxy.
   A) His impeccable behavior resulted in no kudos for the age-worn
   B) His good behavior resulted in no kudos for the age-worn
   C) His good behavior did not bring any praise for the age-worn
   D) His good behavior did not bring any praise for the old
   E) His impeccable behavior did not bring no kudos for the old

9. Everybody wearing gloves on this fishing trip know about the effects of sea water on their hands.
   A) know about the effects of sea water on their hands
   B) knows about the effects of sea water on their hands
   C) have known about the effects of sea water on their hands
   D) have known about the effects of sea water on his hands
   E) knows about the effects of sea water on his hands

10. The manager stated that, although he had given all his workers, who he had respected, a raise, they all complained.
    A) workers, who he had respected, a raise
    B) workers, whom he had respected, a raise
    C) workers who he had respected a raise
    D) workers whom he had respected a raise
    E) workers, who he had been respected, a raise

11. The call for fiscal responsibility is enough to make one think of changing your political affiliation.
    A) one think of changing your
    B) anyone think of changing one's
    C) one thinks of changing your
    D) anyone think of changing his
    E) one think of changing his

12. The lawyer thought that she would either ask for a continuance or press charges immediately.
    A) that she would either ask for a continuance or press
    B) that she either would ask for a continuance or would press
    C) that she either would ask for a continuance or press
    D) that either she would ask for a continuance or press
    E) that she would either ask for a continuance or she would press

13. Instead of ordering chicken for dinner, the activity director, who prided herself on good judgment and who was known for her culinary predilections, when the time came.
    A) who was known for her culinary predilections, when the time came
    B) who had culinary predilections, substituted beef when the time came
    C) who had culinary predilections, when the time came
    D) who had been known for her culinary predilections, when the time came
    E) who came to be known for her culinary predilections, substituted beef when the time came

14. Although the authorities looked everywheres, they were unable to discover who had stolen the masterpiece.
    A) everywheres, they were unable to discover who
    B) everywhere, they were unable to discover whom
    C) everywhere, they were unable to discover who
    D) everywhere, they were unable to discover about whom
    E) everywheres, they were unable to discover whom

15. The old geezer aggravated his younger counterparts by consistently producing more work than them.
   A) The old geezer aggravated his younger counterparts by consistently producing more work than them.
   B) The old geezer aggravated the younger counterparts by consistently producing more work than they.
   C) The old geezer irritated the younger workers by consistently producing more work than them.
   D) The old man irritated the younger workers by consistently producing more work than them.
   E) The old man irritated the younger workers by consistently producing more work than they.

16. Members of the quartermaster corps moved four hundred tons of munitions and supplies two hundred miles in two days, which pleased the commanding officer to no end.
   A) , which pleased the commanding officer to no end
   B) , an achievement which pleased the commanding officer greatly
   C) an achievement which pleased the commanding officer greatly
   D) , an achievement which pleased the commanding officer to no end
   E) which pleased the commanding officer to no end

17. Since Agnostino found the climate of Florida more pleasant after living in New York, he decided to pull up roots and to settle there.
   A) more pleasant after living in New York, he decided to pull up roots and to
   B) pleasant after living in New York, he decided to pull up roots and to
   C) pleasant after living in New York, he decided to
   D) pleasant after having lived in New York, he decided to
   E) more pleasant after having lived in New York, he decided to pull up roots and to

18. Even though she didn't anticipate to implement it, the advertising manager agreed with the personal manager's proposal to strengthen her department
   A) to implement it, the advertising manager agreed with the personal
   B) implementing it, the advertising manager agreed with the personal
   C) implementing it, the advertising manager agreed with the personnel
   D) to implement it, the advertising manager agreed with the personal
   E) implementing it, the advertising manager agreed to the personnel

19. Since Julio was living in Boston for fifteen years, he really didn't want to leave that city last year.
   A) was living in Boston for fifteen years, he really didn't want
   B) had been living in Boston for fifteen years, he really didn't want
   C) had been living in Boston for fifteen years, he really hadn't want
   D) had been living in Boston for fifteen years, he really hadn't wanted
   E) has lived in Boston for fifteen years, he really didn't want

20. The prime minister should have waited for but should not have agreed to the compromise solution offered by the back benchers in parliament.
    A) should have waited for but should not have agreed to the compromise solution offered
    B) should have waited for but did not agree to the compromise solution offered
    C) should have waited but should not have agreed to the compromise solution offered
    D) should have waited for but not agreed to the compromise solution offered
    E) had waited for but did not agree to the compromise solution offered

21. The Miss America Candidate from Arkansas who was so ingenious delivered a speech that brought tears to the eyes of every mother in the audience.
    A) who was so ingenious delivered a speech that
    B) , who was so ingenious, delivered a speech that
    C) who was so ingenuous delivered a speech that
    D) , who was so ingenuous, delivered a speech that
    E) who was such an ingenious person delivered a speech that

22. That kind of problems create a lot of difficulties for the average mathematician.
    A) That kind of problems create a lot of
    B) That kind of problem creates many
    C) Those kinds of problems creates a lot of
    D) Those kinds of problems creates many
    E) That kind of problems creates many

STOP!

If you finish before time is up (25 minutes), you may return to any of the questions in Section 2. Do not turn to any other section of the test.

SECTION 3 Critical Reasoning

16 Questions
Time: 25 minutes

Directions: Select the best answer for each of the following questions.

1. Someone wishes to deduce the conclusion that there are at least two men in Calcutta who have exactly the same number of hairs on their heads. He begins with the premise that there are more men in Calcutta than there are hairs on the head of any one person in the entire world (whether man or woman).

   The desired conclusion can be validly deduced

   A) from the original premise just as it stands.
   B) if we add a premise to the effect that no man in Calcutta is completely bald, but not from the original premise as it stands.
   C) if we add the premise that there are at least as many men in Calcutta as women, but not from the original premise as it stands.
   D) only if we add the premise that no man in Calcutta is completely bald, but not from the original premise as it stands.
   E) only if we add the premise that there are at least as many men in Calcutta as women, but not from the original premise as it stands.

2. In a routine physical exam, Josh McTavish is discovered to have an early-stage malignant tumor. Although McTavish does not feel sick, a cancer specialist advises immediate surgery, and a consultant agrees. So McTavish accepts the surgery, which turns out to be unexpectedly difficult. A few months later a friend asks McTavish, "Do you feel better now than before your operation?" After a little thought, McTavish replies, "No, I really don't. I'm weaker now, and I have some pain. I didn't have any pain before the operation." "I'm sorry to hear that," the friend says. "I guess the surgery wasn't worth it after all." But McTavish immediately objects by saying, "Oh, I wouldn't say that at all!"

   Which of the following things which McTavish might add, assuming that it was a fact, would provide the strongest support for his reaction?

   A) "I feel better now than I would have felt if I hadn't had the surgery."
   B) "I got opinions from two of the foremost cancer specialists in the country."
   C) "A lot of medical practice is a matter of probabilities, and I went along with the best probability."
   D) "Even with the most modern methods and facilities, medicine is still more of an art than a science, and one can't really predict the outcome with any high degree of reliability."
   E) "I made the decision myself, and I have to take the responsibility for it."

3. There is a piece of folk wisdom expressed in the saying, "If it ain't broke, don't fix it." A factory manager who accepted that saying would, on that account, be least likely to
   A) agree to union demands, in the interest of safety, for better lighting in the stairwells and storage areas.
   B) respond to the difficulty of retaining skilled electronic technicians by establishing an on-site day-care center for small children.
   C) order the immediate replacement of windows broken in a strike.
   D) replace the quality control supervisor, after receiving several complaints about defective units in recent shipments from the factory.
   E) institute a program of preventive maintenance for major pieces of production machinery.

<u>Questions 4 and 5 refer to the following scenario</u>.

In a horse race involving six horses, three of the entries were Bag O'Bones, Cold Molasses, and Three-Leg Charlie. All six horses finished, one after the other.

4. No horse finished ahead of Cold Molasses, and no horse finished behind Bag O'Bones. Also, no horse finished between Cold Molasses and Three-Leg Charlie. Therefore,
   A) Cold Molasses finished second or third.
   B) Bag O'Bones came in fourth or better.
   C) Three-Leg Charlie finished second or third.
   D Three-Leg Charlie may have finished first, but at least he did not finish last.
   E) Bag O'Bones finished ahead of Cold Molasses.

5. Four horses finished between Bag O'Bones and Cold Molasses. Therefore,
   A) Cold Molasses finished last.
   B) Bag O'Bones finished second or third.
   C) Bag O'Bones finished fifth.
   D) Three-Leg Charlie did not finish last.
   E) either Bag O'Bones finished fifth, or Three-Leg Charlie came in third.

6. A valid argument is often defined as one in which it is not possible for all the premises to be true and the conclusion false. A circular argument is sometimes defined as one in which one of the premises is identical to the conclusion.

   From these definitions we can infer that . . .

   A) Every circular argument is valid.
   B) Every valid argument is circular.
   C) No circular argument is valid.
   D) Some circular arguments are valid, and some are not.
   E) Some circular arguments are not valid, and some valid arguments are not circular.

7. Typhoid Mary was a typhoid "carrier." That is, she was infected for a long time with the typhoid bacillus, and other people could catch this infection from her. But she herself did not have typhoid fever, and she showed none of the usual symptoms of that disease.

   The case of Typhoid Mary shows that

   A) typhoid fever is not always fatal.
   B) the usual symptoms of typhoid fever are not always a reliable indicator of typhoid fever.
   C) the absence of the usual symptoms of typhoid fever is not always a reliable indicator that one does not have typhoid fever.
   D) typhoid fever sometimes occurs without the typhoid bacillus.
   E) the typhoid bacillus does not always cause typhoid fever when it infects a person.

8. A study of emergency room treatments in the hospitals of a large city showed that, over a recent period of one year, almost twice as many inebriated persons were treated for injuries received while walking as for injuries received while driving a motor vehicle. Some have concluded that, contrary to a widespread belief, drunk pedestrians run more risk of injury than do drunk drivers.

   Before accepting this conclusion, it would probably by wise to get some idea of

   A) the comparative severity of injuries to drunk pedestrians and drunk drivers.
   B) how the numbers of drunk pedestrians and drunk drivers compare.
   C) how many of the injuries to drunk pedestrians were traffic-related.
   D) how many motor-vehicle passengers are injured in accidents involving a drunk driver.
   E) how many of the injured pedestrians were walking because they considered themselves too drunk to drive.

9. In response to widespread expressions of public concern, the spokesperson for a manufacturer of insecticides asserts that there is no evidence that any of their products causes health problems in human beings when used in the recommended way.

   This testimony, if it is assumed to be true, might be a substantial reason for believing that the insecticides were harmless to humans, in their recommended uses if

   A) there was good reason to believe that if the insecticides were harmful, evidence of their bad effects would have been discovered by now.
   B) the insecticides in question meet all of the recently adopted industry standards for safety.
   C) no increased incidence of disease has been traced to the use of these insecticides.
   D) almost the only users of these insecticides are state and federal agencies which deal with agricultural and forestry problems, and these agencies carefully monitor the application of these insecticides.
   E) the spokesperson is speaking in good faith.

10. Arnie O'Malley, a small businessman, is a member of the Starfish Club. At about $50,000 annually, his income puts him in the upper 10% of the membership of that club. He has recently been invited to join the Penguin Club, in which about 70% of the members have incomes over $100,000 annually. The Penguin Club is expensive, but Arnie could afford it if he dropped the Starfish membership. Nevertheless, he is reluctant to join. His wife, however, urges him to make the move, arguing that it will greatly improve his chances of economic success.

Which of the following, if it is a fact, best supports the wife's advice?

A) The probability that a randomly selected Penguin has an income substantially higher than Arnie's present income is much greater than the probability that a randomly selected Starfish surpasses Arnie in income.
B) If Arnie becomes a Penguin, he is likely to make some valuable business and professional contacts there.
C) Arnie has twice before been considered for possible membership in the Penguin Club, but this is the first time he has actually been invited.
D) The Penguin Club regularly sponsors the sort of social events which both Arnie and his wife enjoy.
E) Arnie is also presently a member of the Giraffe Club, and his annual income is in the upper 5% compared to that of other members there.

11. Mr. Frank Loren owns a house in the small town of Rayleigh Harbor, and he owns no other property in the town. It so happens that no one who lives in Rayleigh Harbor pays any local property taxes anywhere else. Also, Rayleigh Harbor exempts residents from local property taxes on their homes if they are over 70 years of age.

What follows from these assumptions?

A) Mr. Loren pays no local property tax in Rayleigh Harbor (though he may pay such taxes elsewhere).
B) Mr. Loren pays no local property taxes anywhere.
C) If Mr. Loren is over 70 years of age, he pays no local property taxes anywhere.
D) If Mr. Loren is over 70 years of age, he pays no local property taxes in Rayleigh Harbor (but perhaps he does elsewhere).
E) None of the preceding conclusions follow from the stated assumptions.

12. In his first senatorial campaign six years ago, Senator LaGrand campaigned extensively and personally in the two major metropolitan centers in his state. He won the election by a narrow margin, but he did less well in the metropolitan areas than in the out-state areas where he did rather little personal campaigning and relied largely on various forms of advertising. In fact, despite his personal campaigning, he received less of the metropolitan vote than did his opponent.

This year LaGrand is running again. His manager advises him to make very few personal appearances in the metropolitan areas. He argues that experience has shown that LaGrand is not effective in personal appearances, and that he gets his case across to the people much better by way of advertising.

In making this argument, the manager seems to be ignoring the possibility that

A) LaGrand's position is comparatively unattractive to metropolitan voters, but his personal campaigning in the large cities enabled him to do much better there than he would have done otherwise.
B) LaGrand's position on the issues is already highly attractive to metropolitan voters, and so one cannot reasonably expect to improve his appeal there very much by advertising.
C) the cost of advertising in metropolitan areas is substantially greater than in rural areas and small towns.
D) since advertising material can be carefully reviewed and revised before presentation it may be more suitable for some candidates than personal campaigning.
E) while LaGrand did not do well in the metropolitan areas in his last campaign, he did not do any better in the out-state areas.

13. Most Brazilian citizens are fluent speakers of Portuguese. Some Brazilian citizens speak Japanese. Therefore, some Brazilian citizens are bilingual (i.e., can speak two languages).

A) The conclusion given above follows conclusively from the stated premises.
B) The conclusion follows from the premises, but it cannot represent the actual situation in Brazil, since the premises cannot both be true.
C) Since the premises of this argument are true, and the conclusion does not follow from them, we can infer that all Brazilian citizens are monolingual (i.e., speak only one language).
D) Since the conclusion of this argument is true, and it follows from the premises, we can infer that the premises are true also.
E) The conclusion of this argument does not follow from the premises, but we cannot thereby infer anything about the truth of either the premises or the conclusion.

14. A social critic, describing what he thought would be an ideal, utopian, state of affairs, wrote "They have no lawyers among them, for they consider them as a sort of people whose professional preoccupation is to disguise matters."

Which of the following does not accurately describe this statement?

A) If this is an argument, then its premise is "they consider them as a sort of people whose professional preoccupation is to disguise matters."
B) If this is an explanation, the thing to be explained is that a utopia has no place for lawyers.
C) If this is an argument, it is intended to establish the fact that a utopia has no place for lawyers.
D) If this is an explanation, the fact to be explained is that the profession of lawyers is to disguise matters.
E) If this is an explanation, it undertakes to explain a fact in terms of beliefs about the profession of lawyers.

15. A recent newspaper feature story listed several factors as "predictors" of the likelihood of premature death. Two of these factors were a sedentary lifestyle without regular physical exercise, and sleeping more than 12 hours daily.

If a person were to respond to this news by both joining an exercise club and buying an alarm clock, that person would probably be

A) mistaking an explanation for an argument.
B) mistaking an argument for an explanation.
C) mistaking a premise for a conclusion.
D) mistaking a cause for an indicator.
E) mistaking an indicator for a cause.

16. Ellen: "All three of Shirley's children have the measles!"

Lois: "As a matter of fact, all three of Shirley's children are fine!"

Accepting the assumption that nobody who has measles is fine, which of the following is true about this exchange?

A) It is possible that both Ellen and Lois are right about Shirley's children.
B) It is possible that both Ellen and Lois are mistaken about Shirley's children.
C) Either Ellen is right about Shirley's children, or Lois is right about them, but they are not both right.
D) Ellen and Lois might both be right about Shirley's children, and they might both be wrong about them.
E) None of these alternatives correctly identifies the possibilities for this scenario.

STOP!

If you finish before time is up (25 minutes), you may return to any of the questions in Section 3. Do not turn to any other section of the test.

SECTION 4 Problem Solving

20 Questions
Time: 30 minutes

<u>Directions</u>: Solve each problem and mark the best answer on the Answer Marking Sheet provided. You may use the open space on the test paper for scratch work (in the actual exam no scratch paper is permitted). Figures are drawn to scale unless otherwise noted. All numbers are real numbers (no imaginary numbers).

1. A student leaves city A at 8:00 a.m., traveling 60 mph toward city B. A second student leaves city B 1000 miles away two hours later, traveling 50 mph toward city A. What time do they meet?

   A) 2 p.m. B) 3 p.m. C) 4 p.m. D) 5 p.m. E) 6 p.m.

2. A cylinder holds 10 liters of water. All of the water is poured into a horizontal cube, 50 cm on a side. What is the depth of the water?

   A) 4 cm B) 10 cm C) 40 cm D) 60 cm E) 100 cm

3. If $x - y = 4$ and $x - 2y = 6$, what is $x + y$?

   A) 2 B) 6 C) 8 D) 12 E) none of these

4. Evaluate $1+\frac{3}{5}\div(1-x)$ if $x=\frac{2}{15}$.

   A) $1\frac{13}{15}$ B) 23/13 C) $1\frac{9}{13}$ D) 1.7 E) none of these

5. The area of a parallelogram is 50 and its 4 sides are of equal length 10. One of the angles in the parallelogram is one of the following.

   A) 30° B) 45° C) 60° D) 90° E) 120°

6. Find the two roots to the equation $x^2 - 5x = 14$.

   A) (7, 6) B) (−7, −2) C) (−7, 2) D) (7, −2) E) none of these

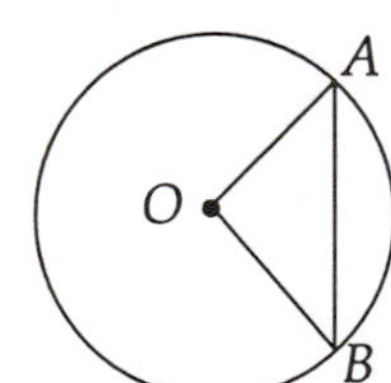

circle of radius 10

7. If arc AB = 120°, find the length $\overline{AB}$ in the circle above.

   A) $10\sqrt{3}$ B) 10 C) $5\sqrt{3}$ D) 15 E) none of these

8. Calculate the acute angle made by the hands of a clock at 3:10 p.m.

   A) 28° B) 32° C) 35° D) 38° E) 46°

9. One worker can do a job in n hours while it takes a second worker m hours to do the same job. How long does it take both workers?

A) $m + n$ B) $\frac{1}{m} + \frac{1}{n}$ C) $(m + n) / mn$

D) $mn / (m + n)$ E) none of these

10. A large cube 10 cm on a side is composed of cubes 1 cm on a side. The large cube is printed red and then all the cubes are mixed in a drum. If one cube is selected, what are the odds that it will have at least one red side?

A) 1 : 6 B) 1 : 5 C) 1 : 4 D) 1 : 3 E) 1 : 2

11. If $x + \frac{1}{2} = y$ and $\frac{x}{y} = 0.1$, find x.

A) 10 B) 4 C) 2 D) 1/9 E) 1/18

<u>Questions 12 and 13 refer to this diagram</u>.

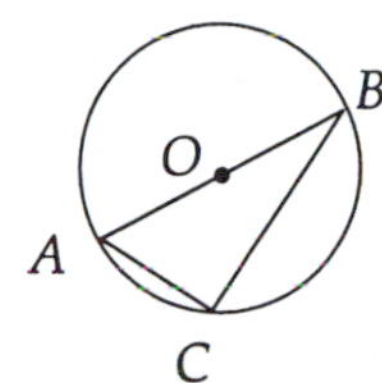

circle with radius = 13

12. If $AC = 10$ in the above triangle calculate the area of triangle ABC.

A) 60 B) 80 C) 90 D) 100 E) 120

13. If arc $BC = 135°$ in the above diagram, estimate the angle BAC.

A) 59.6° B) 61.2° C) 63.4° D) 67.5° E) 69.6°

14. If 280 people, representing 5% of the population in a city, ride bikes, how many people do not ride bikes?

A) 5930 B) 5600 C) 5320 D) 5110 E) 4980

15. If $x - y + z = 4$ and $y - x + 2z = 8$, find z.

A) 0 B) 2 C) 4 D) 6 E) 8

16. Select an equivalent expression to $x^{1/3}\sqrt{x}\left(x^{1/6}\right) \div \sqrt[4]{x^5}$.

A) $x^{1/4}$ B) $x^{1/3}$ C) $x^{1/2}$ D) $x^{-1/2}$ E) $x^{-1/4}$

17. Simplify the product $\frac{x^2 + 3x - 4}{x^2 - 4} \; \frac{x + 2}{x - 1}$.

A) $(x+4)/(x-2)$

B) $(x-4)/(x+2)$

C) $(x-1)/(x-2)$

D) $(x+1)/(x+2)$

E) $(x+4)/(x+2)$

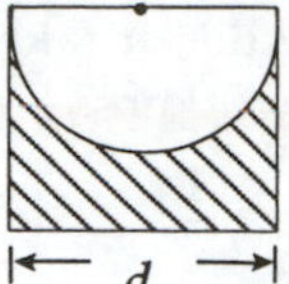

a square and a half circle

18. Approximate the shaded area in the above figure if $d = 10$.
A) 65 B) 63 C) 61 D) 59 E) 57

19. In 10 years Kyle will be as old as Cindy is now. Thirty years ago Cindy was twice Kyle's age. How old is Kyle?
A) 20 B) 30 C) 40 D) 50 E) 60

20. Select the largest number.
A) $4/0.002$
B) 0.01^{-2}
C) $\frac{1}{.0002} + \frac{1}{.0004}$
D) $20^2 + 10^3$
E) $1492.5 + 6713.2 + 1532.9$

STOP!

If you finish before time is up (30 minutes), you may return to any of the questions in Section 4. Do not turn to any other section of the test.

SECTION 5 Analysis of an Issue

Directions: In this section you are asked to analyze and explain your views on the issue presented below. The question has no 'correct' answer. Instead, you should consider various perspectives as you develop your own position on the issue.

Read the statement and directions, and then make any notes in your test booklet that will help you plan a response. Begin writing your response on the separate answer document. Make sure that you use the answer document that goes with this writing task. (For your own informal test essay—to be graded by us or your own service—use three unlined 8.5"x11" pages, writing on front and back sides.)

> There are 100,000 serious injuries every year in American football, ranging from severed spinal chords to broken limbs. This fact strongly supports the argument that the game should be banned or radically modified. Any 'sport' that causes so many injuries is no longer a matter of character-building athletics but it is instead the creator of a serious national health problem.

STOP!

If you finish before time is up (30 minutes), do not turn to any other section of the test.

SECTION 6 Data Sufficiency

20 Questions
Time: 25 minutes

Directions: Each data sufficiency problem includes a question followed by two statements, labeled (1) and (2), that contain certain information. Using your knowledge of mathematics and common facts, you must determine if the information in the statements is sufficient to solve the problem. Select:

A if (1) alone is sufficient, but (2) alone is not sufficient;

B if (2) alone is sufficient, but (1) alone is not sufficient;

C if (1) and (2) together are sufficient, but neither alone is sufficient;

D if each statement alone is sufficient;

E if you cannot solve the problem with the information given.

Numbers: Only real numbers are used; no imaginary numbers are used or implied.

Diagrams: Diagrams reflect the information contained in the question, not necessarily the information contained in the two statements.

1. Can x/y be expressed as in mixed numbers?
   (1) x is a factor of y.
   (2) y is a factor of x.

2. What is the perimeter of this triangle?
   (1) $x = 30°$
   (2) y is a factor of x.

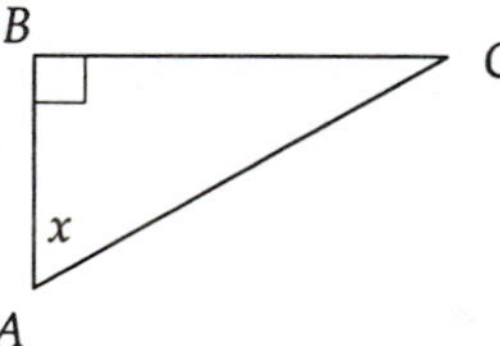

3. What is $x + 2y$?
   (1) $x - 2y = 0$
   (2) $x + y = 6$

4. What is the area inside the parallelogram and outside the circle? $\overline{AB} = \overline{AD} = 10$
   (1) $x = 60°$
   (2) $d = 8$

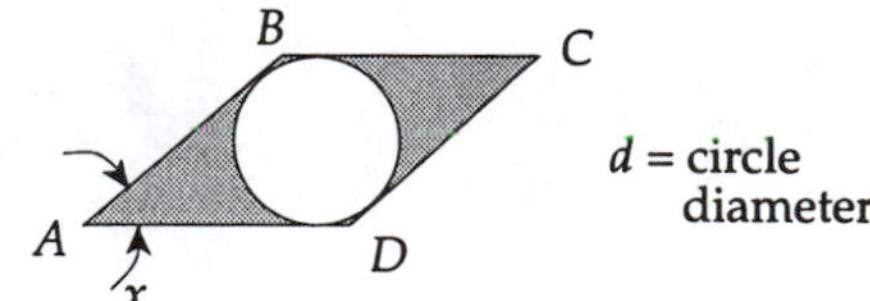

5. A geometric progression is formed by 16, x, y. What is the sum of the three terms?
   (1) $x = 10$
   (2) $y = 2x$

6. A rectangle is 10 units long. What is its area?
   (1) Its diagonal is 20 units long.
   (2) Its diagonals bisect each other.

7. Does a box that measures $20\text{ cm} \times 40\text{ cm} \times 50\text{ cm}$ stand erect?
   (1) One of its diagonals measures 70 cm.
   (2) It holds 35 liters of liquid when filled to the top.

8. What is x?
   (1) $x^2 - 3x - 4 = 0$
   (2) $x > 1$

9. Is $x^2 + 5x - 14 > 0$?
   (1) $x > -7$
   (2) $x < 2$

10. Is $a < b$?
    (1) $x = -1, y = -1$
    (2) $x^2 + y^2 = 25$

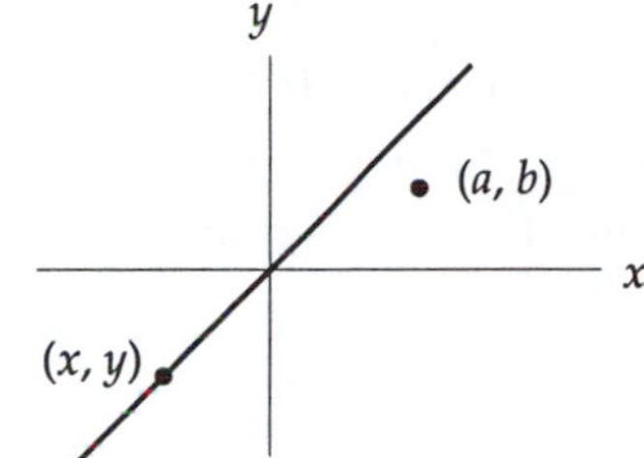

11. Two intersecting lines form four angles. Are the lines perpendicular?
    (1) Two of the angles are equal.
    (2) The sum of three angles is 270°.

12. Is $m \parallel n$?
    (1) $x = 100°$
    (2) $x = 2y$

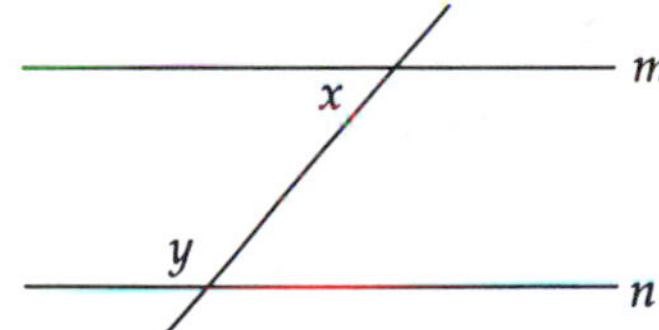

13. What is the ratio of two numbers?
    (1) Their sum is 6.
    (2) One is twice the other.

14. How many quarts of paint are needed to paint the four 8-ft high side walls of a house?
    (1) The house is twice as long as it is wide.
    (2) The perimeter of the house is 140 ft.

15. How far is it from A to C?

(1) Angle B plus Angle C is 150°.

(2) Angle C is 40°.

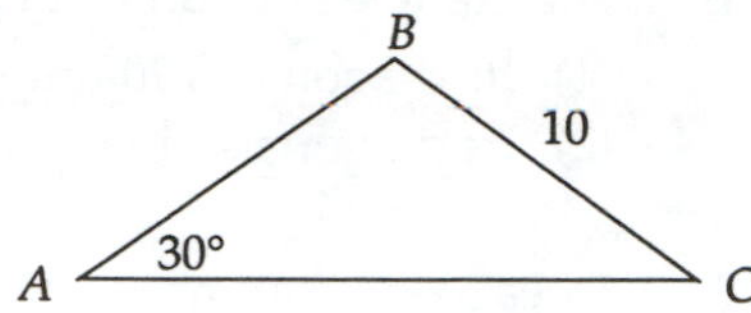

16. Is $xy > 0$?

(1) $x > 0$

(2) $y^2 > 0$

17. What is the cross-hatched area?

(1) The area of the rectangle $ABEC$ is 10 square units.

(2) $\overline{AC} = \frac{1}{2}\overline{AB}$

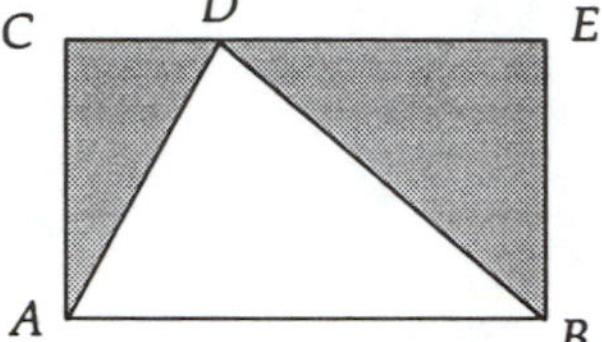

18. What is the value of a fraction if its numerator is its denominator minus 6?

(1) The fraction is positive.

(2) Its denominator is its numerator squared.

19. Is $(a-b)^2$ greater than $a^2 + b^2$?

(1) $a < b$

(2) $b > 0$

20. Carpeting is 12 ft wide. What is the minimum length that should be purchased to cover the floor shown? It cannot be rotated.

(1) $\overline{AF} = \overline{CD} = \overline{AB} = 16$ ft

(2) $\overline{BC} = 9$ ft.

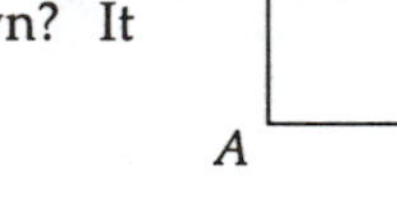

STOP!

If you finish before time is up (25 minutes), you may return to any of the questions in Section 6.
Do not turn to any other section of the test.

SECTION 7 Problem Solving

16 Questions
Time: 25 minutes

<u>Directions</u>: Solve each problem and select the best answer on the Answer Marking Sheet provided. You may use the open space on the test paper for scratch work (in the actual exam no scratch paper is permitted). Figures are drawn to scale unless otherwise noted. All numbers are real numbers (no imaginary numbers).

1. If k is odd, then

   I. k^2 is odd II. $k+2k$ is even III. $2k$ is even

   A) I only B) II only C) II & III D) I & II E) I & III

2. Simplify $\frac{17/16}{\frac{5}{6}-\frac{1}{8}}$.

   A) $\frac{1}{3}$ B) $\frac{3}{2}$ C) $\frac{17}{3}$ D) $\frac{3}{34}$ E) 3

3. The average of three numbers is 60 and the median is 70. What are the three numbers if one of them is 20?

   A) 20, 70, 90 B) 20, 60, 100 C) 20, 80, 80 D) 20, 50, 110 E) 20, 70, 80

4. Jon drives 60 mph for 30 miles, 40 mph for 20 miles, and 70 mph for 35 miles. What is his average speed?

   A) $48\frac{1}{3}$ mph B) 55 mph C) $56\frac{2}{3}$ mph D) $58\frac{1}{3}$ mph E) 60 mph

5. $\left(8x^3y^4\right)^{1/2} \div \left(2xy^2\right)^{3/2} =$

   A) $\sqrt{\frac{4x}{y^2}}$ B) $\sqrt{\frac{4x^2}{y}}$ C) $\sqrt{\frac{4x}{y}}$ D) $\frac{1}{y}$ E) $\sqrt{\frac{2x}{y^2}}$

6. Evaluate $183^2 - 181^2$.

   A) 728 B) 364 C) 6 D) 4 E) 2

7. Simplify $\left(2x^2+3x-2\right)\div\left(x^2-4\right)$.

   A) $\frac{2x-1}{x-2}$ B) $\frac{x+2}{x-2}$ C) $\frac{2x+1}{x-2}$ D) $\frac{2x-1}{x+2}$ E) $\frac{x-1}{x+2}$

8. If $x + y - z = 2$ and $x - y - z = 4$, what is y?

A) –2 B) –1 C) 1 D) 2 E) Can't say

9. Estimate the percentage that utilities contributed to the total budget shown.

A) 15%
B) 17%
C) 19%
D) 21%
E) 23%

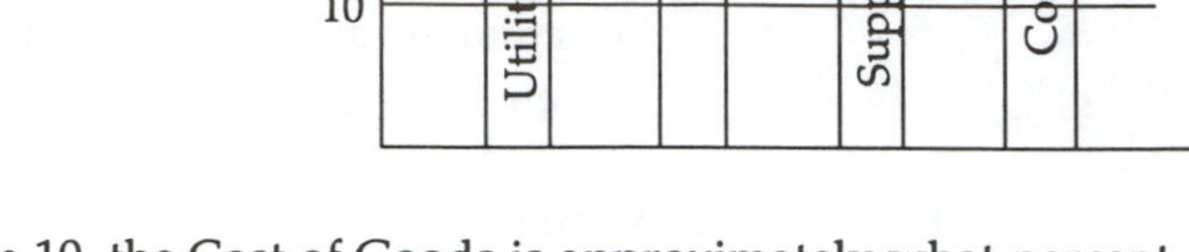

10. Referring to the graph of Problem 10, the Cost of Goods is approximately what percentage of Labor?

A) 17% B) 53% C) 83% D) 117% E) 217%

11. One leg of an isosceles right triangle measures 10 units. How long is the hypotenuse?

A) $5\sqrt{2}$ B) $10\sqrt{2}$ C) $10/\sqrt{2}$ D) $5/\sqrt{2}$ E) 20

12. Select the triangle that connects the points (–4, 3), (1, 3), (4, –1).

A) right B) isosceles C) 5-12-13 D) equilateral E) 3-4-5

13. If $x^2 - 3x > 4$ then

A) $x < 4$ B) $x > -1$ C) $x > -4$ D) $-1 < x < 4$ E) $x < -1$

14. It takes Ron n hours to plow a field. How much of the field remains to be plowed after m hours?

A) $\frac{n}{m}$ B) $\frac{m}{n}$ C) $\frac{n-m}{n}$ D) $\frac{n-m}{m}$ E) $\frac{mn}{n-m}$

15. A telephone worker wishes to attach a rope from a point 20 feet above the level ground to a point 15 feet away from the base of the vertical telephone pole. What is the absolute minimum length of rope required?

A) 35 ft B) 30 ft C) 25 ft D) 20 ft E) 15 ft

16. A house in the form of a spherical dome stands 16 feet high. The geometric center of the dome is 10 feet below ground level. What is the diameter of the circle formed by the dome and the horizontal ground?

A) 48 ft B) 42 ft C) 36 ft D) 30 ft E) 24 ft

A) 5 B) $3 + \sqrt{6}$ C) $3 + 2\sqrt{6}$ D) 6 E) 7

STOP!

If you finish before time is up (25 minutes), you may return to any of the questions in Section 7. Do not turn to any other section of the test.

SECTION 8 Sentence Correction

22 Questions
Time: 25 minutes

Directions: Some part of the following sentences, or the entire sentence, is underlined. The first of the five versions beneath each sentence is identical to the underlined portion. If you think the text is most correct as written in the problem, select (A); otherwise, choose the best sentence correction from the four remaining choices. Follow the requirements of written English when making your selection. Pay attention to grammar, word choice, and general sentence construction. Select the version that expresses most effectively and accurately what is contained in the original sentence.

1. Due to the fact that little rain had fallen during the winter months, the planting was delayed and the farmers waited for a harvest which they expected to be small.
   A) Due to the fact that little rain had fallen during the winter months, the planting was delayed and the farmers
   B) Since little rain had fallen during the winter months, the planting was delayed and the farmers
   C) Due to the fact that little rain had fallen during the winter months, the farmers delayed the planting, and
   D) Since little rain had fallen during the winter months, the farmers delayed the planting and they
   E) Since little rain had fallen during the winter months, the farmers delayed the planting and

2. After all was said and done, the senator being at death's door, his family gathered around to bid him farewell.
   A) After all was said and done, the senator being at death's door, his family gathered around to bid him farewell.
   B) Since the senator was dying in spite of the efforts of the doctor's, his family gathered around to bid him farewell.
   C) Since the senator was dying in spite of the efforts of the doctor's, his family came to bid him farewell.
   D) Since the senator was dying in spite of the efforts of the doctors, his family came to say good-bye to him.
   E) Since the senator was dying in spite of the efforts of the doctor's, his family came to say good-bye to him.

3. The poet had not had much experience or any use for the machinations of his fellow man as they struggled to make a living.
   A) The poet had not had much experience or any use for the machinations of his fellow man
   B) The poet had not had much experience with or any use for the machinations of his fellow man
   C) The poet had not had much experience with nor any use for the machinations of people
   D) The poet had not had much experience with or any use for the machinations of people
   E) The poet had not had much experience or any use for the machinations of people

4. The first of the many agreements that were agreed on by the five trading partners proved to be the most satisfactory.
   A) that were agreed on by the five trading partners proved
   B) that was agreed on by the five trading partners proved
   C) that were signed by the five trading partners proved
   D) that the five trading partners agreed on proved
   E) that the five trading partners signed proved

5. The scientist knew for a long time beyond the shadow of a doubt that she discovered the double helix.
   A) The scientist knew for a long time beyond the shadow of a doubt
   B) For a long time, the scientist had known beyond the shadow of a doubt
   C) For a long time, the scientist had known with great certainty
   D) For a long time, the scientist knew beyond the shadow of a doubt
   E) The scientist had known for a long time beyond the shadow of a doubt

6. Everyone who knew about the injustices done to individuals in Hitler's Germany wished that they could right the wrongs.
   A) Everyone who knew about the injustices done to individuals in Hitler's Germany wished that they
   B) Everyone who knows about the injustices done to individuals in Hitler's Germany wishes that they
   C) The people who knew about the injustices done to individuals in Hitler's Germany wished that they
   D) The people who had been knowing about the injustices done to individuals in Hitler's Germany wished that they
   E) The people who were knowing about the injustices done to individuals in Hitler's Germany wished that they

7. Never in the history of the world has the difference between equality and inequality been as distinct as it is now.
   A) Never in the history of the world has the difference between equality and inequality been as distinct as
   B) The difference between equality and inequality has never been as distinct as
   C) Never in the history of the world has the difference between equality and inequality been so distinct as
   D) The difference between equality and inequality has never been so distinct as
   E) The difference between equality and inequality never had been so distinct as

8. His approach to singing is different than the approach used by any other tenor.
   A) different than the approach used by any other tenor
   B) different from the approach used by any other tenor
   C) different from the approach which is used by any other tenor
   D) different then the approach of any other tenor
   E) different from the approach of any other tenor

9. The mechanic has frequently tried and will ultimately succeed to repair the expensive automobile.
   A) has frequently tried and will ultimately succeed to repair
   B) has frequently tried and will ultimately succeed in repairing
   C) has frequently tried to and will ultimately succeed to repair
   D) has frequently tried to and will ultimately succeed in repairing
   E) has frequently tried to repair and will ultimately succeed to repairing

10. The increasing costs for both materials and labor—the two largest components of the manufacturing process—are going to drive profit margins down.
    A) are going to drive profit margins down
    B) is going to drive profit margins down
    C) are the causes underlying the downward trend of profit margins
    D) are the causes that will drive profit margins down
    E) is the symptom of lowering profit margins down

11. Needless to say the coach expects an one-hundred-and-twenty percent effort from each of the players in today's game which determined the championship.
    A) Needless to say the coach expects an one-hundred-and-twenty percent effort from each of the players in today's game which determined the championship.
    B) The coach expects an one-hundred-and-twenty percent effort from each of the players in today's game which determined the championship.
    C) The coach expects a total effort from each of the players in today's championship game.
    D) The coach expects a one-hundred-and-twenty percent effort from each of the players in today's game which determined the championship.
    E) Needless to say the coach expects a total effort from each of the players in today's championship game.

12. Bill and Arley were captains of the two football teams, the Raiders and the Pirates, respectively.
    A) were captains of the two football teams, the Raiders and the Pirates, respectively
    B) was captain of the two football teams, the Raiders and the Pirates, respectively
    C) were captains of the two football teams, the Raiders and the Pirates, respectfully
    D) was captain of the two football teams, the Raiders and the Pirates, respectfully
    E) was captain of the two football teams, the Raiders and the Pirates, in that order

13. Jerry found the novel replete with interest as the story described the actions of Superhero, a marvelous specimen of humanity.
    A) replete with interest as the story described the actions of Superhero, a marvelous specimen of humanity
    B) interesting as the story described the actions of Superhero, a marvelous specimen of humanity
    C) very interesting as the story described the actions of Superhero, a marvelous human being
    D) very interesting as the story described the actions of Superhero, a marvelous specimen of humanity
    E) replete with interest as the story described the actions of Superhero, a marvelous human being

14. When General MacArthur said, "I shall return", he was making an ungrammatical statement. He should have said, "I will return."
    A) "I shall return", he was making an ungrammatical statement. He should have said, "I will return."
    B) "I shall return", he made a grammatical statement. He should have said, "I shall return."
    C) "I shall return", he had made an ungrammatical statement. He should have said, "I will return."
    D) "I shall return", he was making a grammatical statement. He should have said, "I shall return."
    E) "I shall return", he was making a grammatical statement. But he should have said, "I will return."

15. If the president were not so fat, he would not need to travel first class all the time.
    A) were not so fat, he would not
    B) wasn't so fat, he wouldn't
    C) were not so fat, he would
    D) was not so fat, he would not
    E) weren't so fat, he wouldn't

16. Traveling by ship from New York to London, three weeks were consumed by the time alone.
    A) three weeks were consumed by the time alone
    B) it had taken him three weeks to complete the trip
    C) the time alone consumed three weeks
    D) he took three weeks to complete the trip
    E) it took him three weeks to complete the trip

17. George Washington's notoriety was developed out of the notion that he had become the father of his country.
    A) George Washington's notoriety was developed out of the notion that he had become
    B) George Washington's fame was developed out of the notion that he had become
    C) George Washington's notoriety developed out of the notion that he became
    D) George Washington's fame developed out of the notion that he became
    E) George Washington's fame developed out of the notion that he had become

18. The workers taught theirselves to manage the assembly line, create new products and running the heavy machinery.
    A) theirselves to manage the assembly line, create new products and running
    B) themselves to manage the assembly line, create new products and running
    C) themselves to manage the assembly line, create new products and run
    D) theirselves to manage the assembly line, create new
    E) themselves to have managed the assembly line, create new products and running

19. Josiah saw where the cost of doing business was escalating at an exceedingly alarming rate.
    A) where the cost of doing business was escalating at an exceedingly alarming rate
    B) that the cost of doing business was increasing at a very rapid rate
    C) where the cost of doing business was escalating at a very alarming rate
    D) where the cost of doing business was increasing at a very rapid rate
    E) that the cost of doing business was escalating at an exceedingly alarming rate

20. None of the recently wealthy entrepreneurs remember when he hadn't but a few pennies in his pocket.
    A) None of the recently wealthy entrepreneurs remember when he hadn't but
    B) None of the recently wealthy entrepreneurs remembered when he hadn't but
    C) None of the recently wealthy entrepreneurs remembers when he hadn't but
    D) None of the recently wealthy entrepreneurs remember when he had but
    E) None of the recently wealthy entrepreneurs remembers when he had but

21. Anyone who doesn't like the food in the company dining room brings his own lunch.
    A) Anyone who doesn't like the food in the company dining room brings his own lunch.
    B) Anyone who don't like the food in the company dining room brings his own lunch.
    C) Anyone, who doesn't like the food in the company dining room, brings his own lunch.
    D) Anyone who doesn't like the food in the company dining room brings their own lunch.
    E) Anyone, who doesn't like the food in the company dining room, brings their own lunch.

22. Neither the president nor the vice-president <u>wonder if either the secretary or the treasurer voted their conscience</u> in the matter of raises for themselves.

A) wonder if either the secretary or the treasurer voted their conscience
B) wonders if either the secretary or the treasurer voted their conscience
C) wonders if either the secretary or the treasurer voted his conscience
D) wonder if either the secretary or the treasurer voted his conscience
E) wonder if either the secretary or the treasurer had voted their conscience

STOP!

If you finish before time is up (25 minutes), you may return to any of the questions in Section 8. Do not turn to any other section of the test.

SECTION 9 Analysis of an Argument

Directions: In this section you will write a critique of the argument presented below. You may, for example, consider what questionable assumptions underlie the thinking, what alternative explanations or counter examples might weaken the conclusion, or what sort of evidence could help strengthen or refute the argument. Read the argument and directions, and then make any notes in your test booklet that will help you plan a response. Begin writing your response on the separate answer document. Make sure that you use the answer document that goes with this writing task. (For your own informal test essay—to be graded by us or your own service—use three unlined 8.5"x11" pages, writing on front and back sides.)

During the last fifteen years, the economy of the USA has shifted from a production-based economy to a service-based economy. Symptomatic of this is the fact that McDonalds is now a larger corporation than General Motors. Since service jobs pay less than productions jobs, the average wage earners make less than they did 15 years ago. As a result, the nuclear family with a single wage earner is now a thing of the past.

STOP!

If you finish before time is up (30 minutes), do not turn to any other section of the test.
This is the last section of Test 2.

Answer Key to Test No. 2

Section 1 *Reading*	Section 2 *Sentences*	Section 3 *Reasoning*	Section 4 *Problems*	Section 6 *Data*	Section 7 *Problems*	Section 8 *Sentences*
1. E	1. A	1. B	1. E	1. D	1. E	1. E
2. C	2. C	2. A	2. A	2. E	2. B	2. D
3. C	3. B	3. E	3. E	3. C	3. A	3. C
4. B	4. C	4. C	4. C	4. D	4. C	4. E
5. B	5. D	5. D	5. A	5. D	5. D	5. C
6. A	6. E	6. A	6. D	6. A	6. A	6. C
7. B	7. C	7. E	7. A	7. D	7. A	7. A
8. E	8. D	8. B	8. C	8. C	8. B	8. E
9. C	9. E	9. A	9. D	9. C	9. B	9. D
10. C	10. B	10. B	10. E	10. A	10. D	10. A
11. D	11. D	11. E	11. E	11. B	11. B	11. C
12. A	12. A	12. A	12. E	12. C	12. B	12. A
13. E	13. B	13. E	13. D	13. E	13. E	13. C
14. B	14. C	14. D	14. C	14. E	14. C	14. B
15. A	15. E	15. E	15. C	15. B	15. C	15. A
16. D	16. B	16. B	16. E	16. E	16. A	16. D
17. D	17. D		17. A	17. A		17. E
18. C	18. E		18. C	18. C		18. C
	19. B		19. C	19. E		19. B
	20. A		20. B	20. C		20. E
	21. D					21. A
	22. B					22. C

Note: Sections 5 & 9 are "Writing Analysis," to be completed on 6 separate sheets.

Self-Grading & Score Conversion

Upon completing this Practice Test, it is extremely beneficial for you to grade yourself. This will enable you to identify your weak areas so that you can organize a review that will give you the greatest improvement.

Using the Answer Sheet, determine your Raw Score using the following formula for each of the seven sections of the test and fill in the following table:

$$\text{Raw Score} = \#\ \text{Correct} - \tfrac{1}{4}\ (\#\ \text{Incorrect})$$

Your Rating (Poor to Excellent) in each section is determined using the second table.

Self-Grading Table

Section	Correct	Incorrect	Blank	Raw Score	Rating
1					
2					
3					
4					
6					
7					
8					

Rating Determination (use Raw Scores)

Section	Poor	Fair	Good	Excellent
1	0-6	7-10	11-15	16-18
2	0-8	9-13	14-18	19-22
3	0-6	7-9	10-13	14-16
4	0-8	9-12	13-17	18-20
6	0-8	9-12	13-17	18-20
7	0-6	7-9	10-13	14-16
8	0-8	9-13	14-18	19-22

Your Verbal and Quantitative scores and your total score can be converted to approximate percentile rankings using the following formulas:

Verbal Raw Score = Sum of Raw Scores from Sections 1, 2, and 3
Quantitative Raw Score = Sum of Raw Scores from Sections 4, 6, and 7
Total Score = Sum of Verbal and Quantitative Raw Scores

Top Quarter Percentile	Middle Half Percentile	Bottom Quarter Percentile
Verbal > 37	$31 >$ Verbal > 17	Verbal < 17
Quantitative > 37	$37 >$ Quantitative > 17	Quantitative < 17
Total > 72	$72 >$ Total > 37	Total < 37

Explanations to the Answers

SECTION 1 Reading Comprehension

1. E The correct answer is (E), development of publication policy. (A), (B), (C), and (D) are incorrect, for they name specific features, causes, or effects of DuPont's developing publication policy. Only (E) accurately and comprehensively names the subject of this passage.

2. C (A), (B), (D), and (E) are accurate statements, but none comprehensively states the central idea.

3. C (A), (B), (D), and (E) are incorrect. Although each stands alone as an accurate statement, none is associated with the reversal of the liberal publication policy on research by the Chemical Department.

4. B (A) may be implicitly true according to the information given in the passage, but it fails to address specific reasons for the prohibition. (C) is incorrect, since its truth applies to all departments in DuPont, not solely to the industrial departments. (D) and (E) are incorrect, for nothing in the passage warrants these generalizations.

5. B The passage explicitly declares that industrial department autonomy precluded the creation of a report indexing system. (A), (C), (D), and (E) may accurately name specific impediments, but only industrial department autonomy is identified as having precluded the creation of this system.

6. A (B) is incorrect, since the passage indicates the contrary. (C) is incorrect because the passage does not associate the publication policy of the Chemical Department with company-wide policy on publication. (D) is incorrect, since the passage declares the contrary. (E) is incorrect in its first part because research was thrown away because of the way reports were being handled, not because reporting among departments differed dramatically.

7. B (A) is incorrect, for only the first and the second legislative powers, not all four, are indicated as affecting the private market. (C) is incorrect, for it too broadly generalizes the effect of legislative power over market transactions. (D) is incorrect, for it is not warranted by information given in the passage. (E) is incorrect, since it names only one aspect of one legislative power described in the passage. (B) is the accurate, most comprehensive answer.

8. E (A), (B), (C), and (D) accurately name parts of legislative power, but only (E), the investigatory power, is the broadest, most significant legislative power.

9. C (A), (B), (D), and (E) are incorrect, since each is a part of the legislative taxing power.

10. C The correct answer is (C), evidence of frequency of citation in statute books. (A), (B), (D), and (E) are incorrect, since none is associated with frequency of citation in research.

11. D (A) is incorrect, since administrative agencies are chartered and regulated by the legislative power. (B) and (C) are incorrect, for the passage makes the point that legislation has preempted judge-made (common) law. (E) is incorrect because the private market is an entity regulated by the legislative power, not a body that holds broader authority than the legislative power. Only the constitution-makers hold broader authority in this matter than the legislative power.

12. A (B), (C), (D), and (E) are incorrect, since each is associated with the investigative power. (A) is associated with the legislative power to create new forms of organization for collective action.

13. E (A) is incorrect, for nowhere does the passage attribute investigatory power to the judiciary. (B) is incorrect. Based upon information given in this passage, it too broadly overstates the effect of legislative power. (C) is incorrect, for nowhere does the passage state such a disproportionate influence. (D) is incorrect, since the point of the passage is that legislative power inheres in four major areas. Only (E) is a defensible inference from the information given in the passage.

14. B The subject of each paragraph is the conflict of two objectives. (A), (C), (D), and (E) are incorrect because they name **effects** of the conflict between the two objectives.

15. A (B), (C), (D), and (E) are accurate answers but incomplete. (A) in two parts names the two causes of reduction in fundamental research.

16. D (A), (B), (C), and (E) are incorrect, since each was a project undertaken by DuPont for war agencies. Although the passage mentions manufacture of war gases, it does not explicitly mention weapons.

17. D (A), (B), (C), and (E) may be accurately associated with DuPont's ability to carry out its wartime work, but the passage assigns major responsibility for this ability to "research carried out in time of peace in the various Company laboratories."

18. C (A) is incorrect, for according to information given in the passage, it is inaccurate. (B) is incorrect, since nothing in the passage indicates that this is the case. (D) is incorrect, since the passage explicitly states that executives sought to accomplish both wartime work and commercial development during the prewar and wartime period. (E) is incorrect because most of the products for wartime applications derived from improvement or adaptation of existing products.

SECTION 2 Sentence Correction

1. A The correct word is *elude*, "to escape from"; *allude* is related to *allusion* as in a *poetic allusion*. There is nothing wrong with the participial phrase starting with *having*, since the fighter pilot completed the evasive tactics and eluded the attacker as well.

2. C Infinitives should not be split as in (A), (B) and (E). Preachers would not tell parishioners to love money as in (D); hence, (C) is the correct answer.

3. B *Talk me out of* is colloquial eliminating (A) and (E). (C) has a double negative, *n't* and *nobody*; (D) has *I was you* which is colloquial but not correct as a subjunctive. That leaves (B) as the correct answer.

4. C *Scarcely* and *not* create a double negative, thus eliminating (B) and (D). *Most unique* is an impossibility because *unique* is one of a kind, (A). *Only just* does not express anything that *just* expresses by itself; therefore, *only* is unnecessary, (E).

5. D *More* with *fast* is simply incorrect, (A) and (E). *Hadn't* or *shouldn't ought to* are simply colloquial and hence wrong on the GMAT, (B) and (C).

6. E A verb form in *-ing* is paired with a marked infinitive with *to, to finish*, destroying the parallelism of the sentence, (A), (B) and (D). (C) has unnecessary words in it.

7. C The indefinite *they* lacks a reference; hence (A), (D) and (E) are incorrect. *Accept* is the correct word—how could excepted work be brilliant?

8. D *Kudos* and *age-worn* are clichés. *Impeccable* is unlikely since it means "without sin." Thus (D) is the correct form.

9. E *Everybody* is singular; therefore, only (B) and (E) with *knows*, which is singular, could be correct. Since *everybody* is singular, it can be referred to only with *his*; thus (E) is correct.

10. B The relative pronoun *who* is the object of the verb *respect*; therefore, only (B) and (D) could be correct. Since he gave the raise to all of the workers, the clause does not identify a particular group of workers and thus must only add additional information; therefore, (B) is correct.

11. D The use of *one* and *you* as indefinite pronouns is to be avoided. This leaves only (D) as the correct answer.

12. A There is nothing wrong with the position of *either* since it is in the same position relative to the verb as *or*. (Both come immediately before the verb.) The repetitive *would*, (B), or *she would*, (E), are simply unnecessary.

13. B The basic problem with the sentence is that it is incomplete. It has a subject without a verb. Only (B) and (E) remedy that. (E) has a passive (*be known*).

14. C *Everywheres* is a colloquial term that is not acceptable in writing or on the GMAT. *Who* is the subject and thus cannot have the object marker, *-m*. As a result, the correct answer is (C).

15. E *Geezer* and *counterparts* are jargon and should be avoided. A wound or sore is *aggravated*. A person is *irritated*. *They* is subject of the understood *produce*, not the object. Hence (E) is correct.

16. B *To no end* meaning "greatly," is colloquial and should be avoided. *Which* has no antecedent and thus starts a detached relative clause. The sentence is corrected by giving *which* an antecedent, *achievement*.

17. D *To pull . . . roots* is a colloquialism and should be avoided; besides, it adds little or nothing to sentences (A), (B) and (E). *More* is not necessary in this sentence because there is no comparison with *than*, (A) and (E). The perfect tense is necessary to express a time anterior to that of the main clause.

18. E *Personal* deals with a person's own special things; *Personnel* deals with a lot of people. Verbs like *anticipate* must be followed by a gerund, the verb form in *-ing*. A person *agrees with* another person, not with an inanimate thing such as a proposal. Therefore, (E) is correct.

19. B Since the past perfect tense with *had* is used to express a time before a certain time in the past, it is necessary in this sentence. Since a period of time is also involved, the durative tense with *-ing* is necessary. Thus (B) is correct.

20. A *Should have* cannot be deleted from the clause after *but* because it is not the same as the part before *but*; that is, it contains *not* and *should not have*, (D). Only identical parts can be deleted. Thus, the *for* before *but* cannot be deleted. It is different from the preposition *to* which follows *but*. Therefore, the original is OK.

21. D Since *The Miss America Candidate* is capitalized, it is a proper noun and must be followed with a non-restrictive clause with commas, (B) and (D). *Ingenious* is usually used of things, or devices, which are cleverly constructed. *Ingenuous* is used of humans. Therefore, (D) is the correct form.

22. B Since *those* is plural, *kind* must also be plural to agree with the verb *create*, which is also marked for a plural subject. *A lot of* is colloquial; *many* is better with this kind of noun in a formal context. Therefore, (B) is correct.

SECTION 3 Critical Reasoning

1. B Since nothing is said about how many men there are in Calcutta or how many hairs there are on a head, we can try the problem with some small easy numbers. Suppose that 10 is the maximum number of hairs on a head, and there are 11 men in Calcutta. That will satisfy the terms of the problem. Now, suppose the first man has one hair, the second has two hairs, and so on up to 10. It is tempting to suppose that the eleventh man must then match one of the first ten. But that is not so. For the eleventh man might be completely bald. And in that case no two men would have the same number of hairs. But if we add the premise that no man is bald, then the conclusion follows.

The women have nothing to do with this problem, so neither (C) nor (E) is right. (D) is wrong because there are other premises—e.g., that the number of men in Calcutta exceeds the maximum number of hairs by at least two—which will also yield the conclusion.

2. A The strongest is (A). It directly addresses the question of the results of the surgery, and claims that the surgery did in fact have good results. It did not make McTavish feel better than he did before, but maybe the positive result could not have been achieved by anything else that McTavish might have done. The surgery did, according to (A), make McTavish better than he would have been without it. And so the surgery had a good result.

   All of the other responses are more peripheral to the question of whether the surgery was in fact worth it.

3. E The point of the proverb seems to be that tampering with something which is not problematic is likely to make things worse rather than better. All of the alternatives involve the manager's making some change or taking some action. But the first four represent the manager's action as being a response to a particular existing problem. They are not contrary to the spirit of the proverb. But preventive maintenance, overhauling the machine before it breaks down, seems to be just what the proverb advises against.

4. C Since no horse finished ahead of Cold Molasses, Cold Molasses came in first. Since no horse was between Cold Molasses and Three-Leg Charlie, Three-Leg Charlie must have been second. And if so, obviously he was "either second or third." None of the other alternatives are guaranteed by the given data.

5. D Since there are only six horses in the race, Bag O'Bones and Cold Molasses (with four horses between them) must have been first and last. But there is no indication of which one was first and which one last. But anyway, Three-Leg Charlie could not have been last. The other alternatives are either incompatible with the given data, or not guaranteed by it.

   (Notice, incidentally, that in cases where two or more questions begin with a common scenario, they share the information in the scenario itself, but they do not share the information or premises in the individual questions.)

6. A Some people find this paradoxical, but it follows directly from these common definitions. Since the circular argument has a premise which is identical to its conclusion, it is not possible for all of its premises to be true if its conclusion is false. But that is just what the definition of a valid argument says. (Of course, validity is not the only virtue which an argument can have or need.)

   (C), (D), and (E) are incompatible with (A), and are ruled out. (B) is mistaken because it is easy to find valid arguments whose premises are not identical with their conclusion.

7. E The statement of the problem stipulates that Mary was infected with the bacillus but did not have typhoid fever. So apparently the bacillus does not always cause the fever—it did not in the case of Typhoid Mary.

   Since the problem stipulates that Mary did not have typhoid fever, her unusual case is irrelevant to the other alternatives.

8. B If it should turn out that there are many more drunk pedestrians than drunk drivers, then the cited statistics would not show that drunk pedestrians run a greater risk of injury than drunk drivers.

The questionable conclusion is not about the severity of injuries. Therefore, (A) is irrelevant. Nor is it about how the pedestrians were injured, so (C) is irrelevant. (D) is irrelevant, because the conclusion compares the risks incurred by pedestrians and drivers, so injuries to passengers are irrelevant. And (E) is also irrelevant because the conclusion says nothing about why the pedestrians were walking.

9. A (A) is strongest. This question is really about the conditions under which ignorance that something is true is evidence that it is false. This is not generally the case. But if there is reason to believe that if the thing were true then we would have evidence of it, then the lack of evidence in favor of the claim is itself evidence that the claim is false. That is what (A) adds in this case, and so it strengthens the manufacturer's case.

(B) might be an independent reason for thinking the insecticides to be safe (depending on the stringency of the industry standards), but it does not connect up with the spokesperson's claim in such a way as to make that claim a support for the safety claim. (C) is just one of the things which might lead us to assert (A), and (A) is the more general claim. (D) might assure us that the insecticides are in fact used in the recommended way. But the manufacturer's claim is about what happens if they are used in that way. That requires a different support. (E) might do a little (the spokesperson is sincere), but is not nearly as strong as (A).

10. B (B) suggests a way in which membership in the Penguin Club might lead pretty directly to an improvement in Arnie's financial success.

(A) is true, but it has no bearing on whether changing membership will have an effect on Arnie's income. There is no reason to think that the distribution of incomes in the club is itself a causal factor in the income of the members. (C), so far as we can tell from the scenario, is irrelevant, since we are given no idea of why Arnie was not invited earlier nor why he is invited now. (D) represents a benefit, but not a financial one. And (E) is irrelevant, so far as we know.

11. E This problem is easy, unless you succumb to carelessness in reading it. The crucial point is that it is not specified that Mr. Loren lives in Rayleigh Harbor, but only that he owns a house there. He may live somewhere else, and if so then he may pay property taxes in Rayleigh Harbor, and elsewhere, regardless of his age.

12. A The manager is apparently taking LaGrand's failure to carry the metropolitan areas to be evidence for his lack of effectiveness in personal campaigning. But that failure might be due to other factors—e.g., the unattractiveness of LaGrand's positions for urban voters—and LaGrand's vigorous personal campaign in the urban areas may have contributed much to his victory even though he did not actually carry those areas. The effectiveness of LaGrand's personal campaigning must be measured against some estimate of what would have been the result of a different strategy.

(B) seems rather unlikely in view of LaGrand's failure to carry the metropolitan centers. (C) is irrelevant to the argument about LaGrand's effectiveness in campaigning. (D) would, if anything, strengthen the manager's position; there is no reason to think he is ignoring it. And (E) must be false. LaGrand could not have won the first election if he had not done better in out-state areas than in the big cities.

13. E The Japanese speakers may be few. If so, then even if these Japanese speakers cannot speak Portuguese, the first premise may still be true. So this conclusion does not follow from the stated premises. But that fact itself does not entail anything about the truth or falsity of the premises or the conclusion. For example, the conclusion may be true even if it does not follow from the premises (it might be true even if no Brazilian speaks both Portuguese and Japanese).

14. D (D) is the statement which does not fit the quoted statement. If the quote is an argument (which seems highly unlikely), then its intended premise is almost surely indicated by the "for." And if it is an explanation, then the explaining fact is indicated by the "for." But (D) assigns that as the fact to be explained. So (D) does not accurately represent the quote.

    (A) identifies the premise of the argument as the clause attached to the "for," and (C) identifies the conclusion with the other clause. (B) picks out the thing to be explained as what is expressed in the clause without the "for." And (E) identifies the explaining fact as the one which does have the "for" attached to it.

15. E The given set of alternative responses indicates that the initial scenario is assumed to involve a mistake. The scenario doesn't involve any obvious argument, nor, for that matter, does it appear to propose an explanation for anything. (A), (B), and (C), therefore, seem unlikely. It does, however, say that certain things are "predictors," and that looks much like claiming that they are indicators. And the reaction, buying an alarm clock, looks like the reaction of a person who takes something to be a cause which he can control to achieve (or avoid) a certain effect. (D) and (E), therefore, look like the most promising candidates. Which one? Remember, we are looking for a mistake. The person who buys an alarm clock and joins an exercise club appears to be treating something as a cause. If that is a mistake, then (E) is the correct response. He is probably mistaking an indicator for a cause (i.e., over-sleeping is probably not a cause of premature death, but rather a symptom of some deeper condition which shortens a life span).

16. B Pairs of statements such as these are sometimes called "contraries." They cannot both be true, but they can both be false. The latter would be a reality if, for example, two of Shirley's children had measles and the third one was fine. But no combination of illness and health in Shirley's children will make both Ellen and Lois correct.

SECTION 4 Problem Solving

1. E Sketch a line graph:

    1000 miles

    A → C ← B

    Use $D = VT$. $D_A = 60T_A$, $D_B = 50\ (T_A - 2)$. $D_A + D_B = 1000 = 60T_A + 50(T_A - 2)$. $\therefore 1000 = 60T_A + 50T_A - 100$. $1100 = 110T_A$. $\therefore T_A = 10$ hrs. 8:00 + 10 hours = 6 p.m.

2. A Volume = $.5 \times .5 \times h$ (keep dimensions in meters). There are 1000 liters in a cubic meter. $\therefore 10/1000 = .5 \times .5 \times h$. $\therefore h = 40/1000 = 0.04$ m or 4 cm.

3. E $\left.\begin{aligned} x-y&=4 \\ x-2y&=6. \end{aligned}\right\}$ Subtract the second equation from the first: $y=-2$.
Substitute $y=-2$ back into either equation: $x=2$. $\therefore\ x+y=0$.

4. C $1+\frac{3}{5}\div\left(1-\frac{2}{15}\right)=1+\frac{3}{5}\div\frac{13}{15}=1+\frac{3}{\cancel{5}}\times\frac{\overset{3}{\cancel{15}}}{13}=1+\frac{9}{13}=\frac{22}{13}=1\frac{9}{13}$.

5. A Sketch the parallelogram:

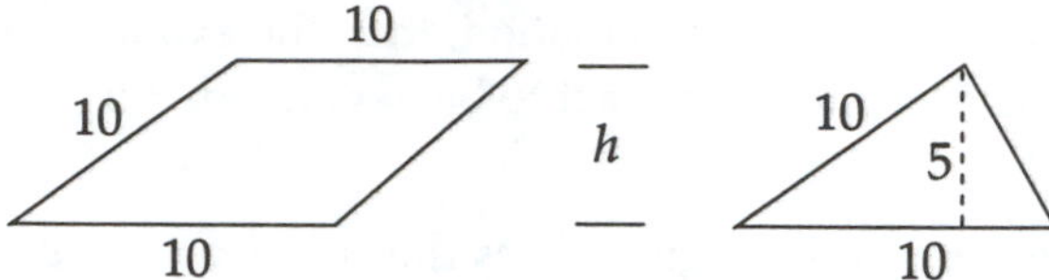

If its area is 50 the height must be 5. A right triangle has an angle of 30° opposite a leg which is half the hypotenuse. Hence, the large angles in the parallelogram are 150° and the small angles are 30°.

6. D Rewrite the equation as $\overline{ED}$ $x^2-5x-14=0$. Factor the equation: $(x-7)(x+2)=0$. $\therefore\ x=7,-2$.

7. A $\angle AOB$ is arc $AB=120°$. A perpendicular to $\overline{AB}$ from O provides a 30°-60°-90° right triangle. $\therefore \angle\ OBA=30°$. The leg adjacent to the 30° (on $\overline{AB}$) is $\sqrt{3}$ if the hypotenuse is 2. The hypotenuse is the radius = 10. $\therefore$ Half of $\overline{AB}$ is $5\sqrt{3}$ so $\overline{AB}$ is $10\sqrt{3}$.

8. C Between each number is 30° (360/12 = 30). The small hand will travel (10/60) × 30 = 5° in 10 minutes. $\therefore$ 30 + 5 = 35°.

9. D Worker A's rate is $1/n$ job/hour. Worker B's rate is $1/m$ job/hour. If T is the total time for the job, then $\left(\frac{1}{n}+\frac{1}{m}\right)T=1$ job, or $\frac{n+m}{nm}T=1$ so that $T=\frac{nm}{n+m}$.

10. E The large cube is made up of 100 cubes on one side, or 1000 small cubes. Of these, there are $8\times 8\times 8=512$ that are inside, with no sides that could get painted. That means there are 488 that have at least one side painted. The odds of selecting one of these are 488 : 1000, or about 1 : 2.

11. E Multiply the first equation by 2: $2x+1=2y$. From the second equation $y=\frac{x}{0.1}=10x$. Substitute this into the first equation: $2x+1=2(10x)=20x$. $\therefore\ 1=18x$ and $x=1/18$.

12. E If a triangle includes a diameter, it is a right triangle. The diameter is 26 and if one leg is 10 the other must be 24 (twice a 5-12-13 right triangle). Thus, $A=\frac{1}{2}bh=\frac{1}{2}(10)(24)=120$.

13. D For such an angle, $\angle BAC=\frac{1}{2}\text{arc } BC=\frac{1}{2}(135)=67.5°$.

14. C $280 = 0.05P.\ \therefore P = \dfrac{280}{.05} = \dfrac{28000}{5} = 5600$ people. $5600 - 280 = 5320$ people.

15. C $\left.\begin{array}{r} x - y + z = 4 \\ -x + y + 2z = 8 \end{array}\right\}$ Add the equations: $3z = 12$. $\therefore z = 4$.

Note: We write the equations so terms of like variables are aligned.

16. E $x^{1/3}x^{1/2}x^{1/6}x^{-5/4} = x^{\left(\frac{1}{3}+\frac{1}{2}+\frac{1}{6}-\frac{5}{4}\right)}$. $\dfrac{1}{3}+\dfrac{1}{2}+\dfrac{1}{6}-\dfrac{5}{4} = \dfrac{4+6+2-15}{12}$

$= \dfrac{-3}{12} = -\dfrac{1}{4}$.

17. A $x^2 + 3x - 4 = (x+4)(x-1)$. $x^2 - 4 = (x-2)(x+2)$

$\dfrac{(x+4)\cancel{(x-1)}}{(x-2)\cancel{(x+2)}} \dfrac{\cancel{x+2}}{\cancel{x-1}} = \dfrac{x+4}{x-2}$

18. C $A_{\text{circle}} = \dfrac{\pi d^2}{4} = \dfrac{100\pi}{4} = 25\pi = (25)\dfrac{22}{7} = \dfrac{550}{7} = 78.5$.

Area of $\frac{1}{2}$ circle $= \dfrac{78.5}{2} = 39.2$.

$A_{\text{square}} = 10 \times 10 = 100$. $100 - 39.2 = 60.8 \cong 61$.

19. C Let x = Kyle's age and y = Cindy's age. The two statements take the algebraic form:

$$\begin{array}{l} x + 10 = y \\ y - 30 = 2(x - 30) \end{array} \quad \text{or} \quad \begin{array}{rl} x - y &= -10 \\ -2x + y &= -30 \\ \hline -x &= -40 \end{array} \quad \therefore x = 40.$$

20. B A) $\dfrac{4}{.002} = \dfrac{4000}{2} = 2000$

B) $.01^{-2} = \dfrac{1}{.01 \times .01} = 100 \times 100 = 10{,}000$

C) $\dfrac{1}{.0002} + \dfrac{1}{.0004} = \dfrac{10000}{2} + \dfrac{10000}{4} = 5000 + 2500 = 7500$

D) $20^2 + 10^3 = 400 + 1000 = 1400$

E) $1500 + 6720 + 1530 = 9750$ (Here, we rounded off a bit on the high side, and it is still smaller than 10,000.)

SECTION 5 Analysis of an Issue

You may wish to have a friend or colleague grade your writing using the scoring guidelines presented on page 136 in 'Analytical Writing.' Or, should you desire a professional assessment of your writings, you may send the two essays to: Great Lakes Press, POB 483, Okemos, MI 48805-0483. Or fax to (517) 339-4455. You must also provide your Visa/MC # and expiration date (or a check or money order). Within 2 weeks, we will return a well-informed GMAT-type score, an evaluation of your writing and some suggestions for improvement for $20. Essays will be graded through an expertly-staffed program managed by Dr. James Ney, the author of this chapter.

SECTION 6 Data Sufficiency

1. D (1) is sufficient since if x is a factor of y then $x = yz$ so that $yz/z = y$, an integer; the answer is "No"; it is not a mixed number. (2) is also sufficient since if y is a factor of x then $y = xw$ and $x/(xw) = 1/w$, a fraction; again, the answer is "No" since a mixed number is an integer plus a fraction.

2. E (1) is not sufficient since the length of one side of a right triangle must be known, in addition to an angle. (2) is not sufficient since two sides must be known if one of the acute angles is not known. (1) and (2) together are also not sufficient since a length is not specified.

3. C To find $x + 2y$ we must find x and y. (1) and (2) provide two equations and two unknowns from which x and y can be determined. (Subtract the first equation from the second: $3y = 6$. $\therefore$ $y = 2$ and $x = 4$; then $x + 2y = 8$.)

4. D Since $\overline{AB} = \overline{AD} = 10$ all sides of the parallelogram are equal and the area can be determined if an angle and a side are known. Since an angle is given in (1) and the sides are of length 10, the area can be determined by (1) alone. Also, since (2) gives d and the sides are known, an angle can be determined and hence the area. ((1) Area $= 10 \times 10 \sin 60°$. (2) $\sin x = d/10 = 0.8$. $\therefore$ Area $= 10 \times 10 \times 0.8$.)

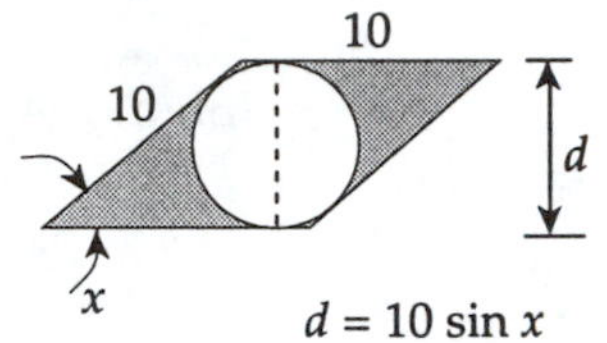

5. D (1) is sufficient since the ratio of two terms gives the common multiple, so all successive terms can be found. ($\frac{10}{16} = \frac{5}{8}$. $\therefore y = 10 \times \frac{5}{8} = \frac{50}{8}$. The sum can be easily found.) (2) is also sufficient since, if $y = 2x$, then the common multiple is $\frac{y}{x} = \frac{2x}{x} = 2$. The terms are 16, 32, 64 and the sum follows.

6. A A diagonal splits a rectangle into two right triangles. If the hypotenuse and a leg are known, the other leg can be found, and subsequently, the area; so (1) is sufficient. ($20^2 = 10^2 + w^2$. $\therefore w^2 = 400 - 100 = 300$ and $w = \sqrt{300}$. Then Area $= 10\sqrt{300}$.) (2) is not sufficient since the diagonals of a rectangle always bisect each other, so this information is not of use.

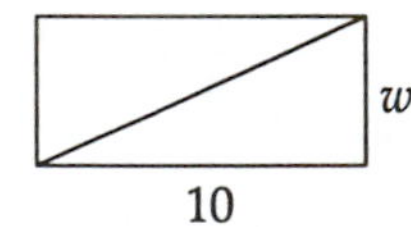

7. D (1) is sufficient since the diagonal from corner to corner of an erect box has length $\sqrt{20^2 + 40^2 + 50^2}$. If this is greater than, or less than 70, then the box is not erect. (2) is sufficient since the erect box would have a volume of $0.2 \times 0.4 \times 0.5 = 0.04$ m^3 or $0.04 \times 1000 = 40$ liters. In both cases, the question can be answered.

8. C Factor the quadratic: $(x - 4)(x + 1) = 0$. $\therefore x = 4, -1$. (1) is not sufficient to decide. With (2) the question can be answered: $x = 4$.

9. C Factor the quadratic: $(x + 7)(x - 2) > 0$? We investigate $x = 2, -7$. If $x < -7$, the question could be answered; but with $x > -7$, the question cannot be answered (if $x = 0$, the product is negative; if $x = 4$, the product is positive). But, with both (1) and (2) the first factor $(x + 7)$ is positive and the second factor $(x - 2)$ is negative, so the product is negative and the answer is "No."

10. A If the line is sloped at a 45° angle, then the y-coordinate is always less than the x-coordinate for all points that lie below the line. (1) is sufficient since a line passing through (0, 0) and (–1, –1) has a 45° angle, so the answer is "No"; a is always greater than b. (2) is not sufficient since it does not fix the line at a 45° angle.

11. B (1) is not sufficient since two of the four angles are always equal. (2) is sufficient since the sum of the four angles is 360° requiring that the fourth angle be 90°; hence, all angles are 90° and the lines are perpendicular.

12. C If the lines are parallel, $x + y = 180°$. Using (1) and (2) we find that $100 = 2y$ so that $y = 50°$ and $x + y = 150°$. The answer is "No."

13. E Let the ratio be x/y. If $x + y = 6$ and $x = 2y$ then $2y + y = 6$ and $y = 2$ so that $x = 4$. But (2) also allows $y = 2x$ so that $x + 2x = 6$ and $x = 2$, $y = 4$. More information is needed to answer the question.

Avg Salary = $\frac{x}{20}$. ($1.1y = 20{,}000 + y$. $\therefore y = 200{,}000$ and $x = 220{,}000$ so that

Avg Salary = $\frac{220{,}000}{20} = \$11{,}000$.)

14. E Neither (1) nor (2) is sufficient since the area covered by a quart of paint is not given.

15. B (1) does not supply information that is not known (three angles of a triangle total 180°). With angle C known, angle B is also known ($\angle B = 180 - 30 - 40 = 110°$) and $\overline{AC}$ can be found since one of the sides is specified in the figure. (It is not necessary to actually make the calculation; just make the correct decision that the calculation can be made.)

16. E From (1), x is positive; but (2) implies that y can be either positive or negative so a decision cannot be made. More information is needed.

17. A (1) is sufficient since the cross-hatched area is one half of the area of the rectangle (Area = $\frac{10}{2} = 5$). (2) is not sufficient since a length is needed.

18. C Let the fraction be x/y. Then $x = y - 6$. (1) states that both x and y are positive or they are negative. (2) states that $y = x^2$ so that $x = x^2 - 6$ or $x^2 - x - 6 = 0$. This is factored: $(x - 3)(x + 2) = 0$. $\therefore$ $x = 3, -2$. If $x = 3$, $y = 9$; if $x = -2$, $y = 4$. Thus, $x = 3$ and $y = 9$ so that $x / y = 1/3$.

19. E $(a - b)^2 = a^2 - 2ab + b^2$. The question is: Is $a^2 - 2ab + b^2 > a^2 + b^2$? Or is $-2ab > 0$? If $a < b$, b could be positive and a either positive or negative, so the question cannot be answered. (2) does not help the situation, so more information is needed.

20. C Whether the carpeting is laid parallel to $\overline{FE}$ or parallel to $\overline{ED}$ the question can be answered using the information contained in (1) and (2). All the dimensions must be known.

SECTION 7 Problem Solving

1. E If k is odd, then k^2 is also odd, $2k$ is even, and $k + 2k$ is odd. So I and III are true.

2. B $\frac{5}{6}-\frac{1}{8}=\frac{40-6}{48}=\frac{34}{48}=\frac{17}{24}$. $\frac{17}{16}\div\frac{17}{24}=\frac{17}{16}\times\frac{24}{17}=\frac{24}{16}=\frac{3}{2}$.

3. A $\frac{x+y+z}{3}=60$ and $y = 70$. Let $x = 20$, then $\frac{20+70+z}{3}=60$. $\therefore 90 + z = 180$ and $z = 90$.

4. C The total time is $\frac{30}{60}+\frac{20}{40}+\frac{35}{70}=0.5+0.5+0.5=1.5$ hours. Distance divided by time gives average speed: $\frac{85}{1.5}=56\frac{2}{3}$ mph.

5. D $\left(2xy^2\right)^3=8x^3y^6$. Then $\frac{\sqrt{8x^3y^4}}{\sqrt{8x^3y^6}}=\frac{1}{\sqrt{y^2}}=\frac{1}{y}$.

6. A Think of this as x^2-y^2 which is equal to $(x-y)(x+y)$. Consequently, $183^2-181^2=(183-181)(183+181)=2\times 364=728$.

7. A Factor: $\left(2x^2+3x-2\right)=(2x-1)(x+2)$; $\left(x^2-4\right)=(x-2)(x+2)$. $\frac{2x^2+3x-2}{x^2-4}=\frac{(2x-1)(x+2)}{(x-2)(x+2)}=\frac{2x-1}{x-2}$.

8. B Solve simultaneously (note that $x - z = w$, that is, $x - z$ is a single variable!) by subtracting the first equation from the second: $-2y = 2$. $\therefore y = -1$.

9. B The total budget is found by adding the four items together: 18 + 29 + 25 + 34 = 106. % utilities = $\frac{18}{106}\times 100=17.0\%$.

10. D Goods = 34 and Labor = 29. The question becomes $34 = 29x$. $\therefore x = \frac{34}{29}=1.17$ or 117%.

11. B An isosceles triangle has two equal sides. If the triangle is a right triangle the legs must be equal. Hence, $10^2+10^2=L^2$ or $L^2=200$ and $L=\sqrt{200}=10\sqrt{2}$. (A sketch is always helpful.)

12. B Make a sketch. The distance a is $a = 1 - (-4) = 5$. The distance b is also 5 since the horizontal leg has length $4 - 1 = 3$ and the vertical leg has length $3 - (-1) = 4$. Two sides are equal so the triangle is isosceles.

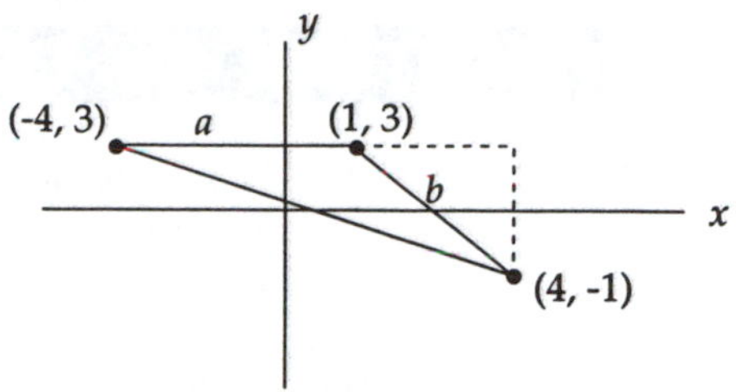

13. E $x^2 - 3x > 4$ is equivalent to $x^2 - 3x - 4 > 0$. Factor: $(x-4)(x+1) > 0$. The two roots are $x = 4, -1$. If $x > 4$ then a positive times a positive is positive; if $x < -1$ then a negative times a negative is also positive. So $x > 4$ or $x < -1$ are acceptable.

14. C Let x be the number of acres in the field. Then Ron plows at the rate of $\frac{x}{n}$ acres per hour. If he plows for m hours he plows $(\frac{x}{n})m$ acres and $\left(x - \frac{x}{n}m\right)$ acres remain to be plowed. This is $\left(1 - \frac{m}{n}\right)x$ or the fraction $\frac{n-m}{n}$.

15. C A quick sketch shows a right triangle that has legs 15 and 20. These are five times the 3-4 legs of a 3-4-5 triangle. Hence, the hypotenuse is $5 \times 5 = 25$ ft long, which is the minimum length.

16. A A sketch shows that the radius of the dome (the sphere) is 26. The right triangle has a 26 ft hypotenuse and a 10 ft leg. This is twice a 5-12-13 triangle. The other leg is thus $12 \times 2 = 24$ and the diameter of the circle formed by the ground and the dome is 48 ft.

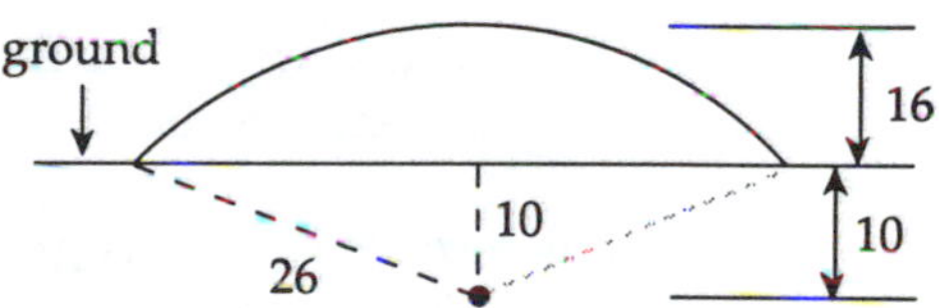

SECTION 8 Sentence Correction

1. E *Due to the fact that* is a wordy version of *since* or *because*. Besides this, the clauses on either side of *and* have a different form; that is, they are not parallel. One of them, *was delayed*, is passive. (E) corrects these problems.

2. D *After all was said and done* and *at death's door* are both rather conventional clichés. These are corrected by (D).

3. C *His fellow man* is a cliché. *Had not had much experience . . . for the machinations* is not grammatical. *Experience* must be followed by *with*. (C) corrects these problems.

4. E It is completely redundant to write about *agreements that were agreed upon*. (D) leaves a stranded preposition at the end of the sentence. (C) is passive. That leaves (E) as the correct selection.

5. C *Beyond the shadow of a doubt* is a cliché and should not be used. The phrase *for a long time* modifies the whole sentence and should be placed at the beginning. Therefore (C) is correct.

6. C *Everyone* is not plural; therefore, it cannot be referenced by a plural pronoun, *they*. Verbs like *know* cannot be used with the progressive tenses.

7. A The sentence starting with *never in the history of the world* has been used so frequently it is now a cliché.

8. E *Different than* is grammatically incorrect. *Different then* has a spelling error, *then* for *than*. *Used by* is a passive. The correct answer is (E).

9. D *Will succeed . . . to repair* is ungrammatical as is *tried . . . in repairing*. The correct forms are: *will succeed . . . in repairing* and *tried . . . to repair*.

10. A *Costs* is plural and needs a plural verb. (C) and (D) are 'wordy' when they are compared to (A), the correct answer.

11. C The basic problem with the sentence is wordiness and the presence of clichés. Thus, *needless to say* and *one-hundred-and-twenty* percent cannot be used. Further, *today's game which determined the championship* can be reduced to *today's championship game*. *An* is used before vowel sounds; *one* starts with the consonant sound *w*.

12. A To link two entities in a list in order, *respectively* is used—not *respectfully*. *Bill* and *Arley* make up a plural subject and must have a plural form of *be* and a plural noun, *captains*, in the predicate. Thus the original sentence is all right.

13. C *Replete with interest* and *specimen of humanity* are wordy clichés and should not be used.

14. B With the past tense *said* and the past progressive *was making*, there is a tense problem, a progressive tense paired with a simple past tense. The action involved with the

verb *said* occurs at the same time as the action of *make*; hence they must have the same tense.

15. A Contractions are to be avoided in writing. The subjunctive *were* should be used with a conditional *if*-clause.

16. D The original has a passive in it, *were consumed*, and the participial phrase, *traveling by ship from New York to London*, is dangling since its subject, *he*, is different from the subject in the main clause. These are corrected by (D).

17. E The use of the passive, *was developed*, should be avoided. George Washington was not *notorious* but *famous*, (A) and (C). The past perfect is all right since Washington's work as father of the nation preceded his becoming famous.

18. C *Theirselves* is a grammatically incorrect, colloquial form of *themselves*. The lack of parallelism between the infinitive and gerund is corrected by (C), the correct answer.

19. B *Escalating at an exceedingly alarming rate* is a wordy cliché and should be abandoned. Similarly, *where* should not be used for *that*.

20. E *None*, the subject of the sentence, is a combination of *no* and *one* and is thus singular so that the verb in the present requires the *-s*, *remembers*. *But* is negative; thus, *hadn't but* is a double negative.

21. A Indefinite pronouns such as *anyone* never have non-restrictive clauses following them. The commas are wrong. *Anyone* is singular and can not be the antecedent for a plural pronoun. Sentence (A) is correct.

22. C Subjects joined by *either . . . or* and *neither . . . nor* are singular and require a singular verb, (B) or (C). As antecedents they are also singular and require a singular pronoun. The answer is (C).

SECTION 9 Analysis of an Argument

You may wish to have a friend or colleague grade your writing using the scoring guidelines presented on page 136 in 'Analytical Writing.' Or, should you desire a professional assessment of your writings, you may send the two essays to: Great Lakes Press, POB 483, Okemos, MI 48805-0483. Or fax to (517) 339-4455. You must also provide your Visa/MC # and expiration date (or a check or money order). Within 2 weeks, we will return a well-informed GMAT-type score, an evaluation of your writing and some suggestions for improvement for $20. Essays will be graded through an expertly-staffed program managed by Dr. James Ney, the author of this chapter.